Everyman, I will go with thee,
and be thy guide

THE EVERYMAN
LIBRARY

*The Everyman Library was founded by J. M. Dent
in 1906. He chose the name Everyman because he wanted
to make available the best books ever written in every
field to the greatest number of people at the cheapest possible
price. He began with Boswell's 'Life of Johnson';
his one-thousandth title was Aristotle's 'Metaphysics',
by which time sales exceeded forty million.*

*Today Everyman paperbacks remain true to
J. M. Dent's aims and high standards, with a wide range
of titles at affordable prices in editions which address
the needs of today's readers. Each new text is reset to give
a clear, elegant page and to incorporate the latest thinking
and scholarship. Each book carries the pilgrim logo,
the character in 'Everyman', a medieval morality play,
a proud link between Everyman
past and present.*

William Shakespeare

HAMLET

Edited by
JOHN F. ANDREWS

Foreword by
DEREK JACOBI

EVERYMAN
J. M. DENT · LONDON
CHARLES E. TUTTLE
VERMONT

First published in Everyman by J. M. Dent 1993
Published by permission of Guild America Books, an imprint
of Doubleday Book and Music Clubs, Inc.

Reprinted 1996, 2000

J. M. Dent
Orion Publishing Group
Orion House, 5 Upper St Martin's Lane,
London WC2H 9EA
and
Tuttle Publishing,
Airport Industrial Park, 364 Innovation Drive,
North Clarendon, VT 05759–9436 USA

Photoset by Deltatype Ltd, Ellesmere Port, Cheshire
Printed in Great Britain by
The Guernsey Press Co. Ltd, Guernsey, C.I.

British Library Cataloguing-in-Publication Data
is available upon request

ISBN 0 460 87176 5

CONTENTS

NOTE ON THE AUTHOR AND EDITOR

WILLIAM SHAKESPEARE is held to have been born on St George's Day, 23 April 1564. The eldest son of a prosperous glove-maker in Stratford-upon-Avon, he was probably educated at the town's grammar school.

Tradition holds that between 1585 and 1592, Shakespeare first became a schoolteacher and then set off for London. By 1595 he was a leading member of the Lord Chamberlain's Men, helping to direct their business affairs, as well as being a playwright and actor. In 1598 he became a part-owner of the company, which was the most distinguished of its age. However, he maintained his contacts with Stratford, and his family seem to have remained there. From about 1610 he seems to have grown increasingly involved in the town's affairs, suggesting a withdrawal from London. He died on 23 April 1616, in his 53rd year, and was buried at Holy Trinity Church on the 25th.

JOHN F. ANDREWS has recently completed a 19-volume edition, *The Guild Shakespeare*, for the Doubleday Book and Music Clubs. He is also the editor of a 3-volume reference set, *William Shakespeare: His World, His Work, His Influence*, and the former editor (1974–85) of the journal *Shakespeare Quarterly*. From 1974–84, he was Director of Academic Programs at the Folger Shakespeare Library in Washington and Chairman of the Folger Institute.

CHRONOLOGY OF SHAKESPEARE'S LIFE

Year[1]	Age	Life
1564		Shakespeare baptized 26 April at Stratford-upon-Avon
1582	18	Marries Anne Hathaway
1583	19	Daughter, Susanna, born
1585	21	Twin son and daughter, Hamnet and Judith, born
1590–1	26	*The Two Gentlemen of Verona* & *The Taming of the Shrew*
1591	27	*2 & 3 Henry VI*
1592	28	*Titus Andronicus* & *1 Henry VI*
1592–3		*Richard III*
1593	29	*Venus and Adonis* published
1594	30	*The Comedy of Errors. The Rape of Lucrece* published
1594–5		*Love's Labour's Lost*
1595	31	*A Midsummer Night's Dream, Romeo and Juliet,* & *Richard II.* An established member of Lord Chamberlain's Men
1596	32	*King John.* Hamnet dies
1596–7		*The Merchant of Venice* & *1 Henry IV*
1597	33	Buys New Place in Stratford

1 It is rarely possible to be certain about the dates at which plays of this period were written. For Shakespeare's plays, this chronology follows the dates preferred by Wells and Taylor, the editors of the Oxford Shakespeare. Publication dates are given for poetry and books.

CHRONOLOGY OF HIS TIMES

Year	Literary Context	Historical Events
1565–7	Golding, Ovid's *Metamorphoses*, tr.	Elizabeth I reigning
1574	*A Mirror for Magistrates* (3rd ed.)	
1576	London's first playhouse built	
1578	John Lyly, *Euphues*	
1579	North, Plutarch's *Lives*, tr.	
	Spenser, *Shepherd's Calender*	
1587	Marlowe, *I Tamburlaine*	Mary Queen of Scots
	Holinshed's *Chronicles* (2nd ed.)	executed
1588		Defeat of Spanish Armada
1589	Kyd, *Spanish Tragedy*	Civil war in France
	Marlowe, *Jew of Malta*	
1590	Spenser, *Faerie Queene*, Bks I–III	
1591	Sidney, *Astrophel and Stella*	Proclamation against Jesuits
1592	Marlowe, *Dr Faustus* & *Edward II*	Scottish witchcraft trials
		Plague closes theatres from June
1593	Marlowe killed	
1594	Nashe, *Unfortunate Traveller*	Theatres reopen in summer
1594–6		Extreme food shortages
1595	Sidney, *An Apologie for Poetry*	Riots in London
1596		Calais captured by Spanish
		Cadiz expedition
1597	Bacon, *Essays*	

Year	Age	Life
1597–8		*The Merry Wives of Windsor* & *2 Henry IV*
1598	34	*Much Ado About Nothing*
1598–9		*Henry V*
1599	35	*Julius Caesar*. One of syndicate responsible for building the Globe in Southwark, where the Lord Chamberlain's Men now play
1599–1600		*As You Like It*
1600–1		*Hamlet*
1601	37	*Twelfth Night*. His father is buried in Stratford
1602	38	*Troilus and Cressida*. Invests £320 in land near Stratford[2]
1603	39	*Measure for Measure*. The Lord Chamberlain's Men become the King's Men. They play at court more than all the other companies combined
1603–4		*Othello*
c.1604	40	Shakespeare sues Philip Rogers of Stratford for debt
1604–5		*All's Well That Ends Well*
1605	41	*Timon of Athens*. Invests £440 in Stratford tithes
1605–6		*King Lear*
1606	42	*Macbeth* & *Antony and Cleopatra*
1607	43	*Pericles*. Susanna marries the physician John Hall in Stratford
1608	44	*Coriolanus*. The King's Men lease Blackfriar's, an indoor theatre. His only grandchild is born. His mother dies
1609	45	*The Winter's Tale*. 'Sonnets' and 'A Lover's Complaint' published
1610	46	*Cymbeline*
1611	47	*The Tempest*
1613	49	*Henry VIII*. Buys house in London for £140
1613–14		*The Two Noble Kinsmen*
1616	52	Judith marries Thomas Quiney, a vintner, in Stratford. On 23 April he dies, and is buried two days later
1623		Publication of the First Folio. His widow dies in August

2 A schoolmaster would earn around £20 a year at this time.

Year	Literary Context	Historical Events
1598	Marlowe and Chapman, *Hero and Leander* Jonson, *Every Man in his Humour*	Rebellion in Ireland
1599	Children's companies begin playing Thomas Dekker's *Shoemaker's Holiday*	Essex fails in Ireland
1601	'War of the Theatres' Jonson, *Poetaster*	Essex rebels and is executed
1602		Tyrone defeated in Ireland
1603	Florio, Montaigne's *Essays*, tr.	Elizabeth I dies, James I accedes Raleigh found guilty of treason
1604	Marston, *The Malcontent*	Peace with Spain
1605	Bacon, *Advancement of Learning*	Gunpowder plot
1606	Jonson, *Volpone*	
1607	Tourneur, *The Revenger's Tragedy* published	Virginia colonized Enclosure riots
1609		Oath of allegiance Truce in Netherlands
1610	Jonson, *Alchemist*	
1611	Authorised Version of the Bible Donne, *Anatomy of the World*	
1612	Webster, *White Devil*	Prince Henry dies
1613	Webster, *Duchess of Malfi*	Princess Elizabeth marries
1614	Jonson, *Bartholomew Fair*	
1616	Folio edition of Jonson's plays	

Biographical note, chronology and plot summary compiled by John Lee, University of Bristol, 1993.

FOREWORD BY DEREK JACOBI

As an actor I thank God for William Shakespeare. An extraordinary, superhuman genius – I mean, where did he come from? And he wrote most of his plays while still a man in his thirties! Where did he get all that knowledge? Where did all that wisdom come from? If you go through all the plays, you find that he knew something about everything. He had a phrase or a sentence, a word for every conceivable human situation and emotion.

I think Shakespeare is for all ages. He is always relevant and exciting. He is loved and understood and respected and thrilled to no matter where you are in the world, no matter what age you are. He's survived four hundred years of reverence and idolatry. And during those four centuries he's also survived a great deal of iconoclasm. You can muck about with Shakespeare. You can do all sorts of things with and to him. It doesn't matter. He always survives.

He was a true man of the theatre, and he wrote wonderful parts. And I so hope he's looking down and approving of what we're doing with his plays when we try to be true to them. Whatever changes we make – textual transpositions, little felicities, whatever – we do so that the play and its characters will shine through. Our job is not to glorify any particular actor or director or designer, but to make the play as fresh and new-minted as we can.

I constantly remind myself that Shakespearean actors should approach their parts, in a sense, as they do contemporary roles. 'Forget it's Shakespeare,' I said to the actors I recently directed in *Hamlet*, and in a certain sense I meant it. When they come to Shakespeare, many actors tend to block off all those wonderful juices that naturally flow into modern parts. They cease to think, imagine, react, and feel as they would do normally. Their voices become different. Their bodies become different.

They must learn to make Shakespeare's language sound like the language they speak every day. They must live in the moment, create the words out of the air. They must forget that Shakespeare wrote them; get rid of the smell of ink; forget that anybody's ever said them before; pluck them out of the feeling and the situation and make them new.

I think that spontaneity comes from the immediacy of emotion. If actors regard these lines as speeches, famous speeches, then that is how they'll come out. Actors must not think that what they say and do is the result of what Shakespeare wrote. What actors say and do must be the result of what they're thinking and feeling, of what is happening in the play as the company has chosen to present it.

Of all of Shakespeare's plays, *Hamlet* probably holds the most interest for an actor. Because one of the things it's about is acting and pretending to be what you're not. It's a play that very much inhabits the world of the imagination: the world of what if, the world of finding out who you are, what you are, where you are in relation to other people and to the universe. This is true of most of Shakespeare, but *Hamlet* in particular comes very close to what acting itself is about, how actors react to a situation and the whole craft of pretence, of being someone else.

Another reason *Hamlet* is so interesting for an actor is that a performance can never be definitive. There are as many *Hamlet*s as there are actors to play Hamlet. Each one is different, because each production, to a great extent, turns on the personality of the actor who is playing Hamlet, and most actors have a Hamlet within them.

Hamlet is probably the clearest and most accessible of all of Shakespeare's plays, largely because it's such a wonderful story, with wonderful dramatic sweep rhythmically throughout the evening. Hamlet goes on a voyage of self-discovery. I don't believe he's ever truly mad. There are three occasions in the play, maybe four, when he drives himself to the edge of madness, but he never actually topples over that edge. He is in control of his own destiny for a great deal of the play.

This play has always been very important to me. Hamlet was the first major role I ever played as a schoolboy. That was when I was seventeen or eighteen. It really started my career as an actor, because my performance got a great deal of press and attention. I was very lucky in that respect. And so I had a very fond memory of the play long before I came to play it professionally in 1977. I played it again in 1979 at the Old Vic. Then I did it for television in 1980. And most recently, in 1988 I directed the very talented young actor Kenneth Branagh in a production for the Renaissance Theatre Company.

Over the years since I first began playing Hamlet, I have become more and more convinced that 'To be or not to be' is to be treated not as a soliloquy, but as a dramatic speech to Ophelia. And my reasons are very much rooted in the text.

The way the Nunnery Scene is set makes it clear that Hamlet is not merely wandering round the Castle with thoughts of death on his mind. Claudius has just told Ophelia that 'We have closely sent for Hamlet hither.' So Hamlet is on his way to a particular place at a certain time to fulfil an appointment.

The person he sees when he gets there is the person he least expected to see. For the last few weeks, every time he's met Ophelia she's run the other way; she's avoided him. If he saw her at the end of the corridor, she would turn the other way and off she'd go. Now he sees her and she doesn't run away. Of course, the last thing Polonius has said to her is 'Walk you here. Read on this book.' But most Ophelias have to not 'walk you here' but go to the wings or hide behind a pillar, or do something to get out of Hamlet's way, whereas the whole point of the scene is for her to confront him.

If we presuppose that they have been lovers, that they are in love, then what better opportunity for him to be able to say, 'This is where my head is at the moment: I'm thinking about committing suicide.' He speaks at her, through her, around her. He soliloquizes to her, if you like.

Well, what does Ophelia do while he's doing this? Does she just sit there? Yes indeed. What else can she do? She's in a very false situation, having been placed there by her father and the King. She knows they are listening behind the curtain. She doesn't want to be there. She knows she's a decoy. It's a completely false situation to her. Hamlet is the man she loves.

I played Hamlet this way with two Ophelias, and both said it helped them with their character. Because the irony is that the speech is about the very things that happen to Ophelia – madness and suicide. She goes mad, and commits suicide, virtually. Hamlet talks about both but experiences neither. In effect, though, hearing this speech plants the seed in Ophelia's mind.

The speech ends with 'Soft you now, the fair Ophelia.' This line is usually taken to mean 'Oh look, there's Ophelia,' but I take it to be one of those little titles he gives her, that we all give each other: the tedious Polonius, the villainous King. This is the way he sees her and he wants her to know it. Then he goes on to call her 'Nymph'. What he is saying is 'Soft you now . . .' 'I don't need you to say anything. Now you know where I am. Just remember me in your prayers. Now, off you go.'

But of course, she's been placed there by her father and the King, so she's got to keep him there, however she can. 'Oh, good my Lord,' she blurts out, 'how does your Honour for this many a day?' 'How have you been lately?'

So the first thing she says is false, and immediately Hamlet knows that the whole situation is phoney. We don't have to see the curtains moving to know that Hamlet senses Polonius' presence. From the beginning of the scene Hamlet has suspected that something is wrong, something is out of kilter. 'She didn't run away like she usually does. She's had the most extraordinary reaction to what I've just said. Then she goes on to give back all these tokens of love and remembrance. Something is extremely wrong.' And then when he confirms it by testing her, by asking her, 'Where's your father?' and she answers, 'At home, my Lord,' in spite of the fact that everything in her being might be struggling to tell him the truth, their relationship, and their lives, can never be the same again.

From this point on, Hamlet realizes that there is no one in his world that he can trust. Everyone is acting, and survival will depend on choosing and playing one's own role as shrewdly as possible.

DEREK JACOBI has acted in three professional productions of *Hamlet*, including one at the Old Vic and one that permitted him to perform the title role in Elsinore. In 1988 he made his directorial debut with the play in England. A veteran of the Royal Shakespeare Company, Mr Jacobi has won the theatre's most coveted awards, and his television credits include such BBC series as *I, Claudius* and *The Shakespeare Plays* (for which he played both Hamlet and Richard II).

EDITOR'S INTRODUCTION TO
Hamlet

In an eloquent tribute to *Ulysses*, the most celebrated novel of the twentieth century, T. S. Eliot praised the brilliance with which James Joyce had deployed classical myth and legend to convey 'the immense panorama of futility and anarchy which is contemporary history'. What Eliot applauded in the work of his fellow writer was what he himself was endeavouring to accomplish in *The Waste Land*, our century's most famous poem. And something akin to what both authors attempted was what Shakespeare appears to have undertaken more than three centuries earlier in *The Tragedy of Hamlet, Prince of Denmark*.

Of all the plays he penned, *Hamlet* is the one that has most persistently been described as 'modern'.* Its hero is a figure of

---

* A close second is *Troilus and Cressida*, a travesty of the *Iliad* that crushes all the grandeur of Antiquity into a squalid 'Argument' about 'a Whore and a Cuckold' (II.iii.82–83). From all indications *Troilus and Cressida* was completed in late 1601 or early 1602, a time-frame that suggests some overlap with *Hamlet*, and the little we know about its production history would seem to make it the perfect Shakespearean analogue for what the Prince of Denmark depicts as a drama that 'was never acted, or if it was, not above once', because 'it pleas'd not the Million'.

When the copyright for *Troilus and Cressida* was registered in 1602, the work was listed as a 'History' that had been performed by Shakespeare's company at the Globe. That designation remained on the initial title-page for the quarto that was printed in 1609. A different title-page was substituted before the print run finished, however, and in the new 'Epistle' that commended Shakespeare's text to sophisticated readers *Troilus and Cressida* was advertised as a 'Comedy' that had never been 'stal'd with the Stage' or 'clapper-claw'd with the Palms of the Vulgar'.

A little more than a decade later, when the publishers of the First Folio began printing the work for the collection that would be issued in 1623, their original plan was to put *Troilus and Cressida* in the part of the volume reserved for 'Tragedies'. Owing to some problem that developed after typesetting commenced, they abandoned this intention, withheld the pages that had gone to press, and eventually repositioned the play in a no-man's-land of its own between the 'Histories' and the 'Tragedies'.

In many ways the publishing history of the title has proven prophetic. Some of today's scholars group *Troilus and Cressida* with the Comedies and some with the Tragedies. Others point to its affinities with those histories that are now labelled Roman Plays. But most have classified the work with the 'Comical Satires' that enjoyed a brief vogue during the outbreak of thespian mudslinging known as the War of the Theatres (see *Hamlet*, II.ii.358–95). No doubt Polonius would have been able to fit *Troilus and Cressida* into one of the ludicrously composite genres he catalogues in II.ii.424–31 of *Hamlet*.

dazzling wit and complexity, a uniquely attractive if tantalizingly elusive personality, and for many interpreters the 'Mystery' (III.ii.392–402) that shrouds him has made the brooding Prince an epitome of man's problematic identity in the post-medieval world. For all his charm, and for all the sympathy he evokes through the soliloquies he shares with the audience, Shakespeare's introspective Prince can be a dark, impulsive, and even savage protagonist. But that has seldom dismayed his admirers. In his clouded mirror entire nations have claimed to see their psyches registered. And so multifarious are the intellectual and artistic progeny of the melancholy Dane that the commentary on *Hamlet* and its offshoots is now a significant body of literature in its own right.

Shakespeare probably wrote the first of his four 'great tragedies' between 1599 and 1601 (quite possibly in two or more increments, since some of the material about the upstart children's companies in II.ii may have been a later addition to the script). It has close affinities with *Julius Caesar*, a title it echoes at several points, and it could well have alternated in the repertory with the playwright's rendering of history's most famous assassination. If so, theatregoers who'd seen the earlier drama would have been amused by Polonius' remark that he'd played Caesar and been 'kill'd i'th' Capital' (III.ii.110–11), because in all likelihood the same actors who had taken the parts of Brutus and his victim in the tragedy that preceded *Hamlet* were now exchanging comments as the Prince and a later ruler's chief counsellor.

Like *Julius Caesar*, and like several of the other plays Shakespeare wrote between 1595 and 1603, *Hamlet* reflects the waning of the Elizabethan era whose glories were receding into gloom. As the sixteenth century yielded to the seventeenth, many of Shakespeare's contemporaries grew increasingly anxious as the ageing, heirless Queen refused to forestall a social and political maelstrom by designating her successor. In the absence of a vigorous, fully involved monarch and a ratified arrangement for the transition to a new head of state when Elizabeth died, Englishmen who'd never regarded their island's defences as secure began bracing themselves for a new onslaught of armadas, coup attempts, and assassination conspiracies. Meanwhile, for those who kept abreast of what was happening in intellectual circles, fears about the country's dynastic instability were being compounded by other concerns of a more cosmic nature. As people looked about them and saw their old verities succumbing to the 'new philosophy', a corrosive scepticism that was said to cast 'all in doubt', there were many who wondered if the human race was abandoning its traditional moorings. Virtually everyone was apprehensive, and theatregoers on the Bankside would have heard reverberations of their own doubts when they listened to a funereally attired actor's remarks about how quickly 'this goodly Frame the Earth' had deteriorated to a 'sterile Promontory', 'a foul and pestilent Congregation of Vapours' (*Hamlet*, II.ii.318– 24). If the Prince's sentiments could be applied to England, the 'Other Eden' a nostalgic John of Gaunt had described a few years earlier as a 'demi-Paradise' (in *Richard II*, II.i.42) was coming more and more to resemble a rank, 'unweeded Garden' whose caretakers were permitting it to go 'to Seed' (*Hamlet*, I.ii.135–36).

In a way that links it with *Troilus and Cressida*, *All's Well That Ends Well*, *Measure for Measure*, and *Othello*, *Hamlet* details the lusts – the perversions of reason and will – that undermine civic harmony and bring great kingdoms to ruin. It focuses on appetite as the cause, and disease as one of the consequences, of fatal error. And in the fiery rhetoric the Prince and the leading Player declaim about the downfall of Troy in II.ii.479–553, it hints at ominous correspondences between the corrupt, prison-like Elsonoure* of Shakespeare's play and the embattled Ilium of Homeric and Virgilian epic.

As it happened, Troy was a citadel with symbolic ties to the London in which *Hamlet* was being performed by late 1600 or

---

* Elsinore. Here as elsewhere the Everyman text preserves the Shakespearean word-forms to be found in the 1604/5 Second Quarto of *Hamlet* (as explained in the section on 'The Everyman Text of *Hamlet*'). Other proper names whose Everyman spellings may be unfamiliar to today's reader are *Fortinbrasse* (*Fortinbras* in the 1623 First Folio and in most modern editions), *Gertrard* (*Gertrude*), *Ostricke* (*Osric* or *Osrick*), and *Rosencraus* (*Rosencrantz*).

early 1601. According to an account popularized by the twelfth-century chronicler Geoffrey of Monmouth, the 'Troy-nauvaunt' that bestrode the Thames had been established by a great-grandson of the same Aeneas that Virgil's *Aeneid* had immortalized as founder of a 'new Troy' in Latium. The voyager who'd planted a third Troy on the site of what was in Shakespeare's day the largest city in Europe had supposedly bestowed his name, Brutus, on the land that became known as Britain. In the process he'd forged a kinship, both lineal and spiritual, that extended back from London through Rome (whose Republic had been instituted by another Brutus, Lucius Junius, in 509 BC, and defended by a third, Marcus Junius, in 44 BC) to the Trojan fortress that fronted the plains of Phrygia.

Given the legends they knew about their nation's early history, when Elizabethans heard allusions to the fall of Troy they were predisposed to connect that cataclysmic event both with the settlement of their own capital and with the cautionary moral that vigilance alone could preserve a latter-day Troy from the same fate that had overtaken the two cities London counted as its ancient forebears. To a cultivated member of Shakespeare's audience, then, 'the matter of Troy' was intimately related both to 'the matter of Britain' (which the playwright had already explored in nine 'chronicle histories' about the dynastic struggles that had brought about the Tudor order) and to 'the matter of Rome' (which the poet had been dramatizing in *Julius Caesar* as he began his preparations for *Hamlet*).

But Troy's import was in no sense limited to these patrilineal bonds. Like Rome, Troy was also an instance of what St Augustine had defined, by contrast with his *City of God*, as 'the City of Man'. As such it could serve as an archetype, not only for human societies in general, but for specific nations and individual human beings in particular.

In a number of his plays Shakespeare treats Troy as a figure for what the title character of *Macbeth* calls the 'Single State of Man' (I.iii.138). Troy's walls become symbols of the bulwark a soul must maintain against the forces of temptation, and for women especially those walls represent the virtue required to maintain chastity and honour. At the same time, Troy's towers, her 'wanton Tops' (*Troilus and Cressida*, IV.v.218), are emblems of pride, particularly as that primal sin manifests its potency in the unruliness of male assertion. And Troy's undoing can be viewed as a reiteration of the biblical Fall of Man.*

In many ways the ramparts and turrets of Elsonoure Castle function as Danish equivalents of the battlements surrounding Troy, and it is thus very much to the point when the Prince asks one of 'the Tragedians of the City' to resurrect an old play and narrate Aeneas' tale about 'Priam's Slaughter' (II.ii.352, 482). Hamlet calls for this speech because he believes his uncle has slain his father, and he yearns to model his vengeance on the mayhem a 'hellish Pyrrhus' (II.ii.498) delivers in retaliation for *his* father's death at the hands of the Trojans. In Pyrrhus' 'Cause', as the Prince will later say of Laertes', the title character sees an 'Image' of his own (V.ii.77–78). Eventually, following a lengthy delay that recapitulates Pyrrhus' 'Pause' (II.ii.522), Hamlet succeeds in his aim to emulate the deed, if not all the gory trappings, of his classical predecessor. As he does so, however, he himself is struck down by the treachery of Claudius and Laertes, and what is left of the royal court 'Stoops' to its 'Base' (II.ii.511) as Elsonoure collapses around its poisoned deliverer.

The unplanned but perhaps fitting result of Hamlet's Pyrrhic victory is that the sceptre he has been trying to wrest from the murderer of his father devolves to a youthful Norwegian who has been skirting the borders of Denmark in search of an opening that will enable him to avenge *his* father's death and territorial losses at the hands of the elder Hamlet. With no Dane of noble blood remaining to ascend Elsonoure's throne once the crown prince has drawn his last breath, the expiring Hamlet correctly surmises that 'th' Election lights / On Fortinbrasse'.

Just what an Elizabethan audience would have thought about

---

* For a sampling of Shakespearean reminders of the Troy paradigm, see *1 Henry VI*, V.vii.103–8, *2 Henry VI*, I.iv.19, III.iii.100–4, *3 Henry VI*, II.i.50–52, III.ii.185–89, IV.viii.25, *Titus Andronicus*, III.i.68–69, V.iii.83–84, *2 Henry IV*, I.i.170–75, and *All's Well That Ends Well*, I.i.133–36 (a passage that parallels *Hamlet*, i.iii.19–44).

Denmark's default to Fortinbrasse is impossible to say, but it seems likely that at least some of the Globe's more judicious patrons would have seen it as confirmation that a Troy-like Elsonoure had sown its own destruction through vices analogous to those that had proven disastrous to the original Ilium. Anyone who stopped to consider the broader implications of the Hamlet–Pyrrhus parallel, moreover, would probably have found it interesting that the Prince's role model is not a Trojan but a Greek. The effect of the playwright's inclusion of the Troy story, then, is to align Hamlet with those who reconnoitre and eventually invade the 'Pales and Forts' (I.iv.27) of his own castle. In other words, the Troy motif defines Denmark's heir apparent as the unwitting agent of an adversary* who enters Elsonoure at the end of the action only to discover that his enemies have already slaughtered themselves and made his battalions unnecessary.

Hamlet has often been called the most enigmatic of Shakespeare's tragedies, and the Pyrrhus narrative that prompts the Prince to 'cleave the general Air with horrid Speech' (II.ii.600) is characteristic of its conundrums. Little or nothing in this drama can be taken for what it superficially appears to be, and it is in keeping with the play's ironies and ambiguities that the title character's name means 'imbecile' or 'fool'. This fact is by no means lost on the paronomastic Prince, of course, and he plays upon it when he dons an 'Antic Disposition' (I.v.163) to lull his 'Mighty Opposites' (III.iv.62) into the confidence that they needn't trouble themselves over-much about the disconnected ramblings of a harmless madman. Hamlet picks up on the significance of his name a second time when he tells Polonius that 'It was a Brute part' for Brutus 'to kill so Capital a Calf' (III.ii.110–13) in the Roman Capitol. In this quip what sounds like a crude, throwaway pun conceals a veiled warning, because the name 'Brutus' carries the same connotations as the name

---

* Whether Hamlet considers Fortinbrasse an adversary is less than clear. In the soliloquy he delivers just before he departs for England (a speech that occurs only in the Second Quarto printing of the text), he paints his Norwegian counterpart as 'a delicate and tender Prince, / Whose Spirit, with divine Ambition puff'd, / Makes Mouths at the invisible Event' (IV.iv.45–47).

'Hamlet'. With the boldness his eccentric 'Disposition' gives him licence to exercise, the Prince is informing anyone with ears to hear that he too is engaged in a 'Brute part', and one that depends upon an artful combination of two distinct but related 'antique Roman' roles (V.ii.353). One is the persona Lucius Junius Brutus devised when he feigned idiocy to outwit a suspicious autocrat, avenge the death of his father, and expel the tyrannical Tarquins from a Rome that was thereafter to enjoy nearly five hundred years as a republic. The second is the role Marcus Junius Brutus took upon himself half a millennium later when he helped cut off a new dictator who seemed poised to restore the oppression a previous Brutus had abolished.

Like the Troy legend, the Hamlet story was a tale from the murky past. Although the story probably goes back to at least the tenth century, the earliest surviving narrative dates from the late twelfth century, when a Danish chronicler, Saxo Grammaticus, incorporated it in a Latin anthology that came to be known as the *Historiae Danicae*. It seems doubtful that Shakespeare had read Saxo, even though he might have had access to the *Historiae* in a version that was printed in Paris in 1524. But the playwright was probably aware of a sixteenth-century French adaptation of Saxo's narrative, the redaction François de Belleforest published in the 1570 edition of his *Histoires Tragiques*. Meanwhile Shakespeare was certainly familiar with an English dramatization of the tale, evidently not printed and thus no longer extant, that scholars have denominated the *Ur-Hamlet* ('prior *Hamlet*').

Prose writer Thomas Nashe referred to this revenge tragedy in his preface to Robert Greene's *Menaphon*, published in 1589. Theatre impresario Philip Henslowe recorded a performance of it in a June 1594 entry for his Diary. And Thomas Lodge alluded to the play in 1597 in his book *Wit's Misery*. Who wrote the *Ur-Hamlet* we can only speculate, but the leading candidate is Thomas Kyd, whose popular *Spanish Tragedy* (c. 1589) anticipated several of the dramaturgical devices – among them the Ghost who visits the hero to tell him how his father died, and the 'Mousetrap' the protagonist later stages in an effort to substantiate the Ghost's testimony – that Shakespeare is believed to have borrowed from the older drama.

Even more than the works that preceded it in the author's career, *Hamlet* is a play about various forms of acting. Almost everyone in the world it presents is adept in the craft of pretence,* and one of the predicaments each character faces is how to read and react to the roles adopted by others. A similar problem confronts the audience. To what extent are we to infer that the persons of the drama, as distinguished from the actors impersonating those persons, are 'merely Players' (*As You Like It*, II.vii.140) at given moments in the plot?

The Prince poses this question in the first scene at Court when he calls attention to the word 'Seems'. What Hamlet appears to mean when he says, 'I know not Seems' (I.ii.75) is that he is incapable of – and indeed totally inexperienced with – 'Show'. Unlike others, he implies disingenuously, he is unwilling to participate in 'Actions that a man might Play' to deceive onlookers into thinking that he is something he may seem to be but knows himself not to be (I.ii.75–86). Later in the play, when the Prince looks in on a Claudius who has bent himself into the posture of a man at prayer (and, as the audience knows, is genuinely trying to invest that posture with its conventional meaning), Hamlet shows that he knows not 'Seems' in another sense. He assumes that in this instance 'the Action lies / In his true Nature' (III.iii.61–62), and he therefore spares for now a 'Villain' whose would-be slaughterer mistakenly takes him to be engaged 'in the Purging of his Soul' (III.iii.76, 85).

Like the Troy that Shakespeare depicts in *Troilus and Cressida*, the 'State' the hero seeks to set right in *Hamlet* is 'rotten' at the core (I.iv.89). For the Prince as for Thersites in the other play, the

---

* For Polonius it is axiomatic that to be human is to be a creature of guile. When he tells his son, 'To thine own Self be True' (I.iii.78), the cagey old statesman is not advising Laertes to adhere to the highest principles of virtue so much as telling him to protect himself in a deceptive and dangerous world by keeping his own thoughts and motives under lock and key. To be sure that the young man is heeding his counsel, Polonius commissions a friendly spy to follow Laertes to Paris and report back on the young man's behaviour. In characteristic fashion, Polonius recommends that Reynaldo use 'Forgeries' (lies invented for the purpose) as a way of extracting information about Laertes from supposedly idle conversations with the young man's acquaintances.

'Argument' is largely about 'a Whore and a Cuckold'. But of course in this case the cuckold is the hero's dead father, and his cuckolder is also a murderer and a usurper; and that, for Hamlet, is the 'necessary Question of the Play' (III.ii.49–50).

Once the Prince fixes his mind upon the task he regards himself as commissioned to undertake, he concludes that there is but one detail to be disposed of before he proceeds; to eliminate any possibility that the accused King is innocent, Hamlet must subject the unknowing suspect to a diagnostic test to determine whether the Ghost has spoken truthfully about how the elder Hamlet died (II.ii.626–43). Hamlet presumes that the Ghost's veracity is the only issue that needs to be resolved before the King's executioner knows his 'Course'. But it seems likely that Shakespeare expected his audiences – or at least 'those with Judgements in such Matters' (II.ii.470–71) – to ponder a couple of additional issues: first, whether Hamlet should infer that even a truth-telling Ghost is necessarily 'Honest' in a sense that would call for it to be received at face value and obeyed, and, second, whether Hamlet would not be well advised to weigh the Ghost's command in the light of biblical injunctions (see Romans 12:17–13:7) and statutory prohibitions against private vengeance.*

The opening scenes of the play draw a significant contrast between the Prince's response to the Ghost and the reactions of more cautious observers such as Horatio and the Danish guard. And a number of Hamlet's speeches suggest that the Prince's orientation to what he considers a sacred duty is difficult to reconcile with Christian precepts that are shown to be applicable elsewhere in the action. In the Prayer Scene, for example, Shakespeare contrives to have Hamlet come upon Claudius at a moment when the King's 'Conscience' has been caught (II.ii.626–43) in a way the Prince had not expected and would not have

---

* The laws that forbade English citizens to take justice into their own hands were paralleled by similar statutes in Denmark and in other nations. But as Fredson Bowers points out in *Elizabethan Revenge Tragedy, 1587–1642* (Princeton: Princeton University Press, 1942), Renaissance codes of honour were often hard to square with official pronouncements against duelling and other unauthorized means of righting individual wrongs. See Anne Barton's introduction to the New Penguin Shakespeare edition of *Hamlet* (Harmondsworth: Penguin Books, 1980) for a discussion of the ambivalence Elizabethans felt about private vengeance.

sought. At this juncture it is possible that even so wicked a man as Claudius might repent. We are surely meant to be surprised at this development, and to ask ourselves what kind of 'Consummation' is now 'Devoutly to be wished' (III.i.61). Then, a moment later, we are probably meant to ask whether Hamlet's decision to postpone his 'Purgation' (III.ii.331) until some occasion when the King's 'Heels may kick at Heaven' (III.iii.93) isn't one that raises doubts about the Prince's own relationship with Heaven. In similar fashion we are no doubt intended to be brought up short when Hamlet tells Horatio that he has arranged for Rosencraus and Guildenstern to be 'put to sudden Death, / Not Shriving-time allow'd', and then says that 'They are not near my Conscience' (V.ii.46–47, 58).

The Prince's dealings with his former schoolmates offer an instructive insight into the way *Hamlet* operates as a work of drama. On the one hand we have the Prince's view of Rosencraus and Guildenstern as 'Adders fang'd' (III.iv.199), willing and presumably knowing tools of the King's cunning. On the other hand we have what might be said to be the play's more objective portrayal of them, as a pair of courtiers who come to Elsonoure at the request of Hamlet's mother and uncle, who seek to help the Queen find out why her son is acting so strangely, and who then comport themselves in accordance with what they perceive to be the legitimate interests of a monarch to whom they owe loyal obedience. So far as we can demonstrate, they know nothing of what Claudius has done in the past and they are never made privy to the King's designs against his nephew.*

Like Polonius, and indeed like virtually every other character in this world of intrigue and counter-intrigue, Hamlet attempts 'by Indirections' to 'find Directions out' (II.i.63). More often than not, for the Prince as for others, those 'Indirections' either result in or contribute tragically to 'Purposes mistook / Fall'n on th' Inventors' Heads' (V.ii.396–97). To what extent Hamlet himself

---

* In *Rosencrantz and Guildenstern Are Dead*, Tom Stoppard's witty recasting of the Hamlet story from the perspective of two minor players in the action, the hero's schoolmates are puzzled dupes in an absurdist psychodrama.

is to be held accountable for the consequences of his misjudge-
ments – for the products of his frequently rough-hewn 'Ends'
(V.ii.10–11) – is a matter of interpretation. But in the encounters
that draw the drama to a close he acts with a nobility that elicits
the most touching benediction a tragic hero ever received. For
most audiences Horatio's prayer for 'Flights of Angels' to 'sing' a
'sweet Prince' to his 'Rest' (V.ii.371–72) is sufficient to assure 'the
yet unknowing World' (V.ii.391) that the Prince has at last found
the way 'rightly to be Great' (IV.iv.50). For others it is simply a
final reminder that, for this as for many of the other questions
Hamlet raises, the only answer the play proffers with any clarity is
'Silence' (V.ii.370).

THE TEXT OF THE EVERYMAN SHAKESPEARE

―――――――

Background

THE EARLY PRINTINGS OF SHAKESPEARE'S WORKS

Many of us enjoy our first encounter with Shakespeare when we're introduced to *Julius Caesar* or *Macbeth* at school. It may therefore surprise us that neither of these tragedies could ever have been read, let alone studied, by most of the playwright's contemporaries. They began as scripts for performance and, along with seventeen other titles that never saw print during Shakespeare's lifetime, they made their inaugural appearance as 'literary' works seven years after his death, in the 1623 collection we know today as the First Folio.

The Folio contained thirty-six titles in all. Of these, half had been issued previously in the small paperbacks we now refer to as quartos.* Like several of the plays first published in the Folio, the most trustworthy of the quarto printings appear to have been set either from Shakespeare's own manuscripts or from faithful copies of them. It's not impossible that the poet himself prepared some of these works for the press, and it's intriguing to imagine him reviewing proof-pages as the words he'd written for actors to speak and embody were being transposed into the type that readers would filter through their eyes, minds, and imaginations. But, alas, there's no indisputable evidence that Shakespeare had any direct involvement with the publication of these early editions of his plays.

What about the scripts that achieved print for the first time in

―――――――

* Quartos derived their name from the four-leaf units of which these small books were comprised: large sheets of paper that had been folded twice after printing to yield four leaves, or eight pages. Folios, volumes with twice the page-size of quartos, were put together from two-leaf units: sheets that had been folded once after printing to yield four pages.

the Folio? Had the dramatist taken any steps to give the permanency of book form to those texts? We don't know. All we can say is that when he fell fatally ill in 1616, Shakespeare was denied any opportunities he might otherwise have taken to ensure that his 'insubstantial Pageants' survived the mortal who was now slipping into the 'dark Backward and Abysm of Time'.

Fortunately, two of the playwright's colleagues felt an obligation, as they put it, 'to procure his Orphans Guardians'. Sometime after his death John Heminge (or Heminges) and Henry Condell made arrangements to preserve Shakespeare's theatrical compositions in a manner that would keep them vibrant for all time. They dedicated their endeavour to two noblemen who had helped see England's foremost acting company through some of its most trying vicissitudes. They solicited several poetic tributes for the volume, among them a now-famous eulogy by fellow writer Ben Jonson. They commissioned an engraved portrait of Shakespeare to adorn the frontispiece. And they did their utmost to display the author's dramatic works in a style that would both dignify them and make them accessible to 'the great Variety of Readers'.

As they prepared Shakespeare's plays for the compositors who would set them into stately Folio columns, Heminge and Condell (or editors designated to carry out their wishes) revised and augmented many of the entrances, exits, and other stage directions in the manuscripts. They divided most of the works into acts and scenes.* For a number of plays they appended 'Names of the Actors', or casts of characters. Meanwhile they made every effort to guarantee that the Folio printers had reliable copy-texts for each of the titles: authoritative manuscripts for the plays that had not been published previously, and good quarto printings (annotated in some instances to insert staging details, mark script changes, and add supplementary material) for the ones that had been issued prior to the Folio. For several titles they supplied texts

---

* The early quartos, reflecting the unbroken sequence that probably typified Elizabethan and Jacobean performances of the plays, had been printed without the structural demarcations usual in Renaissance editions of classical drama.

that were substantively different from, if not always demon-
strably superior to, the quarto versions that preceded them.

Like even the most accurate of the printings that preceded it, the
Folio collection was flawed by minor blemishes. But it more than
fulfilled the purpose of its generous-minded compilers: 'to keep
the memory of so worthy a Friend and Fellow alive as was our
Shakespeare'. In the process it provided a publishing model that
remains instructive today.

MODERN EDITIONS OF THE PLAYS AND POEMS
When we compare the First Folio and its predecessors with the
usual modern edition of Shakespeare's works, we're more apt to
be impressed by the differences than by the similarities. Today's
texts of Renaissance drama are normally produced in conformity
with twentieth-century standards of punctuation and usage; as a
consequence they look more neat, clean, and, to our eyes, 'right'
than do the original printings. Thanks to an editorial tradition
that extends back to the early eighteenth century and beyond,
most of the rough spots in the early printings of Shakespeare have
long been smoothed away. Textual scholars have ferreted out
redundancies and eradicated inconsistencies. They've mended
what they've perceived to be errors and oversights in the
playscripts, and they've systematically attended to what they've
construed as misreadings by the copyists and compositors who
transmitted these playscripts to posterity. They've added '[With-
in]' brackets and other theatrical notations. They've revised stage
directions they've judged incomplete or inadequate in the initial
printings. They've regularized disparities in the speech headings.
They've gone back to the playwright's sources and reinstated the
proper forms for many of the character and place names which a
presumably hasty or inattentive author got 'wrong' as he
conferred identities on his dramatis personae and stage locales.
They've replaced obsolete words like *bankrout* with their modern
heirs (in this case *bankrupt*). And in a multitude of other ways
they've accommodated Shakespeare to the tastes, interests, and
expectations of latter-day readers.

The results, on the whole, have been splendid. But interpreting the artistic designs of a complex writer is always problematical, and the task is especially challenging when that writer happens to have been a poet who felt unconstrained by many of the 'rules' that more conventional dramatists respected. The undertaking becomes further complicated when new rules, and new criteria of linguistic and social correctness, are imposed by subsequent generations of artists and critics.

To some degree in his own era, but even more in the neoclassical period (1660–1800) that came in its wake, Shakespeare's most ardent admirers thought it necessary to apologise for what Ben Jonson hinted at in his allusion to the 'small Latin, and less Greek' of an untutored prodigy. To be sure, the 'sweet Swan of Avon' sustained his popularity; in fact his reputation rose so steadily that by the end of the eighteenth century he'd eclipsed Jonson and his other coevals and become the object of near-universal Bardolatry. But in the theatre most of his plays were being adapted in ways that were deemed advisable to tame their supposed wildness and bring them into conformity with the decorum of a society that took pride in its refinement. As one might expect, some of the attitudes that induced theatre proprietors to metamorphose an unpolished poet from the provinces into something closer to an urbane man of letters also influenced Shakespeare's editors. Persuaded that the dramatist's works were marred by crudities that needed expunging, they applied their ministrations to the canon with painstaking diligence.

Twentieth-century editors have moved away from many of the presuppositions that guided a succession of earlier improvers. But a glance at the textual apparatus accompanying virtually any modern publication of the plays and poems will show that emendations and editorial procedures deriving from such forebears as the sets published by Nicholas Rowe (1709), Alexander Pope (1723–25, 1728), Lewis Theobald (1733, 1740, 1757), Thomas Hanmer (1743–45, 1770–71), Samuel Johnson (1765), Edward Capell (1768), George Steevens (1773), and Edmond Malone (1790) retain a strong hold on today's renderings of the playwright's works. The consequence is a 'Shakespeare' who offers the tidiness we've come to expect in our libraries of treasured authors, but not necessarily the playwright a 1599 reader of the Second Quarto of *Romeo and Juliet* would still be able to recognize as a contemporary.

OLD LIGHT ON THE TOPIC

Over the last two decades we've learned from art curators that paintings by Old Masters such as Michelangelo and Rembrandt look a lot brighter when centuries of grime are removed from their surfaces – when hues that had become dulled with soot and other extanaeous matter are allowed to radiate again with something approximating their pristine luminosity. We've learned from conductors like Christopher Hogwood that there are aesthetic rewards to be gained from a return to the scorings and instruments with which Renaissance and Baroque musical compositions were first presented. We've learned from twentieth-century experiments in the performance of Shakespeare's plays that an open, multi-level stage, analogous to that on which the scripts were originally enacted, does more justice to their dramaturgical techniques than does a proscenium auditorium devised for works that came later in the development of Western theatre. We've learned from archaeological excavations in London's Bankside area that the foundations of playhouses such as the Rose and the Globe look rather different from what many historians had expected. And we're now learning from a close scrutiny of Shakespeare's texts that they too look different, and function differently, when we accept them for what they are and resist the impulse to 'normalize' features that strike us initially as quirky, unkempt, or unsophisticated.

The Aims that Guide the Everyman *Text*

Like other modern editions of the dramatist's plays and poems, The Everyman Shakespeare owes an incalculable debt to the scholarship that has led to so many excellent renderings of the author's works. But in an attempt to draw fresh inspiration from the spirit that animated those remarkable achievements at the outset, the Everyman edition departs in a number of respects from the usual post-Folio approach to the presentation of Shakespeare's texts.

RESTORING SOME OF THE NUANCES OF
RENAISSANCE PUNCTUATION

In its punctuation, Everyman attempts to give equal emphasis to sound and sense. In places where Renaissance practice calls for heavier punctuation than we'd normally employ – to mark the caesural pause in the middle of a line of verse, for instance – Everyman sometimes retains commas that other modern editions omit. Meanwhile, in places where current practice calls for the inclusion of commas – after vocatives and interjections such as 'O' and 'alas', say, or before 'Madam' or 'Sir' in phrases such as 'Ay Madam' or 'Yes Sir' – Everyman follows the original printings and omits them.

Occasionally the absence of a comma has a significant bearing on what an expression means, or can mean. At one point in *Othello*, for example, Iago tells the Moor 'Marry patience' (IV.i.90). Inserting a comma after 'Marry', as most of today's editions do, limits Iago's utterance to one that says 'Come now, have patience.' Leaving the clause as it stands in the Folio, the way the Everyman text does, permits Iago's words to have the additional, agonizingly ironic sense 'Be wed to Patience'.

The early texts generally deploy exclamation points quite sparingly, and the Everyman text follows suit. Everyman also follows the early editions, more often than not, when they use question marks in places that seem unusual by current standards: at the ends of what we'd normally treat as exclamations, for example, or at the ends of interrogative clauses in sentences that we'd ordinarily denote as questions in their entirety.

The early texts make no orthographic distinction between simple plurals and either singular or plural possessives, and there are times when the context doesn't indicate whether a word spelled *Sisters*, say, should be rendered *Sisters*, *Sisters'*, or *Sister's* in today's usage. In such situations the Everyman edition prints the word in the form modern usage prescribes for plurals.

REVIVING SOME OF THE FLEXIBILITY OF
RENAISSANCE SPELLING

Spelling had not become standardized by Shakespeare's time, and that meant that many words could take a variety of forms. Like James Joyce and some of the other innovative prose and verse stylists of our own century, Shakespeare revelled in the freedom a largely unanchored language provided, and with that in mind Everyman retains original spelling forms (or adaptations of those forms that preserve their key distinctions from modern spellings) whenever there is any reason to suspect that they might have a bearing on how a word was intended to be pronounced or on what it meant, or could have meant, in the playwright's day. When there is any likelihood that multiple forms of the same word could be significant, moreover, the Everyman text mirrors the diversity to be found in the original printings.

In many cases this practice affects the personalities of Shakespeare's characters. One of the heroine's most familiar questions in *Romeo and Juliet* is 'What's in a Name?' For two and a half centuries readers – and as a consequence actors, directors, theatre audiences, and commentators – have been led to believe that Juliet was addressing this query to a Romeo named 'Montague'. In fact 'Montague' *was* the name Shakespeare found in his principal source for the play. For reasons that will become apparent to anyone who examines the tragedy in detail, however, the playwright changed his protagonist's surname to 'Mountague', a word that plays on both 'mount' and 'ague' (fever). Setting aside an editorial practice that began with Lewis Theobald in the middle of the eighteenth century, Everyman resurrects the name the dramatist himself gave Juliet's lover.

Readers of *The Merchant of Venice* in the Everyman set will be amused to learn that the character modern editions usually identify as 'Lancelot' is in reality 'Launcelet', a name that calls attention to the clown's lusty 'little lance'. Like Costard in *Love's Labour's Lost*, another stage bumpkin who was probably played by the actor Will Kemp, Launcelet is an upright 'Member of the Commonwealth'; we eventually learn that he's left a pliant wench 'with Child'.

Readers of *Hamlet* will find that 'Fortinbras' (as the name of the Prince's Norwegian opposite is rendered in the First Folio and in most modern editions) appears in the earlier, authoritative 1604 Second Quarto of the play as 'Fortinbrasse'. In the opening scene of that text a surname that meant 'strong in arms' in French is introduced to the accompaniment of puns on *brazen*, in the phrase 'brazon Cannon', and on *metal*, in the phrase 'unimprooued mettle'. In the same play readers of the Everyman text will encounter 'Ostricke', the ostrich-like courtier who invites the Prince of Denmark to participate in the fateful fencing match that draws *Hamlet* to a close. Only in its final entrance direction for the obsequious fop does the Second Quarto call this character 'Osrick', the name he bears in all the Folio text's references to him and in most modern editions of Shakespeare's most popular tragedy.

Readers of the Everyman *Macbeth* will discover that the fabled 'Weird Sisters' appear only as the 'weyward' or 'weyard' Sisters. Shakespeare and his contemporaries knew that in his *Chronicles of England, Scotland, and Ireland* Raphael Holinshed had used the term 'weird sisters' to describe the witches who accost Macbeth and Banquo on the heath; but no doubt because he wished to play on *wayward*, the playwright changed their name to *weyward*. Like Samuel Johnson, who thought punning vulgar and lamented Shakespeare's proclivity to seduction by this 'fatal Cleopatra', Lewis Theobald saw no reason to retain the playwright's weyward spelling of the witches' name. He thus restored the 'correct' form from Holinshed, and editors ever since have generally done likewise.

In many instances Renaissance English had a single spelling for what we now define as two separate words. For example, *humane* combined the senses of 'human' and 'humane' in modern English. In the First Folio printing of *Macbeth* the protagonist's wife expresses a concern that her husband is 'too full o'th' Milke of humane kindnesse.' As she phrases it, *humane kindnesse* can mean several things, among them 'humankind-ness', 'human kindness', and 'humane kindness'. It is thus a reminder that to be true to his or her own 'kind' a human being must be 'kind' in the sense we now attach to 'humane'. To disregard this logic, as the protagonist and his wife will soon prove, is to disregard a principle as basic to the cosmos as the laws of gravity.

In a way that parallels *humane*, *bad* could mean either 'bad' or 'bade', *borne* either 'born' or 'borne', *ere* either 'ere' (before) or 'e'er' (ever), *least* either 'least' or 'lest', *lye* either 'lie' or 'lye', *nere* either 'ne'er' or 'near' (though the usual spellings for the latter were *neare* or *neere*), *powre* either 'pour' or 'power', *then* either 'than' or 'then', and *tide* either 'tide' or 'tied'.

There were a number of word-forms that functioned in Renaissance English as interchangeable doublets. *Travail* could mean 'travel', for example, and *travel* could mean 'travail'. By the same token, *deer* could mean *dear* and vice versa, *dew* could mean *due*, *hart* could mean *heart*, and (as we've already noted) *mettle* could mean *metal*.

A particularly interesting instance of the equivocal or double meanings some word-forms had in Shakespeare's time is *loose*, which can often become either 'loose' or 'lose' when we render it in modern English. In *The Comedy of Errors* when Antipholus of Syracuse compares himself to 'a Drop / Of Water that in the Ocean seeks another Drop' and then says he will 'loose' himself in quest of his long-lost twin, he means both (a) that he will release himself into a vast unknown, and (b) that he will lose his own identity, if necessary, to be reunited with the brother for whom he searches. On the other hand, in *Hamlet* when Polonius says he'll 'loose' his daughter to the Prince, he little suspects that by so doing he will also lose his daughter.

In some cases the playwright employs word-forms that can be translated into words we wouldn't think of as related today: *sowre*, for instance, which can mean 'sour', 'sower', or 'sore', depending on the context. In other cases he uses forms that do have modern counterparts, but not counterparts with the same potential for multiple connotation. For example, *onely* usually means 'only' in the modern sense; but occasionally Shakespeare gives it a figurative, adverbial twist that would require a nonce word such as 'one-ly' to replicate in current English.

In a few cases Shakespeare employs word-forms that have only seeming equivalents in modern usage. For example, *abhominable*, which meant 'inhuman' (derived, however incorrectly, from *ab*, 'away from', and *homine*, 'man') to the poet and his contemporaries, is not the same word as our *abominable* (ill-omened, abhorrent). In his advice to the visiting players Hamlet complains about incompetent actors who imitate 'Humanity so abhominably' as to make the characters they depict seem unrecognizable as men. Modern readers who don't realize the distinction between Shakespeare's word and our own, and who see *abominable* on the page before them, don't register the full import of the Prince's satire.

Modern English treats as single words a number of word-forms that were normally spelled as two words in Shakespeare's time. What we render as *myself*, for example, and use primarily as a reflexive or intensifying pronoun, is almost invariably spelled *my self* in Shakespeare's works; so also with *her self*, *thy self*, *your self*, and *it self* (where *it* functions as *its* does today). Often there is no discernible difference between Shakespeare's usage and our own. At other times there is, however, as we are reminded when we come across a phrase such as 'our innocent self' in *Macbeth* and think how strained it would sound in modern parlance, or as we observe when we note how naturally the self is objectified in the balanced clauses of the Balcony Scene in *Romeo and Juliet*:

> Romeo, doffe thy name,
> And for thy name, which is no part of thee,
> Take all my selfe.

Yet another difference between Renaissance orthography and our own can be exemplified with words such as *today*, *tonight*, and *tomorrow*, which (unlike *yesterday*) were treated as two words in Shakespeare's time. In *Macbeth* when the Folio prints 'Duncan comes here to Night', the unattached *to* can function either as a preposition (with *Night* as its object, or in this case its destination) or as the first part of an infinitive (with *Night* operating figuratively as a verb). Consider the ambiguity a Renaissance reader would have detected in the original publication of one of the most celebrated soliloquies in all of Shakespeare:

> To morrow, and to morrow, and to morrow,
> Creeps in this petty pace from day to day,
> To the last Syllable of Recorded time:
> And all our yesterdayes, have lighted Fooles
> The way to dusty death.

Here, by implication, the route 'to morrow' is identical with 'the way to dusty death', a relationship we miss if we don't know that for Macbeth, and for the audiences who first heard these lines spoken, *to morrow* was not a single word but a potentially equivocal two-word phrase.

RECAPTURING THE ABILITY TO HEAR WITH OUR EYES
When we fail to recall that Shakespeare's scripts were designed initially to provide words for people to hear in the theatre, we sometimes overlook a fact that is fundamental to the artistic structure of a work like *Macbeth*: that the messages a sequence of sounds convey through the ear are, if anything, even more significant than the messages a sequence of letters, punctuation marks, and white spaces on a printed page transmit through the eye. A telling illustration of this point, and of the potential for ambiguous or multiple implication in any Shakespearean script, may be found in the dethronement scene of *Richard II*. When Henry Bullingbrook asks the King if he is ready to resign his crown, Richard replies 'I, no no I; for I must nothing be.' Here the punctuation in the 1608 Fourth Quarto (the earliest text to print this richly complex passage) permits each *I* to signify either 'ay' or 'I' (*I* being the usual spelling for 'ay' in Shakespeare's time).

Understanding *I* to mean 'I' permits additional play on *no*, which can be heard (at least in its first occurrence) as 'know'. Meanwhile the second and third soundings of *I*, if not the first, can also be heard as 'eye'. In the context in which this line occurs, that sense echoes a thematically pertinent passage from Matthew 18:9: 'if thine eye offend thee, pluck it out'.

But these are not all the implications *I* can have here. It can also represent the Roman numeral for '1', which will soon be reduced, as Richard notes, to 'nothing' (o), along with the speaker's title, his worldly possessions, his manhood, and eventually his life. In Shakespeare's time, to become 'nothing' was, *inter alia*, to be emasculated, to be made a 'weaker vessel' (1 Peter 3:7) with 'no thing'. As the Fool in *King Lear* reminds another monarch who has abdicated his throne, a man in want of an 'I' is impotent, 'an O without a Figure' (I.iv.207). In addition to its other dimensions, then, Richard's reply is a statement that can be formulated mathematically, and in symbols that anticipate the binary system behind today's computer technology: '1, 0, 0, 1, for 1 must 0 be.'

Modern editions usually render Richard's line 'Ay, no; no, ay; for I must nothing be'. Presenting the line in that fashion makes good sense of what Richard is saying. But as we've seen, it doesn't make total sense of it, and it doesn't call attention to Richard's paradoxes in the same way that hearing or seeing three undifferentiated *I*'s is likely to have done for Shakespeare's contemporaries. Their culture was more attuned than ours is to the oral and aural dimensions of language, and if we want to appreciate the special qualities of their dramatic art we need to train ourselves to 'hear' the word-forms we see on the page. We must learn to recognize that for many of what we tend to think of as fixed linkages between sound and meaning (the vowel 'I', say, and the word 'eye'), there were alternative linkages (such as the vowel 'I' and the words 'I' and 'Ay') that could be just as pertinent to what the playwright was communicating through the ears of his theatre patrons at a given moment. As the word *audience* itself may help us to remember, people in Shakespeare's time normally spoke of 'hearing' rather than 'seeing' a play.

In its text of *Richard II*, the Everyman edition reproduces the title character's line as it appears in the early printings of the tragedy. Ideally the orthographic oddity of the repeated *I*'s will encourage today's readers to ponder Richard's utterance, and the play it epitomizes, as a characteristically Shakespearean enigma.

OTHER ASPECTS OF THE EVERYMAN TEXT

Now for a few words about other features of the Everyman text.

One of the first things readers will notice about this edition is its bountiful use of capitalized words. In this practice as in others, the Everyman exemplar is the First Folio, and especially the works in the Folio sections billed as 'Histories' and 'Tragedies'.* Everyman makes no attempt to adhere to the Folio printings with literal exactitude. In some instances the Folio capitalizes words that the Everyman text of the same passage lowercases; in other instances Everyman capitalizes words not uppercased in the Folio. The objective is merely to suggest something of the flavour, and what appears to have been the rationale, of Renaissance capitalization, in the hope that today's audiences will be made continually aware that the works they're contemplating derive from an earlier epoch.

Readers will also notice that instead of cluttering the text with stage directions such as '[Aside]' or '[To Rosse]', the Everyman text employs unobtrusive dashes to indicate shifts in mode of address. In an effort to keep the page relatively clear of words not supplied by the original printings, Everyman also exercises restraint in its addition of editor-generated stage directions. Where the dialogue makes it obvious that a significant action occurs, the Everyman text inserts a square-bracketed phrase such as '[Fleance escapes]'. Where what the dialogue implies is subject

---

* The quarto printings employ far fewer capital letters than does the Folio. Capitalization seems to have been regarded as a means of recognizing the status ascribed to certain words (*Noble*, for example, is almost always capitalized), titles (not only King, Queen, Duke, and Duchess, but Sir and Madam), genres (tragedies were regarded as more 'serious' than comedies in more than one sense), and forms of publication (quartos, being associated with ephemera such as 'plays', were not thought to be as 'grave' as the folios that bestowed immortality on 'works', writings that, in the words of Ben Jonson's eulogy to Shakespeare, were 'not of an age, but for all time').

to differing interpretations, however, the Everyman text provides a facing-page note to discuss the most plausible inferences.

Like other modern editions, the Everyman text combines into 'shared' verse lines (lines divided among two or more speakers) many of the part-lines to be found in the early publications of the plays. One exception to the usual modern procedure is that Everyman indents some lines that are not components of shared verses. At times, for example, the opening line of a scene stops short of the metrical norm, a pentameter (five-foot) or hexameter (six-foot) line comprised predominantly of iambic units (unstressed syllables followed by stressed ones). In such cases Everyman uses indentation as a reminder that scenes can begin as well as end in mid-line (an extension of the ancient convention that an epic commences *in media res*, 'in the midst of the action'). Everyman also uses indentation to reflect what appear to be pauses in the dialogue, either to allow other activity to transpire (as happens in *Macbeth*, II.iii.87, when a brief line 'What's the Business?' follows a Folio stage direction that reads 'Bell rings. Enter Lady') or to permit a character to hesitate for a moment of reflection (as happens a few seconds later in the same scene when Macduff responds to a demand to 'Speak, speak' with the reply 'O gentle Lady, / 'Tis not for you to hear what I can speak').

Everyman preserves many of the anomalies in the early texts. Among other things, this practice pertains to the way characters are depicted. In *A Midsummer Night's Dream*, for example, the ruler of Athens is usually identified in speech headings and stage directions as 'Theseus', but sometimes he is referred to by his title as 'Duke'. In the same play Oberon's merry sprite goes by two different names: 'Puck' and 'Robin Goodfellow'.

Readers of the Everyman edition will sometimes discover that characters they've known, or known about, for years don't appear in the original printings. When they open the pages of the Everyman *Macbeth*, for example, they'll learn that Shakespeare's audiences were unaware of any woman with the title 'Lady Macbeth'. In the only authoritative text we have of the Scottish tragedy, the protagonist's spouse goes by such names as 'Macbeth's Lady', 'Macbeth's Wife', or simply 'Lady', but at no time is she listed or mentioned as 'Lady Macbeth'. The same is true of the character usually designated 'Lady Capulet' in modern editions of *Romeo and Juliet*. 'Capulet's Wife' makes appearances as 'Mother', 'Old Lady', 'Lady', or simply 'Wife'; but she's never termed 'Lady Capulet', and her husband never treats her with the dignity such a title would connote.

Rather than 'correct' the grammar in Shakespeare's works to eliminate what modern usage would categorize as solecisms (as when Mercutio says 'my Wits faints' in *Romeo and Juliet*), the Everyman text leaves it intact. Among other things, this principle applies to instances in which archaic forms preserve idioms that differ slightly from related modern expressions (as in the clause 'you are too blame', where 'too' frequently functions as an adverb and 'blame' is used, not as a verb, but as an adjective roughly equivalent to 'blameworthy').

Finally, and most importantly, the Everyman edition leaves unchanged any reading in the original text that is not manifestly erroneous. Unlike other modern renderings of Shakespeare's works, Everyman substitutes emendations only when obvious problems can be dealt with by obvious solutions.

The Everyman *Text of* Hamlet

Like several of Shakespeare's other works, *Hamlet* made its initial foray into print in a volume that was published without the permission of its author and the theatre company he represented as shareholder, performer, and resident dramatist. From all indications the basis of the garbled 1603 First Quarto (Q1) of Shakespeare's tragedy was a playbook that had been assembled from memory. Scholars now believe the text's compiler to have been an actor who'd played minor roles as a hired man for the Lord Chamberlain's troupe at the Globe, and if they are right the copy he supplied for Q1 *Hamlet* was a script he'd cobbled together for a reduced cast to employ during tours of the provinces.

The First Quarto confers idiosyncratic identities on several of the play's characters. Polonius becomes Corambis, for example (a name the Q1 pirate might have taken from the 'Corambus' a hired man would have played in *All's Well That Ends Well*), Reynaldo becomes Montano (a name the compiler might have imported from *Othello*, another work a man in Shakespeare's company could have appeared in shortly before the emergence of the 1603 *Hamlet*), and the Prince's former schoolmates become Rossencraft and Gilderstone.* Thematically, Q1 puts considerable emphasis on Hamlet's madness. It positions his 'To be or not to be' meditation earlier in the action than do later printings of the tragedy. It depicts his mother as a stronger and less culpable woman than the frail creature tradition has bequeathed to posterity. And it features several passages (including a brief scene in which Horatio tells the Queen about the Prince's return from his voyage to England) without precise counterparts in the editions that superseded it.

Because of its differences from later publications of *Hamlet*, Q1 is sometimes thought to bear witness to authorial first thoughts (if it is assumed to reflect an early version of the play we know through more reliable channels) or revisions (if it is assumed to reflect an adaptation subsequent to the scripts that made their way into later printings) that would otherwise have gone unrecorded. Perhaps so, but many interpreters find it easier to believe that any 'originality' to be detected in Q1 testifies primarily to the invention necessity would have enjoined upon the person responsible for so uneven a text. Lacking the memory skills to recreate, or even competently paraphrase, large segments of a

---

* A bit player who'd never seen the full promptbook of *Hamlet* might well have forgotten the names of these characters, if indeed he'd ever have had occasion to learn them. We should bear in mind, too, that a compiler's ability to reconstruct a script from memory was dependent on what his ears had taken in, and that an actor in even a full-text *Hamlet* would have had no more than five opportunities a performance to hear the name 'Polonius' in the dialogue and three opportunities (all in one conversation) to hear 'Reynaldo' – a handicap that would have been even more severe if the actor was offstage when these *dramatis personae* were being addressed. 'Rossencraft' sounds like a felicitous mishearing of 'Rosencraus' (the Second Quarto's name for the courtier who becomes 'Rosincrance' in the First Folio printing). Meanwhile 'Gilderstone', echoing the 'Guyldersterne' of two lines in the Q2 text of II.ii, may preserve one of the ways this name was pronounced in the theatre.

work that has become proverbial for its complexity, he probably had no choice but to supplement whatever he could recall from the dialogue with additional matter of his own devising.*

The First Quarto of *Hamlet* provides a vivid illustration of the way popular plays could be appropriated for unlicensed uses in Shakespeare's time. It offers an independent, and at times valuable, source of information about some of the language and staging details of a multifaceted drama. But otherwise it contributes little of significance to a modern editor's rendering of the tragedy.

Less than two years after the appearance of Q1, a Second Quarto of *Hamlet*, this one undoubtedly authorized by the playwright and his colleagues, began advertising itself to London bookbuyers as 'Newly imprinted and enlarged to almost as much againe as it was, according to the true and perfect Coppie'. The Q2 printing appears to have been completed as 1604 gave way to 1605: of the seven examples of the book that survive, three bear the earlier date and four the later.

The Second Quarto *Hamlet* is nearly twice as long as its predecessor (3,764 lines, as opposed to the 2,154 in Q1), and in all probability it was published directly from the author's manuscript of the play. It's a fascinating document, and it constitutes the lengthiest and by far the most coherent seventeenth-century printing of Shakespeare's tragedy.

Unfortunately, for all its virtues, the Q2 *Hamlet* is not altogether self-sufficient. Like other texts that appear to have been set from the author's incompletely polished 'foul papers', it lacks punctuation (or at least adequate punctuation) in places, and in a handful of instances it is marred by lacunae that have to be filled in with words and phrases from elsewhere (in this case the 1623 First Folio edition of the play). At times, moreover, Q2's readings suggest that the manuscript its compositors had before them was difficult to decipher.

---

* Some scholars believe that more than one 'reporter' was involved in the preparation of the script published as Q1 *Hamlet*. And it is not inconceivable that the text was creacted by someone other than an actor, or group of actors, who'd worked for the Lord Chamberlain's Men.

Not surprisingly, given these circumstances, the extant copies of the Second Quarto disclose a scattering of stop-press alterations. Of the baker's dozen that are usually classified as substantive, roughly a third can be described as repairs of inadvertent omissions or compositorial miscues. The remaining two-thirds focus on what evidently impressed the Q2 printers as obscurities in the author's copy, and with many of these alterations it is hard to determine whether the emended passages bring the Second Quarto text into greater conformity with Shakespeare's script or replace uncommon but authentic features of the dramatist's artistry with an overlay of conjectural 'corrections'. In many instances modern editions (including the Everyman Shakespeare) adopt unaltered Q2 word-forms in preference to the ones that have been substituted for them in revised states of the affected Second Quarto pages.

The text of the First Folio printing of *Hamlet* probably derived from a playhouse manuscript, and in all likelihood it was a sloppily prepared one that stood at least two removes from Shakespeare's own pen. There can be little doubt that the 1623 printing incorporates a number of authorial revisions. But there can also be little doubt that it contains stage directions, phrasing variants, sophistications (minor stylistic 'refinements', such as the replacement of 'my' with 'mine' before words beginning with vowels), and patches of dialogue from non-Shakespearean hands. To complicate the situation further, the Folio text is riddled with errors. Some can probably be blamed on the scribe or scribes who prepared the copy from which F1 was printed; others can surely be attributed to the Folio's editors and typesetters, among them the notoriously high-handed Compositor B.

The Folio adds 83 spoken lines to the version of the tragedy preserved in the Second Quarto. At the same time it omits 222 of the lines Q2 had included. In all it contains 3,535 lines, 139 fewer than the Second Quarto.*

---

* Like the line numbers supplied earlier, these figures come from the introduction to Philip Edwards' New Cambridge edition of *Hamlet* (Cambridge: Cambridge University Press, 1985).

Some if not all of the Folio's lengthy additions may have been restorations of copy that had been inadvertently omitted, if not deliberately excised, from the Second Quarto printing: the give-and-take about 'Ambition' in II.ii.250–84, for instance, or the Prince's remarks about 'Conscience' in V.ii.68–80, or the gossip about the children's companies in II.ii.361–88 (a Folio passage that is usually construed as a later interpolation). Similarly, many of the briefer additions may represent copy that would have been available for publication in 1604/5 but for some reason was not included in Q2: the line 'For he himself is subject to his Birth' in I.iii.18, for example, or the comments about 'the Clown' in II.ii.347–48, or the absurd generic mixtures (II.ii.426–28) in Polonius' catalogue of dramatic entertainments, or the phrase 'of us all' in III.i.80. On the other hand, many of the Folio additions could just as readily have resulted from authorial decisions to flesh out or further develop portions of the script sometime after it achieved print in Q2: the phrase 'suddenly contrive the means of Meeting between him and' in II.ii.220–21 may exemplify such an amplification.

The Folio additions that give modern editors the most pause are brief ones, usually a line or less in length, that could be authorial but could also have originated either in the theatre as actors' improvisations (for example, the exclamation 'Oh Vengeance!' in II.ii.570) or in the printing shop as editors' or compositors' gestures towards a smoother and more decorous, if more pedestrian, text than the one they found in their copy; see II.ii.222, where the Folio expands Polonius' 'My Lord, I will take my leave of you' into the more deferential 'My honourable Lord, I will most humbly / Take my leave of you.'

The Folio deletions present modern editors with at least as many quandaries as do the Folio additions. In a way that parallels the First Folio text of *King Lear*, which cut some 300 of the lines that had been present in the 1608 First Quarto of that tragedy, the 1623 *Hamlet* omits a number of the Second Quarto's reflective or discursive speeches. Among the Q2 passages missing from the Folio printing are Horatio's account of the portents that signalled the fall of 'the mightiest Julius' (see I.i.103–20), Hamlet's observations about the flaws that undermine 'particular Men' (I.iv.16–37), several of his statements in the Closet Scene with his mother (III.iv.69–74, 76–79, 158–62, 164–67, 198–206), including his promise to outfox the 'Adders fang'd' who'll accompany him to England, the exchanges in IV.iv.8–63 that culminate in the Prince's soliloquy about all the 'Occasions' that 'inform against' him, Claudius' report of the 'Envy' a Frenchman's praise of Laertes prompted in the Queen's son (IV.ii.68–80), the King's exhortation about 'Abatements and Delays' (IV.vii.68–80), and some of the more extravagant rhetorical flourishes in Hamlet's conversation with the foppish courtier who brings him word that the Danish monarch has proposed to host a fencing competition (V.ii.109–41, 144–49, 204–19).

Taken together with the Folio's lengthy additions, these F1 omissions alter the contours of the play, especially from III.iv to the end. Some of the cuts may have been inadvertent, owing, say, to scribal inattention or to such factors in the printing house as compositorial mistakes in estimating the amount of manuscript copy that would fit on particular pages. Others may have been dictated by theatrical considerations such as the need to shorten the time required for performances of the tragedy. But most if not all of the Folio deletions appear likely to have been made by Shakespeare himself, and for artistic reasons having to do with the shape he eventually wished his play to have.

In places the disparities between Q2 and F1 point to different ways of staging particular moments.* In the process they suggest that what we've tended to think of as *Hamlet* might more accurately be described as a succession of *Hamlets*, each with the traits required to bring it into conformity with a given setting and occasion. It would be nice if we could capture one *Hamlet* in all its integrity and particularity, and even nicer if the one we captured were the *Hamlet* that most fully realized a sage dramatist's ripest thoughts about how his masterwork should be presented and

---

* See the facing-page commentary for the Everyman text at III.i.52 and at the beginning of IV.i.

interpreted. But alas, the publishing history of the tragedy makes it unthinkable for us to aspire to so lofty an objective.

The Second Quarto brings us as near as we can hope to get to the original *Hamlet* of the author's imagination, the *Hamlet* Shakespeare conceived in the first instance as a scriptwriter. But it doesn't preserve all the revisions he would have made as he and his fellow thespians rehearsed, performed, and revived the play in a diversity of venues over the balance of its creator's professional life. The First Folio text brings us as near as we can expect to get to the *Hamlet* of the playwright's maturity. But it is so compromised and contaminated by non-authorial material that there is no way a modern editor can be completely confident about any procedure designed to sift the Shakespearean wheat from the non-Shakespearean chaff in F1's presentation of the playscript.

So what is today's editor to do? One option is to base a text entirely upon the Second Quarto *Hamlet*. A second is to base a text entirely upon the First Folio *Hamlet*. A third is to produce an eclectic text that draws upon both of these seventeenth-century printings.

Since the eighteenth century most editors have taken the third option, and during the last six decades the majority have identified the Second Quarto as their primary control text. They've retained all the Q2 passages deleted from the Folio; meanwhile they've spliced in all, or nearly all, of the Folio additions, and they've drawn without restraint upon F1's variants for readings they have judged to be in some way superior to those in Q2.

In recent years one prominent edition, the single-volume *William Shakespeare: The Complete Works* by Stanley Wells and Gary Taylor (Oxford: Clarendon Press, 1986), has taken a different tack. It has chosen the First Folio *Hamlet* as its control text, and it has relegated to an appendix the major Q2 passages deleted from F1. But it too has adopted eclectic principles in its approach to variant readings (with Q2 words and phrases freely substituted for F1 readings that the editors regard as inferior to those in the quarto), and the result is much the same as that in the editions that found their texts upon the Second Quarto.

The Everyman Shakespeare offers an eclectic *Hamlet* of a different kind. This edition is based on the Second Quarto, a script that is far more subtle in its nuances than even its staunchest advocates have fully appreciated. Because it is impossible to be certain about why various Q2 passages were omitted from the Folio, Everyman retains them all and leaves the final judgement on such issues with the reader. Everyman also incorporates most, though by no means all, of the *Hamlet* lines peculiar to the Folio.* Unlike other twentieth-century editions, however, Everyman emends the seventeenth-century texts very sparingly, and it substitutes Folio readings for Q2 readings only when the quarto version of a passage is untenable or seems manifestly less suited to the dramatic context than does the Folio version.

In some instances, no doubt, the Everyman text forgoes genuine authorial revisions in the Folio for Q2 readings that do not convey the playwright's final intentions. But by focusing primarily on one text of unquestioned authenticity and keeping it relatively clear of elements from other sources, Everyman minimizes the difficulties that arise when incompatible strands are woven into what will almost inevitably turn out to be a motley fabric. By taking the route it does Everyman lowers the risk of canonizing Folio words and phrases that are not authorial in origin, and it greatly reduces the number of situations in which an editor is forced to determine, on what can only be uncertain, subjective criteria, which word or phrase is the 'better' one in the scores of instances in which Q2 and F1 both provide acceptable sense.

In places (among them a number of celebrated lines in what is arguably the most frequently quoted work in English) the *Hamlet* the Q2-anchored Everyman edition presents will strike some observers as bizarre. But those who suspend their disbelief long

---

* The Everyman text adopts only those Folio additions that seem compatible with the *Hamlet* preserved in the Second Quarto printing. The passages Everyman incorporates fit neatly into place, and many of them patch holes in the Q2 fabric. For readers who wish to contemplate the Second Quarto *Hamlet* without the Folio additions, however, the textual apparatus in the pages that follow includes a roster of all the Folio passages inserted into the Everyman edition. Similarly, for readers who wish to contemplate a *Hamlet* without the Q2 material deleted from the Folio text, the apparatus includes a roster of passages unique to the Second Quarto.

enough to give its unfamiliar language a chance to work upon them will find that what initially seems 'weyward' (*Macbeth*, I.iii.30) in the Second Quarto *Hamlet* is 'rich and strange' in the ways we've learned to associate with Shakespeare's unfathomable capacity to take even the most unpromising of materials and subject them to a wondrous 'Sea-change' (*The Tempest*, I.ii.398–400). The Q2 *Hamlet* is characterized by a remarkable degree of internal consistency, and those who resist the impulse to dismiss its oddities or to tinker with it unnecessarily will discover that it offers an abundance of surprising, and deeply satisfying, rewards.

One of the first things readers will notice about the Everyman *Hamlet* is that several of its characters bear names that look unusual. Hamlet's mother, who had been 'Gertred' in the First Quarto and was to become 'Gertrude' in the First Folio text and in modern editions, is referred to in the Second Quarto, and thus in the Everyman edition, as 'Gertrard'. In similar fashion the 'Fortinbras' of the Folio and of most modern editions is named 'Fortinbrasse' in Q2 (paralleling the 'Fortenbrasse' of Q1), and hence in the Everyman text. The character identified as 'Rosincrance' in the Folio, and 'Rosencrantz' in the twentieth-century editions behind Tom Stoppard's delightful play about Hamlet's former schoolfellows, is presented here as 'Rosencraus', the name he carries in Q2. And finally, the character identified as 'Osricke' in the Folio, and 'Osrick' or 'Osric' in most modern editions, is introduced in the Second Quarto, and thus here, as 'Ostricke'; it is not until his final appearance in the Q2 text that he evolves into 'Osrick'.

The location of the action in Q2, and thus in the Everyman text, is not 'Elsinore', as in most of today's editions, but the 'Elsonoure' of the Second Quarto; the Folio alternates between 'Elsenour' and 'Elsonower'. The distinction is not a major one, but as with the proper names Shakespeare employs in his other plays it illustrates the working methods of an artist who is less interested in being geographically or historically accurate than in producing a verbal pattern that will have the desired effect upon the ears of his audience.

In accordance with its usual practice, the Everyman text also retains a number of Shakespearean spelling forms for other words: among the ones not recorded elsewhere in this textual apparatus are *dooes* (does), *Embassadors* (ambassadors), *despight* (despite), *foorth* (forth), *hast* (haste), *hether* (hither), and *thether* (thither).

As noted above, the control text for the Everyman edition of *Hamlet* is the Second Quarto. In a number of passages, however, Everyman supplements the Q2 text with material that occurs only in the First Folio edition of the play. The Folio additions adopted by the Everyman *Hamlet* are as follows (with speech headings printed, here as elsewhere, in small capital letters, and copy from stage directions printed in italics).

I.i.	121	*again*
	137	*Exit Ghost.*
I.ii.	41	*Exeunt [Exit] Voltemand and Cornelius.*
	58	He
	177	see
I.iii.	18	For ... Birth
I.v.	119	my Lord.
II.i.	28	no
II.ii.	90	since
	172	*reading on a Book*
	220–21	suddenly ... and
	250–84	Let ... attended.
	324	a
	331	no
	347–48	the ... Sere;
	361–88	HAMLET ... too.
	426–28	Tragical ... Pastoral
	509	Then senseless Ilium,
	516	And
	570	*Exit Polonius.*
	619	Oh Vengeance!
III.i.	80	of us all
	119	to
	128	all

V.ii. 57 Why . . . Employment:
       68–80 To . . . here?
       171 impon'd, as
       192–93 yours. He
       234 now
       237 *and . . . it*
       252 Sir . . . Audience
       262 keep
       266 , come on
       298–99 A . . . Touch,
       337 murd'rous
       361 *and shout within*
       373 *with . . . Attendants*
       391 th'
       415 *marching . . . off*

For the reasons provided in the foregoing discussion, the Everyman *Hamlet* retains all the Second Quarto material deleted from the First Folio text of the tragedy. The passages in the Everyman text that occur only in the Second Quarto are as follows.

I.i.   10 ho
        103–20 BARNARDO . . . Countrymen.

I.ii.   58–60 wroung . . . Consent

I.iv.   16–37 This . . . Scandal.
        74–77 The . . . beneath.

I.v.   153 by his Sword

II.ii. 17 Whether . . . thus,
        478–79 as wholesome . . . Fine
        500 So . . . you.

III.ii. 190–91 Women . . . And
        192 Either None,
        195–96 Where . . . there.
        242–43 To . . . Scope,
        356 Impart
        399 speak

III.iv. 69–74 Sense . . . Difference.
        76–79 Eyes . . . mope.
        158–62 That . . . on.
        164–67 the next more . . . Potency

	177	One . . . Lady.
	198–206	HAMLET . . . meet.
IV.i.	4	Bestow . . . while.
	41–44	Whose . . . Air
IV.iii.	19	politic
	25–28	KING . . . Worm
IV.iv.	8–63	*Enter . . . Exit.*
IV.v.	33	O ho.
	38	all
	67	He answers
	80	and now behold
	101	Attend, (The Folio adds a line before this: 'QUEEN Alack, what noise is this?')
	197	was
IV.vii.	8	Greatness
	35	*with Letters*
	41	Of . . . them
	68–80	LAERTES . . . Graveness.
	97–99	the . . . them.
	111–20	There . . . Ulcer,
V.i.	277	ALL Gentlemen.
	287	Woo't fast?
V.ii.	100	But yet
	109–41	here . . . Sir.
	144–49	HAMLET . . . unfellowed.
	162–63	HORATIO . . . done.
	204–19	*Enter . . . me.*
	236–37	Let be.

In a few passages the Everyman *Hamlet* adopts readings from the First Folio text in preference to those in the Second Quarto. In the following list the first entry, in boldface type, is the Everyman reading, derived from the Folio, and the second entry is the rejected Q2 reading.

I.i.	12	**Soldier** soldiers
	82	**Heraldry** heraldy (so also in II.ii.491)
	156	**abroad** abraod (so also in III.iii.81)
I.ii.	66	**you?** you.

	79	**Hire and Salary** base and silly
III.iv.	19	**Inmost** most
	75	**Hoodman** hodman
	162	**refrain to night** to refrain night
IV.iii.	34	**there** thrre
IV.v.	110	**They** The
	154	**Let** LAERTES Let
	159	**Till** Tell (so also in II.ii.282, V.i.313)
IV.vi.	9	**and't** and
	28	**Bore** bord
IV.vii.	6	**proceeded** proceed
	14	**conjunctive** conclive
	22	**loud a Wind** loved Arm'd
	61	**checking** the King
	146	**Weigh** Wey
V.i.	77	**intill** into
	259	**t' have** have
	297	**thus** this
V.ii.	52	**Subscrib'd** Subscribe
	167	**might be** be might (Q2 revised)
	197	**comply** sir (Q2 unrevised) *or* so sir (Q2 revised)
	284	**Union** Unice (Q2 unrevised) or Onyx (onixe Q2 revised)
	329	**thy** my
	338	**thy Union** the Onyx
	376	**proud** prov'd (prou'd)

In a handful of other instances, the Everyman text emends Q2 readings in ways that do not derive from the Folio. Three of the readings listed below occur in Q2 passages omitted from the Folio (I.ii.75, IV.iv.16, IV.vii.77). For each entry the first listing, in boldface type, is the emendation adopted in the Everyman text; the second is the rejected reading from the Second Quarto.

I.i.	45	**march?** march, (march: F1)
I.ii.	75	**thee?** thee.
	208	**Where as** Whereas
I.v.	57	**scent** sent

II.ii	461	**Faulc'ners** (Q3, 1611) Fankers (Q2), Faulconers (F1)
	537	**ah** a
III.ii.	37	**Gait** gate
IV.iv.	16	**Name.** name
IV.v.	145	**Looser?** looser.
IV.vii.	77	**too** to

In the following passages Everyman adheres to the control text (Q2 except for the Folio passages identified in the first list of this textual apparatus) in ways that set it apart from many of today's other editions of *Hamlet*. For each entry the first item, in boldface type, is the Everyman reading, and the second is the reading to be found in some if not most other editions. When the alternative reading derives from another seventeenth-century edition, the second entry in this list is followed by a bracketed abbreviation for that edition.

I.i.	4	**twelfe** twelve (F1; so also in I.ii.246, I.iv.3)
	17	**HORATIO** MARCELLUS (F1)
	24	**Apparision** apparition (F1; so also in I.ii.210)
	40	**horrows** harrows (F1)
	41	**Speak to** Question (F1)
	46	**stauks** stalks (F1; compare I.i.61)
	58	**smot** smote
		sleaded sledded (F1)
	61	**Stauk** stalk (F1)
	68	**with** why (F1)
		cost cast (F1)
	71	**devide** divide (F1; compare II.ii.428, V.ii.117)
	73	**joint** joint- (F1)
	83	**these** those (F1)
	86	**return** return'd (F1)
	88	**Comart** cov'nant (F1)
	89	**desseign** design (F1) *or* design'd (F2, 1632)
	93	**lawless** landless (F1)
	114	**Empier** empire
	116	**fear** fear'd
	133	**your** you (F1)
	135	**strike** strike at (F1)
	146	**shrill** shrill- (F1)
	156	**stir** walk (F1)
	168	**Duty.** duty? (F1)
	170	**convenient** conveniently (F1)

I.ii.
 11 **an auspitious and a** one auspicious and one (F1)
 24 **Bands** bonds (F1)
 29 **Bed-red** bed-rid (F1)
 31 **Gate** gait (compare III.ii.37)
 38 **delated** dilated (F1)
 50 **My dread** Dread my (F1)
 67 **in the Son** i'th' Sun (F1)
 72 **common** common, (F1)
 74 **I** Ay (So in I.v.95, 119, II.i.16, 36, 52, II.ii.575, 580, 586, III.ii.80, 305, 324, 371, IV.ii.15, IV.vii.58, V.ii.37)
 77 **coold** good (F1)
 82 **Chapes** shapes (shewes F1)
 83 **devote (deuote)** denote (F1)
 85 **passes** passeth (F1)
 96 **or** or a (F1)
 105 **Course** corse (Coarse F1)
 114 **retrogard** retrograde (F1)
 118 **loose** lose (F1; compare I.iii.31, 76, II.ii.167, III.i.85, III.ii.424, IV.v.145, V.i.166, V.ii.220)
 125 **jocond** jocund
 127 **Heaven** heavens (F1)
     brute bruit (F1)
 129 **sallied** sullied *or* solid (F1)
 132 **seal** self (F1)
 133 **wary** weary (F1)
 137 **merely that** merely. That (F1)
     thus to this: (F1)
 143 **remember,** remember?
     should would (F1)
 147 **Month** month, (F1)
 149 **she –** she, even she – (F1)
 156 **married,** married. (F1)
     Speed; speed, (F1)
 157 **incestious,** incestuous (F1)
 159 **break** break,
 174 **for to drink** to drink deep (F1)
 176 **Studient** student (F1)
 194 **Marvile** marvel (F1)
     hear? hear. (F1) *or* hear!
 197 **Wast** waste (compare II.ii.242) *or* vast (Q1)
 199 **Capapea** cap a pe (F1)
 203 **Troncheon's** truncheon's (F1)
 212 **watch** watch'd (F1)
 222 **Indeed** Indeed, indeed (F1)

227 **What** What, (F1)
228 **then** than (so also in I.iii.125, II.i.115, II.ii.562, III.i.79, III.iii.31, V.ii.353)
231 **a maz'd** amaz'd (F1)
232 **Very like** Very like, very like (F1)
233 **Hundreth** hundred (F1)
241 **hetherto** hitherto (F1; compare I.iv.150)
246 **a leaven** eleven (F1)
251 **Fond** Foul (F1)

I.iii.   1 **inbark'd** embark'd (imbark't F1)
           3 **Convay, in** Convoy is (F1)
             assistant assistant, (assistant; F1)
          10 **so.** so?
          12 **Bulks** bulk (F1)
          17 **way'd** weigh'd (F1; compare I.iii.29, IV.iii.6)
          21 **Safety** sanctity (F1)
          26 **particular Act and Place** peculiar sect and force
          29 **way** weigh (F1)
          31 **chast** chaste (so also in III.i.137, IV.v.122)
          39 **galls** falls (F1)
          45 **the** th' (F1)
          48 **step** (Q2 unrevised) steep (Q2 revised, F1)
          49 **Whiles** Whilst like (F1)
          51 **reaks** recks
             Reed rede
          63 **unto** to (F1)
          65 **Courage** comrade (F1)
          68 **thy** thine (F1)
          74 **Or** Are (F1)
          75 **Boy** be (F1)
          77 **dulleth** dulls the (F1)
          83 **invests** invites (F1)
         104 **I will** I'll (F1)
         122 **Parle** parley (F1)
         124 **Tider** tether (F1)
         129 **Bonds** bawds
         130 **beguide** beguile (F1)

I.iv.   1 **shroudly** shrewdly (F1)
           2 **nipping** a nipping (F1)
          14 **borne** born (so also in I.v.180, III.iii.71, V.i.155)
          16 **Reveale** revel
          17 **tradust** traduc'd

	26	**their** the
	35	**Eale** evil
	48	**interr'd** enurned (F1)
	52	**glimses** glimpses (F1)
	59	**curteous** courteous (F1)
	60	**waves** wafts (F1; so also in line 77)
	69	**Somnet** summit (Sonnet F1)
		Cleef cliff (F1)
	70	**bettles** beetles (F1)
	71	**horrable** horrible (F1)
	81	**Arture** artire (F1)

I.v.	1	**Whether** Whither (Where F1)
	19	**fearful** fretful (F1)
	25	**Murther.** murther? (F1)
	32	**roots** rots (F1)
	43	**Wit** wits
	44	**wonne** won (F1)
	55	**sort** sate (F1)
	56	**pray** prey (F1)
	61	**Hebona** hebenon (F1)
	66	**Allies** alleys
	67	**possess** posset (F1)
	71	**Lazer** lazar (F1)
	76	**unhuzled** Unhousled (unhouzzled F1)
		unannel'd unnaneel'd (unnaneld F1)
	90	**adiew** adieu (adue F1; compare I.v.110, II.ii.125, IV.vii.185)
	93	**Sinows** sinews (F1)
	94	**swiftly** stiffly (F1)
	108	**I am** I'm (F1)
	111	HORATIO HORATIO AND MARCELLUS *within* (F1; placed before *Enter Horatio and Marcellus*.)
	123	**in the** i'th' (F1)
	129	**I will go** Look you, I'll go (F1)
	131	**I am** I'm (F1)
		hartily heartily (F1; compare III.i.59, III.ii.395, 424, III.iii.70, III.iv.153, V.ii.371)
	150	**hether** hither (F1)
	161	**so mere** so ere (F1)
	165	**encomb'red** encumber'd
		this thus (F1)
	170	**do swear** not to do (F1)
	171	**help you.** help you, swear. (F1)

II.i. 3 **merviles** marvellous (marvels F1; compare III.ii.325)
31 **breath** breathe (so also in II.i.43, III.iv.195, IV.vii.65)
quently quaintly (F1)
38 **Wit** warrant (F1)
39 **Sallies** sullies (sulleyes F1)
40 **with** i'th' (F1)
46 **or** and (F1)
51 **Consequence.** consequence; / At friend, or so, and Gentleman. (F1)
52 **I marry** ay, marry
53 **closes** closes with you (F1)
56 **a Gaming there, or took** he gaming, there o'ertook (F1)
60 **take** takes
62 **Windlesses** windlasses (F1)
64 **Advise** advice (F1; compare II.ii.150, III.ii.236, IV.vii.63)
73 **sowing** sewing
75 **Stockins** stockings (F1)
101 **Passions** passion (F1)
108 **coted** quoted (F1)
109 **beshrow** beshrew (F1)

II.ii. 13 **voutsafe** vouchsafe (so also in III.ii.320)
20 **is** are (F1)
43 **I assure** Assure you, (F1)
57 **hasty** o'er-hasty (F1)
Enter Embassadors. Enter Polonius, Voltemand, and Cornelius. (F1)
97 **he's** he is (F1)
104 **thus** thus. (F1)
120 **Lier** liar
130 **about** above (F1)
137 **hote** hot (F1; so also in III.ii.421, IV.vii.153)
142 **working** winking, (F1)
147 **Prescripts** precepts (F1)
148 **her Resort** his resort (F1)
154 **Lightness** a lightness (F1)
157 **this** 'tis this (F1)
158 **I would** I'd (F1)
186 **good** god
194 **far gone;** far gone, far gone; (F1)
209 **your self** you your self (F1)
210 **shall grow** should be (F1)
219 **Sanctity** sanity (F1)

222 **My** My honourable (F1)
     will will most humbly (F1)
223 **cannot** cannot, Sir (F1)
224 **will not** will (F1)
233 **extent** excellent (F1)
238 **ever happy** over-happy: (F1)
239 **Lap** cap (F1)
242 **Wast** waist (waste F1, vast Q1)
247 **but** but that (F1)
288 **ever** even
295 **Any thing but** Why anything. But (F1)
323 **nothing** no other thing (F1)
326 **Moving,** moving (F1)
327 **Admirable** admirable, (admirable? F1)
     Action, action
     Angel angel, (Angel? F1)
328 **Apprehension,** apprehension
331 **Women** woman (F1)
336 **me.** me? (F1)
343 **on** of (F1)
348 **tickl'd** tickle
349 **black** blank
353 **travail** travel (compare III.i.77, IV.vii.70)
367 **be-rattled** be-rattle (F2, 1632)
375 **like most** most like
391 **Mouths** mows (F1)
392 **Duckets** ducats (F1; compare IV.iv.17, 23)
428 **Indevidable** individable (F1; compare I.i.71)
456 **by** by'r (F1)
459 **uncurrant** uncurrent
461 **friendly** French (F1)
462 **strait** straight (F1; so also in III.iv.1)
463 **Tast** taste
476 **indite** indict
477 **Affection** affectation (F1)
480 **Talk** Tale (F1)
480–81 **there about** thereabout (F1)
481 **when** where (F1)
484 **Ircanian** Hyrcanian
489 **th' omynous** the ominous (F1)
491 **dismal** dismal: (F1)
     Foot, foot

496 **rosted** roasted
497 **o'er-cised** o'er-sized (F1; compare III.ii.194)
514 **reverent** reverend (F1)
530 **Follies** fellies (Fallies F1)
532 **Fiends** fiend's *or* fiends'
539 **good.** good, 'mobled Queen' is good. (F1)
541 **Bison** bisson (F1)
554 **where** whe'er
560 **Abstract** abstracts (F1)
576 **hate** ha't (so also in IV.vii.153, V.ii.355)
577 **dozen Lines,** dozen (F1)
591 **the** his (F1)
      wand wanned *or* waned (warm'd F1)
592 **in his** in's (F1)
596 **to her** to Hecuba (F1)
601 **appale** appal
609 **a cross** across (a-cross F1)
621 **a Deer** a dear father (Q3, 1611; the Deer F1)
625 **Stallion** scullion (F1)
626 **Braves** (Q2 unrevised) brains (Q2 revised) *or* brain (F1)
637 **Deale** devil (Divel F1)

III.i.   1 **Conference** circumstance (F1)
          18 **here about** about (F1)
          25 **into** on to (F1)
          26 **two** too (F1)
          29 **my self** my self, lawful espials, (F1)
          30 **We'll** Will (F1)
          40 **here, gracious** here. Gracious (F1)
          43 **Lowliness** loneliness (F1)
             too blame to blame (so also in IV.v.64, V.ii.333)
          52 **withdraw** let's withdraw (F1)
          57 **die** die, (F1)
          59 **Hart-ache** heartache (F1)
          61 **wish'd to** wish'd. To (F1)
             die die,
          69 **despis'd** dispriz'd (F1)
          76 **Borne** bourne
          77 **Traviler** Traveller (F1)
          78 **have,** have
          81 **Hew** hue (hiew Q2, hew F1)
          82 **sickled** sicklied (F1)
          89 **you well.** you: well, well, well. (F1)

139 **Nunn'ry, farewell** Nunnery. Go, farewell (F1)
144 **Heavenly** O heavenly (F1)
145 **well** too, well (F1)
147 **gig and** jig, you (gidge, you F1)
    list lisp (F1)
149 **Wantonness** wantonness your (F1)
151 **moe** more (F1)
    Marriage marriages (F1)
156 **Expectation** expectancy (F1)
160 **Music'd** music (F1)
161 **what** that (F1)
162 **Time** tune (F1)
163 **Stature** feature (F1)
166 **Love, Love?** (F1)
192 **unmatch'd** unwatch'd (F1)

III.ii.   11 **Totters** tatters (F1)
          12 **spleet** split (F1)
          27 **Feature** own feature (F1)
          30 **makes** make (F1)
          32 **which** the which (F1)
          35 **prais'd** praise (F1)
          43 **us.** us, Sir. (F1)
          48 **barrain** barren (F1)
          62 **ere** e'er (so also in IV.iii.68)
             copt cop'd (coap'd F1)
          71 **distinguish . . . Election,** distinguish, . . . election (F1)
          72 **S'hath** Hath (F1)
          76 **co-meddled** co-mingled (F1)
          96 **detected** detecting (F1)
         105 **mine now** mine. Now (F1)
             Lord. Lord, (F1)
         109 **What** And what (F1)
         160 **munching is** Miching (F1)
             Mallico mallecho (Malicho F1)
         165 **keep** keep counsel (F1)
         194 **ciz'd** siz'd (F1)
         205 **That's Wormwood** Wormwood, wormwood (F1)
         214 **the** like (F1)
         223 **griefes** grieves (F1)
         243 **And** An

247 **once I be a** once a (F1)
I be a I be (F1)
261 **Mary** Marry (F1)
267 **unwrong** unrung (F1)
277 **Murtherer, leave** murderer. Pox, leave (F1)
281 **Considerate** Confederate (F1)
283 **Hecat's** Hecate's
invected infected (F1)
285 **usurps** usurp (F1)
Powres *pours*
286 **for his** for's (F1)
292 **Fire.** fire?
297 **strooken** strucken (F1)
303 **provincial** two provincial (F1)
304 **Players** Players, sir (F1)
308 **raigns** reigns (F1)
328 **with** rather with (F1)
332 **more** far more (F1)
334 **stare** start (F1)
340 **Curtesy** courtesy (compare I.iv.59)
346 ROSENCRAUS GUILDENSTERN (F1)
401–2 **fret me not** can fret me (F1)
420 **breaks** breathes (breaths F1)
422 **Business** bitter business (F1)
bitter Day day (F1)

III.iii.
6 **near's** near us (dangerous F1)
15 **Cesse** cease (F1)
17 **it; or it** it. It (F1)
22 **Rain** ruin (F1; compare III.iii.45)
24 **Viage** voyage (F1)
33 **Farre** Fare (F1)
50 **pardon** pardon'd (F1)
58 **guilded** gilded (F1)
73 **, but** pat, (F1)
89 **Drunk,** drunk (F1)

III.iv.
5 **round** round with him (F1)
wait warrant (F1)
6 **Withdraw . . . coming.** Many editions precede this line
with the Folio insertion '*Hamlet within*: Mother,
Mother, Mother.'
17 **boudge** budge

21	**Help, how** help, help, ho
	how, help ho, help, help, help
28	**it was** 'twas (F1)
34	**Penitrable** penetrable (F1)
35	**bras'd** braz'd (F1)
46	**dooes** doth (F1)
47	**O'er** Yea (F1)
48	**heated** tristful (F1)
50	HAMLET **That** That
57	**Heave, a** heaven- (F1)
86	**pardons** panders (F1)
87	**my very** mine (F1)
	Soul very soul (F1)
88	**grieved** gained (F1)
89	**leave there** not leave (F1)
90	**inseemed** enseamed (F1)
95	**twenti'th** twentieth (F1)
	Kyth tithe (F1)
125	**Least** Lest (so also in V.ii.144, 406)
155	**leave** live
176	**This** Thus (F1)
179	**blowt** bloat (blunt F1)
183	**rovel** ravel (F1)
209	**good night indeed. This** good night. Indeed this (F1)
211	**most foolish** foolish (F1)

IV.i.	1	**Sighs, these** sighs. These
		Heaves, heaves (F1)
	9	**some thing** something (F1)
	35	**dregg'd** dragg'd (F1)
	40	**doone** done (F1; compare IV.ii.5)

IV.ii.	6	**Compound** Compounded (F1)
	18	**like an Apple** like an ape an apple (like an Ape F1)

IV.iii.	6	**wayed** weigh'd (F1; compare I.iii.17, 29)
	15	**How,** Ho, Guildenstern (F1; compare *how* in III.iv.21,
		V.ii.317)
		the my (F1)
		They enter. Enter Hamlet and Guildenstern. (F1)
	29	**King. What** What
	52	**so** and so (F1)
	64	**congruing** conjuring (F1)
	68	**will nere begin** were ne'er begun (F1)

IV.v.	9	**yawn** aim (F1)
	16	**Let** QUEEN Let

36 **Shrowd** shroud (compare V.i.99)
39 **Ground** grave (F1)
42 **good** God (F1)
60 **Indeed** Indeed la? (F1)
68 **'a** ha' (F1)
76 **God** good (F1; so also in line 77)
93 **this** his (F1)
100 *A Noise within.* Most editions add a line from the Folio after this stage direction: 'QUEEN Alack, what noise is this?'
101 **is** are (F1)
104 **impitious** impetuous (Q3, F2)
122 **Brow** brows
139 **World's** (worlds) world (F1)
144 **Soopstake** swoopstake
153 **'pear** (peare) pierce (F1)
158 **paid with** paid by (F1)
162 **a Poor** an old (F1)
174 **Maister's** masters (F1)
184–85 **you may** O, you must (F1)
190 **Afflictions** affliction (F1)
202 **Christians'** (Christians) Christian (F1)
    Souls, souls, I pray God (F1)
216 **Trophy** (trophe) Trophy, (F1)
217 **Right** rite (F1)

IV.vi.
23 **Turn good** turn (F1)
26 **thine** your (F1)
32 **So** He (F1)

IV.vii.
7 **Criminal** crimeful (F1)
8 **Safety, Greatness** safety (F1)
20 **Work** Would (F1)
21 **Gives** Gyves (F1)
24 **But** And (F1)
    have had (F1)
37 **These** This (F1)
46 **you Pardon, thereunto** your pardon thereunto, (F1)
47 **sudden** sudden, and more strange (F1)
    Return. return. Hamlet (F1)
52 **devise** advise (F1)
53 **I am** I'm (F1)
56 **didst** diddest (F1) *or* diest
76 **Ribaud** riband (Q3)

82	**I have** I've (F1)
87	**topp'd, me (topt me)** topp'd my (past my F1)
90	**Lamord** Lamound (F1)
95	**especial** especially (F1)
102	**you** him (F1)
112	**Weeke** wick
119	**Spendthrift's** spendthrift
122	**indeed** in deed
131	**o'er** on (F1)
135	**pace** pass (F1)
155	**prefarr'd** preferr'd *or* prepar'd (F1)
162	**ascaunt** askant *or* aslant (F1)
	the a (F1)
163	**hoary** hoar (F1)
164	**Therewith** There with (F1)
	make come (F1)
167	**cull-cold** cold (F1)
168	**Cronet** crownet *or* coronet (F1)
173	**Lauds** tunes
175	**indewed** indued (F1) or endued
179	**drown'd** drown'd? (F1)
186	**a'** of
187	**drowns** doubts (F1)

V.i.	4	**sate** sat
	9	**so offended** *Se offendendo* (F1)
	12–13	**to perform, or all** and to perform; argall (F1)
	63	**in** to Yaughan (F1)
		soope stoupe (F1)
	67	**a** ah (so also in V.i.68; compare II.ii.537, V.ii.19)
	74	**Dintier** daintier (F1)
	83	**o'er-reaches** o'er-offices (F1)
	89	**went** meant (F1)
	93	**Chop-less (Choples)** chapless (F1)
		Massene mazard (F1)
	105	**mad** rude (F1)
	114	**Purchases and Doubles** purchases, and double ones too (F1)
	119	**iot** jot
	125	**or** O (F1)
		made. made / For such a guest is meet.
	150	**Of** Of all (F1)
	154	**that very** the very (F1)
	181	**now hath** now: this skull hath

193 **Alas,** Let me see. Alas, (F1)
195 **bore** borne (F1)
203 **Table** chamber (F1)
229 **Water's** winter's (F1)
230 **soft a while** soft, aside (F1)
239 DOCTOR PRIEST (F1; so also in line 248)
242 **been** have (F1)
250 **a** sage (F1)
260 **double** treble (F1)
267 **blew** blue
274 **spleenative** splenitive, and (F1)
276 **Wisdom** wiseness (F1)
289 **Doost** Dost thou (F1)
299 **Cuplets** couplets (Cuplet F1)
310 **thereby** (Q2 revised) shortly (F1; thirty Q2 unrevised)

V.ii.   6 **Bilbo** bilboes (F1)
            , rashly . Rashly
          9 **fall** pall (paule F1)
         17 **unfold** unseal (F1)
         19 **A** Ah *or* Oh (F1)
         29 **Villains** villainies
         36 **Yeman's** yeoman's (F1)
         43 **As Sir** Ases (Assis F1)
         63 **think** thinkst (F1)
            upon? upon –
         67 **Cus'nage** cozenage (coosenage F1)
         73 **Interim's** interim is
         78 **count** court
         80 **a** *Courtier* young Osric (F1)
         94 **your** put your (F1)
        100 **Sully** sultry (soultry F1; so also in line 102)
        101 **or** for (F1)
        102 **Soultery** sultry
        103 **My** But my (F1)
        104 **bad** bade
        108 **my Ease** mine ease (F1)
        112 **sellingly** (Q2 unrevised) feelingly (fellingly Q2 revised)
        118 **dazzy** (Q2 revised) dozy (dosie Q2 unrevised)
            Arithmatic arithmetic
        119 **Raw** (Q2 revised) yaw (Q2 unrevised)
        120 **Saile** sail
        132 **do't** (Q2 revised) to't (Q2 unrevised)
        143 **is.** is at his Weapon. (F1)

147 **this** his (Q4, 1676)
156 **Hanger** hangers (F1)
164 **Carriage** carriages (F1)
165 **German (Ierman)** Germaine (F1)
171 **impon'd** impawn'd
188 **deliver** redeliver (F1)
     so e'en so (F1)
198 **Breed** bevy (F1)
200 **out of an** outward (F1)
201 **histy** yeasty (yesty F1)
202 **profane** fann'd *or* fond (F1)
203 **trennowed** winnowed (F1)
220 **loose** lose this wager, (F1)
227 **Gamgiving** gain-giving (F1)
235–36 **of ought he leaves knows** knows of aught he leaves
239 **I have** I've (F1)
261 **President** precedent
262 **all** till (F1)
275 **better** better'd (F1)
277 **Length.** length?
310 **third,** third. (F1)
312 **sure** affeard (F1)
326 **Hamlet;** Hamlet. Hamlet (F1)
328 **hour's** hour of (F1)
338 **of** off (F1)
357 **I leave** live (F1)
370 **Silence.** silence. O, o, o, o. (F1)
386 **Commandement** commandment (command'ment F1)
395 **for no** forc'd (F1)
404 **no** on
411 **Right** rites (F1)

HAMLET

NAMES OF THE ACTORS

CLAUDIUS, King of Denmark
GERTRARD [GERTRUDE], Queen of Denmark and Mother to
  Hamlet
HAMLET, Prince of Denmark and Nephew to the King

POLONIUS, Lord Chamberlain
LAERTES, Son to Polonius
OPHELIA, Daughter to Polonius

HORATIO, Friend to Hamlet

ROSENCRAUS [ROSENCRANTZ]
GUILDENSTERN
VOLTEMAND   } Courtiers
CORNELIUS
OSTRICKE (OSRICK)

MARCELLUS ⎱ Officers of the Court
BARNARDO ⎰

FRANCISCO, a Soldier

REYNALDO, Servant to Polonius

FORTINBRASSE [FORTINBRAS], Prince of Norway
NORWEGIAN CAPTAIN
DOCTOR OF DIVINITY
PLAYERS
TWO CLOWNS, Gravediggers
ENGLISH AMBASSADORS

GHOST

LORDS, LADIES, OFFICERS, SOLDIERS, SAILORS,
  MESSENGERS, and ATTENDANTS

I.i   The opening scene begins in the dark of midnight on the battlements of Elsinore Castle in Denmark. Barnardo is reporting for guard duty, relieving Francisco, whose watch is now scheduled to conclude.

S.D.   **Barnardo**   This spelling, a variant of *Bernardo*, occurs in both of the authoritative early texts, and reflects the way *Bernardo* would have been pronounced in Elizabethan England.

1   **Nay answer me**   The emphatic *me* in this sentence suggests that there is an unusual tension in the air. Under normal circumstances the incoming guard would not be challenging another figure to identify himself, as Barnardo has just done; and under normal circumstances the guard awaiting relief would not feel the need to question the identity of a man appearing at the appointed 'Hour' (line 3).
     unfold   disclose, reveal.

2   **Long live the King**   Whether or not this is a watchword, it identifies Barnardo not as an enemy but as a friend to Denmark.

3   **carefully**   cautiously, nervously.

4   **strook twelfe**   struck twelve. These spellings are likely to reflect Shakespeare's pronunciation of these words.

6   **Sick at Heart**   We are given no reason for Francisco's sense of despondency, but the phrase provides another suggestion that all is not well.
     quiet   uneventful.

7   **Not . . . stirring**   A later poet, Clement C. Moore, would adapt this vivid phrase for the opening lines of ''Twas the Night Before Christmas'.
     Well   that's good.

9   **Rivals**   partners. Like *competitors*, this word frequently had a significance in Shakespeare's time that is the opposite of its present meaning.

11   **ground**   land, territory.
     Liegemen to   loyal servants of.
     the Dane   the King of Denmark.

12   **Give**   God give.

ACT I

Scene 1

Enter Barnardo and Francisco, two Sentinels.

BARNARDO Who's there?
FRANCISCO   Nay answer me. Stand and unfold
  Your self.
BARNARDO Long live the King.
FRANCISCO   Barnardo.
BARNARDO   He.
FRANCISCO You come most carefully upon your Hour.
BARNARDO 'Tis now strook twelfe: get thee to Bed,
  Francisco.
FRANCISCO For this Relief much thanks: 'tis
  bitter cold.   5
  And I am Sick at Heart.
BARNARDO   Have you had quiet Guard?
FRANCISCO Not a Mouse stirring.
BARNARDO   Well, good night.
  If you do meet Horatio and Marcellus,
  The Rivals of my Watch, bid them make haste.

Enter Horatio and Marcellus.

FRANCISCO I think I hear them. — Stand ho: who is
  there?   10
HORATIO Friends to this Ground.
MARCELLUS   And Liegemen to the Dane.
FRANCISCO Give you good night.

15 **A piece of him.** This is probably Horatio's ironic way of saying that his heart is not in this visit to the guard's post on such a cold night; as we learn in line 22, he is here only because Marcellus has 'entreated him along' (urged him to come).

17 **this Thing** Horatio's phrasing conveys scepticism.
to night tonight. But here as elsewhere the Elizabethan spelling permits implications the modern one-word form inhibits.

21 **Touching** concerning.
dreaded awesome, terrifying.

23 **watch** both (a) observe, and (b) stay awake for.

25 **approve our Eyes** verify that our eyes have not been deceived by a seizure of 'Fantasy' (here meaning delusion).
speak to it Marcellus and Barnardo have been afraid to confront the 'Apparision' (apparition). By implication, Horatio, being a scholar (line 38), will know how to address it without endangering either his life or his soul. In Shakespeare's time, Protestants assumed that apparitions were likely to be demonic spirits. Catholics, who believed in Purgatory, were more inclined to think that ghosts might be the spirits of departed human beings; but Catholics too urged caution, because everyone knew that 'Satan himself' could appear to be 'an angel of light' (2 Corinthians 11:14). See the note to line 45.

27 **assail** assault. Barnardo uses a military metaphor to suggest that Horatio's ears are walled behind a battlement.

31 **Last Night of all** this very last night. This short line is indented here to indicate that Barnardo commences his narrative only after a brief pause for Barnardo, Marcellus, and Horatio to settle into sitting positions.

32 **Pole** the Pole (North) Star.

33 **his** its. In Shakespeare's time 'his' and 'it' were the normal forms for the neuter possessive pronoun.
illume light up.

MARCELLUS   O farewell, honest Soldier;
  Who hath reliev'd you?
FRANCISCO   Barnardo hath my place;
  Give you good night.   *Exit*.
MARCELLUS   Holla, Barnardo.
BARNARDO   Say,
  What, is Horatio there?
HORATIO   A piece of him.   15
BARNARDO   Welcome, Horatio; welcome, good Marcellus.
HORATIO   What, has this Thing appear'd again
  to night?
BARNARDO   I have seen nothing.
MARCELLUS   Horatio says 'tis but our Fantasy,
  And will not let Belief take hold of him,   20
  Touching this dreaded Sight twice seen of us:
  Therefore I have entreated him along,
  With us to watch the Minutes of this Night,
  That if again this Apparision come
  He may approve our Eyes and speak to it.   25
HORATIO   Tush, tush, 'twill not appear.
BARNARDO   Sit down a while,
  And let us once again assail your Ears,
  That are so fortified against our Story,
  What we have two Nights seen.
HORATIO   '   Well, sit we down,
  And let us hear Barnardo speak of this.   30
BARNARDO   Last Night of all,
  When yond same Star that's Westward from the Pole
  Had made his Course t'illume that part of
    Heaven
  Where now it burns, Marcellus and my self,
  The Bell then beating One —   35

Enter Ghost.

MARCELLUS   Peace, break thee off, look where it
  comes again.

37 **Figure** shape, appearance.

40 **horrows** The Folio prints *harrows*, the reading most editions accept here. The Second Quarto's word would seem more likely to be Shakespeare's; like *horrors* (the reading in the First Quarto), it means 'horrifies'.

41 **It would be spoke to** Barnardo's line suggests that the Ghost is trying to establish communication; it was commonly believed that ghosts were not able to address living mortals until they were first spoken to.

42 **usurp'st** Horatio's verb suggests that he regards the Ghost's appearance as illegitimate, both because the spirit intrudes upon the night without warrant and because it borrows the apparel of the dead King. It will soon emerge that the Ghost's mission relates to another usurpation.

43 **fair** handsome, impressive. But *fair* can also mean 'peaceable' and 'benign' (the opposite of *warlike*), as well as 'good' (the opposite of *foul*, as in *Macbeth*, I.i.9).

44 **buried Denmark** the buried King of Denmark.

45 **sometimes** both (a) on occasion, and (b) at one time.
By Heaven Christians were told to 'believe not every spirit, but try the spirits whether they are of God' (1 John 4:1). When Horatio says 'I charge [command] thee speak' in the name of Heaven, then, he is following orthodox procedure.

46 **It is offended** Marcellus appears to believe that the Ghost is annoyed at Horatio's words, and particularly at his reference to Heaven.
staukes stalks (the spelling in the Second Quarto text). Compare line 61.

51–52 **I might / Not this believe** I would not be able to believe this.

52 **sensible** both (a) through the senses, and (b) intelligent.

53 **true avouch** reliable testimony.

56 **Norway** King of Norway.
combated fought; accented on the first and third syllables.

57 **angry Parle** fierce argument. This may refer to either (a) a heated verbal altercation, or (b) a hand-to-hand combat.

BARNARDO   In the same Figure like the King that's
    dead.
MARCELLUS   Thou art a Scholar; speak to it, Horatio.
BARNARDO   Looks 'a not like the King? Mark it,
    Horatio.
HORATIO   Most like, it horrows me with Fear and
    Wonder.   40
BARNARDO   It would be spoke to.
MARCELLUS   Speak to it, Horatio.
HORATIO   — What art thou that usurp'st this Time of
    Night,
  Together with that fair and warlike Form
  In which the Majesty of buried Denmark
  Did sometimes march? By Heaven I charge thee
    speak.   45
MARCELLUS   It is offended.
BARNARDO   See, it staukes away.
HORATIO   Stay, speak, speak, I charge thee, speak.
                                                Exit Ghost.

MARCELLUS   'Tis gone, and will not answer.
BARNARDO   How now, Horatio? You tremble and
    look pale:
  Is not this something more than Fantasy?   50
  What think you on't?
HORATIO   Before my God I might
  Not this believe without the sensible
  And true avouch of mine own Eyes.
MARCELLUS   Is it
  Not like the King?
HORATIO   As thou art to thy self.
  Such was the very Armour he had on   55
  When he the ambitious Norway combated;
  So frown'd he once, when in an angry Parle

58 **smot ... Pollax** probably either (a) struck the ice with his studded poleaxe (a long-handled weapon), or (b) smote (slew) the sled-borne Polacks (Polish soldiers). *Smot* (smote) is one of several Shakespearean forms that lack the final *e* normal in modern spelling; others are *bad* (bade), *breath* (breathe), *chast* (chaste), *hast* (haste), and *wast* (waste). On the other hand forms such as *hote* (hot) and *sate* (sat) illustrate the opposite principle. The Everyman text preserves many of these spelling peculiarities.

60 **jump** exactly. Compare V.ii.387; also see *Othello*, II.iii.399–400.

62–64 **In ... State** Although I'm as yet unable to formulate a precise reason for my hunch, the general drift of my thinking is that this appearance portends something to be feared.

65 **Good now** now good sirs.

67 **toils the Subject** requires toil of the subjects.

68 **cost** expense. The Folio prints *cast* (casting).
 brazen both (a) brass, and (b) bold and aggressive.

69 **Mart** marketing, trading.

70 **Impress** impressment, forced labour.
 sore Task grievous burden, unceasing workload.

71 **devide** divide. But here as elsewhere (see *Othello*, I.i.21–22), the Shakespearean spelling incorporates senses that relate to *devise*, 'deploy' strategically.

72 **toward** in the offing, in the near future.

77 **Fortinbrasse** The First Folio spelling (*Fortinbras*) reproduces a French word for 'strong arm' or 'strong in arms'. The earlier Quarto spelling, adopted here, suggests an additional link with 'brass' (brazen mettle), reinforced by lines 68 and 91.

78 **prick'd on** incited, motivated. The verb Horatio employs here often refers to a rider's spurring of a steed; but it can also allude to the 'Pride' that signifies virility.
 emulate envious, rivalrous.

81 **seal'd Compact** official agreement; here pronounced 'com-páct'.

82 **Well ratified ... Heraldry** properly subscribed to by the councils and heraldic officials of both countries.

He smot the sleaded Pollax on the Ice.
'Tis strange.

MARCELLUS   Thus twice before, and jump at this
   dead Hour,   60
With Martial Stauke hath he gone by our Watch.

HORATIO   In what particular Thought to work I know
   not,
But in the gross and scope of mine Opinion,
This bodes some strange Eruption to our State.

MARCELLUS   Good now sit down, and tell me, he that
   knows,   65
Why this same strict and most observant Watch
So nightly toils the Subject of the Land,
And with such daily cost of brazen Cannon
And foreign Mart, for Implements of War;
Why such Impress of Shipwrights, whose sore Task   70
Does not devide the Sunday from the Week;
What might be toward that this sweaty Haste
Doth make the Night joint Labourer with the Day?
Who is't that can inform me?

HORATIO   That can I;
At least the Whisper goes so. Our last King,   75
Whose Image even but now appear'd to us,
Was, as you know, by Fortinbrasse of Norway,
Thereto prick'd on by a most emulate Pride,
Dar'd to the Combat; in which our valiant
   Hamlet
(For so this side of our known World esteem'd
   him)   80
Did slay this Fortinbrasse, who by a seal'd
   Compact
Well ratified by Law and Heraldry
Did forfeit, with his Life, all these his Lands

84   **Which ... seiz'd of**   which he stood to lose.

85   **Moi'ty competent**   equivalent (competing) portion (of land).

86   **gaged**   engaged; pledged, staked.

88–89 **as ... desseigne**   as by the same mutual agreement and tenor of
     the articles designed and designated for this purpose. Instead
     of *Comart* (bargain), many editions adopt the Folio's
     Cov'nant here. Most also amend *desseigne* (which reflects the
     French *dessein*, design, scheme, or intention) to *design'd*, a
     reading that first appears in the Second Folio, though a few
     adopt the First Folio's *design*.

91   **unimproved Mettle**   both (a) unproven, unfinished raw virtue,
     not yet put to profitable use, and (b) untempered *metal* (a
     word that was yet to be fully distinguished from *mettle*), such
     as brass or steel that is still being treated to make it durable.

93   **Shark'd ... Resolutes**   scavenged up (like a ravenous shark) an
     indiscriminate collection of desperadoes from the fringes of
     society. Here many editions substitute the Folio's *landless*, a
     concept implicit in the Quarto's *lawless*.

95   **a Stomach**   both (a) an appetite (in keeping with the food
     metaphor), and (b) a touch of bravery (guts).

101 **Head**   both (a) source, and (b) reason, heading (as in a list of
     topics).

102 **Post-haste and Romage**   intense haste (roamage) and bustling
     activity (rummage). *Romage* anticipates 'Rome' (line 108).

104 **Well may it sort**   may it accord well (be a favourable sign).
     portentous   ominous, prophetic.

107 **Moth**   mote, tiny particle. Compare Matthew 7:3.

108 **palmy**   victorious, flourishing. See *Julius Caesar*, I.ii.126–29.

113 **Disasters**   literally, 'malign stars' in the Heavens.
     the Moist Star   the Moon, which controls Neptune's empire
     (the sea, whose ruling deity was known as Poseidon to the
     Greeks and Neptune to the Romans).

114 **Empier**   empire. The Second Quarto spelling suggests wordplay
     on *pier*.

116 **fear**   fearful, feared.

Which he stood seiz'd of to the Conqueror;
Against the which a Moi'ty competent   85
Was gaged by our King, which had return
To the Inheritance of Fortinbrasse,
Had he been Vanquisher; as by the same Comart
And Carriage of the Article desseigne,
His fell to Hamlet. Now Sir, young Fortinbrasse,   90
Of unimproved Mettle, hot and full,
Hath in the Skirts of Norway here and there
Shark'd up a List of lawless Resolutes
For Food and Diet to some Enterprise
That hath a Stomach in't, which is no other,   95
As it doth well appear unto our State,
But to recover of us by Strong Hand
And Terms Compulsatory, those foresaid Lands
So by his Father lost; and this, I take it,
Is the main Motive of our Preparations,   100
The Source of this our Watch, and the chief Head
Of this Post-haste and Romage in the Land.
BARNARDO   I think it be no other but e'en so:
  Well may it sort that this portentous Figure
  Comes armed through our Watch so like the King   105
  That was and is the Question of these Wars.
HORATIO   A Moth it is to trouble the Mind's Eye.
  In the most high and palmy State of Rome,
  A little ere the mightiest Julius fell,
  The Graves stood tenantless, and the sheeted
    Dead   110
  Did squeak and gibber in the Roman Streets
  As Stars with trains of Fire, and dews of Blood,
  Disasters in the Sun; and the Moist Star,
  Upon whose Influence Neptune's Empier stands,
  Was sick almost to Doomsday with Eclipse.   115
  And even the like Precurse of fear Events,

117   **still**   always. So also in I.ii.104.
      the Fates   the three Goddesses who determine human destiny
        (the fates of human beings and their states).

118   **the . . . on**   coming on the events foretold by the 'Harbingers'.

120   **Climatures**   climes, region. Lines 108–20 echo *Julius Caesar*,
      I.iii.1–78, 126–30, II.ii.1–104.

122   **cross it**   literally, cross its path; confront it (perhaps with arms
        spread to form a cross-like figure).
      blast   either (a) wither, or (b) blow away.
      Illusion   apparition. Horatio is not suggesting that it is illusory.

S.D.   **his**   its. See the note to line 33.

125–   **If . . . Ease**   Horatio's 'if' clause indicates that he is testing to
26   see whether the Ghost claims to be a departed human spirit
      who cannot rest until something he left undone has been
      attended to. See the note to line 45.

129   **happily**   both (a) by chance, and (b) fortunately.

131   **uphoorded**   hoarded and buried.

132   **Extorted**   wrested by force.

135   **Partizan**   partisan, a long-handled spear or pike.

138   **being so Majestical**   both (a) since it is so king-like, and (b)
      acting so imperiously in our effort to protect our sovereign
      state against usurpation. Marcellus' words are a reminder that
      Denmark's sentinels are seeking to keep their castle securely
      'fortified against' (line 28) more than one kind of invasion.

139   **offer it the show**   threaten it with a display.

140   **invulnerable**   incapable of being harmed.

141   **vain**   useless, empty; in vain.
      malicious Mockery   a defiant threat of malice.

As Harbingers preceding still the Fates
And Prologue to the Omen coming on,
Have Heaven and Earth together demonstrated
Unto our Climatures and Countrymen.   120

Enter Ghost again.

But soft, behold, lo where it comes again.
I'll cross it though it blast me. – Stay,
   Illusion,   *It spreads his Arms.*
If thou hast any Sound or use of Voice,
Speak to me.
If there be any good thing to be done   125
That may to thee do Ease, and Grace to me,
Speak to me.
If thou art privy to thy Country's Fate,
Which happily Foreknowing may avoid,
O speak.   130
Or if thou hast uphoorded in thy Life
Extorted Treasure in the Womb of Earth,
For which they say your Spirits oft walk in
   Death,   *The Cock crows.*
Speak of it, stay and speak. – Stop it,
   Marcellus.
MARCELLUS Shall I strike it with my Partizan?   135
HORATIO Do if it will not stand.
BARNARDO   'Tis here.
HORATIO   'Tis here.
                         Exit Ghost.
MARCELLUS 'Tis gone.
  We do it wrong, being so Majestical,
  To offer it the show of Violence,
  For it is as the Air, invulnerable,   140
  And our vain Blows malicious Mockery.
BARNARDO It was about to speak when the Cock crew.
HORATIO And then it started like a Guilty Thing,

144 **Upon a fearful Summons** upon receiving a frightening summons (either to trial or to execution). Elizabethans would have been reminded of the guilty disciple, Peter, who thrice denied his Lord before the crowing of the cock. See Matthew 26:33–35, 69–75.

147 **Awake the God of Day** bring on the dawn by waking up the Sun.

149 **Th' extravagant and erring Spirit** the wandering spirit that has strayed beyond its appointed bounds.
hies hastens.

151 **made Probation** offered proof, evidence. *Probation* echoes lines 24–25.

153 **'gainst that Season comes** in anticipation of the coming of that time. See the note to line 7.

155 **This Bird of Dawning** the Cock.

157 **wholesome** free from contagion (hale or whole, healthy), and shielded from the powers of evil.
strike harm by pernicious influence. In this phrase Marcellus alludes to the belief, from astrology, that the stars and planets conditioned human behaviour.

158 **No Fairy takes** no fairy bewitches or captures. This line is a reminder that in Shakespeare's time fairies were often regarded as malevolent spirits; among other things, they were said to take human infants and leave 'changelings' (bad children, or children possessed by evil fairy spirits) in their place. See V.ii.53.
charm enslave, bewitch.

159 **hallowed** holy, sanctified.
gratious gracious, blessed. The Second Quarto spelling retains the flavour of the Latin word *gratia*, grace, charm, favour, which would have brought to mind such liturgical prayers as *Ave Maria, gratia plena*, 'Hail, Mary, full of grace' (a derivative of Luke 1:28 and John 1:14).

161 **in russet Mantle clad** cloaked in a coarse, reddish cloth. *Mantle* echoes *Julius Caesar*, III.ii.172, 189.

163 **Advise** advice. The Quarto spelling appears to reflect Shakespeare's usual rendering of this word.

166 **dumb** speechless.

Upon a fearful Summons. I have heard
The Cock that is the Trumpet to the Morn   145
Doth with his lofty and shrill sounding Throat
Awake the God of Day, and at his Warning,
Whether in Sea or Fire, in Earth or Air,
Th' extravagant and erring Spirit hies
To his Confine; and of the Truth herein   150
This present Object made Probation.

MARCELLUS   It faded on the crowing of the Cock.
Some say that ever 'gainst that Season comes
Wherein our Saviour's Birth is celebrated
This Bird of Dawning singeth all Night long,   155
And then they say no Spirit dare stir abroad;
The Nights are wholesome, then no Planets
    strike,
No Fairy takes, nor Witch hath power to charm,
So hallowed and so gratious is that Time.

HORATIO   So have I heard, and do in part believe it;   160
But look, the Morn in russet Mantle clad
Walks o'er the Dew of yon high Eastward Hill;
Break we our Watch up, and by my Advise
Let us impart what we have seen to night
Unto young Hamlet; for upon my Life,   165
This Spirit, dumb to us, will speak to him.

170 **convenient** conveniently, readily. *Convenient* literally means
'coming together'.

I.ii The scene takes place at the Court in Elsinore Castle.

S.D. **Claudius** Apart from this opening stage direction and the
initial speech assignment, Claudius is referred to solely as
'King'. Shakespeare probably drew the name from that of a
Roman Emperor (AD 41–54) who married his niece
Agrippina (mother of Nero) and was notorious for the vice
and corruption of his reign.
Gertrad a variant of *Gertrard*, as the Queen's name is normally
spelled in the Second Quarto. *Gertrude* is the spelling in the
First Folio text and in most modern editions.
cum Aliis with others.

2 **green** fresh.

4 **contracted in** constrained or compressed into. The legal sense
of *contracted* ('Well ratified by Law', I.i.82) will soon
reverberate with an ironic undertone.

5 **Discretion** prudence; the judgement of the 'wisest' (line 6).

8 **sometime Sister** former sister-in-law.

9 **Jointress** inheritor. Claudius implies that the Queen has
inherited the kingdom as a jointure (estate settled on a widow
for the time she survives her husband), and that he has joined
(grafted) himself to her and to the kingship as a 'joint
Labourer' (I.i.73) by a matrimonial contract. The root word
joint echoes the marriage service in the Book of Common
Prayer (1549), 'Those whom God hath joined together, let no
man put asunder' (Matthew 19:6), and epitomizes the other
perversions of 'marriage' described in lines 10–14; meanwhile
it anticipates the images in I.ii.20 and I.v.179.

10 **as 'twere** as it were, so to speak.

11 **auspitious** auspicious, happy, uplifted (contrast *dropping*,
downcast). The literal meaning of *auspicious* is 'ominous'
(normally 'well-omened'), from the Latin *avispex*
(bird-watching for purposes of divination, prophecy). See
I.i.60–63, 107–20, 152–59, and compare *Julius Caesar*,
V.i.70–85. The Second Quarto spelling suggests wordplay on
piteous; compare *impiteous* in IV.v.104.

Do you consent we shall acquaint him with it
As needful in our Loves, fitting our Duty.
MARCELLUS   Let's do't, I pray, and I this Morning
   know
Where we shall find him most convenient.   *Exeunt.*   170

Scene 2

Flourish. Enter Claudius, King of Denmark, Gertrad the Queen, Council: as Polonius, and his Son Laertes, Hamlet, cum Aliis.

CLAUDIUS   Though yet of Hamlet our dear Brother's
   Death
The Memory be green, and that it us befitted
To bear our Hearts in Grief, and our whole
   Kingdom
To be contracted in one Brow of Woe,
Yet so far hath Discretion fought with Nature   5
That we with wisest Sorrow think on him
Together with Remembrance of our selves:
Therefore our sometime Sister, now our Queen,
Th' imperial Jointress to this warlike State,
Have we, as 'twere with a defeated Joy,   10
With an auspitious and a dropping Eye,
With Mirth in Funeral, and with Dirge in
   Marriage,

13   **Dole**   grieving, sorrow (from an earlier form of the modern
      French word *deuil*). Ironically, *Dole* can also mean 'division'
      (an implication that will soon become pertinent). And it can
      refer to the dealing out of benefits (a reminder that Claudius is
      in a position to dole out favours only because he has been the
      recipient of the kind of 'Dole' noted at line 11).

14   **barr'd**   excluded, acted without.

18   **weak Supposal**   low estimate. Claudius implies that
      Fortinbrasse's 'Supposal' is 'weak' (ill-founded) if it is
      postulated on the presumed weakness of 'this warlike State'
      (line 9).

20   **out of Frame**   both (a) out of socket (like a disjointed limb),
      and (b) disordered. Compare *Julius Caesar*, II.i.18–19, where
      Brutus says that 'Th' Abuse of Greatness is when it dis-joins /
      Remorse from Power.' Compare line 9.

21   **Co-leagued**   joined, linked.
      Dream   illusory hope. See *Julius Caesar*, I.ii.23.

23   **Importing**   both (a) concerning, and (b) importuning (pestering
      with demands for).

24   **Bands**   bonds, binding contracts. At the conclusion of this
      sentence (following line 25), the Folio inserts the stage
      direction '*Enter Voltemand and Cornelius.*' In the Second
      Quarto, apparently, these two ambassadors are to be regarded
      as members of the Court party who enter at the
      commencement of the scene; if so, Claudius probably signals
      for them to step forward.

28   **Norway**   the King of Norway.

29   **impotent and Bed-red**   feeble and bed-ridden. Compare line 18.

31   **Gate**   both (a) gait, proceeding, and (b) encroachment with a
      threat of forced entry. See I.i.90–102.
      Levies   conscripted troops. So also with 'Lists' and
      'Proportions' in line 32.

33   **Subject**   subjects (as in I.i.67).

37   **To**   to do.
      Scope   prescribed range.

38   **delated**   dilated, detailed at length.
      Articles   written provisions.

In equal Scale weighing Delight and Dole,
Taken to Wife; nor have we herein barr'd
Your better Wisdoms, which have freely gone   15
With this Affair along. For all, our Thanks.
Now follows that you know young Fortinbrasse,
Holding a weak Supposal of our Worth,
Or thinking by our late dear Brother's Death
Our State to be Disjoint, and out of Frame,   20
Co-leagued with this Dream of his Advantage,
He hath not fail'd to pester us with Message
Importing the Surrender of those Lands
Lost by his Father, with all Bands of Law
To our most valiant Brother; so much for him.   25
Now for our self, and for this Time of Meeting,
Thus much the Business is: we have here writ
To Norway, Uncle of young Fortinbrasse,
Who, impotent and Bed-red, scarcely hears
Of this his Nephew's Purpose, to suppress   30
His further Gate herein, in that the Levies,
The Lists, and full Proportions are all made
Out of his Subject, and we here dispatch
You, good Cornelius, and you, Voltemand,
For Bearers of this Greeting to old Norway,   35
Giving to you no further personal Power
To Business with the King, more than the Scope
Of these delated Articles allow.

39   **commend**   speak for, be a witness to.

41   **nothing**   not at all.

43   **Suit**   request.

44   **the Dane**   the King (the embodiment of all Denmark). Compare
        I.i.11.

45   **lose your Voice**   waste your breath, fail to obtain what you
        request. Here *Voice* means 'authority', the power to effect a
        political outcome. So also in I.iii.23.

47   **native to**   born with, linked to as part of the same organism.

48   **instrumental to**   an instrument (servant) of. In lines 47–49
        Claudius says that the Heart (Laertes' father) and the Mouth
        (Laertes in his role as a 'Voice' making a request) are so
        powerful in the Body Politic of Denmark that they rule the
        Head (the King's mind and authority) and the Hand (the
        King's power to bestow favour).

51   **Fraunce**   France. Here and elsewhere, this edition adopts the *au*
        spellings in the Second Quarto, which may well have been set
        from Shakespeare's own manuscript of the play and is likely
        to reflect the pronunciations he preferred in particular
        contexts.

56   **bow**   submit. Combined with *bend* (incline) in line 55, this verb
        suggests that as Laertes bends his knee to the King he also
        bends in the direction of France. Compare *Julius Caesar*,
        III.i.39–43.
        Leave   permission (for Laertes to leave).

58   **wroung**   wrung.

60   **Upon . . . Consent**   This erotic suggestiveness of Polonius'
        phrasing prepares the way for Hamlet's allusions to the 'hard
        Consent' his mother's 'Will' gave to the brother of her late
        husband. *Will* can refer both to sexual desire and to the
        genitalia of either gender. Like other words with *con* sounds,
        Consent echoes a vulgar English derivative of the Latin word
        cunnus (female pudendum). The Prince plays on that sense in
        III.ii.122.

Farewell, and let your Haste commend your Duty.
CORNELIUS, VOLTEMAND   In that, and all things, will
   we show our Duty.   40
KING   We doubt it nothing: heartily farewell.
                        Exeunt Voltemand and Cornelius.
  – And now, Laertes, what's the News with you?
  You told us of some Suit, what is't, Laertes?
  You cannot speak of Reason to the Dane
  And lose your Voice; what would'st thou beg,
    Laertes,   45
  That shall not be my Offer, not thy Asking?
  The Head is not more native to the Heart,
  The Hand more instrumental to the Mouth,
  Than is the Throne of Denmark to thy Father.
  What would'st thou have, Laertes?
LAERTES   My dread Lord,   50
  Your Leave and Favour to return to Fraunce,
  From whence, though willingly I came to Denmark
  To show my Duty in your Coronation,
  Yet now I must confess, that Duty done,
  My Thoughts and Wishes bend again toward
    Fraunce,   55
  And bow them to your gracious Leave and Pardon.
KING   Have you your Father's Leave, what says
  Polonius?
POLONIUS   He hath, my Lord, wroung from me my
  slow Leave
  By laboursome Petition, and at last
  Upon his Will I seal'd my hard Consent.   60
  I do beseech you give him leave to go.
KING   Take thy fair Hour, Laertes, Time be thine,
  And thy best Graces spend it at thy Will.
  – But now, my Cousin Hamlet, and my Son.

65 **A . . . Kind** What Hamlet appears to mean is that, as a result of his uncle's marriage to his mother, he is more 'Kin' to the King than he wishes, since he is 'less than Kind' (less than a real 'Son' to this newly crowned 'Father'). Hamlet does not want to be considered the 'kind' of man the King is. Many editions mark this line as an aside; whether it is to be so treated is a matter of interpretation.

67 **Son** Hamlet puns on *Sun* (the word to be found in the Folio), a traditional symbol of kingship.

70 **vailed** both (a) lowered, and (b) veiled, as with the 'Clouds' (black clothes) that hide the Sun (Son) in a 'nighted Colour'. The Folio prints *veyled*. Lines 69–71 echo line 11.

71 **in the Dust** by looking to the ground. The Queen echoes Genesis 3:19 ('dust thou art, and unto dust shalt thou return').

74 **I** both (a) I [know], and (b) Ay.
common a universally shared experience. But Hamlet is also alluding to the 'it' of his mother; see the note to line 60.

75 **so** both (a) thus, and (b) so intensely.
particular with thee peculiar to you, or especially so to you. But *particular* can also refer to a genital 'part' that responds to a 'tickler' (see *Troilus and Cressida*, II.ii.8–12, III.i.120–26, V.ii.45–47), and that sense informs Hamlet's reply in line 76. No doubt he also supplies a copulative sense of *die* (achieve orgasm) to line 72 (see *Troilus and Cressida*, III.i.115–36).

77 **coold** either (a) cool'd, or (b) cold. Modern editions normally adopt the Folio's *good*, and that is no doubt the word Hamlet expects his mother's cooled and dulled ears to register. See 2 *Henry IV*, I.ii.75–145, and *Julius Caesar*, I.ii.21–23, 207–10, for related instances of the spiritual deafness defined in such New Testament passages as Matthew 11:13–19 and John 5:24–25. Hamlet is exasperated by the corrupted Queen's capacity for dispassionate philosophizing: what the Lord Chief Justice in 2 *Henry IV* commends as 'cold Considerance' (V.ii.97).

79 **Suspiration** exhaling, sighing.

81 **Haviour** behaviour, expression. *Dejected* (downcast) recalls lines 68–71, and anticipates lines 106–7.

HAMLET   A little more than Kin, and less than Kind.   65
KING   How is it that the Clouds still hang on you?
HAMLET   Not so, my Lord, I am too much in the Son.
QUEEN   Good Hamlet, cast thy nighted Colour off
   And let thine Eye look like a Friend on
      Denmark;
   Do not for ever with thy vailed Lids   70
   Seek for thy noble Father in the Dust;
   Thou know'st 'tis common all that lives must
      die,
   Passing through Nature to Eternity.
HAMLET   I Madam, it is common.
QUEEN   If it be,
   Why seems it so particular with thee?   75
HAMLET   Seems, Madam, nay it is; I know not Seems.
   'Tis not alone my Inky Cloak, coold Mother,
   Nor customary Suits of solemn Black,
   Nor windy Suspiration of forc'd Breath,
   No, nor the fruitful River in the Eye,   80
   Nor the dejected Haviour of the Visage,

82 **Chapes** Modern editions normally emend to *shapes* (for which the Second Quarto spelling may be either a variant or a pun); but *chapes* (plural for the metal plate protecting the end of a scabbard from the point of the blade 'within', line 85) suits the context with equal precision.

83 **devote** Today's editions normally adopt the Folio's *denote* instead of the Quarto's *deuote*; but *devote* (consecrate, as with a monastic habit similar to Hamlet's 'Suits of Woe') is by no means untenable here. Compare *Romeo and Juliet*, III.iii.110, where the Second Quarto's *deuote* is almost certainly a misprint for *denote*.

85 **passes** surpasses.

92 **obsequious** funereal (from *obsequies*, rites for the dead).

96 **unfortified** unprotected [against the assaults of grief and the despair it can induce]. Hamlet regards the hearts of his mother and uncle as *too* fortified. In due course Claudius will attempt to solicit Heaven for a 'Heart unfortified', a conscience that is not too hardened by sin to be receptive to the ministrations of Heaven's angels; see II.iii.67–71, 97–98.

97 **simple** naive, infantile; undisciplined by the schooling of the catechism.

99 **vulgar** common to all people. Claudius' phrasing keeps us focused on the kind of erotic 'Understanding' (see *The Two Gentlemen of Verona*, II.v.20–36) that troubles Hamlet: the fact that his mother's will has become 'as common / As any the most vulgar thing to Sense'.

100 **peevish** obstinately childish.

101 **a Fault to Heaven** an offence against God. Here and elsewhere the King rejects Hamlet's implication that his 'Trappings' of grief are signs of filial and religious devotion. As Claudius depicts them, they are the very opposite: a rejection of Heaven's will, and thus an impious sin against God, Nature, Reason, and even the deceased himself. Once again Claudius' word choice runs counter to his design. *Fault*, whose literal meaning is 'flaw' or 'crack', is a term for the genital deficiency (the 'nothing', the 'no thing') of a 'weaker vessel' (1 Peter 3:7).

Together with all Forms, Moods, Chapes of
   Grief,
That can devote me truly. These indeed Seem,
For they are Actions that a man might Play;
But I have that within which passes Show,   85
These but the Trappings and the Suits of Woe.
KING 'Tis sweet and commendable in your Nature,
   Hamlet,
To give these Mourning Duties to your Father;
But you must know your Father lost a Father,
That Father lost, lost his, and the Survivor
   bound   90
In filial Obligation for some Term
To do obsequious Sorrow. But to persever
In obstinate Condolement is a Course
Of impious Stubbornness; 'tis unmanly Grief;
It shows a Will most incorrect to Heaven,   95
A Heart unfortified, or Mind impatient,
An Understanding simple and unschool'd;
For what we know must be, and is as common
As any the most vulgar thing to Sense,
Why should we in our peevish Opposition   100
Take it to Heart? Fie, 'tis a Fault to Heaven,
A Fault against the Dead, a Fault to Nature,
To Reason most absurd, whose Common Theme
Is Death of Fathers, and who still hath cried

105 **Course** both (a) course (echoing line 93), lifetime, and (b) corse, corpse.
 to day today. But here, as in I.i.17, the Elizabethan orthography is open to additional interpretations. Compare line 125, where, as here, *day* can function as the object of the preposition *to*.

107 **unprevailing** unavailing, ineffectual.

109 **the most immediate to our Throne** the next in succession.

113 **Wittenberg** This German university, founded in 1502 and made famous in 1517 as the place where Martin Luther launched the Protestant Reformation, was the most popular institution of higher learning for Danes studying abroad in the later sixteenth century.

114 **retrogard** a variant of *retrograde*, moving in a contrary direction. Unlike Laertes, whose request to return to Paris was granted immediately, Hamlet will not be encouraged in his suit to leave Denmark. The Second Quarto spelling hints at *guard* and thereby plays on *unfortified*; see the note to line 96.

115 **bend you** bow yourself, humble your stubborn, stiff will. Compare lines 55–56.

118 **loose her Prayers** be denied her wishes by having them set loose for nought. Compare line 45.

123 **Accord** consent. The King is relieved that Hamlet has chosen not to be 'retrogard' to the 'Desire' of Gertrard.

125 **jocond Health** jocund (cheerful) toast. *Cannon* (line 126) recalls I.i.68 and anticipates lines 131–32.

127 **Rouse** carouse; here a 'Health' pledged by the King.
 brute again bruit back, proclaim in reply (with a loud reverberation). The Quarto spelling hints that 'the Heaven' may play a 'Brute part' (III.ii.112) that discountenances the 'Earthly Thunder' (line 128) of an overweening 'Denmark' (line 125).

129 **sallied** a variant of *sullied*, blemished, defiled. The Folio prints *solid*, and Hamlet may be combining the two senses in an image of bloated flesh. Compare II.i.39.

130 **a Dew** both (a) a liquid state, and (b) 'Adew' (adieu), farewell. See I.v.110. Compare the imagery in lines 70–71.

From the first Course till he that died to day   105
This must be so. We pray you throw to Earth
This unprevailing Woe, and think of us
As of a Father, for let the World take note
You are the most immediate to our Throne,
And with no less Nobility of Love   110
Than that which dearest Father bears his Son
Do I impart toward you. For your Intent
In going back to School in Wittenberg,
It is most retrogard to our Desire,
And we beseech you bend you to remain   115
Here in the Cheer and Comfort of our Eye,
Our chiefest Courtier, Cousin, and our Son.
QUEEN   Let not thy Mother loose her Prayers, Hamlet:
I pray thee stay with us, go not to Wittenberg.
HAMLET   I shall in all my best obey you, Madam.   120
KING   Why 'tis a loving and a fair Reply:
Be as our self in Denmark. – Madam, come;
This gentle and unforc'd Accord of Hamlet
Sits smiling to my Heart, in Grace whereof
No jocond Health that Denmark drinks to day   125
But the great Cannon to the Clouds shall tell.
And the King's Rouse the Heaven shall brute
    again,
Respeaking Earthly Thunder; come away.
                    Flourish. Exeunt all but Hamlet.
HAMLET   O that this too too sallied Flesh would
    melt,
Thaw, and resolve it self into a Dew;   130
Or that the Everlasting had not fix'd

132   **Cannon** both (a) an aimed and firmly placed ('fix'd') weapon, and (b) an unbending divine law (*canon*, the spelling adopted by most modern editions).

     seal Slaughter The Second Quarto's *seale* may be a misreading of *sealf* or *sealfe* or simply a variant of *self* (the word in the Folio text). But it is just as likely to be a Shakespearean play on *self* and *seal* (the insignia of a self, and particularly a monarch). If so, this line can refer to two options, both forbidden by 'the Everlasting': suicide and regicide (see Romans 12:17–13:7).

133   **wary** (a) perilous, (b) cursed, and (c) weary (the Folio reading).

137– **merely . . . dead** either (a) 'solely to bring it to this unkempt,
38   overgrown, weed-infested state within two months of its caretaker's death' (assuming that the Quarto's lack of punctuation reflects the way this passage should be read and interpreted), or (b) 'completely; that it should deteriorate to this point; only two months dead' (assuming that semicolons should be inserted after *merely* and *thus*, to approximate the punctuation in the Folio text).

     come thus arrive at this point. Modern editions normally follow the Folio and print *come to this*.

138   **But . . . dead** only two months after the demise of its gardener.

140   **Hyperion to a Satyr** the Sun God in comparison to a creature half human and half goat. Like goats, satyrs were proverbial for lechery. The Quarto spelling, *satire*, reinforces Hamlet's point that the present monarch is ludicrously unfit for the role he is trying in vain to play.

141   **beteem** permit.

146   **Frailty** Hamlet alludes to the commonplace that a woman is a 'weaker vessel'; see the note to line 101.

147   **or ere** either (a) before (compare line 182), or (b) or before.

149   **Niobe** a heroine in Greek myth who wept so uncontrollably for her children (slain by Apollo and Diana) that she became a stone from which tears continued to flow. Ovid depicted her in Book VI of his *Metamorphoses*.

153   **Hercules** a Greek hero proverbial for his strength. According to later traditions he became a god, and his virtues and labours were allegorized in such a way that he became a symbol of Christ in victory. He also appears to have been an emblem for the Globe playhouse and its actors; see II.ii.387–88.

His Cannon 'gainst seal Slaughter; O God, God,
How wary, stale, flat, and unprofitable
Seem to me all the Uses of this World?
Fie on't, ah fie, 'tis an unweeded Garden   135
That grows to Seed: things rank and gross in
   Nature
Possess it merely that it should come thus
But two Months dead, nay not so much, not two;
So excellent a King, that was to this
Hyperion to a Satyr, so loving to my Mother   140
That he might not beteem the Winds of Heaven
Visit her Face too roughly. Heaven and Earth,
Must I remember, why she should hang on him
As if Increase of Appetite had grown
By what it fed on, and yet within a Month –   145
Let me not think on't (Frailty, thy name is
   Woman) –
A little Month or ere those Shoes were old
With which she followed my poor Father's Body
Like Niobe all Tears, why she –
O God, a Beast that wants Discourse of Reason   150
Would have mourn'd longer – married with my Uncle,
My Father's Brother, but no more like my Father
Than I to Hercules. Within a Month,

154 **unrighteous** both (a) unworthy, and (b) insincere. *Salt* refers to the brinish composition of tears. But used as an adjective, *salt* could mean 'lustful', as in *Othello*, II.i.247–48.

155 **Had . . . Eyes** had finished washing the red out of her irritated eyes. *Galled* (spelled *gauled* here and elsewhere in the Quarto) can mean (a) afflicted with galls (painful swellings), (b) chafed from rubbing, or (c) filled with gall (either bitter bile or the substance from which ink derives).

156 **post** hasten. Compare I.i.102.

157 **incestious** incestuous. In accordance with such biblical passages as Leviticus 18:16 and 20:21, Hamlet regards as incestuous a union between a woman and her former husband's brother. His views would have had the support of both Catholics and Anglicans in Shakespeare's time. The matter was somewhat sensitive, because Queen Elizabeth was a product of the second marriage of Henry VIII, whose first wife, Catherine of Aragon, was the widow of Henry's brother Arthur.

163 **Sir my good Friend** Hamlet refuses to allow Horatio to describe himself as a 'poor Servant'. Horatio can be welcomed only on equal terms as a 'good' (true) 'Friend'. In II.ii.233–407 two other erstwhile 'Friends' prove unworthy of the opportunity to 'change that Name' with the Prince.
change exchange.

164 **what make you from** what brings you from, what are you doing away from.

166 **Good even, Sir** This greeting is probably addressed to Barnardo. The word *even* indicates that it is now after noon.

168 **truant** wayward, irresponsible. Horatio's self-description implies more than a disposition to play hooky from school.

170 **do . . . Violence** abuse my ear. Hamlet's phrasing anticipates a report that will soon unleash real 'Violence'. See the note to line 77, and compare I.i.19–29, I.ii.26–33, 118–28, I.v.33–37.

173 **Elsonoure** the usual Quarto spelling for what modern editions normally render as *Elsinore*. Here the Folio spelling is *Elsenour*.

174 **for to drink** how to drink thoroughly. The Folio's 'to drink deep' has the same implications and is preferred by most modern editions.

Ere yet the Salt of most unrighteous Tears
Had left the Flushing in her galled Eyes,   155
She married, O most wicked Speed; to post
With such Dexterity to incestious Sheets,
It is not, nor it cannot come to, Good.
But break my Heart, for I must hold my
    Tongue.

Enter Horatio, Marcellus, and Barnardo.

HORATIO   Hail to your Lordship.
HAMLET   I am glad to see you well;   160
    Horatio, or I do forget my self.
HORATIO   The same, my Lord, and your poor Servant
    ever.
HAMLET   Sir my good Friend, I'll change that Name
    with you,
    And what make you from Wittenberg, Horatio?
    — Marcellus.
MARCELLUS   My good Lord.   165
HAMLET   I am very glad to see you, good even,
    Sir.
    — But what in faith make you from Wittenberg?
HORATIO   A truant Disposition, good my Lord.
HAMLET   I would not hear your Enemy say so,
    Nor shall you do my Ear that Violence   170
    To make it Truster of your own Report
    Against your self: I know you are no Truant.
    But what is your Affair in Elsonoure?
    We'll teach you for to drink ere you depart.

176 **prethee** prithee, pray thee. This spelling is the one to be found throughout the Second Quarto.
Studient student; this spelling occurs frequently in Shakespeare's texts. *Mock* recalls I.i.141.

178 **hard upon** quickly thereafter. Compare the similarly suggestive phrasing in lines 58–60. Here, as in lines 83–84, *indeed* plays on 'in deed', with *deed* alluding to what Shylock calls 'the Deed of Kind' in *The Merchant of Venice*, I.iii.86.

179 **Meats** food, not limited to meat in the modern sense.

180 **coldly** Hamlet means this literally; in lines 179–80 he is saying that the wedding was so soon after the funeral that the leftovers from the food served hot on the first occasion were served cold on the second. As in line 77, however, *coldly* also refers to an inappropriately unfeeling attitude.

181 **Would . . . Heaven** The sentiments Hamlet expresses here will be echoed later in the play. Compare III.iii.73–95 and V.ii.37–47.

182 **Or ever** before. Compare line 147.

185 **'a** he.

188 **yesternight** last night.

191 **Season your Admiration** moderate your amazement.

192 **attent** attentive; probably accented on the second syllable.

194 **Marvile** marvel. The Quarto spelling may involve wordplay on *vile*.

197 **dead Wast and Middle** Horatio means midnight, the time when night is most still (dead), and when the spirits of the dead are most likely to walk. *Wast* (waste), the spelling to be found in both the Second Quarto and the First Folio, plays on *waist* (another kind of middle) and on *vast* (which is etymologically related to *waste*, and which appears at this point in the 1603 First Quarto). Compare II.ii.238–46.

199 **at Point** precisely in every respect.
Cap a pea the Quarto's metrical rendering of *cap-a-pe* (cap-à-pied), French for 'head to foot'. Compare line 225.

201 **stately** literally, 'state-like', in the imperial manner of a monarch. *Slow* (slowly) echoes line 58.

202 **surprised** ambushed, overtaken by surprise.

HORATIO   My Lord, I came to see your Father's
   Funeral.   175
HAMLET   I prethee do not mock me, fellow Studient,
   I think it was to see my Mother's Wedding.
HORATIO   Indeed, my Lord, it followed hard upon.
HAMLET   Thrift, thrift, Horatio: the funeral bak'd
   Meats
   Did coldly furnish forth the Marriage Tables.   180
   Would I had met my dearest Foe in Heaven
   Or ever I had seen that Day, Horatio;
   My Father, me thinks I see my Father.
HORATIO   Where,
   My Lord?
HAMLET   In my Mind's Eye, Horatio.
HORATIO   I saw him once, 'a was a goodly King.   185
HAMLET   'A was a Man, take him for all in all,
   I shall not look upon his like again.
HORATIO   My Lord I think I saw him yesternight.
HAMLET   Saw, who?
HORATIO   My Lord, the King your Father.
HAMLET   The King my Father?   190
HORATIO   Season your Admiration for a while
   With an attent Ear till I may deliver
   Upon the Witness of these Gentlemen
   This Marvile to you.
HAMLET   For God's Love, let me hear?
HORATIO   Two Nights together had these Gentlemen,   195
   Marcellus and Barnardo, on their Watch
   In the dead Wast and Middle of the Night
   Been thus encount'red: a Figure like your Father,
   Arm'd at Point, exactly Cap a pea,
   Appears before them, and with solemn March   200
   Goes slow and stately by them; thrice he walk'd
   By their oppress'd and Fear-surprised Eyes

203 **Troncheon** truncheon, a short, thick staff symbolizing military authority.

205 **dumb** speechless.

206 **dreadful** full of fear.

211 **like** like each other than the Ghost is like your Father. *Apparision* (apparition) recalls I.i.24.

215 **it** its. See the note to I.i.33.

216 **like as** as if.

217 **even then** at that very moment.

222 **Indeed, Sirs** This phrase can either refer back to what Horatio has just said (with Hamlet commending the sense of duty the three men have demonstrated) or intensify what follows (with Hamlet saying 'This troubles me indeed'). Expressions 'Looking before and after' (IV.iv.34) are characteristically Shakespearean.

223 **to night** tonight. Compare lines 105, 125, 236.

227 **Beaver** visor.
What . . . frowningly? It is not clear how this line is to be spoken. Among the possibilities are 'What, look'd he frowningly?' and 'What look'd he, frowningly?' In the second version *What* would mean 'how'.

228 **then** than. But here as elsewhere *then* could fit the context as well. Only rarely does *than* appear in the early texts of Shakespeare.

Within his Troncheon's length, whil'st they, distill'd
Almost to Jelly with the Act of Fear,
Stand dumb and speak not to him. This to me   205
In dreadful Secrecy impart they did,
And I with them the third Night kept the Watch,
Where as they had deliver'd, both in Time,
Form of the Thing, each Word made true and good,
The Apparision comes. I knew your Father,   210
These Hands are not more like.
HAMLET   But where was this?
MARCELLUS   My Lord, upon the Platform where we
   watch.
HAMLET   Did you not speak to it?
HORATIO   My Lord, I did,
But Answer made it none; yet once me thought
It lifted up it Head, and did address   215
It self to Motion like as it would speak:
But even then the Morning Cock crew loud,
And at the Sound it shrunk in haste away
And vanish'd from our Sight.
HAMLET   'Tis very Strange.
HORATIO   As I do live, my honour'd Lord, 'tis true,   220
And we did think it writ down in our Duty
To let you know of it.
HAMLET   Indeed, Sirs, but
This troubles me. Hold you the Watch to night?
ALL   We do, my Lord.
HAMLET   Arm'd, say you?
ALL   Arm'd, my Lord.
HAMLET   From Top to Toe?
ALL   My Lord, from Head to Foot.   225
HAMLET   Then saw you not his Face?
HORATIO   O yes, my Lord,
He wore his Beaver up.
HAMLET   What look'd he frowningly?
HORATIO   A Countenance more in Sorrow then in
   Anger.

231 **a mazed**   amazed. The Quarto spelling could be construed 'have mazed'.

232 **like**   likely, probably.

233 **tell a Hundreth**   count to a hundred.

234 **grisl'd**   grizzled, mingled with grey.

236 **Sable silver'd**   black mixed with grey.
to night   tonight. See lines 223, 243.

238 **assume**   take on. Hamlet seems perilously close to assuming that if the spirit assumes his 'Father's person' (appearance), it must be his father's spirit in fact. Horatio and the two watchmen have been much more cautious about drawing any conclusions about the Ghost.

239 **gape**   open its mouth widely. This verb is often used to describe an infant bird eagerly awaiting food.

241 **hetherto**   hitherto. As with *thither* and *whither*, Shakespeare seems to have preferred the *e*-form.

242 **tenable**   held tightly.

243 **what somever**   whatsoever.

244 **Give . . . Tongue**   note it but say nothing about it to anyone.

245 **requite**   reward.

246 **a leaven**   eleven.

250 **doubt**   fear, suspect.

HAMLET   Pale, or Red?

HORATIO   Nay very Pale.

HAMLET   And fix'd
His Eyes upon you?

HORATIO   Most constantly.

HAMLET   I would   230
I had been there.

HORATIO   It would have much a maz'd you.

HAMLET   Very like, stay'd it long?

HORATIO   While one
With moderate Haste might tell a Hundreth.

BOTH   Longer, longer.

HORATIO   Not when I saw't.

HAMLET   His Beard was grisl'd, no.

HORATIO   It was as I have seen it in his Life,   235
A Sable silver'd.

HAMLET   I will watch to night:
Perchaunce 'twill walk again.

HORATIO   I warr'nt it will.

HAMLET   If it assume my noble Father's person,
I'll speak to it though Hell it self should gape
And bid me hold my Peace. I pray you all,   240
If you have hetherto conceal'd this Sight,
Let it be tenable in your Silence still,
And what somever else shall hap to night,
Give it an Understanding but no Tongue;
I will requite your Loves; so fare you well.   245
Upon the Platform 'twixt a leaven and twelfe
I'll visit you.

ALL   Our Duty to your Honour.

HAMLET   Your Loves as mine to you: farewell.

                              Exeunt [all but Hamlet].

– My Father's Spirit, in Arms, all is not well;
I doubt some Foul Play, would the Night were
   come.   250

251 **Fond** Most editions print *Foul*, the word in the First Folio (as well as in the First Quarto). Here *Fond* means 'foolish' or 'mad' (referring to deeds an evildoer rashly expected to go undetected and unpunished). In Shakespeare's time *fond* was also a variant spelling for 'found', and Hamlet could well be punning on that implication as a way of emphasizing the folly of the 'Foul Play' (line 250) that is now to be found out.

252 **o'erwhelm** literally, bury, cover over; suppress, overpower.

I.iii This scene probably takes place in or near the chamber of Polonius.

1 **Necessaries** necessities.
inbark'd embarked, loaded aboard (literally, into) the ship.

3 **Convay** conveyance, means of transport; accented on the first syllable.
in assistant in assisting them. Most of today's editions adopt the Folio's *Convoy is assistant*.

5 **For** as for.

6 **Hold it a Fashion** regard it as a passing fancy.
a Toy in Blood an idle prompting of his youthful passions.

7 **primy Nature** [human] nature in its springtime.

8 **Forward** over-eager (and thus likely to wither prematurely).

9 **Suppliance of a Minute** something that supplies the needs of a brief moment and no more.

10 **so** thus. Although the early texts do not so indicate, modern editions normally punctuate this speech as a question.

11 **cressant** crescent; growing, increasing. Laertes hints at the 'Virtue' (literally, manliness) of Hamlet's 'Will' (line 16). See the notes to I.ii.60, 75, 178, and compare I.ii.251.
alone solely.

12 **Thews and Bulks** strength and stature.
Temple waxes body grows. Laertes alludes to 1 Corinthians 6:19, 'know yet not that your body is the temple of the Holy Ghost which is in you, which ye have of God, and ye are not your own?'

14 **Grows wide withal** develops along with it. But *wide* also hints at 'wide of the mark', out of kilter.

– Till then sit still, my Soul. Fond Deeds will
  rise,
Though all the Earth o'erwhelm them to men's
  Eyes.   *Exit.*

Scene 3

Enter Laertes and Ophelia, his Sister.

LAERTES   My Necessaries are inbark'd, farewell,
  And Sister, as the Winds give Benefit
  And Convay, in assistant do not sleep
  But let me hear from you.
OPHELIA   Do you doubt that?
LAERTES   For Hamlet, and the Trifling of his Favour,   5
  Hold it a Fashion, and a Toy in Blood,
  A Violet in the Youth of primy Nature,
  Forward, not Permanent, Sweet, not Lasting,
  The Perfume and Suppliance of a Minute,
  No more.
OPHELIA   No more but so.
LAERTES   Think it no more: 10
  For Nature cressant does not grow alone
  In Thews and Bulks, but as this Temple waxes
  The inward Service of the Mind and Soul
  Grows wide withal. Perhaps he loves you now,

15   **Soil nor Cautel**   blemish nor deceitfulness. Compare *Julius Caesar*, II.i.127–38.

17   **way'd**   (a) given its way, allowed free rein, (b) straying from the way, the 'Course' proper to it (I.ii.105), or (c) weigh'd (the Folio reading), taken into account. Laertes implies that Hamlet is an 'extravagant and erring Spirit' (I.i.149); compare I.ii.50–61, 112–20, 168.

19   **Unvalued Persons**   people of no consequence to the well-being of the 'State'.

21   **Safety**   Here the Folio reads *sanctity*. If *Safety* is correct, either (a) the word is probably to be pronounced with three syllables, or (b) *Health* is to be preceded by *the*.

23   **Body**   body politic; the 'whole State' and those with the 'Voice' (authority) to speak its corporate mind.

29   **way**   both (a) map out, consider, and (b) weigh, calculate. Compare line 17.

30   **credent**   credulous, gullible.
     list   listen to, heed.

31   **loose**   release (and thereby lose control over). Compare I.ii.118.
     chast   virgin. Here the Second Quarto spelling permits a second reading as well: *chas'd*, pursued. Compare *A Midsummer Night's Dream*, II.i.161–62.

32   **Importunity**   demanding persistence. The Latin root of this word refers to an urgent suit to gain admission to a port or entrance.

34   **keep you in the Rear of your Affection**   keep your 'chast Treasure' (maidenhead) away from the front lines of battle, so that neither your 'Affection' (emotions and desires) nor Hamlet's may endanger its security.

36   **Chariest**   literally, stingiest, most sparing; most modest.
     Prodigal   extravagant, spendthrift. The quotation marks, adapted from those in the Second Quarto text, indicate that Laertes is parroting proverbial love, probably 'Precepts' (line 58) bequeathed him by his father.

37   **Moon**   The Moon was associated with Cynthia (Diana), Goddess of Chastity.

38   **scapes**   escapes.
     calumnious Strokes   the blows of calumny (malicious scandal).

And now no Soil nor Cautel doth besmirch   15
The Virtue of his Will; but you must fear,
His Greatness way'd, his Will is not his own;
For he himself is subject to his Birth;
He may not, as Unvalued Persons do,
Carve for himself, for on his Choice depends   20
The Safety and Health of this whole State,
And therefore must his Choice be circumscrib'd
Unto the Voice and Yielding of that Body
Whereof he is the Head; then if he says he
    loves you,
It fits your Wisdom so far to believe it   25
As he in his particular Act and Place
May give his Saying deed, which is no further
Than the main Voice of Denmark goes withal.
Then way what Loss your Honour may sustain
If with too credent Ear you list his Songs,   30
Or loose your Heart, or your chast Treasure
    open
To his unmast'red Importunity.
Fear it, Ophelia, fear it, my dear Sister,
And keep you in the Rear of your Affection
Out of the Shot and Danger of Desire.   35
'The Chariest Maid is Prodigal enough
If she unmask her Beauty to the Moon.'
'Virtue it self scapes not calumnious Strokes.'

39   **Canker** cankerworm, a larva feeding on the buds ('Buttons') of flowers. *Galls* (injures) recalls I.ii.155.

42   **Contagious . . . imminent** the danger of contagion from withering blasts of air (the cause of blight) is most urgent. *Blastments* recalls I.i.122; *wary*, I.ii.133; *Safety*, I.iii.20; *Fear*, I.i.40, 116.

47   **ungracious Pastors** ministers (literally, shepherds) lacking in grace (spiritual discipline). Compare I.i.159.

48   **step** stairstep. Modern editors normally follow the revised version of the Second Quarto here and print *steep*, of which *step* may be an authorial variant.

49   **a puff'd and reckless Libertine** as a proud and heedlessly licentious young gallant.

50   **Dalliance** wanton pleasure.

51   **reaks not his own Reed** both (a) heeds (recks) not his own 'rede' (advice, reading), and (b) fails to remember that he himself is, or is armed with, nothing more substantial than a reed. Reeds were proverbial for their frailty; see *Antony and Cleopatra*, II.vii.13–14, and *Cymbeline*, IV.ii.265–66. Ophelia's rejoinder to her brother recalls the admonition Jesus gives his disciples about the weakness of the flesh in Matthew 26:41.
    fear me not don't worry about me.

58   **Precepts** proverbs, wise sentences (from Latin *sententiae*).

59   **character** inscribe or engrave. As we have just seen from Laertes' advice to Ophelia, he has already 'charactered' a large stock of his father's prudent maxims. See the note to line 36.

60   **unproportion'd** unsuitable, inordinate. Compare I.ii.32–33.

61   **Familiar** friendly, informal, open.
    Vulgar common, loose, indiscriminate. See I.ii.99.

62   **and their Adoption tried** once they have been proven trustworthy.

63   **Grapple** grasp, embrace.

64   **entertainment** hospitable reception.

65   **unfledg'd Courage** ardent 'hearts' too young to fly. *Courage* derives from *cor*, the Latin word for 'heart'.

'The Canker galls the Infants of the Spring
Too oft before their Buttons be disclos'd,   40
And in the Morn and liquid Dew of Youth
Contagious Blastments are most imminent.'
Be wary then, best Safety lies in Fear;
Youth to it self rebels, though none else near.

OPHELIA   I shall the effect of this good Lesson
    keep   45
As Watchman to my Heart; but good my Brother,
Do not as some ungracious Pastors do,
Show me the step and thorny way to Heaven
Whiles a puff'd and reckless Libertine
Himself the Primrose Path of Dalliance treads   50
And reaks not his own Reed.

Enter Polonius.

LAERTES   O fear me not.
I stay too long, but here my Father comes:
A double Blessing is a double Grace,
Occasion smiles upon a second Leave.
POLONIUS   Yet here, Laertes? Aboard, aboard, for
    shame,   55
The Wind sits in the Shoulder of your Sail,
And you are stay'd for; there my Blessing
    with thee,
And these few Precepts in thy Memory
Look thou character. Give thy Thoughts no
    Tongue,
Nor any unproportion'd Thought his Act.   60
Be thou Familiar, but by no means Vulgar.
Those Friends thou hast, and their Adoption
    tried,
Grapple them unto thy Soul with Hoops of Steel;
But do not dull thy Palm with entertainment
Of each new-hatch'd unfledg'd Courage. Beware   65

66 **Quarrel** dispute requiring you to uphold your honour in a duel.

68 **Voice** (a) thoughts, opinions, (b) commitment, endorsement, and (c) 'Censure' or 'Judgement'. Compare line 23 and I.i.123, I.ii.44–45. Lines 68–69 and lines 59–60 echo I.ii.243–44.

69 **Censure** counsel, opinions, criticism.
reserve thy Judgement both (a) make up your own mind, and (b) keep your opinions to yourself.

70 **Habit** apparel.

71 **express'd in Fancy** displayed in ostentatious finery.

74 **Generous** highborn, noble (from Latin *generosus*). Here 'class of men' is implied. Compare the elliptical phrasing in lines 70–71.
Chief in that most renowned for tasteful elegance.

75 **Lender, Boy** Here the Folio reads *Lender be*. In the Second Quarto version Polonius continues his word-sparing discourse and leaves 'be' to be supplied by the hearer.

76 **Lone** loan (but here spelled in a way that emphasizes the 'lone', self-protective approach to life that Polonius commends). The Quarto reading, *loue* (love), may well be correct (see the note to I.ii.83), but the Folio's *lone* fits the context more tidily. *Looses* (both 'releases' and 'loses') echoes line 31.

77 **Husbandry** personal economy, thrifty management.

81 **season** make palatable, preserve, and ripen. Compare I.ii.191.

83 **invests you** clothes you (making you ready). Compare the imagery in I.i.1–2, 42–45, 161–62, I.ii.66–68, 77–86, 195–201, 224–25, 238–40, I.iii.5–6, 36–37, 62–63, 70–74.
tend attend, wait on you.

89 **So** if it.
touching concerning. Compare I.i.21.

90 **Marry well bethought** Indeed, I'm glad you reminded me of that. Originally *marry* was an oath referring to the Virgin Mary.

92 **private Time** time alone. In Shakespeare's time maidens were often forbidden to spend unchaperoned time with young men. See lines 123–25. *Private* is suggestive; compare II.ii.238–46.

93 **Audience** willingness to hear. Compare I.ii.170.

Of entrance to a Quarrel, but being in,
Bear't that the Opposed may beware of thee.
Give every man thy Ear, but few thy Voice;
Take each man's Censure, but reserve thy
    Judgement.
Costly thy Habit as thy Purse can buy,   70
But not express'd in Fancy; Rich, not Gaudy,
For the Apparel oft proclaims the Man,
And they in Fraunce of the best Rank and Station,
Or of a most Select and Generous, Chief in that.
Neither a Borrower nor a Lender, Boy: 75
For Lone oft looses both it Self and Friend,
And Borrowing dulleth Edge of Husbandry.
This above all, to thine own Self be True,
And it must follow as the Night the Day
Thou canst not then be False to any Man.   80
Farewell, my Blessing season this in thee.
LAERTES   Most humbly do I take my Leave, my Lord.
POLONIUS   The Time invests you, go, your Servants
    tend.
LAERTES   – Farewell, Ophelia, and remember well
What I have said to you.
OPHELIA   'Tis in my Memory lock'd   85
And you your self shall keep the Key of it.
LAERTES   Farewell.   *Exit.*
POLONIUS   What is't, Ophelia, he hath said to you?
OPHELIA   So please you, something touching the
    Lord Hamlet.
POLONIUS   Marry well bethought,   90
'Tis told me he hath very oft of late
Given private Time to you, and you your self
Have of your Audience been most free and
    bounteous;

94   **put** pressed. Polonius' phrasing recalls I.ii.58–60, 178.

97   **behooves** befits.
    my Daughter the daughter of a respected counsellor such as I.
    Honour both (a) chastity, and (b) reputation.

99   **Tenders** offers, here gestures of tenderness.

101   **green** unripe, naive.
    unsifted unproven. Polonius probably alludes to Luke 22:31,
    where Jesus says, 'Satan hath desired to have you, that he may
    sift you as wheat.'

102   **perilous** the word was probably pronounced 'parlous' in
    Shakespeare's time. Compare the imagery in lines 101–2 with
    that in lines 19–24.

103–4 **I . . . think** Ophelia's words echo lines 5–10, and they make it
    clear that her 'Choice' is so 'circumscrib'd' by her father and
    her older brother that she has no way to 'carve' for herself
    (lines 18–23).

106   **Sterling** legitimate currency; what would now be called 'legal
    tender'.

107   **Tender . . . dearly** hold (value) yourself at a higher rate.

108   **Phrase** word.
    roaming it thus leading it about in this roundabout fashion.
    Roaming comes from the Folio printing; the Second Quarto
    reads *wrong*, and most editions emend to *wringing, wronging,*
    or *running*.

109   **tender me a Fool** probably (a) give me a fool for a daughter,
    (b) give me a fool (baby) for a grandchild, and (c) make me a
    fool to the world.

110   **Importun'd me** sought my favour. Compare line 32.

111   **go to** an expression of dismissal, like our 'come now!' *Fashion*
    echoes lines 5–9.

112   **Countenance** literally, face; assurance, warranty. Compare
    I.ii.228.

114   **Springes** snares.
    Woodcocks birds proverbial for their stupidity. *Prodigal* (line
    15) recalls lines 36–37.

116   **Blazes** bright flames. Polonius puns on *blazons* (see I.v.20),
    proclamations, trumpetings. Compare *Julius Caesar*, II.ii.31.

If it be so, as so 'tis put on me,
And that in way of Caution, I must tell you,   95
You do not understand your self so clearly
As it behooves my Daughter, and your Honour;
What is between you, give me up the Truth.

OPHELIA   He hath, my Lord, of late made many
 Tenders
Of his Affection to me.

POLONIUS   Affection, puh,   100
You speak like a green Girl unsifted in
Such perilous Circumstance. Do you believe
His Tenders, as you call them?

OPHELIA   I do not know,
My Lord, what I should think.

POLONIUS   Marry I will teach you.
Think your self a Baby, that you have ta'en   105
These Tenders for true Pay which are not Sterling;
Tender your self more dearly, or (not to crack
The Wind of the poor Phrase, roaming it thus)
You'll tender me a Fool.

OPHELIA   My Lord, he hath
Importun'd me with Love in honourable fashion.   110

POLONIUS   Ay, Fashion you may call't; go to, go to.

OPHELIA   And hath given Countenance to his Speech,
My Lord, with almost all the holy Vows
Of Heaven.

POLONIUS   Ay, Springes to catch Woodcocks. I
Do know when the Blood burns, how prodigal   115
The Soul lends the Tongue Vows; these Blazes,
 Daughter,

117 **extinct** extinguished.

118 **a making** in the act of being made.

121 **Intreatments** both (a) your treatment of him, your willingness
to give him audience; and (b) your willingness to receive his
entreaties to you [to surrender].

122 **a Commaund to Parle** a call for a parley, a conference to
negotiate the terms for a truce (in this case one that depends
upon the yielding of a stronghold).

124 **larger Tider** longer tether.

125 **Then** than (as in I.ii.228). Polonius' phrasing will prove
prophetic; in short order 'a larger Tider' will be 'given'
Ophelia.

126 **Brokers** untrustworthy panders (rather than honest business
agents).

127 **Die** probably both (a) dye (colour), and (b) gambling die.
Investments show apparel (outward appearance) indicates.
Compare line 83.

128 **Implorators** suitors imploring you to be persuaded.

129 **Bonds** ratified 'Bands' (I.ii.24) or agreements.

130 **beguide** Modern editions normally follow the Folio and print
beguile (deceive, cheat). That is the sense called for here; but
beguide may be a Shakespearean coinage to combine such
senses as 'misguide', 'beguile', and 'beguild' (gild over).
Compare *Macbeth*, II.ii.52–54. All of these implications
would fit with the seemingly 'pious Bonds' (holy pledges or
contracts) that Polonius accuses Hamlet of tendering to
disguise the 'unholy Suits' he implores (lines 128–29).
Whereas Laertes has counselled Ophelia to beware of
Hamlet's 'Blood' (line 6), his youthful passion, and her own,
the more cynical Polonius warns her against the Prince's
cunning. It never occurs to him that Hamlet's intentions might
be honourable, his feelings sincere.

132 **moment** moment's.

134 **charge** command.
come your ways come along now.

Giving more Light than Heat, extinct in both
Even in their Promise as it is a making,
You must not take for Fire. From this Time
Be something scanter of your Maiden Presence,   120
Set your Intreatments at a higher Rate
Than a commaund to Parle; for Lord Hamlet,
Believe so much in him, that he is Young,
And with a larger Tider may he walk
Then may be given you. In few, Ophelia,   125
Do not believe his Vows, for they are Brokers,
Not of that Die which their Investments show,
But mere Implorators of unholy Suits
Breathing like sanctified and pious Bonds
The better to beguide. This is for all: 130
I would not, in plain Terms, from this Time
    foorth
Have you so slaunder any moment Leisure
As to give Words or Talk with the Lord Hamlet.
Look to't, I charge you, come your ways.
OPHELIA   I shall obey, my Lord.   *Exeunt.*   135

I.iv   This scene returns us to the battlements on which the play began.

1   **shroudly**   shrewdly (the Folio spelling); cursedly, sharply. The form of the word in the Second Quarto suggests that the air chafes Hamlet's skin in a manner that puts him in mind of a burial shroud.

2   **eager**   bitter.

4   **strook**   struck.

5   **Season**   period of time. This word echoes I.iii.81.

6   **wont**   custom, habit.

S.D.   **Pieces goes off**   cannon are fired.

7   **to night**   both (a) to night, and (b) tonight. Compare I.ii.236, 243.
takes his Rouse   carouses. See I.ii.121–28.

8   **Wassel**   wassail, a word that derives from an Anglo-Saxon toast meaning 'be hale [whole, healthy]'.
up-spring Reels   The up-spring was a wild dance, and reels are swirling, swaggering movements, as in Scottish dancing.

9   **Rennish**   Rhenish (Rhine) wine.

11   **The Triumph of his Pledge**   his quaffing the entire cup after each toast.

14   **borne**   both (a) born, and (b) carried, made accustomed.

15   **More . . . Observance**   that would be more honoured by being broken than by being observed. In modern parlance the phrase is usually given a satirical twist that reverses its original thrust.

16   **Reveale**   both (a) revel (the usual interpretation), and (b) reveille (the French word for a brass or drum call to awaken or assemble troops); see line 8. For Hamlet and 'other Nations' (line 17), it is also a revealing sound, a 'bray' that makes the Danes seem ass-like if not 'Swinish' (lines 10, 18).

17   **tradust**   traduc'd; insulted, scorned. The Quarto spelling suggests play on 'tread' and 'dust'; compare I.iii.49–51, I.ii.68–71.
tax'd   vilified, censured.

18   **clip**   both (a) clepe, call, and (b) nickname (thereby clipping short 'our Addition', line 19).

Scene 4

Enter Hamlet, Horatio, and Marcellus.

HAMLET   The Air bites shroudly, it is very cold.
HORATIO   It is nipping, and an eager Air.
HAMLET   What Hour now?
HORATIO   I think it lacks of Twelfe.
MARCELLUS   No, it is strook.
HORATIO   Indeed; I heard it not.
  It then draws near the Season wherein the Spirit   5
  Held his wont to walk.
            A Flourish of Trumpets, and two Pieces goes off.
                    What does this mean, my Lord?
HAMLET   The King doth wake to night, and takes his
    Rouse.
  Keeps Wassel and the swagg'ring up-spring Reels;
  And as he drains his drafts of Rennish down,
  The Kettle-drum and Trumpet thus bray out   10
  The Triumph of his Pledge.
HORATIO   Is it a Custom?
HAMLET   Ay marry is't,
  But to my Mind, though I am Native here
  And to the Manner borne, it is a Custom
  More honour'd in the Breach than the Observance.   15
  This heavy headed Reveale East and West
  Makes us tradust, and tax'd of other Nations:
  They clip us Drunkards, and with Swinish Phrase

19 **Soil our Addition** befoul any titles or epithets they apply to us.
Soil echoes I.iii.14–17, where Laertes traduces Hamlet.

21 **The Pith . . . Attribute** the core of our good reputation.

22 **So . . . Men** similarly it happens with individual men.
Particular recalls I.ii.75, I.iii.24–28.

23 **for . . . them** because of some natural blemish in them.

26 **Complexion** humour (an imbalance in one's disposition).

27 **Pales** fences. This word is echoed in III.i.82. Compare
I.i.26–28, I.iii.5–44, 114–34.

28–29 **some . . . Manners** some vice that spoils pleasing manners.
Habit echoes I.iii.70–74; *O'er-leavens* recalls I.ii.245–47.

31 **Being . . . Star** either (a) resulting from Nature (wearing her
livery, uniform) or deriving from a malignant star (or planet)
that sways one's fortune, or (b) otherwise being a designated
servant of Nature itself, or the Pole Star at the apogee of
Fortune (compare I.i.31–34). It is not clear whether this line is
meant to illustrate 'Defect' or 'Grace' (lines 30, 32); see the
note to I.ii.222.

34 **in . . . Corruption** in general opinion be judged corrupt.
Censure echoes I.iii.69.

35–37 **the . . . Scandal** a drop of oil (symbolizing evil) clouds all their
nobility of soul with a dubious character that scandalizes it,
giving it a bad name. *Eale* probably means both 'oil' and
'evil'; compare II.ii.636, where *Deale* appears as the spelling
for *Devil*.

40 **Blasts** both (a) loud gusts of wind and fire, and (b) blights.
Compare I.i.122, I.iii.42.

41 **charitable** good, in keeping with *caritas* (Latin for 'Christian
love').

42 **Questionable** The preceding phrases prepare us to interpret
Questionable here as 'ambiguous' or 'dubious'; but Hamlet
appears to mean 'to be questioned' in a more positive sense.
Rather than 'try the spirit' as Horatio has done in I.i.45,
Hamlet simply assumes that it is his father's ghost and
proceeds to question it on that basis. See I.ii.238–40.

Soil our Addition; and indeed it takes
From our Achievements, though perform'd at
    Height,   20
The Pith and Marrow of our Attribute.
So oft it chaunces in particular Men,
That for some vicious Mole of Nature in them,
As in their Birth, wherein they are not guilty
(Since Nature cannot choose his Origin),   25
By their o'er-growth of some Complexion
Oft breaking down the Pales and Forts of
    Reason,
Or by some Habit that too much o'er-leavens
The Form of Plausive Manners, that these Men
Carrying, I say, the Stamp of one Defect,   30
Being Nature's Livery, or Fortune's Star,
His Virtues else be they as pure as Grace,
As infinite as Man may undergo,
Shall in the general Censure take Corruption
From that particular Fault: the Dram of Eale   35
Doth all the Noble Substance of a Doubt
To his own Scandal.

Enter Ghost.

HORATIO   Look, my Lord, it comes.
HAMLET   Angels and Ministers of Grace defend us.
  – Be thou a Spirit of Health, or Goblin damn'd,
Bring with thee Airs from Heaven, or Blasts
    from Hell,   40
Be thy Intents wicked, or charitable,
Thou com'st in such a Questionable Shape
That I will speak to thee, I'll call thee
    Hamlet,
King, Father, Royal Dane; O answer me,
Let me not burst in Ignorance, but tell   45

46 **canoniz'd** sanctified; buried with the prescribed rites. In order to preserve the metre in this line, *canoniz'd* either needs to be syncopated to 'can'niz'd' or accented on the second syllable.
hearsed coffined; here pronounced as a two-syllable word.

47 **Cerements** apparently a Shakespearean coinage that combines 'cerecloth' (waxed burial cloth) and 'ceremonies'.

51 **Corse** corpse. Compare I.ii.105.
in complete Steel in full armour; here pronounced 'cómplete'.

52 **the glimses of the Moon** This phrase reminds us that the Ghost is from a realm the Moon does not reach with its beams. It also suggests that the light of the Moon is pale and intermittent on this ominous night. *Glimses*, the Second Quarto spelling for *glimpses*, may reflect the way Shakespeare wanted the actor playing Hamlet to pronounce this word here.

53 **hideous** terrifying.
Fools of Nature mere mortals, subject to Nature's whims.

54 **Disposition** This word echoes I.ii.168 and anticipates I.v.162–63, where it is coloured by the sense of *disposed* that means 'inclined to merriment and mockery'; see *Love's Labour's Lost*, II.i.247, and compare *Julius Caesar*, I.iii.33, II.ii.127.

56 **What should we do?** Hamlet's question reflects the belief that ghosts sometimes revisited the living in order to get them to perform some unfinished task. Compare Ophelia's remark in I.iii.103–4.

58 **Impartment** communication. This word plays on *particular* (line 22), and it suggests that what the Ghost imparts will become so imbedded in Hamlet that it will be a part of him and of the part (role) he plays from this point forward.

59 **curteous** courteous. Shakespeare frequently associates 'courtesy' with the 'base Spaniel Fawning' (*Julius Caesar*, III.i.43) of hypocritical, treacherous curs (see *The Merchant of Venice*, I.iii.112–30), and here the Second Quarto spelling reinforces Marcellus' warning against putting too much trust in the Ghost.

60 **removed** remote, isolated. *Ground* recalls I.i.11.

62 **then** therefore.

64 **Fee** value.

Why thy canoniz'd Bones, hearsed in Death,
Have burst their Cerements? why the Sepulchre,
Wherein we saw thee quietly interr'd
Hath op'd his ponderous and marble Jaws
To cast thee up again? What may this mean   50
That thou, dead Corse, again in complete Steel
Revisits thus the glimses of the Moon,
Making Night hideous, and we Fools of Nature
So horridly to shake our Disposition
With Thoughts beyond the reaches of our Souls?   55
Say why is this, wherefore, what should we do?

         Ghost beckons Hamlet.

HORATIO It beckons you to go away with it
 As if it some Impartment did desire
 To you alone.
MARCELLUS Look with what curteous Action
 It waves you to a more removed Ground,   60
 But do not go with it.
HORATIO   No, by no means.
HAMLET It will not speak, then I will follow it.
HORATIO Do not, my Lord.
HAMLET   Why what should be the Fear?
 I do not set my Life at a Pin's Fee,

65   **what can it do to that**   Horatio provides the conventional
Elizabethan answer to this question in the speech that follows.

68   **toward**   here a one-syllable word.
Flood   sea.

69   **Somnet**   summit.
Cleef   cliff. Horatio alludes to the notion that devils often lured
troubled souls to promontories, where they could induce them
to surrender to despair and commit suicide (a damnable act,
as Hamlet has noted in I.ii.130–32). Shakespeare treats this
subject again in IV.vi.11–59 of *King Lear*; there Edgar tells
Gloucester a 'Fiend' has led him to the cliff from which the
suicidal old man believes he has leaped.

70   **bettles**   beetles, overhangs. The word may derive from
beetle-brows; or it may derive from a likeness between an
overhanging precipice and a beam (beetle) used as a battering
ram.

71   **horrable**   horrible; both abhorrent and horrifying.

72   **deprive . . . Reason**   drive your lordship mad, separating you
from the 'Reason' that makes human beings sovereign over
the world's other creatures. Compare II.ii.224–30,
III.i.161–64, IV.iv.30–36.

74   **Toys of Desperation**   desperate impulses (towards despair and
self-slaughter). *Toys* echoes I.iii.5–9.

76   **Fadoms**   fathoms (lengths of six feet).

81   **Arture**   artery. To a theatre audience this word might have
sounded similar to 'archer'; like the title character in *Macbeth*
(I.vii.79–80), Hamlet is 'settled', and is steeling himself to
'bend up / Each corporal Agent to their terrible Feat'.

82   **Nemean Lion**   a mythical creature slain by Hercules as the first
of his twelve labours.
Nerve   sinew, muscle.

84   **lets**   impedes.

85   **I . . . away**   This clause is presented here as one that Hamlet
addresses to his companions; but it could just as readily be
directed to the Ghost. Compare the ambiguity in line 31.

And for my Soul, what can it do to that,   65
Being a Thing Immortal as it self?
It waves me forth again, I'll follow it.
HORATIO   What if it tempt you toward the Flood, my
    Lord?
Or to the dreadful Somnet of the Cleef
That bettles o'er his Base into the Sea,   70
And there assume some other horrable Form
Which might deprive your Sovereignty of Reason,
And draw you into Madness? Think of it:
The very Place puts Toys of Desperation,
Without more Motive, into every Brain   75
That looks so many Fadoms to the Sea
And hears it roar beneath.
HAMLET   It waves me still.
— Go on, I'll follow thee.
MARCELLUS   You shall not go, my Lord.
HAMLET   Hold off your Hands.
HORATIO   Be rul'd, you shall not go.
HAMLET   My Fate cries out   80
And makes each petty Arture in this Body
As hardy as the Nemean Lion's Nerve;
Still am I call'd, unhand me, Gentlemen;
By Heaven I'll make a Ghost of him that lets
    me;
I say away. — Go on, I'll follow thee.   85
                              Exeunt Ghost and Hamlet.

86   **Imagination**   irrational fantasies. Compare *A Midsummer Night's Dream*, V.i.1–27, where Theseus and Hippolyta debate the merits of 'strong Imagination' and the 'Tricks' it can play on 'cool Reason'. *Waxes* recalls I.iii.11–14; *desperate* echoes lines 74–77.

88   **Have after**   Proceed, and I'll follow.

89   **Something . . . Denmark**   Marcellus uses a now-familiar olfactory figure to convey what Horatio has said in I.i.62–64. Up to this point most of the play's imagery has focused on sights and sounds; this allusion to the senses of smell, taste, and feeling marks a transition to the more visceral discourse of the Ghost in the scene that follows.

90   **it**   the issue, outcome (line 88).

I.v   This scene continues immediately on the heels of I.iv. As Hamlet and the Ghost re-enter, we are to assume that they have arrived at the 'removed Ground' referred to in I.iv.60.

1   **Whether**   both (a) whither, and (b) where. See the note to I.ii.241.

2   **My Hour is almost come**   The Ghost means that dawn is now approaching. See I.i.142–59.

3   **sulph'rous and tormenting Flames**   This description of the Ghost's residence is compatible with pre-Shakespearean renderings of both Purgatory and Hell. But lines 10–12 suggest that the Ghost is referring to Purgatory. Since Elizabethans were no longer legally permitted to be Catholics (being enjoined to worship in an Anglican Church that generally followed the reformers in denying the existence of Purgatory), it seems likely that many of them would have inferred that the Ghost is merely deceiving Hamlet by implying that he comes from somewhere other than Hell. It was a commonplace that the Devil was the Father of Lies and was capable of transforming himself 'into an angel of light' to mislead the unwary (2 Corinthians 11:14). In the final analysis, the origin and nature of the Ghost in *Hamlet* remain profoundly ambiguous, like much else in this most enigmatic of Shakespearean tragedies. The issue of the Ghost's 'honesty' re-emerges in III.ii.311.

6   **unfold**   disclose. Compare I.i.1–2, and see line 14.
    bound   pledged, committed. This word recalls the 'pious Bonds' of I.iii.129–30.

HORATIO   He waxes desperate with Imagination.

MARCELLUS   Let's follow, 'tis not fit thus to obey
  him.

HORATIO   Have after; to what Issue will this come?

MARCELLUS   Something is rotten in the State of
  Denmark.

HORATIO   Heaven will direct it.

MARCELLUS   Nay let's follow him.   90

                                    Exeunt.

Scene 5

Enter Ghost and Hamlet.

HAMLET   Whether wilt thou lead me, speak; I'll go no
  further.

GHOST   Mark me.

HAMLET   I will.

GHOST   My Hour is almost come
  When I to sulph'rous and tormenting Flames
  Must render up my self.

HAMLET   Alas poor Ghost.

GHOST   Pity me not, but lend thy serious Hearing   5
  To what I shall unfold.

HAMLET   Speak, I am bound
  To hear.

GHOST   So art thou to Revenge, when thou
  Shalt hear.

HAMLET   What?

GHOST   I am thy Father's Spirit,
  Doom'd for a certain Term to walk the Night
  And for the Day confin'd to fast in Fires   10
  Till the foul Crimes done in my Days of Nature

12 **But** except.

15 **harrow up** fill with horror (compare I.i.40). One of the early
doctrines of the Church was that between the Crucifixion and
the Resurrection, Jesus descended into the underworld for the
'Harrowing of Hell'. On this expedition, he harried
(despoiled) the underworld and gathered up the souls of the
Old Testament patriarchs and other pre-Christian saints for
eternal rewards in Heaven. Though the Ghost uses the phrase
harrow up in a very different sense here, the echo of Christ's
harrowing would have probably given his words additional
poignancy to some members of Shakespeare's original
audience. *Harrow* could also mean (a) vex or rob, (b) cry out
or plead (see *Macbeth*, I.iii.100), (c) plough up with a harrow
(a heavy spiked frame), and (d) lacerate. All those senses are
pertinent here.

16 **start** jump.
Spheres eye-sockets, with an analogy to the concentric spheres
in which the stars were thought to revolve around the globe.

18 **an end** on end. *Particular* echoes I.iv.22.

19 **fearful Porpentine** frightened (and frightening) porcupine.

20 **eternal Blazon** catalogue of the horrors of eternity. The word
blazon was associated with heraldry (where it denoted a coat
of arms or a description there of), but it also referred to a
proclamation. Here its first syllable keeps us mindful of the
blazing flames of the Underworld. See the note to I.iii.116.

21 **List** listen and mark (as in I.iii.30). But *list* can also mean 'lean'
or 'incline', as in *The Tempest*, III.ii.20–21, and *The Winter's
Tale*, IV.iv.555.

24 **Murther** murder. *Foul* recalls I.ii.249–52.

29 **Meditation** thought. Here the choice of words picks up on
murther by alliteration.

30 **apt** ready, eager, attentive.

31 **fat Weed** a weed that has grown large and lethargic through
overfeeding.

32 **Lethe Wharf** the bank of Lethe, the River of Forgetfulness in
the classical Hades. Compare *Julius Caesar*, III.i.205–7.

34 **given out** reported.

Are burnt and purg'd away. But that I am forbid
To tell the Secrets of my Prison-house,
I could a Tale unfold whose lightest Word
Would harrow up thy Soul, freeze thy young
   Blood,   15
Make thy two Eyes like Stars start from their
   Spheres,
Thy knotted and combined Locks to part,
And each particular Hair to stand an end
Like Quills upon the fearful Porpentine;
But this eternal Blazon must not be   20
To Ears of Flesh and Blood. List, list, O list:
If thou didst ever thy dear Father love.
HAMLET   O God.
GHOST   Revenge his foul, and most unnatural Murther.
HAMLET   Murther.   25
GHOST   Murther most foul, as in the best it is;
   But this most foul, strange, and unnatural.
HAMLET   Haste me to know't, that I with Wings as
   swift
As Meditation, or the Thoughts of Love,
May sweep to my Revenge.
GHOST   I find thee apt,   30
   And duller should'st thou be than the fat Weed
   That roots it self in ease on Lethe Wharf
   Would'st thou not stir in this. Now Hamlet hear.
   'Tis given out that, sleeping in my Orchard,

35   **Serpent** snake. Because this murder is elsewhere described as 'primal' (III.iii.37), it is appropriate that it be introduced here with an image that associates it with the Fall of Man (Genesis 3) and with the Devil, who took the sinuous form of a beguiling serpent to tempt Eve (here to be seen as a prototype of Hamlet's mother). Shakespeare frequently compares snakes to the male member (see *Love's Labour's Lost*, V.i.140–51, and *Antony and Cleopatra*, V.ii.240–59), and in *As You Like It*, II.vii.65–66, Duke Senior calls Jaques 'a Libertine, / As sensual as the Brutish Sting it self'. *Ear* recalls I.ii.170, I.iii.51, 68, 93.

36   **forged Process** counterfeited account.

37   **Rankly abus'd** egregiously deceived. But here *Rankly* carries associations with overgrowth, corruption and disease, and *abus'd* also means 'misused'. Compare I.ii.133–38.

41   **adulterate** This adjective suggests that in addition to committing incest by marrying his brother's widow, Claudius also committed adultery with her before he killed the elder Hamlet. Since *adultery* was a word that could refer to licentiousness in general, however, there are other ways of interpreting this passage.

43   **Wit** Like *will*, *wit* could refer to sexual desire and to the genitalia. See the note to I.i.60, and compare *Romeo and Juliet*, I.iii.42.

44   **wonne** both (a) wooed, and (b) won. Compare *Troilus and Cressida*, I.ii.307–8, where the heroine notes that 'Things woone are done' in the Quarto version of the play, and 'Things won are done' in the Folio.

51   **To** compared to.

52   **But . . . moved** but just as Virtue can never be seduced.

55   **sort** situate, place (compare I.i.104). Most editions today adopt the Folio's *sate*.

56   **pray on** (a) pray while kneeling upon, (b) pray to, beseech, while clinging to, and (c) prey upon (consume). Compare line 129 for another pun on *pray*.

60   **secure** free from cares. Elsewhere in Shakespeare this word refers to a condition of negligence resulting from overconfidence. See *Macbeth*, III.v.32–33, where Hecat says that 'Security / Is Mortals chiefest Enemy.'

A Serpent stung me; so the whole Ear of Denmark   35
Is by a forged Process of my Death
Rankly abus'd; but know, thou Noble Youth,
The Serpent that did sting thy Father's Life
Now wears his Crown.
HAMLET   O my prophetic Soul!
    My Uncle?   40
GHOST   Ay that incestuous, that adulterate Beast,
    With Witchcraft of his Wits, with traitorous
        Gifts,
    O wicked Wit, and Gifts, that have the power
    So to seduce; wonne to his shameful Lust
    The Will of my most seeming virtuous Queen;   45
    O Hamlet, what a falling off was there
    From me whose Love was of that Dignity
    That it went Hand in Hand, even with the Vow
    I made to her in Marriage, and to decline
    Upon a Wretch whose Natural Gifts were poor   50
    To those of mine.
    But Virtue as it never will be moved,
    Though Lewdness court it in a Shape of Heaven,
    So Lust, though to a radiant Angel link'd,
    Will sort it self in a Celestial Bed   55
    And pray on Garbage.
    But soft, me thinks I scent the Morning Air:
    Brief let me be. Sleeping within my Orchard,
    My Custom always of the Afternoon,
    Upon my secure Hour thy Uncle stole   60

61 **Hebona** ebony, a tree associated with blackness and possibly also with poison in Shakespeare's time. But Shakespeare may also have been thinking of another poison, henbane, and perhaps merging the names poetically.

63 **leaperous** leprous, designed to produce scales on the body similar to those caused by leprosy. The spelling in the early texts reinforces the leaping 'Quicksilver' imagery of line 65.

66 **Allies** both (a) alleys (the usual emendation in modern editions), and (b) allies (with the implication that Claudius' 'traitorous Gifts' were so charming that they could 'seduce' even the body's own guardians to yield its 'Gates' (lines 42, 44, 66).

67 **possess** Most editors adopt the Folio's *posset* here, a word meaning much the same thing as *curd* (coagulate) in the next line.

68 **eager** sour. Compare I.iv.2.

70 **Tetter** scab-like eruption. This word echoes *Tider* (tether) in I.iii.124

71 **Lazer** lazar, leper.

76 **Unhuzled** unhousled, without having received the Eucharist (the Housel), the last communion.
disappointed unprepared, without having confessed and received forgiveness for my sins.
unannel'd unaneled; literally, unanointed; deprived of extreme unction. The Quarto spelling provides a reminder that, lacking anelement, the elder Hamlet departed unrenewed (without the cleansing that would prepare his soul for Heaven).

77 **Reck'ning** absolution (forgiveness of sins confessed).
Account judgment-day

82 **Luxury** lust and other forms of sensual indulgence.

85 **ought** aught, anything.

86–87 **And . . . her** The Ghost refers to what Macbeth's Lady calls the 'compunctious Visitings of Nature' (*Macbeth*, I.v.47). But the 'Thorns' of conscience (alluding to the Apostle Paul's 'thorn in the flesh', 2 Corinthians 12:7) are described in a way that suggests homeopathic medicine (fighting fire with fire), since 'prick' and 'sting' are both words that point to the Queen's own 'Luxury' (line 82). See the notes to I.i.78 and I.v.35.

With Juice of cursed Hebona in a Vial,
And in the Porches of my Ears did pour
The leaperous Distilment, whose Effect
Holds such an Enmity with Blood of Man
That swift as Quicksilver it courses through   65
The natural Gates and Allies of the Body,
And with a sudden Vigour it doth possess
And curd, like eager droppings into Milk,
The thin and wholesome Blood. So did it mine,
And a most instant Tetter bark'd about,   70
Most Lazer-like, with vile and loathsome Crust,
All my smooth Body.
Thus was I sleeping by a Brother's Hand
Of Life, of Crown, of Queen at once dispatch'd,
Cut off even in the Blossoms of my Sin,   75
Unhuzled, disappointed, unannel'd,
No Reck'ning made, but sent to my Account
With all my Imperfections on my Head,
O horrible, O horrible, most horrible.
If thou hast Nature in thee, bear it not,   80
Let not the Royal Blood of Denmark be
A Couch for Luxury and damned Incest.
But howsomever thou pursues this Act,
Taint not thy Mind, nor let thy Soul contrive
Against thy Mother ought; leave her to Heaven,   85
And to those Thorns that in her Bosom lodge
To prick and sting her. Fare thee well at once,

88 **Matin** morning. *Matin* (from Old French) is associated with morning prayers.

89 **uneffectual Fire** a light that gives off no heat (compare I.iii.117) and is unable to hold its own in broad daylight. *Pale* echoes I.iv.27; it also recalls I.i.49 and I.ii.229.

90 **Adiew** adieu (French for 'to God'). See the note to I.ii.130, and compare line 110, where the Second Quarto prints *Adew*.

92 **couple** add in; join.

93 **Sinows** sinews, muscles.

95 **I** both (a) I [will], and (b) Ay. Compare line 119 and I.ii.74.

96 **this distracted Globe** this distraught head. But in its original performances this line would also have reminded the audience of the theatre in which the first Hamlet (Richard Burbage) was acting frenzied.

97 **Table** both (a) tablet, notebook, and (b) picture (painted scene).

98 **fond** foolish, idle. Compare I.ii.251–52.
Records accented on the second syllable here.

99 **Saws** wise sayings. See the notes to I.iii.36, 58, 59, and compare *As You Like It*, II.vii.153–56.
Forms images.
Pressures impressions, characters (as in I.iii.59).

102 **Book and Volume** Hamlet may be referring to different divisions of a larger work; he may be distinguishing between a book (the written text) and the volume (the bound cover) that contains it; or he may simply be using the terms with deliberately redundant duplication, as he and other speakers so often do in this play. In any event his decision to obey the Ghost parallels the commitment Ophelia has made to her father at the conclusion of the preceding scene.

103 **Baser Matter** This term was often used to refer to the kinds of metal (often iron or lead) that alchemists sought to transform into gold. Compare *Julius Caesar*, I.i.66, I.ii.312–14, I.iii.108–11.

106 **meet it is I set it down** it is appropriate for me to record. Except for the Ghost's commission, Hamlet says, his mind will henceforth be a *tabula rasa*, a blank slate.

The Glowworm shews the Matin to be near,
And 'gins to pale his uneffectual Fire.
Adiew, adiew, adiew, remember me.   *Exit.*   90
HAMLET   – O all you Host of Heaven, O Earth,
      what else,
And shall I couple Hell? – O fie, hold, hold, my
      Heart,
And you, my Sinows, grow not instant Old,
But bear me swiftly up. – Remember thee,
I, thou poor Ghost, whiles Memory holds a Seat   95
In this distracted Globe, remember thee;
Yea, from the Table of my Memory
I'll wipe away all trivial fond Records,
All Saws of Books, all Forms, all Pressures past
That Youth and Observation copied there,   100
And thy Commandment all alone shall live
Within the Book and Volume of my Brain
Unmix'd with Baser Matter; yes, by Heaven.
– O most pernicious Woman.
– O Villain, Villain, smiling damned Villain.   105
– My Tables, meet it is I set it down
That one may smile, and smile, and be a
      Villain,
At least I am sure it may be so in Denmark.

109 **my Word** my watchword, my charge. Hamlet's 'too too sallied
Flesh' will now 'resolve it self' into 'Adew, adew, remember
me.'

112 **secure him** protect him from evil (see Matthew 6:13). Compare
I.i.45, I.iv.38. *Secure* echoes lines 60–61.
So be it This 'amen' is assigned to Marcellus in the Folio text.

113 **Illo** hello. In his next speech Hamlet plays on Horatio's
greeting and implicitly compares it to a falconer's call to his
hawk.

115 **wonderful** to be wondered at.

118 **think it,** Many editors replace the Quarto's comma with a dash
here; the Folio text employs a question mark. The usual
interpretation is that Hamlet is on the verge of disclosing
what he has just seen and then stops himself in mid-sentence.

124 **Circumstance** elaboration, ceremony. This word recalls
I.iii.101–2.

126 **Business and Desire** Hamlet is probably alluding to the erotic
senses of these two terms. In *Romeo and Juliet*, Romeo jokes
that 'my Business was great, and in such a Case as mine a
Man may strain Curtesy' (II.iii.56–58). Here *fit* (line 125) and
point reinforce the genital innuendo.
point both (a) direct, and (b) appoint.

129 **I will go pray** These words are often taken literally. But it
seems more likely that Hamlet is simply implying that he will
set off in a different direction. His primary purpose at this
moment is not to communicate his intentions but to get rid of
his companions as quickly as possible so that he can 'go prey'
on his father's murderer. Compare line 56.

– So Uncle, there you are. – Now to my Word:
It is 'Adew, adew, remember me.'   110
I have sworn't.

Enter Horatio, and Marcellus.

HORATIO   My Lord, my Lord.
MARCELLUS   Lord Hamlet.
HORATIO   Heavens secure him.
HAMLET   So be it.
HORATIO   Illo, ho, ho, my Lord.
HAMLET   Hillo, ho, ho,
   Boy; come, Bird, come.
MARCELLUS   How is't, my Noble Lord?
HORATIO   What News, my Lord?
HAMLET   O wonderful.   115
HORATIO   Good my Lord, tell it.
HAMLET   No, you will reveal it.
HORATIO   Not I, my Lord, by Heaven.
MARCELLUS   Nor I, my Lord.
HAMLET   How say you then, would Heart of Man once
      think it,
   But you'll be secret.
BOTH   I, by Heav'n, my Lord.
HAMLET   There's never a Villain dwelling in all
      Denmark   120
   But he's an arrant Knave.
HORATIO   There needs no Ghost,
   My Lord, come from the Grave to tell us this.
HAMLET   Why right, you are in the right,
   And so, without more Circumstance at all,
   I hold it fit that we shake Hands and part,   125
   You as your Business and Desire shall point you,
   For every man hath Business and Desire,
   Such as it is, and for my own poor part
   I will go pray.

131 **hartily** heartily, but here with play on *hart*, a term Shakespeare frequently associates with nobility and manliness. See *Julius Caesar*, III.i.205–11, where Mark Antony calls the slain title character a 'brave Hart' and addresses him as 'a Deer, stroken by many Princes'. The usual spelling of *heart* in the Second Quarto of *Hamlet* is *hart*, so it is often difficult to determine when the playwright is referring to a hart in the sense modern usage restricts to a stag. See the note to II.ii.621, and compare III.ii.297–98.

133 **by Saint Patrick** Saint Patrick (ca. 389–461), the patron saint of Ireland, was proverbial as the spiritual keeper of 'Purgatory', an Irish cave visited by pilgrims who wished to have their sins purged. He was also credited with ridding Ireland of all its serpents, and that association would relate to lines 38–39.

134 **Touching this Vision here** with regard to this apparition we have seen. *Touching* recalls I.iii.89.

135 **Honest** good, genuine. Hamlet means that the Ghost is what it presents itself as being, not a demon counterfeiting the spirit of a deceased king. Later (II.ii.636–43) it occurs to the Prince to doubt what he has said here, but for now he seems to speak with complete assurance about the Ghost's reliability.

136 **us** Hamlet and the Ghost

137 **O'ermaster** overcome, suppress.

139 **poor** paltry.

140 **to night** tonight. Compare I.iv.7

143 **Upon my Sword** With its hilt the sword formed a cross. Hamlet demands that his companions place their right hands on it as they vow to keep secret what they have seen.

145 **Truepenny** Hamlet's name for the Ghost is one that means 'honest or trusty fellow'.

146 **Cellarage** the area below the stage. Like other Elizabethan amphitheatres, the Globe probably had a trapdoor to the cellarage; whether it was used in these scenes with the Ghost is uncertain.

149 **Hic et ubique** Latin for 'here and everywhere'. This phrase (and the capacity for omnipresence) was associated with both God and Satan.

HORATIO   These are but wild and whirling Words, my
Lord.   130
HAMLET   I am sorry they offend you, hartily:
Yes faith, hartily.
HORATIO   There's no Offence, my Lord.
HAMLET   Yes, by Saint Patrick, but there is, Horatio,
And much Offence too; touching this Vision here,
It is an Honest Ghost, that let me tell you;   135
For your desire to know what is between us,
O'ermaster't as you may; and now, good Friends,
As you are Friends, Scholars, and Soldiers,
Give me one poor Request.
HORATIO   What is't, my Lord, we will.
HAMLET   Never make known what you have seen
to night.   140
BOTH   My Lord, we will not.
HAMLET   Nay but swear't.
HORATIO   In faith,
My Lord, not I.
MARCELLUS   Nor I, my Lord, in faith.
HAMLET   Upon my Sword.
MARCELLUS   We have sworn, my Lord, already.
HAMLET   Indeed, upon my Sword, indeed.
GHOST   *cries under the Stage*   Swear.
HAMLET   Ha, ha, Boy, say'st thou so, art thou there,
Truepenny?   145
– Come on, you hear this Fellow in the Cellarage,
Consent to swear.
HORATIO   Propose the Oath, my Lord.
HAMLET   Never to speak of this that you have seen
Swear by my Sword.
GHOST   Swear.
HAMLET   *Hic et ubique,*

150   **Then ... ground**   Just why Hamlet wants to move to another site for the swearing is unclear. One possibility is that he wants to be directly over the Ghost; another is that he wants to be away from where the Ghost is. *Ground* echoes I.iv.60.

154   **old Mole**   Whether this nickname means anything other than that Hamlet is comparing the Ghost to a burrowing mammal is subject to debate. Some interpreters have suggested that the name would have associated the Ghost with the Devil. Compare I.iv.22–37, where *Mole* refers to a 'vicious' defect in character.

155   **Pioner**   miner; a soldier who dug trenches and tunnels to undermine enemy fortifications.

156   **O Day ... Strange**   Horatio's reaction is surely meant to be shared by the audience. Hamlet's response (line 157) means 'give it the welcome one is expected to give a stranger'. See 1 Chronicles 29:15, Psalm 146:9, Proverbs 5:17, Isaiah 14:1, Ephesians 2:19, Hebrews 11:13, and especially Matthew 25:35 ('I was a stranger, and ye took me in') and Hebrews 11:13 and 13:2 ('Be not forgetful to entertain strangers: for thereby some have received angels into their houses unawares', as the Geneva Bible renders the latter passage). Some commentators have interpreted this episode merely as Shakespeare's means of providing comic relief. Others, noting that the 'Cellarage' (see line 146) was frequently associated with Hell in early English drama, have suggested that the episode is intended to serve a more ominous purpose.

159   **Philosophy**   In Shakespeare's time this word was associated with all the branches of natural science.

161   **so mere**   both (a) some'er, so e'er, and (b) so merely (simply, mindlessly). Compare I.ii.135–38.
    bear my self   conduct myself, appear in public.

163   **To put ... on**   to adopt the mannerisms of an idiot or a madman. *Antic* could refer to any kind of eccentric behaviour. Since *antic* (*anticke* in the early texts at this point) could also be spelled *antique*, and vice versa, Hamlet is also adopting an 'antique disposition', one modelled after the pretended idiocy Lucius Junius Brutus deployed to outwit the tyrannical Tarquins and drive them from Rome in 509 BC. Hamlet alludes to his own 'Brute part' in III.i.112. See the note on *Disposition* at I.iv.54.

Then we'll shift our ground. Come hether, Gentlemen,   150
And lay your Hands again upon my Sword;
Swear by my Sword never to speak of this
That you have heard.

GHOST   Swear by his Sword.

HAMLET   Well said, old Mole, canst work i'th' Earth so
    fast?
A worthy Pioner. – Once more remove, good Friends.   155

HORATIO   O Day and Night, but this is wondrous
    Strange.

HAMLET   And therefore as a Stranger give it Welcome.
There are more things in Heaven and Earth, Horatio,
Than are dreamt of in your Philosophy. But come,
Here as before, never, so help you Mercy   160
(How strange or odd so mere I bear my self,
As I perchance hereafter shall think meet
To put an Antic Disposition on),
That you at such times seeing me never shall

165   **encomb'red**   encumbered, folded.

168   **list**   wished. See the note to line 21.

170   **ought**   aught, anything. This word echoes line 85.

174   **commend me**   offer myself. Compare I.i.39.

176   **Friending**   friendliness.

178   **still**   continually, always.

179   **out of Joint**   This phrase can mean 'out of socket' or 'out of frame'; here its implication is that Denmark is in a state of utter disorder. The *joint* imagery echoes Claudius' opening speech, particularly I.ii.9, 20.
        Spight   spite, injury.

180   **borne**   born; brought into this world. Compare I.iv.14.

181   **Nay come, let's go together**   Hamlet is reassuring his companions that it is all right for them to accompany him. It may be that he has separated himself from the group for a moment to speak lines 179–80 as a private reflection. Or it may be that they have held back in order to let him precede them as they exit. In either case he insists on treating them as equals; compare I.ii.160–65.

With Arms encomb'red thus, or this Head shake,   165
Or by pronouncing of some doubtful Phrase,
As 'Well, well, we know', or 'We could and if we
    would',
Or 'If we list to speak', or 'There be and if they might',
Or such ambiguous giving out, to note
That you know ought of me. This do swear,   170
So Grace and Mercy at your most need help you.
GHOST   Swear.
HAMLET   Rest, rest, perturbed Spirit. – So Gentlemen,
With all my Love I do commend me to you;
And what so poor a Man as Hamlet is   175
May do t'express his Love and Friending to you,
God willing, shall not lack. Let us go in together,
And still your Fingers on your Lips, I pray.
The Time is out of Joint. O cursed Spight
That ever I was borne to set it right.   180
Nay come, let's go together.   *Exeunt.*

II.i This scene takes place in Polonius' quarters. The Second Quarto stage direction, reproduced here, suggests that Shakespeare originally conceived the scene in such a way that Polonius' 'Man' (Reynaldo) could be accompanied by another servant. The Folio reads 'his man Reynaldo'.

3 **merviles** marvellous[ly]. Compare I.ii.194.

7 **Inquire me** Here *me* has the force of 'for me'. It is an illustration of what grammarians call the 'ethic dative', a form that Shakespeare uses to convey a colloquial familiarity or informality or to imitate the manner of the person being 'presented'.
Danskers Danish fellows.

8 **keep** stay, lodge.

10 **By this . . . Question** by these roundabout and yet subtly directed inquiries. *Encompassment* suggests a circling motion; *Drift* (which is related to 'drive') implies a thrusting home, as in fencing (compare line 37) or a casting and drifting of the angler's line and hook, as in fishing (see lines 37–38, 59–63).

11 **more nearer** closer to home.

12 **particular Demaunds** individual, pointed questions. *Particular* recalls I.v.18.

13 **Take you . . . him** adopt as your posture the perspective of someone who knows him from afar, as a distant acquaintance. Having just heard Hamlet speak of donning a persona (an 'Antic Disposition') for his purposes, we now hear Polonius advise Reynaldo to do something similar for Polonius' as yet undisclosed purposes.

16 **I** both (a) I [do], and (b) Ay. Compare I.v.95, 119, and see line 36.

18 **Wild** self-willed, unruly. See I.iii.5–51, where Laertes warns Ophelia against 'Nature cressant' and she in turn advises him not to be 'a puff'd and reckless Libertine' himself.

19 **put on him** literally, clothe him in. See the note to I.iii.83, and compare I.iv.28–31, I.v.159–70.

20 **Forgeries** made-up tales.
rank corrupting, excessive. Compare I.v.33–37.

ACT II

Scene 1

Enter Old Polonius, with his Man or Two.

POLONIUS   Give him this Money, and these Notes,
    Reynaldo.
REYNALDO   I will, my Lord.
POLONIUS   You shall do merviles wisely, good
    Reynaldo,
Before you visit him, to make inquire
Of his Behaviour.
REYNALDO   My Lord, I did intend it.   5
POLONIUS   Marry well said, very well said. Look you,
    Sir,
Inquire me first what Danskers are in Paris,
And how, and who; what means, and where they keep;
What company, at what expense; and finding
By this Encompassment, and Drift of Question,   10
That they do know my Son, come you more nearer
Than your particular Demaunds will touch it;
Take you as 'twere some distant Knowledge of him,
As thus, 'I know his Father and his Friends,
And in part him'. Do you mark this, Reynaldo?   15
REYNALDO   I, very well, my Lord.
POLONIUS   'And in part him', but you may say
    'not well,
But if't be he I mean, he's very Wild,
Addicted so and so', and there put on him
What Forgeries you please; marry none so rank   20
As may dishonour him, take heed of that,

22   **usual Slips**   common lapses or vices. The phrase 'Of general Assault' (line 35) has the same implications.

23   **noted**   commonly observed ('most known'), and thus regularly associated with.

24   **Gaming**   Polonius probably means gambling.

26   **Drabbing**   whoring, resorting to prostitutes.

28   **as you may season it in the Charge**   since you may flavour or temper it in the way you imply the accusation. *Season* recalls I.iv.5.

30   **Incontinency**   uncontrolled, habitual vice; libertinism. *Scandal* echoes I.iv.22–37.

31   **breath**   give breath to, breathe. See the note to I.i.58 and compare I.ii.79.
        quently   quaintly, artfully, with wit and urbanity. In this context, the word probably also has bawdy connotations; *quent* was one form of a common English derivative from the Latin *cunnus* (see the note to I.ii.60).

33   **Flash . . . Mind**   sudden eruptions of a disposition comprised primarily of the noblest of the four elements, Fire.

34   **unreclaimed Blood**   as yet untamed passions.

35   **of general Assault**   a temptation to which everyone is susceptible. See the note to I.iii.51. *Assault* plays on *salt* (which can mean 'lust', as in *Antony and Cleopatra*, II.i.21) and recalls the imagery of a besieged fortress or of a battalion under attack in I.iii.24–44.

38   **a Fetch of Wit**   a clever device. A *Fetch* was a trick or subterfuge; and *Wit* refers to any kind of cunning or intelligence. Here many editors follow the Folio, which substitutes *Warrant* for *Wit*. See the note to I.v.43.

39   **Sallies**   probably both (a) sullies, blemishes, and (b) assaults. Compare I.ii.129.

40   **As . . . Working**   as if he were something that has become a bit soiled from use (but is no worse for wear). *Soil'd* recalls I.iv.16–19.

42   **prenominate Crimes**   aforementioned vices.

But Sir, such wanton, wild, and usual Slips
As are Companions noted and most known
To Youth and Liberty.
REYNALDO   As Gaming, my Lord.
POLONIUS   Ay, or Drinking, Fencing, Swearing,   25
    Quarrelling, Drabbing; you may go so far.
REYNALDO   My Lord, that would dishonour him.
POLONIUS   Faith no, as you may season it in the
        Charge.
    You must not put another Scandal on him,
    That he is open to Incontinency,   30
    That's not my Meaning; but breath his Faults so
        quently
    That they may seem the Taints of Liberty,
    The Flash and Out-break of a Fiery Mind,
    A Savageness in unreclaimed Blood,
    Of general Assault.
REYNALDO   But my good Lord.   35
POLONIUS   Wherefore should you do this?
REYNALDO   I, my Lord,
    I would know that.
POLONIUS   Marry Sir, here's my Drift,
    And I believe it is a Fetch of Wit:
    You laying these slight Sallies on my Son,
    As 'twere a thing a little soil'd with Working,   40
    Mark you, your Party in Converse, him you
        would sound,
    Having ever seen in the prenominate Crimes

43 **breath** speak. Here as in line 31, both early texts print *breath*, which may convey the Shakespearean pronunciation.

44 **closes with you** concludes with you, confides to you.
in this Consequence in the following way (as a result of what you have said to him).

47 **Of Man and Country** the name of the addressee and his country. *Addition* (designation, title) recalls I.iv.16–19.

49–51 **What . . . leave?** Amusingly, when Polonius loses track of what he was saying, he also drifts away from regular verse into something more like prose.

52 **I marry** Polonius means 'ay indeed' (see the note on *marry* at I.iii.90), but here as elsewhere the usual modern senses of *I* and *marry* provide amusing and unwitting reinforcement for 'closes in the Consequence'. Compare lines 16, 36.

56 **a** he. Modern editions usually render this line as it appears in the Folio, which reads: 'There was he gaming, there o'retooke in's Rouse.' In the Second Quarto phrase *a Gaming*, the word *a* can mean either (a) a, or (b) 'a (he). The Quarto phrasing echoes I.iv.7.

57 **falling out** quarrelling. Compare I.iii.65–67.

59 **Videlizet** namely; from Latin *videlicet*.

61 **Reach** apprehension.

62 **Windlesses** windlasses (hoists), roundabout means.
Assays of Bias trials of the bias (curving course) on a bowl (a bowling ball with an off-centre weight designed to prevent it from rolling in a straight line). See the note to III.i.62.

63 **By Indirections find Directions out** by indirect means arrive at our desired destination. Compare lines 9–12. Appropriately, Polonius' entire discourse has been a series of 'Indirections'; only now does Reynaldo get his 'Drift' (line 37).

64 **Advise** advising, advice.

65 **have** understand.

66 **God buy ye** God be with you (the ancestor of 'goodbye'), the English equivalent of *adieu* (see I.v.90).

The Youth you breath of Guilty, be assur'd
He closes with you in this Consequence:
'Good Sir', or so, or 'Friend', or 'Gentleman',   45
According to the Phrase, or the Addition
Of Man and Country –
REYNALDO   Very good, my Lord.
POLONIUS   And then, Sir, dooes 'a this, 'a dooes –
   What was I about to say?
   By th' Mass, I was about to say something,   50
   Where did I leave?
REYNALDO   At 'closes in the Consequence'.
POLONIUS   At 'closes in the Consequence', I marry,
   He closes thus: 'I know the Gentleman;
   I saw him yesterday', or 'th'other day',
   Or then or then, with such or such, and 'as
         you say,   55
   There was a Gaming there, or took in's Rouse',
   'There falling out at Tennis', or perchance
   'I saw him enter such a House of Sale',
   Videlizet, a Brothel, or so foorth. See you now,
   Your Bait of Falsehood take this Carp of Truth,   60
   And thus do we of Wisdom, and of Reach,
   With Windlesses and with Assays of Bias,
   By Indirections find Directions out;
   So by my former Lecture and Advise
   Shall you my Son; you have me, have you not?   65
REYNALDO   My Lord, I have.
POLONIUS   God buy ye, fare ye well.

67–68 **Observe . . . self** Be observant of his disposition, and adapt your own behaviour to his moods. This counsel will be applied to a different situation in the next scene (II.ii.10–18).

69 **And let him ply his Music** Give him a full-length 'Tider' (I.iii.124) to follow his own inclination. Music in the literal sense would have been one of the skills and pastimes of an accomplished courtier such as Laertes.

73 **sowing** sewing. Here as elsewhere, the spelling in the early printings permits implications that become obscured by modernization. Ophelia's seclusion in her 'Closet' was a consequence of the 'sowing' (planting) of her father (see I.iii.114–35), and Elizabethans would have known that 'whatsoever a man soweth, that shall he also reap' (Galatians 6:7). Compare *Coriolanus*, I.iii.56, and *Othello*, III.iv.72.
Closet private chamber.

74 **his Doublet all unbrac'd** his jacket all unlaced.

75 **his Stockins foul'd** his stockings soiled and unkempt.

76 **down gyved** fallen down so that they resembled the gyves (fetters) around a prisoner's ankles.

78 **Purport** implication. Since we hear only Ophelia's account of this episode, we are at a loss to determine its significance. Whether it reveals the 'real' Hamlet, Hamlet in his 'antic' mode, or some combination thereof is left ambiguous.

86 **Perusal** careful examination.

87 **draw it** Ophelia probably means 'draw a portrait of it'. But two other senses may also be pertinent: (a) pull it along with him, or to him, and (b) suck it up and drink it.

88 **a little shaking of mine Arm** while shaking my arm slightly. Compare I.v.159–70.

90 **profound** from the depths of his being.

91 **Bulk** body. Compare I.iii.11–14.

REYNALDO Good my Lord.
POLONIUS   Observe his Inclination
  In your self.
REYNALDO I shall, my Lord.
POLONIUS And let him ply his Music.
REYNALDO   Well, my Lord.

Enter Ophelia.

POLONIUS Farewell.   *Exit Reynaldo.*
  – How now, Ophelia? What's the matter?   70
OPHELIA O my Lord, my Lord, I have been so
  affrighted.
POLONIUS With what, i'th' name of God?
OPHELIA My Lord, as I was sowing in my Closet,
  Lord Hamlet, with his Doublet all unbrac'd,
  No Hat upon his Head, his Stockins foul'd,   75
  Ungart'red, and down gyved to his Ankle,
  Pale as his Shirt, his Knees knocking each
      other,
  And with a Look so piteous in Purport
  As if he had been loosed out of Hell
  To speak of Horrors, he comes before me.   80
POLONIUS Mad for thy Love?
OPHELIA   My Lord, I do not know.
  But truly I do fear it.
POLONIUS   What said he?
OPHELIA He took me by the Wrist, and held me hard,
  Then goes he to the length of all his Arm,
  And with his other Hand thus o'er his Brow   85
  He falls to such Perusal of my Face
  As 'a would draw it; long stay'd he so;
  At last, a little shaking of mine Arm,
  And, thrice his Head thus waving up and down,
  He rais'd a Sigh so piteous and profound   90
  As it did seem to shatter all his Bulk,

95 **a' Doores** The spellings in the early printings *(adoores* in the
Quarto, *adores* in the Folio) provide poignant reminders that
if Hamlet still adores Ophelia, he is now forced to keep such
emotions out of the way, both because of Polonius' protective
custody and because of Hamlet's perceived need to 'wipe
away' any 'Pressures past' that might interfere with his
adhering to the Ghost's 'Commandment all alone'
(I.v.97–103).
Helps assistance.

98 **Ecstasy** seizure. Polonius uses a Greek word whose literal
meaning is to be beside oneself, in a state that suspends the
normal operations of reason and apprehension.

99 **Whose . . . self** whose nature is to take hold of a self with such
violence as to undo it.

100 **to desperate Undertakings** to extremes of behaviour. Here the
word *desperate* suggests that Polonius believes Hamlet to be
suicidal. Compare I.iv.74–77, 86.

102 **dooes** does. Modern grammar would call for *do*. Elizabethan
usage allowed for many constructions that would now be
considered violations of subject–verb agreement. Here as
elsewhere, the *Everyman* text preserves the word forms
(including the *oo-* spellings) to be found in the original
printings.

103 **hard** harsh, unfriendly. Polonius' adjective recalls I.ii.178.

108 **coted** observed; often spelled *quoted*, as at this point in the
Folio.

109 **wrack** wreck, ruin. To an audience, the meanings associated
with *rack* would also be pertinent: (a) put on the rack (shelf)
as a conquest, and (b) stretch flat, as on a rack (instrument of
torture). Compare *King Lear* V.iii.311, and *The Merchant of
Venice*, I.i.181.
beshrow my Jealousy curse (beshrew) my suspiciousness.

110 **it . . . Age** it is as much a part of being old (my age).

111 **To . . . Opinions** to overshoot, to allow our anxieties to carry
us too far. See the note to II.i.10, and compare V.ii.252–56.

113 **Discretion** prudence, judgement (as in I.ii.5).

And end his Being; that done, he lets me go,
And, with his Head over his Shoulder turn'd,
He seem'd to find his way without his Eyes,
For out a' Doors he went without their Helps,   95
And to the last bended their Light on me.

POLONIUS   Come, go with me, I will go seek the King:
This is the very Ecstasy of Love,
Whose violent Property fordooes it self
And leads the Will to desperate Undertakings   100
As oft as any Passions under Heaven
That dooes afflict our Natures. I am sorry;
What, have you given him any hard Words of late?

OPHELIA   No, my good Lord, but as you did commaund
I did repel his Letters and denied   105
His Access to me.

POLONIUS   That hath made him mad.
I am sorry that with better Heed and Judgement
I had not coted him. I fear'd he did but trifle
And meant to wrack thee, but beshrow my Jealousy:
By Heaven it is as proper to our Age   110
To cast beyond our selves in our Opinions
As it is common for the Younger Sort
To lack Discretion. Come, go we to the King:

114   **close**   secret. Polonius' phrasing is a reminder that Ophelia's
       being 'kept close' (secluded from Hamlet's 'Access', line 106)
       appears to be related to what the old man interprets as a
       'lack' of 'Discretion' in the Prince (line 113). Polonius now
       construes a 'consequence' in the 'closes' (II.i.51–52) he has
       imposed; see the note to line 73.

115   **More . . . Love**   more grief (and grievance, reproach) from our
       hiding it than displeasure over the love we show by speaking
       openly about Hamlet's love-malady. Here again, the *then*
       spelling, preceded by a comma in both the Quarto and Folio
       texts, permits an ambiguity that subsequent events will prove
       pertinent. Compare I.iii.125, and see *Macbeth*, III.ii.7,
       III.iv.13.

II.ii   This scene takes place at Court. In the opening stage direction
         cum Aliis (from the Folio version) means 'with others'. In the
         two preceding scenes, we have heard first Hamlet and then
         Polonius talk about the use of indirect means to achieve ends
         that will not lend themselves to more direct approaches. Now
         we hear the King and Queen give similar instructions to two
         of Hamlet's former schoolmates, who have been summoned
         to see if they can be of assistance by helping to find out why
         the Queen's son is acting so strangely. *Rosencraus* is the
         Second Quarto's rendering of a name that is usually spelled
         Rosincrance in the Folio and *Rosencrantz* (German for 'rose
         garland') in modern editions. *Rosencraus* can be construed as
         either 'crispy rose' or 'rose frill'. *Guildenstern* means 'gilded
         star' or 'gold star'.

2   **Moreover that**   in addition to the fact that.

5   **Transformation**   Here the metrical context calls for the King to
       stretch the word out to its full five syllables.

6   **Sith**   since, because. In line 12, the word may have the
       additional meaning of 'since that time'.

9   **th' Understanding of himself**   his normal self, his proper use of
       his reasoning faculties. *Understanding* recalls I.ii.97, 244,
       I.iii.96.

11   **of so young Days**   from an early age.

12   **Haviour**   behaviour. Compare I.ii.81, II.i.4–5.

13   **voutsafe your Rest**   vouchsafe (condescend) to stay.

14   **so**   in order.

This must be known, which being kept close
  might move
More grief to hide, then hate to utter Love.   115
Come.   *Exeunt.*

Scene 2

Flourish. Enter King and Queen, Rosencraus and Guildenstern,
cum Aliis.

KING   Welcome, dear Rosencraus and Guildenstern;
  Moreover that we much did long to see you,
  The need we have to use you did provoke
  Our hasty Sending. Something have you heard
  Of Hamlet's Transformation; so call it,   5
  Sith nor th' Exterior nor the Inward Man
  Resembles that it was. What it should be,
  More than his Father's Death, that thus hath
    put him
  So much from th' Understanding of himself
  I cannot dream of. I entreat you both   10
  That, being of so young Days brought up with
    him,
  And sith so neighbour'd to his Youth and Haviour,
  That you voutsafe your Rest here in our Court
  Some little Time, so by your Companies
  To draw him on to Pleasures, and to gather   15

16 **glean** gather (like those who pick up leftover grain after the reapers have harvested a field). Claudius' advice ('draw him on to Pleasures') echoes what Polonius has said in the previous scene to Reynaldo (compare II.i.67–69); and gleaning is another form of indirection (II.i.63). *Draw* recalls II.i.87.

17 **ought** aught, anything (as in I.v.170).

18 **open'd** Claudius means 'disclosed'. But the medical metaphor implied by 'Remedy' also suggests the lancing of a boil or the opening of a patient's veins to rid his blood of infection.

21 **adheres** clings.

22 **Gentry** gentle behaviour; the courtesy characteristic of gentlemen.

24 **the Supply and Profit of our Hope** the fulfilment and reward of our hopes.

25 **Visitation** visit, sojourn. But *visitation* can also mean 'plague', as in the afflictions visited on the Pharaoh for his refusal to allow the Children of Israel to leave Egypt (see Exodus 5–14), and Hamlet will soon take that view of this visit. Compare *The Winter's Tale*, I.i.6–8, and *The Tempest*, III.i.31–32.

26 **Remembrance** gratitude for services rendered.

27 **of** over.

28 **dread** fearful; to be held in awe and reverence. Compare I.i.21, I.ii.50.

30 **in the full Bent** Guildenstern probably bows fulsomely as he speaks, thereby imitating a bow bent to the utmost to discharge an arrow. Compare I.ii.55–56, 115–16, II.i.96.

38 **Practices** endeavours. But the word often connoted deceits and tricks.

40 **Embassadors** ambassadors, emissaries.

42 **still** both (a) yet, and (b) always.

So much as from Occasion you may glean,
Whether ought to us unknown afflicts him thus,
That open'd lies within our Remedy.
QUEEN   Good Gentlemen, he hath much talk'd of you,
And sure I am, two Men there is not living   20
To whom he more adheres: if it will please you
To shew us so much Gentry and Good Will,
As to expend your Time with us a while,
For the Supply and Profit of our Hope,
Your Visitation shall receive such Thanks   25
As fits a King's Remembrance.
ROSENCRAUS   Both your Majesties
Might by the Sovereign Power you have of us
Put your dread Pleasures more into Commaund
Than to Entreaty.
GUILDENSTERN   But we both obey,
And here give up our selves in the full Bent   30
To lay our Service freely at your Feet
To be commaunded.
KING   Thanks, Rosencraus and gentle Guildenstern.
QUEEN   Thanks, Guildenstern and gentle Rosencraus.
And I beseech you instantly to visit   35
My too much changed Son. – Go some of you
And bring these Gentlemen where Hamlet is.
GUILDENSTERN   Heavens make our Presence and our
    Practices
Pleasant and helpful to him.
QUEEN   Ay Amen.
                    Exeunt Rosencraus and Guildenstern.

                    Enter Polonius.

POLONIUS   Th' Embassadors from Norway, my good
    Lord,   40
Are joyfully return'd.
KING   Thou still hast been the Father of good News.

44   **I . . . Soul** my duty to you is just as important to me as the state of my soul in the eyes of God. Polonius alludes to the commonplace that the King was to be regarded as God's deputy on Earth (a doctrine derived from Romans 13:1–7).

47   **Policy** This word often refers to statecraft, but here it probably means something closer to 'sound judgement'. Polonius' hunting metaphor is yet another variation on the types of cunning he has commended in I.iii.59–60, 65–69, 125–30, and in II.i.1–69.

52   **Fruit** dessert. Polonius refers to the 'banquet', a course of fruits and wine that followed the main course of a feast.

53   **do grace** show proper courtesy. Claudius is probably alluding to the 'grace' to be said before a meal. But he refers primarily to the bounty a magnanimous host shows a guest; see the note to lines 568–69.

55   **Head and Source** Both words mean 'origin'. Compare I.i.99–102, where Horatio uses similar terminology. *Head* echoes I.iii.19–24, I.v.77–78, and II.i.75, 89–96.
    Distemper malady. The word literally means 'lacking in temper' (balance or governance), and it derives from the view that a person's disposition was determined by how successfully the mind controlled the four humours that constituted a human body.

56   **doubt** suspect, fear.
    the Main the problem that has been troubling him all along.

57   **hasty** Most of today's editions adopt the Folio's *o'erhasty* here. But at this point it is not clear that the Queen regards the marriage as *over*hasty. The Folio reading would appear to improve the metre; but if *our* is treated as a two-syllabic word, the metre in the Second Quarto is perfectly regular.

58   **sift** winnow, glean from (line 16). Polonius has used similar imagery in I.iii.101–2.

60   **fair** agreeable, harmonious. Compare I.i.43–45.

61   **Upon our first** as soon as we had delivered our message.

62   **Levies** pressing men into military service. See I.ii.27–33.

65   **griev'd** aggrieved, offended. Compare II.i.114–15.

67   **falsely borne in hand** dishonestly manipulated.
    Arrests restraining orders, summons to appear before the King.

POLONIUS Have I, my Lord? I assure my good Liege
I hold my Duty as I hold my Soul,
Both to my God and to my gracious King;   45
And I do think, or else this Brain of mine
Hunts not the trail of Policy so sure
As it hath us'd to do, that I have found
The very cause of Hamlet's Lunacy.
KING O speak of that, that do I long to hear.   50
POLONIUS Give first admittance to th' Embassadors;
My News shall be the Fruit to that great Feast.
KING Thy self do grace to them, and bring them in.
– He tells me, my dear Gertrard, he hath found
The Head and Source of all your Son's
    Distemper.   55
QUEEN I doubt it is no other but the Main,
His Father's Death and our hasty Marriage.

Enter Embassadors.

KING Well, we shall sift him. – Welcome, my good
    Friends.
Say, Voltemand, what from our Brother Norway?
VOLTEMAND Most fair return of Greetings and
    Desires.   60
Upon our first, he sent out to suppress
His Nephew's Levies, which to him appear'd
To be a Preparation 'gainst the Polack,
But, better look'd into, he truly found
It was against your Highness; whereat griev'd   65
That so his Sickness, Age, and Impotence
Was falsely borne in hand, sends out Arrests

68 **in brief** both (a) quickly, and (b) to make a long story short.

69 **in fine** finally, in the end.

71 **assay** trial, threat. Polonius has used this word in II.i.62.

75 **as** as noted.
Polack both (a) the King of Poland, and (b) Poland's territories.

76 **shone** exhibited, displayed, shown.

77 **to give quiet Pass** to permit peaceful passage.

79 **Regards of Safety** provisions for Denmark's security. *Safety* recalls I.iii.20–21, where Laertes says that 'on his Choice depends / The Safety and Health of this whole State'.
Allowance authorization [by Denmark].

80 **likes** pleases.

81 **at our more consider'd Time** when we have time to consider it more thoroughly.

82 **Answer** reply.

84 **at night we'll Feast together** No doubt one of Shakespeare's purposes in including this detail is to show Claudius' ability to be gracious in hospitality; another is to remind us once again of how much the King indulges in food and drink. See I.iv.7–37.

86 **expostulate** expound upon.

89 **waste** Here as elsewhere (see I.ii.197), the Second Quarto spelling (and in all likelihood the playwright's) is *wast*. Compare line 242.

90 **Brevity** The metre calls for a witty abbreviation of this word to 'brev'ty'.

91 **And Tediousness . . . Flourishes** Appropriately, a line about tediousness (a boringly lengthy exposition) is two syllables longer than the pentameter norm, even when *Tediousness* is rendered as a three-syllable word. The superfluous syllables illustrate the 'outward Flourishes' they denote.

94 **is't** Here *it* refers to 'true Madness'.

95 **Art** a display of rhetorical devices to convey one's wit.

97 **'tis Pity** it is a pity.

On Fortinbrasse, which he in brief obeys,
Receives Rebuke from Norway, and in fine
Makes Vow before his Uncle never more   70
To give th' assay of Arms against your Majesty:
Whereon old Norway, overcome with Joy,
Gives him three thousand Crowns in annual Fee
And his Commission to employ those Soldiers
So levied (as before) against the Polack,   75
With an Entreaty herein further shone
That it might please you to give quiet Pass
Through your Dominions for this Enterprise
On such Regards of Safety and Allowance
As therein are set down.

KING   It likes us well,   80
And at our more consider'd Time we'll read,
Answer, and think upon this Business.
Mean time we thank you for your well took
    Labour.
Go to your Rest: at night we'll Feast together.
Most welcome home.   *Exeunt Embassadors.*

POLONIUS   This Business is well ended.   85
My Liege and Madam, to expostulate
What Majesty should be, what Duty is,
Why Day is Day, Night Night, and Time is Time,
Were nothing but to waste Night, Day, and Time:
Therefore, since Brevity is the Soul of Wit   )   90
And Tediousness the Limbs and outward   )
    Flourishes,
I will be brief. Your Noble Son is mad.
Mad call I it, for to define true Madness
What is't but to be nothing else but mad;
But let that go.

QUEEN   More Matter with less Art.   95

POLONIUS   Madam, I swear I use no Art at all.
That he's mad 'tis true, 'tis true 'tis pity,

98 **Figure** figure of speech. Polonius probably refers to his use of what rhetoricians called *antimetabole*, the repetition of words or phrases in reverse order (in a chiasmic or crossing pattern named after the Greek letter *chi*, X). But he may also be referring to other schematic 'figures' such as *ploce* (the repetition of a word with others in between), *epizeuxis* (the immediate repetition of a word), and *anadiplosis* (the repetition of a word at the end of one unit and the beginning of the next). In the lines that follow, after promising that he will 'use no Art', Polonius parades such schemes as *traductio* (the repetition of a word in varying grammatical forms, as with 'Defect' / 'Defective,' and 'remains,' / 'remainder') and *antithesis* (the use of repetition or parallel structure to draw attention to contrasting elements, as with the phrases ending in 'Effect' and 'Defect' in lines 101–2).

105 **Perpend** weigh, consider. Line 106 anticipates what Polonius will say in line 167, and what Hamlet will say to Ophelia's father in lines 432–50.

111– **That's . . . Phrase** Polonius implies that Hamlet displays 'no
12   Art at all' (line 96). But, given the Prince's remarks in I.v.159–70, we are probably to infer that any 'doubtful Phrase' (I.v.166) he uses is likely to be an 'Effect Defective' that 'comes by Cause'; if so, it is probably designed to deceive Polonius into thinking he has caught a 'Carp of Truth' (II.i.60).

117 **stay** wait, be patient.
    faithful as good as my word.

120 **Doubt** suspect. Elsewhere in this passage *doubt* is used in the normal modern sense. Compare line 56.
    Lier liar. The spellings in the early texts (*lyer* in the Second Quarto, *Lier* in the First Folio) suggest a pun on the copulative sense of *lie* (here alluding to infidelity in love); compare III.ii.118–25, V.i.126–35.

122 **ill at these Numbers** inept at these verses. *Ill* echoes line 111.

123 **reckon** count. Hamlet plays on the more usual sense of 'Numbers'. *Art* recalls lines 95–96.
    Groans love pangs. Hamlet uses the word in a more bawdy sense in III.ii.273.

124 **O . . . it** either (a) believe it absolutely, or (b) O thou Best of all Ladies, believe it.

And pity 'tis 'tis true: a foolish Figure,
But farewell it, for I will use no Art.
Mad let us graunt him then, and now remains   100
That we find out the Cause of this Effect,
Or rather say, the Cause of this Defect,
For this Effect Defective comes by Cause:
Thus it remains, and the Remainder thus
Perpend.   105
I have a Daughter, have while she is mine,
Who in her Duty and Obedience, mark,
Hath given me this. Now gather and surmise:
    'To the Celestial and my Soul's Idol, the
    most beautified Ophelia – '   110
That's an ill Phrase, a vile Phrase;
'beautified' is a vile Phrase. But you shall
hear:
    'thus in her excellent white Bosom, these
    &c.'   115
QUEEN   Came this from Hamlet to her?
POLONIUS   Good Madam, stay awhile, I will be
    faithful.
        'Doubt thou the Stars are Fire,
        Doubt that the Sun doth move,
        Doubt Truth to be a Lier,
        But never doubt I love.   120
    O dear Ophelia, I am ill at these Numbers,
    I have not Art to reckon my Groans, but
    that I love thee best, O most best believe

125 **adew** adieu. See the note to I.v.109.

127 **whilst this Machine is to him** while this body belongs to him. Here *machine* is used in the Renaissance sense of a complex mechanism. Like the behaviour described in II.i.73–96, Hamlet's letter is subject to interpretation. Is it a sincere love-note, or is it a ruse (in keeping with the Prince's 'Antic Disposition', I.v.163) to convey the impression that Hamlet is mad from love-sickness?

130 **more about** Most of today's editions adopt the Folio's *more above* here; but it is difficult to derive any better sense from that phrasing. In this line Polonius appears to mean 'and still more she hath shown me about his entreaties'.

131 **fell out** occurred, were delivered to her [in the form of letters dropped outside her chamber].

136 **fain** gladly, eagerly.

137 **hote** hot. Here as in III.ii.421 and IV.vii.153, the Everyman text retains the spelling in the Second Quarto. It probably reflects Shakespeare's pronunciation, and it suggests wordplay on *haute* (French for 'high'). Compare I.iii.14–28, and see lines 146–47.

141 **play'd the Desk or Table Book** Polonius' metaphor means 'encouraged their wooing by cooperating as readily as if I were a desk or writing-tablet to aid and abet their communications'. *Table* recalls I.v.97, 106.

142 **Or given . . . dumb** or turned my heart into an instrument that failed to report what it perceived. Most editions substitute the Folio's *winking* (blindfolding or eye-shutting) for *working*; but the word in the Second Quarto would seem more compatible with *Heart* (a word that could refer to the eye's perceptions, but usually implied all the senses). *Working* recalls I.i.62–64 and II.i.40.

143 **Idle Sight** either (a) dysfunctional eyes, or (b) neglectful eyes that chose not to register what they saw (and were thus irresponsible).

145 **bespeak** both (a) speak to, and (b) order (like an article of clothing reserved to be rented or acquired at a later date). Compare *The Merchant of Venice*, II.iv.4. Like Capulet in *Romeo and Juliet*, Polonius treats his 'young Mistress' as if she were an automaton, a pliant, reliable instrument of his will. See I.iii.103–5.

   it, adew.   125
         Thine evermore, most dear Lady,
            whilst this Machine is to him.
                        Hamlet.'

This in Obedience hath my Daughter shown me,
And more about hath his Solicitings   130
As they fell out by Time, by Means, and Place,
All given to mine Ear.

KING But how hath she receiv'd his Love?

POLONIUS What do you think of me?

KING As of a Man faithful and honourable.   135

POLONIUS I would fain prove so; but what might
   you think,
When I had seen this hote Love on the wing,
As I perceiv'd it (I must tell you that)
Before my Daughter told me, what might you,
Or my dear Majesty your Queen here, think,   140
If I had play'd the Desk or Table Book,
Or given my Heart a working mute and dumb,
Or look'd upon this Love with Idle Sight,
What might you think? No, I went round to
   work,
And my young Mistress thus I did bespeak: 145

146 **out of thy Star** beyond your sphere (based on the belief that each star or planet occupied its own crystalline sphere as it revolved around the Earth).

147 **Prescripts** orders, prescribings.

148 **from her Resort** from where she is usually to be found, and where he could partake of her company. Most editions adopt the Folio's *his resort*. Compare II.i.104–6.

149 **Tokens** gifts, favours, expressions of affection. Compare I.iii.5–9, 99–109.

150 **Advise** advice (as in II.i.64).

151 **repell'd** Here the elision derives from the Second Quarto text. Fittingly, it makes 'a short Tale' of this line, which is one metrical foot briefer than the pentameter norm; compare lines 90–91.

152 **a Fast** Forlorn lovers were proverbially unable or unwilling to eat.

153 **a Watch** a habitual sleeplessness.
    a Weakness a weakened, vulnerable condition.

154 **Lightness** mental distraction, a lack of rational 'gravity'.
    Declension decline, deterioration. Polonius describes Hamlet's malady in terminology that Elizabethans would have associated with the study of grammar. Compare *The Merry Wives of Windsor*, IV.i.75–76.

161 **Take this from this** Polonius probably gestures as he refers to his head and his neck.

164 **the Centre** the centre of the Earth.

166 **Lobby** anteroom, or vestibule adjacent to the chamber in which state occasions take place. For another indication of its placement in the palace, see IV.iii.35–37.

167 **loose** release (from the tether, the restraints, that Polonius has imposed on her). This verb frequently refers to a man's setting a woman at liberty (to be accosted by male wooers). Compare I.iii.31, 76.

168 **Arras** a large tapestry, named after a town in northern France.

170 **thereon** because of that (his love for Ophelia).

171 **Assistant for a State** counsel to the throne.

'Lord Hamlet is a Prince out of thy Star,
This must not be.' And then I Prescripts gave
   her
That she should lock her self from her Resort,
Admit no Messengers, receive no Tokens;
Which done, she took the Fruits of my Advise,   150
And he repell'd, a short Tale to make,
Fell into a Sadness, then into a Fast,
Thence to a Watch, thence into a Weakness,
Thence to Lightness, and by this Declension
Into the Madness wherein now he raves   155
And we all mourn for.

KING   – Do you think this?

QUEEN   – It may be very like.

POLONIUS   Hath there been such a time, I would fain
   know that,
That I have positively said ''Tis so'
When it prov'd otherwise?

KING   Not that I know.   160

POLONIUS   Take this from this, if this be otherwise;
If Circumstances lead me, I will find
Where Truth is hid, though it were hid indeed
Within the Centre.

KING   How may we try it further?

POLONIUS   You know sometimes he walks four Hours
   together   165
Here in the Lobby.

QUEEN   So he dooes indeed.

POLONIUS   At such a time I'll loose my Daughter to
   him,
Be you and I behind an Arras then,
Mark the Encounter; if he love her not,
And be not from his Reason fall'n thereon,   170
Let me be no Assistant for a State

172   **Carters** drivers of farm carts.

175   **board** accost, approach (a nautical term that usually referred to one ship's pulling alongside another).
presently immediately.
give me leave pardon me (for interrupting you).

178   **Fishmonger** fish merchant. But because *fish* is frequently a word with sexual implications in Shakespeare's plays, it seems likely that Hamlet is also hinting at a less respectable profession. In view of what Polonius has said in line 167, the innuendo is apt. Compare II.i.59–60, and see the notes to II.i.10, II.ii.111–12.

180   **Honest** virtuous, with a play on 'chaste' as well. Compare I.v.135. In the next scene Hamlet will ask Polonius' daughter if she is honest (III.i.100–43).

186   **a good kissing Carrion** a good corpse to kiss. In the context of his reference to breeding maggots (fly larvae), Hamlet's image suggests that he is now depicting the Sun as a lover who sates his lust on putrefying flesh. The image may be meant to recall I.v.54–56 and I.ii.140 (Hamlet's reference to Hyperion, the Sun God), and thus to suggest that in Claudius' rotten Denmark the Sun (a traditional symbol for the King, as noted in I.ii.67) is even more loathsome than a satyr. In the past, many editors emended *good* to *God*.

189   **Let . . . Sun** In light of the previous image, Hamlet's implication is 'don't let her become a piece of breeding carrion'.

190   **conceive** become pregnant. Polonius and Laertes have done their best to prevent Ophelia from conceiving, not only in that sense, but in the sense that means 'think for herself'; see the notes to lines 145, 217.

194   **'a** he.

199   **matter** Polonius means 'subject matter'. In the next line Hamlet mis-takes him to mean 'quarrel'. See I.iii.65–67.

But keep a Farm and Carters.
KING   We will try it.

Enter Hamlet, reading on a Book.

QUEEN   But look where sadly the poor Wretch comes
    reading.
POLONIUS   Away, I do beseech you both away,
    I'll board him presently, oh give me leave.   175
                              Exeunt King and Queen.
    – How dooes my good Lord Hamlet?
HAMLET   Well, God 'a mercy.
POLONIUS   Do you know me, my Lord?
HAMLET   Excellent well, you are a Fishmonger.
POLONIUS   Not I, my Lord.
HAMLET   Then I would you were so Honest a Man.   180
POLONIUS   Honest, my Lord?
HAMLET   Ay Sir, to be Honest as this World goes is
    to be One Man pick'd out of Ten Thousand.
POLONIUS   That's very true, my Lord.
HAMLET   For if the Sun breed Maggots in a dead Dog,   185
    being a good kissing Carrion – Have you a
    Daughter?
POLONIUS   I have, my Lord.
HAMLET   Let her not walk i'th' Sun. Conception is
    a Blessing, but as your Daughter may conceive,   190
    Friend, look to't.
POLONIUS   – How say you by that? Still harping on
    my Daughter. Yet he knew me not at first, 'a
    said I was a Fishmonger; 'a is far gone; and
    truly in my Youth I suff'red much Extremity   195
    for Love, very near this. I'll speak to him
    again. – What do you read, my Lord?
HAMLET   Words, words, words.
POLONIUS   What is the matter, my Lord?
HAMLET   Between who?   200

204 **purging** discharging.

205 **Amber** a brownish-yellow resin, similar to the gum (sap) from a plumtree.

207 **Hams** rear thighs and hips.

208 **potently** a synonym for 'powerfully'.
Honesty virtue, decent behaviour. Hamlet is saying 'I do not regard it as honesty [good manners] to be so brutally honest.'

210 **old** Hamlet probably means 'as old' (that is, as young); that appears to be how Polonius takes his words. But since Hamlet is in his 'Antic Disposition' (I.v.163), it is not necessary to assume that his remarks conform to normal logic. He is pretending to describe himself as 'old' here and Polonius as young.

211 **go backward** walk backwards (probably with the implication 'go backwards in time'). Hamlet is alluding to the common-place that as men grow old they experience a 'Declension' (line 154) into what the melancholy Jaques calls 'Second Childishness' (*As You Like It*, II.vii.165), if not 'mere Oblivion'.

213 **Method** pattern, form, a kind of rationality. The joke, of course, is that Polonius has no 'Conception' (line 189) of the 'Method' behind the Prince's 'Madness'. The 'Purpose' of Hamlet's 'Playing' (III.ii.24) eludes this 'foolish prating Knave' entirely (III.iv.211). See the note to lines 111–12.
out of the Air inside (with the implication that outside air is unhealthy, particularly for invalids). Hamlet's reply (line 215) implies a pun on *heir*; see I.ii.64–65, 109, 129–59, III.ii.99–105.

217 **Pregnant** full of meaning. Polonius' words are true in a literal sense that is probably lost on him; see lines 185–91.
a Happiness a chance (lucky) aptness.

219 **Sanctity** virtue, holiness of life. Here the Folio reads *sanity*. See the note to I.iii.21.

224 **withal** with.

POLONIUS   I mean the matter that you read, my Lord.

HAMLET   Slaunders, Sir, for the Satirical Rogue says
here that Old Men have Grey Beards, that their
Faces are Wrinkled, their Eyes purging thick
Amber and Plumtree Gum, and that they have a   205
plentiful lack of Wit, together with most weak
Hams; all which, Sir, though I most powerfully
and potently believe, yet I hold it not Honesty
to have it thus set down. For your self, Sir,
shall grow old as I am: if like a Crab you   210
could go backward.

POLONIUS   – Though this be Madness, yet there is
Method in't. – Will you walk out of the Air,
my Lord?

HAMLET   Into my Grave.   215

POLONIUS   Indeed, that's out of the Air. – How
Pregnant sometimes his Replies are, a Happiness
that often Madness hits on, which Reason and
Sanctity could not so prosperously be delivered
of. I will leave him and suddenly contrive the   220
means of Meeting between him and my Daughter.
– My Lord, I will take my leave of you.

HAMLET   You cannot take from me any thing that I
will not more willingly part withal: except my
Life, except my Life, except my Life.   225

Enter Guildenstern and Rosencraus.

POLONIUS   Fare you well, my Lord.

HAMLET   – These tedious old Fools.

POLONIUS   – You go to seek the Lord Hamlet, there
he is.

ROSENCRAUS   God save you, Sir.   *[Exit Polonius.]*   230

GUILDENSTERN   My honour'd Lord.

ROSENCRAUS   My most dear Lord.

233 **extent** both (a) extant (still alive), and (b) extended (as your extravagant gestures of friendship would seem to signify). Most of today's editions adopt the Folio's *excellent* in this passage, but *extent* is more compatible with the effusiveness these 'Good Gentlemen' (line 19) display in their efforts to please the King and Queen. One meaning of *extent* is 'protuberant' (a sense that fits with the bawdiness of lines 238–46); another is 'out-stretch'd' (line 277).

236 **indifferent** ordinary. Normally in Shakespeare *indifferent* means 'not different', without pejorative connotations.

238– **Happy . . . Lap** blessed in that we are not too well endowed
39 and treated by Fortune. It was a commonplace of Christian theology that a person's happiness should not be judged by his fortune (his worldly possessions, position, or favour). Indeed, according to Boethius' *Consolation of Philosophy* (a classic treatise on Fortune written while the author awaited execution in the year 524), Fortune was most kind to a person when she seemed most unkind; then a person was forced to recognize that worldly happiness could never be relied upon, that the only lasting fulfilment derived from one's favour and union with God. Queen Elizabeth herself had translated Boethius' treatise from Latin to English, and Shakespeare's audience probably included many who knew it well. Most of today's editions follow the Folio, which prints 'not over-happy: on Fortune's Cap, we are not the very Button.'

239 **Button** knob, head, crown, or cap. Guildenstern probably uses 'Button' with phallic implications. One meaning of *Lap* is 'pudendum', as Hamlet makes clear in III.ii.118–32, and to be 'the very Button' would be to be mounted 'on Fortune's Lap'.

242 **Wast** waist, with play on *waste* (excretion), the word in the Folio. See the note to I.ii.197.

243 **middle** Hamlet plays on at least two senses: (a) midpoint (frequently associated with the Aristotelian mean between two extremes, the idea that a virtue could be defined as the avoidance of vices at either end of an ethical spectrum), and (b) midst (mingling with and encompassed by).

246 **Strumpet** whore, one whose 'Secret Parts' (line 245) are 'common' (I.ii.72–74, 95–106).

247 **but** but that.

HAMLET   My extent good Friends. – How doost
thou, Guildenstern? – Ah Rosencraus. – Good Lads,
how do you both?   235
ROSENCRAUS   As the indifferent Children of the
Earth.
GUILDENSTERN   Happy, in that we are not ever happy
on Fortune's Lap, we are not the very Button.
HAMLET   Nor the Soles of her Shoe.   240
ROSENCRAUS   Neither, my Lord.
HAMLET   Then you live about her Wast, or in the
middle of her Favours.
GUILDENSTERN   Faith, her Privates we.
HAMLET   In the Secret Parts of Fortune, oh most   245
true, she is a Strumpet. What News?
ROSENCRAUS   None, my Lord, but the World's grown
Honest.

249 **Then is Doomsday near** Hamlet is probably alluding to the
peaceful millennium to precede the Last Judgement (the
thousand years during which Satan is to be bound, 'that he
should deceive the people no more', Revelation 20:3). Only
then, Hamlet implies, will the world have 'grown Honest'
(lines 247–8).

252 **Prison** Hamlet's image may be another allusion to 'the
bottomless pit' into which Satan will be cast and 'bound',
according to Revelation 20:1–3. Compare line 266.

262 **but** unless, except when.

264 **Ambition** Rosencraus is fishing to find out if Hamlet's being
passed over for the monarchy is what troubles him. Hamlet
recognizes Rosencraus' crude and ill-disguised indirections for
what they are, and immediately begins toying with him in a
way that resembles the Prince's satirical treatment of
Polonius.

270 **Substance** desired condition or position.

271 **Shadow** image (not limited to what Shakespeare sometimes
refers to as a 'shade', though Hamlet focuses on that meaning
in lines 276–78).

274 **Light** both (a) insubstantial, and (b) frivolous.

276– **Then . . . Shadows** Hamlet takes Rosencraus' image of
78 'Ambition' as a 'Shadow's Shadow' and implies that
'Monarchs' (overgrown or 'out-stretch'd' shadows) are but
the shades cast by beggars. One of his points is that beggars,
who have no ambition and who are normally thought to be
nothing more than 'shadows' (insignificant human beings),
are actually more substantial than monarchs (who personify
ambition). Hamlet reduces all ambition (worldly pride and
aspiration) to the nothing that the word 'vanity' literally
denotes. But the Prince is also picking up on the word *Airy*
(see the second note to line 213) with the implication that the
'Ambition' of one 'Airy' monarch (Claudius) is but a
'Shadow' of the true heir to the throne. Those who appear to
be 'Beggars' (Hamlet) are the legitimate 'Bodies'
(embodiments of Danish royalty), whereas those who now
appear to be 'out-stretch'd Heroes' (overextended pretenders
to monarchy) are really things of 'nothing' (see IV.ii.26–31).

278 **Fey** both (a) fay, faith, and (b) fate (playing on *fey* as an
adjective meaning 'fated to die').

HAMLET   Then is Doomsday near; but your News is
not true. Let me question more in particular.   250
What have you, my good Friends, deserv'd at the
hands of Fortune, that she sends you to Prison
hither?

GUILDENSTERN   Prison, my Lord?

HAMLET   Denmark's a Prison.   255

ROSENCRAUS   Then is the World one.

HAMLET   A goodly one, in which there are many
Confines, Wards, and Dungeons; Denmark being
one o' th' worst.

ROSENCRAUS   We think not so, my Lord.   260

HAMLET   Why then 'tis none to you; for there is
nothing either Good or Bad but Thinking makes
it so. To me it is a Prison.

ROSENCRAUS   Why then your Ambition makes it one:
'tis too Narrow for your Mind.   265

HAMLET   O God, I could be bounded in a Nutshell
and count my self a King of Infinite Space;
were it not that I have Bad Dreams.

GUILDENSTERN   Which Dreams indeed are Ambition:
for the very Substance of the Ambitious is   270
merely the Shadow of a Dream.

HAMLET   A Dream it self is but a Shadow.

ROSENCRAUS   Truly, and I hold Ambition of so Airy
and Light a Quality that it is but a Shadow's
Shadow.   275

HAMLET   Then are our Beggars Bodies; and our
Monarchs and out-stretch'd Heroes the Beggars'
Shadows. Shall we to th' Court: for by my Fey
I cannot reason.

BOTH   We'll wait upon you.   280

281 **No such matter** That's out of the question. Hamlet says that he
refuses to regard his old friends as 'Servants' (line 282) who
'wait upon' him (attend to his needs). He pretends to speak
this as a compliment to them (compare I.ii.160–66), but what
he probably means privately is that he wouldn't trust these
sycophants to be his most menial servants, let alone remain
his friends.

283– **dreadfully attended** (a) poorly served, (b) accompanied by
84   feelings of dread and melancholy (line 268), and (c)
accompanied by companions (namely the two he addresses)
he considers unworthy of his attendance.

284 **Beaten Way** well trodden path. Hamlet's phrasing reflects his
sense that his former schoolmates have treated the 'Way of
Friendship' contemptuously.

285 **what make you at** what brings you to. *Visit* (line 286) echoes
line 25 and anticipates lines 291–92.

290 **too dear a Halfpenny** too expensive at a halfpenny. In other
words, I can't even afford a halfpenny's worth of thanks to
you [and besides that, you'll be thanked by the person who
sent for you]. *Inclining* (line 291) recalls II.i.67–68.

292 **free** both (a) of your own free will, and (b) free of any
obligation and payment that may derive from your pleasing
someone else.

295 **but to th' Purpose** either (a) so long as it is to the point, or (b)
except for something that would be to the point. The
implication of the phrase depends upon whether Hamlet is to
be thought of as (a) exhorting his former schoolmates to tell
him the truth, or (b) telling them that he knows that anything
they say will be a lie. Compare III.ii.23–29.

297 **Modesties** self-control, dignity. Hamlet is referring to the skill
with which actors adhere to their roles: the 'colour' (disguise)
they have donned for their parts. See lines 466–73, and
compare *The Taming of the Shrew*, Induction. i.66–68,
94–99.

304–5 **by ... withal** by any higher claim a dearer friend may invoke.
Hamlet is giving Rosencraus and Guildenstern a final
opportunity to renew their allegiance to one who is in fact 'a
better Proposer' despite his present reduction to the role of a
'Beggar' (line 288, echoing lines 272–78).

HAMLET   No such matter. I will not sort you with
the rest of my Servants: for to speak to you
like an Honest Man, I am most dreadfully
attended. But in the Beaten Way of Friendship,
what make you at Elsonoure?   285

ROSENCRAUS   To visit you, my Lord, no other
Occasion.

HAMLET   Beggar that I am, I am ever poor in Thanks,
but I thank you; and sure, dear Friends, my
Thanks are too dear a Halfpenny. Were you not   290
sent for? Is it your own Inclining? Is it a
free Visitation? Come, come, deal justly with
me; come, come, nay speak.

GUILDENSTERN   What should we say, my Lord?

HAMLET   Any thing but to th' Purpose: you were sent   295
for, and there is a kind of Confession in your
Looks, which your Modesties have not Craft
enough to colour. I know the good King and
Queen have sent for you.

ROSENCRAUS   To what end, my Lord?   300

HAMLET   That you must teach me; but let me conjure
you, by the Rights of our Fellowship, by the
Consonancy of our Youth, by the Obligation of
our ever preserved Love; and by what more dear
a better Proposer can charge you withal, be   305
even and direct with me whether you were sent
for or no.

ROSENCRAUS   – What say you?

HAMLET   Nay then I have an Eye of you: if you love

310 **hold not off** do not hold back from me.

313 **prevent your Discovery** forestall your having to (a) disclose to me the terms of your commission from my mother and uncle, and (b) discover what the King and Queen have sent you to find out about me.

313– **your ... Feather** your secret mission for the King and Queen
14 be accomplished to your full credit, without so much as the loss of a feather.

316 **forgone ... Exercises** given up my normal athletic pursuits (such as fencing, archery, and horsemanship).

319 **Promontory** jutting ('o'erhanging') piece of rock. Compare I.iv.67–77.

320 **brave** splendid.

321 **Firmament** the Heavens. As the original Hamlet spoke these lines, he probably gestured not only to the sky but to the 'Canopy' or 'Roof' above the Globe stage.

322 **fretted with Golden Fire** adorned with the Sun and stars. Shakespeare is probably alluding to the decorations on the underside of the canopy.

324 **Congregation of Vapours** cluster of illuminated gases (such as the *ignis fatuus*, the will-o'-the-wisp).
Piece of Work artistic creation. Compare III.ii.54, 264–65. Hamlet alludes to such biblical passages as Psalm 8:4–6, where the poet asks God, 'What is man, that thou art mindful of him? and the son of man that thou visitest him? For thou hast made him a little lower than the angels, and hast crowned him with glory and honour. Thou madest him to have dominion over the works of thy hands; thou hast put all things under his feet.'

326 **Express** probably both (a) precise, and (b) expressive.

329 **Paragon** touchstone, highest exemplar.

330 **Dust** This word echoes I.ii.71, I.iv.17, and anticipates IV.ii.6.

338 **Lenten Entertainment** the sparse hospitality provided during Lent.

339 **coted** either (a) noted, or (b) overtook, encountered. Compare II.i.108.

343 **Tribute on** reward from.

me, hold not off.   310

GUILDENSTERN   My Lord, we were sent for.

HAMLET   I will tell you why, so shall my
Anticipation prevent your Discovery, and your
Secrecy to the King and Queen moult no Feather.
I have of late, but wherefore I know not, lost   315
all my Mirth, forgone all Custom of Exercises;
and indeed it goes so heavily with my
Disposition that this goodly Frame the Earth
seems to me a sterile Promontory, this most
excellent Canopy the Air, look you, this brave   320
o'erhanging Firmament, this majestical Roof
fretted with Golden Fire, why it appeareth
nothing to me but a foul and pestilent
Congregation of Vapours. What a Piece of Work
is a Man, how Noble in Reason, how Infinite in   325
Faculties, in Form and Moving, how Express and
Admirable in Action, how like an Angel in
Apprehension, how like a God. The Beauty of
the World; the Paragon of Animals; and yet to
me, what is this Quintessence of Dust? Man   330
delights not me, no, nor Women neither, though by
your Smiling you seem to say so.

ROSENCRAUS   My Lord, there was no such stuff in my
Thoughts.

HAMLET   Why did ye laugh then, when I said 'Man   335
delights not me'.

ROSENCRAUS   To think, my Lord, if you delight not
in Man, what Lenten Entertainment the Players
shall receive from you. We coted them on the
way, and hether are they coming to offer you   340
Service.

HAMLET   He that plays the King shall be welcome,
his Majesty shall have Tribute on me; the

344 **Foil** light fencing sword.

345 **Target** small shield (targe).

345– **the Humourous Man** the man subject to humours (obsessions
46   or caprices), here probably either desperate choler (wrath), or
      suicidal melancholy.

348 **tickled a'th' Sere** easily (a) fired off [easily provoked to laugh],
    like a gun whose sere (catch) is easily triggered, or (b) tickled
    by sere (dry, withered) leaves or stems or by sere (thin, worn)
    thread. Most editions emend *tickled* to *tickle*.

349 **black Verse** The Second Quarto's *black* may be a misprint for
    blank (the word in the Folio), meaning 'unrhymed'; most
    modern editors adopt the Folio reading. But *black* may be
    used here with a metaphorical sense, meaning either (a) sad,
    mournful, funereal, or (b) black-letter (a term for gothic or
    'Old English' type).

351 **wont** accustomed. So also with *wonted* in line 363.

353 **travail** both (a) travel, and (b) suffer hardship.

356 **their Inhibition** their inability to perform at home. Hamlet
    alludes to the fact that because of 'the late Innovation' (the
    rise of children's companies), the adult acting companies have
    lost prestige ('Estimation', line 358) and 'profit'.

359 **so followed** thus regarded [still].

363 **Aery** eyrie, nest. Compare lines 273–78.

364 **Eyases** baby hawks. Hamlet refers to the schoolboy actors.

364– **cry . . . Question** scream contentiously at the tops of their
65   voices, and on the loftiest themes.

366– **and . . . Stages** and they have so terrorized the public
67   playhouses.

368– **many . . . Goose-quills** many rapier-bearing gallants are afraid
69   of ridicule from the pens of the poets writing satirical plays
      for the boys' companies to perform.

371 **escoted** supported. The word comes from *scot*, payment.

372 **Quality** profession (acting). Compare lines 273–75.
    no longer than they can sing The actors in the London boys'
    companies were choristers associated with such institutions as
    St Paul's Cathedral and the Chapel Royal.

adventurous Knight shall use his Foil and
Target; the Lover shall not sigh Gratis; the   345
Humourous Man shall end his Part in Peace;
the Clown shall make those laugh whose Lungs
are tickled a'th' Sere; and the Lady shall say
her Mind freely: or the black Verse shall halt
for't. What Players are they?   350

ROSENCRAUS   Even those you were wont to take
such Delight in, the Tragedians of the City.

HAMLET   How chances it they travail? Their
Residence both in Reputation and Profit was
better both ways.   355

ROSENCRAUS   I think their Inhibition comes by the
means of the late Innovation.

HAMLET   Do they hold the same Estimation they did
when I was in the City? Are they so followed?

ROSENCRAUS   No indeed, are they not.   360

HAMLET   How comes it? Do they grow Rusty?

ROSENCRAUS   Nay, their Endeavour keeps in the
wonted Pace. But there is, Sir, an Aery of Children,
little Eyases, that cry out on the Top of
Question, and are most tyrannically clapp'd   365
for't; these are now the Fashion, and so
be-rattled the Common Stages (so they call
them) that many wearing Rapiers are afraid of
Goose-quills and dare scarce come thither.

HAMLET   What are they Children? Who maintains   370
'em? How are they escoted? Will they pursue
the Quality no longer than they can sing? Will
they not say afterwards, if they should grow
themselves to Common Players (as it is

374– **like most**   most likely for most of them.
75

377   **their own Succession**   the 'Common Players' (professional
actors) they will become once they grow up. Hamlet's point is
that they will become 'the indifferent children of the Earth'
(lines 236–37) instead of the stars they now find themselves
'most tyrannically clapp'd for'.

378   **to do**   ado.

380   **tarre**   incite, encourage.

381   **bid for Argument**   paid for themes (plays), here ones taking
sides in an ongoing dispute.

382   **in the Question**   over the matter at issue.

387–   **Hercules and his Load too**   Hercules relieved Atlas of his load
88   (the world) while Atlas went in search of the apples of the
Hesperides. The motto of Shakespeare's own playhouse
probably depicted Hercules bearing the Globe. Now that the
boys 'carry it away' (line 386), Hercules and Globe alike, the
common players have no choice but to perform elsewhere.

389   **It . . . strange**   Hamlet says that the 'late Innovation' in the
theatres has its parallel in the new King's usurpation of
another kind of globe (the orb that is a symbol of royalty).

392   **Duckets**   ducats, gold coins whose name reflected their ducal
origin in Italy.

393   **Picture in Little**   portrait in miniature. Lines 393–95 recall
I.v.158–59.
   'sblood   a contraction of 'God's blood', an oath referring to the
Crucifixion.

400   **Extent**   extension of welcome. Hamlet is complying with the
'Garb' (outward form) that pertains to 'Fashion and
Ceremony' (a 'show' of etiquette) as he takes the hands of his
schoolmates to bid them a formal welcome. See the note to
line 233.

401–2 **show . . . outwards**   appear to the external observer to be
especially cordial.

406   **I . . . Northwest**   I am mad only when the wind is blowing from
the north northwest.

like most if their Means are no better), their   375
Writers do them wrong, to make them exclaim
against their own Succession.

ROSENCRAUS   Faith there has been much to do on
both Sides; and the Nation holds it no Sin to
tarre them to Controversy. There was for a   380
while no Money bid for Argument unless the Poet
and the Player went to Cuffs in the Question.

HAMLET   Is't possible?

GUILDENSTERN   O there has been much throwing
about of Brains.   385

HAMLET   Do the Boys carry it away?

ROSENCRAUS   Ay that they do, my Lord, Hercules
and his Load too.

HAMLET   It is not very strange, for my Uncle is
King of Denmark, and those that would make   390
Mouths at him while my Father lived give
twenty, forty, fifty, a hundred Duckets a piece
for his Picture in Little; 'sblood, there is
something in this more than Natural, if
Philosophy could find it out.   *A Flourish.*   395

GUILDENSTERN   There are the Players.

HAMLET   Gentlemen, you are welcome to Elsonoure.
Your Hands, come then: th' Appurtenance of
Welcome is Fashion and Ceremony. Let me
comply with you in this Garb, lest my Extent to   400
the Players, which I tell you must show fairly
outwards, should more appear like Entertainment
than yours. You are welcome: but my Uncle-
Father and Aunt-Mother are deceived.

GUILDENSTERN   In what, my dear Lord?   405

HAMLET   I am but mad North Northwest; when the

407   **a Hauke from a Handsaw** Here *Hauke* can refer to (a) a hack
,   (a mattock or pickaxe), or (b) a hawk (the Folio spelling is
      Hawke), which can mean either the bird of that name or a
      small plasterer's tool. *Handsaw* can refer to another
      implement, a cutting blade, or to a hernshaw or heronshaw, a
      bird preyed upon by hawks. Hamlet's point is that he has not
      lost the ability to make discriminations.

411   **Swaddling Clouts** the cloths used to wrap an infant. See the
      note to line 211.

412   **Happily** haply, perhaps.

415   **Mark it** Most of today's editions attach this phrase to the
      preceding clause. The Quarto's characteristically light
      punctuation is ambiguous; the phrase is suspended between
      the two halves of Hamlet's speech by parenthetical commas
      (see the note to I.ii.222). The Folio precedes the phrase with a
      full stop, to indicate that it initiates the 'Buzz, buzz' Hamlet
      feigns as Polonius draws within hearing distance. See the note
      to line 421.

419   **Rossius** Roscius, the most celebrated of Roman actors.

421   **Buzz, buzz** both (a) a phrase of contemptuous dismissal,
      indicating that Polonius' report contains no new information
      and (b) a phrase, equivalent to 'blah blah', that imitates the
      murmur actors improvise as filler when occasion demands.
      Hamlet may also be punning on *buzzard*. One version of the
      proverb he uses in lines 406–7 is 'between hawk and
      buzzard', and he may be suggesting that he can tell the
      difference between a true Roscius and an 'Actor' who can
      only 'Buzz buzz' like a scavenging buzzard or a pesky
      humming insect (see *The Taming of the Shrew*, II.i.208–15).
      In III.ii.105–13 Hamlet engages Polonius in a conversation
      about the old chamberlain's brief career as a thespian during
      his university days.

423   **on his Ass** Hamlet may be quoting from a contemporary poem
      or ballad.

428   **Scene Indevidable** It is not clear whether this refers to a play
      that cannot be sorted into constituent elements (such as
      'Pastoral'), a play that is unclassifiable, or a play that is not
      divided into separate scenes or settings. 'Poem Unlimited'
      could be anything from a synonym to an opposite of 'Scene
      Indevidable'. See the note on *devide* at I.i.71.

Wind is Southerly, I know a Hauke from a Handsaw.

Enter Polonius.

POLONIUS   Well be with you, Gentlemen.

HAMLET   — Hark you, Guildenstern, and you too (at
  each Ear a Hearer): that great Baby you see   410
  there is not yet out of his Swaddling Clouts.

ROSENCRAUS   Happily he is the second time come to
  them, for they say an Old Man is twice a Child.

HAMLET   I will prophesy, he comes to tell me of the
  Players. Mark it, you say right, Sir, a Monday   415
  morning, 'twas then indeed.

POLONIUS   My Lord, I have News to tell you.

HAMLET   My Lord, I have News to tell you:
  When Rossius was an Actor in Rome —

POLONIUS   The Actors are come hether, my Lord.   420

HAMLET   Buzz, buzz.

POLONIUS   Upon my Honour.

HAMLET   Then came each Actor on his Ass.

POLONIUS   The best Actors in the World, either for
  Tragedy, Comedy, History, Pastoral, Pastoral-   425
  Comical, Historical-Pastoral, Tragical-
  Historical, Tragical-Comical-Historical-
  Pastoral, Scene Indevidable, or Poem Unlimited.
  Seneca cannot be too heavy, nor Plautus too

430   **for ... Liberty** for the 'rules' (the laws of probability) governing Senecan tragedy, and the freedom from such restraints in Plautine comedy and in the Polonian (and Shakespearean) medley of mixed genres in lines 425–28.

431   **these ... Men** these are the best players.

432   **Jeptha** Hamlet alludes to Jephthah (Judges 11), an Israelite magistrate who vowed that if the Lord would grant him a victory over the Ammonites he would sacrifice whatever emerged from his house to greet him on his return from battle. That turned out to be his only child, a maiden daughter, and after she had been given two months to 'bewail' her 'virginity' in the mountains, the grieving Jephthah offered her up to God.

441   **passing** surpassingly. *Passing* can also mean 'dying' (as in the phrase 'Passing Bell' in line 702 of *Venus and Adonis*); see III.iii.86, and compare *King Lear*, IV.vi.47, where Edgar uses *pass* to mean 'die'. And *well* is frequently used to refer to those who have achieved bliss in Heaven; see *Romeo and Juliet*, V.i.12–19, 34.

442   **Nay ... not** Hamlet says that a man's being a Jephthah does not prove him to be a father who genuinely and wisely loves his daughter.

445   **As by lot, God wot** Like the other quotations here, this one is from a ballad about Jephthah and his daughter. Its implication is that God's will was done 'by lot' (by random chance) as a result of Jephthah's rash vow.

449   **Row** stanza.
       pious Chanson religious song.

449–50   **will show you more** will tell you more about the moral of this story.

450   **my Abridgement** the players, who (a) abridge (cut off) Hamlet's story, and (b) promise to abridge (shorten or bridge) the time. Compare *A Midsummer Night's Dream*, V.i.39–41.

453   **Valanc'd** fringed. Hamlet then plays on *beard* (confront). Compare lines 608–18.

456   **by Lady** The Folio prints *byrlady* (a contraction of 'by our Lady'), and that may be what Hamlet means. But the Prince could be varying the usual expression and swearing by the 'Lady' (the nearly grown male actor) before him.

light for the Law of Writ, and the Liberty: 430
these are the only Men.
HAMLET   O Jeptha, Judge of Israel, what a Treasure
hadst thou?
POLONIUS   What a Treasure had he, my Lord?
HAMLET   Why   435
'One fair Daughter and no more,
The which he loved passing well.'
POLONIUS   — Still on my Daughter.
HAMLET   Am I not i'th' Right, old Jeptha?
POLONIUS   If you call me Jeptha, my Lord, I have a   440
Daughter that I love passing well.
HAMLET   Nay that follows not.
POLONIUS   What follows then, my Lord?
HAMLET   Why
'As by lot, God wot,'   445
and then you know
'It came to pass,
As most like it was.'
The first Row of the pious Chanson will show
you more, for look where my Abridgement comes.   450

Enter the Players.

— You are welcome, Maisters, welcome all. I am
glad to see thee well, welcome good Friends.
— Oh old Friend, why thy Face is Valanc'd since
I saw thee last: com'st thou to beard me in
Denmark? — What, my young Lady and Mistress: 455
by Lady, your Ladyship is nearer to Heaven
than when I saw you last by the altitude of a

458   **Chopine** a high-soled woman's shoe. Hamlet is alluding to
female roles he has seen this 'Lady' play.

459   **uncurrant Gold** a gold coin that will no longer be accepted as
currency because it has been 'cracked' or clipped enough to
penetrate the 'Ring' surrounding the Sovereign's engraved
head. Hamlet puns on the 'ring' of a boy's high-pitched voice;
he may also be noting that if a female's 'ring' (virginity) has
been 'cracked', she can no longer pass as a maiden. Compare
I.ii.101, 146, and see lines 370–77.

460   **Maisters** masters (from the Latin *magister*).

461   **friendly** enthusiastic, undiscriminating. Modern editions
normally adopt the Folio's *French*, evidently a word with
similar import. Compare IV.vii.61.

462   **strait** straight, right away.

463   **Tast** both (a) taste, and (b) test (trial, demonstration). Soon
Hamlet will be using the Player's artistry to 'Tast' the
'Quality' of another actor; see the note to III.ii.94.
Quality expertise. Compare lines 273–75, 371–72.

469   **'twas Caviary to the General** it was like offering a delicacy
(caviare) to the undiscriminating general populace. *General*
recalls I.iv.34, II.i.34–35.

471   **cried in the top of mine** proclaimed with even more vehemence
and authority than my judgement could claim. *Top* echoes
lines 364–65.

473   **Modesty** decorum, restraint. See the note to line 297.
Cunning probably both (a) skill (literally, 'knowing'), and (b)
cleverness.

474   **Sallets** salads; spicy morsels, such as shallots and other herbs.

476–   **indite . . . Affection** both (a) inscribe the author in the annals
77   of criticism as a man too susceptible to his affections (the
senses and emotions that impair judgement, as noted in
I.iii.24–51 and I.iv.16–37), and (b) indict the author for his
affectations, his irresponsible 'Liberty' from 'the Law of Writ'
(line 430). *Method* echoes lines 212–13.

478–   **more . . . Fine** more disciplined and straightforward than
79   overrefined.

484   **Ircanian Beast** a tiger from Hyrcania in the Caucasus. The
Folio prints *Hyrcanian*.

Chopine. Pray God your Voice, like a piece of
uncurrant Gold, be not crack'd within the Ring.
– Maisters, you are all welcome. We'll e'en   460
to't like friendly Faulc'ners, fly at any
thing we see. We'll have a Speech strait:
come give us a Tast of your Quality, come, a
passionate Speech.

PLAYER   What Speech, my good Lord?   465

HAMLET   I heard thee speak me a Speech once, but it
was never acted, or if it was, not above once,
for the Play I remember pleas'd not the Million,
'twas Caviary to the General; but it was, as I
received it, and others, whose Judgements in   470
such Matters cried in the top of mine, an
excellent Play, well digested in the Scenes,
set down with as much Modesty as Cunning. I
remember one said there were no Sallets in the
Lines, to make the Matter savoury, nor no Matter   475
in the Phrase that might indite the Author of
Affection, but call'd it an Honest Method,
as Wholesome as Sweet, and by very much, more
Handsome than Fine. One Speech in't I chiefly
loved, 'twas Aeneas' Talk to Dido, and there   480
about of it especially when he speaks of
Priam's Slaughter. If it live in your Memory,
begin at this Line, let me see, let me see:
'The rugged Pyrrhus like th' Ircanian Beast – '
'Tis not so, it begins with
                                        'Pyrrhus,   485

486 **Sable Arms** black armour (and blackened arms). Compare
I.ii.236, III.ii.136–37, IV.vii.76–80.

489 **couched** crouched, ready to spring.
th' omynous Horse the ominous Trojan Horse. Shakespeare
draws this and many other details from Book II, 'Aeneas' Talk
to Dido' (line 480) in Virgil's *Aeneid*. There Pyrrhus avenges
the death of his father, Achilles, by leading the assault that
destroys Troy. Here the Folio prints 'the Ominous'. The
wrenched pronunciation the Quarto version calls for seems
more likely to convey the artificial 'Affection' (see the note to
lines 476–77) of a speech whose extravagances illustrate
something more than the 'Honest Method' Hamlet professes
to admire in it. See the notes to lines 98, 111–12, 213.

492 **total Gules** totally blood-red. In keeping with the vocabulary
of 'Heraldry' (line 491), Pyrrhus is described as if his body
were a coat of arms, originally smeared all black ('Sable
Arms', line 487) and now 'trick'd' (adorned) in blood.

494 **parching** burning. Once they got their wooden horse inside the
walls, the Greeks emerged under cover of darkness and set
Troy on fire.

495 **tyrannous** Here and elsewhere, Shakespeare uses *tyrannous* to
mean 'cruel and merciless'. Compare lines 363–66.

496 **rosted** roasted. The Quarto spelling parallels that in *Macbeth*,
II.iii.17.

497 **o'er-cised** coated as with sizing (glaze).
coagulate Gore congealed blood.

498 **Carbuncles** fiery red jewels, thought to glow in the dark.

502 **Discretion** judgement, discipline. Compare I.ii.5, II.i.112–13,
III.ii.19–20.

504 **antic** both (a) antique, old-fashioned, and (b) foolish. Priam,
the aged King of Troy, is here depicted as lacking either the
strength or the weapon to withstand the onslaught of the 'fell'
(fierce) invaders. See the note to I.v.163.

506 **Repugnant to Commaund** resisting the will of its master.
Unequal match'd matched with a defenceless old man.

508 **fell** fierce, savage, merciless.

509 **senseless Ilium** the insensible (inanimate) citadel of Troy.

The rugged Pyrrhus, he whose Sable Arms,
Black as his Purpose, did the Night
   resemble,
When he lay couched in th' omynous Horse,
Hath now this dread and black Complexion
   smear'd   490
With Heraldry more dismal Head to Foot,
Now is he total Gules, horridly trick'd
With Blood of Fathers, Mothers, Daughters,
   Sons,
Bak'd and impasted with the parching Streets,
That lend a tyrannous and a damned Light   495
To their Lord's Murther; rosted in Wrath
   and Fire,
And thus o'er-cised with coagulate Gore,
With Eyes like Carbuncles, the hellish
   Pyrrhus
Old Grandsire Priam seeks.'
So proceed you.   500
POLONIUS   'Fore God, my Lord, well spoken, with
good Accent and good Discretion.
PLAYER   'Anon he finds him;
   Striking too short at Greeks, his antic
      Sword,
Rebellious to his Arm, lies where it falls,   505
Repugnant to Commaund; unequal match'd,
Pyrrhus at Priam drives, in Rage strikes wide;
But with the Whiff and Wind of his fell
   Sword
Th' unnerved Father falls. Then senseless
   Ilium,
Seeming to feel this Blow, with flaming Top   510

511   **Stoops to his Base**   collapses to its foundations. Compare *Julius Caesar*, III.ii.185–94, where Mark Antony describes Caesar's death 'at the Base of Pompey's Statue'. *Top* (line 510) echoes line 471.

513   **milky**   milk-white. In *Macbeth*, I.v.19, milk is associated with 'Humane Kindness'. Compare *King Lear*, I.iv.355, where Goneril rebukes her husband for his 'milky Gentleness'.

516   **a Neutral to his Will and Matter**   one caught midway between his intent and his execution of it. See the note to I.ii.222. The brevity of line 517 indicates a moment of silence, to convey 'Pyrrhus' Pause' (line 522). See the notes to lines 90, 91, 111–12, 489 for related instances of the playwright's 'Art'.

518   **against**   in anticipation of; just before.

519   **the Rack**   the mass of clouds broken up by the wind.

520   **Orb**   globe (Earth). Compare III.ii.179.

521   **anon**   shortly.

524   **Cyclops' Hammers**   The Cyclopes (one-eyed giants) were the smiths in Vulcan's shop who made armour for Mars, the God of War.

525   **forg'd for Proof eterne**   made so durable as to be eternally proof against penetration.

526   **Remorse**   pity.

529   **Synod**   assembly, council. (The governing body of the Church of England is still called General Synod.) *General* echoes line 469. The phrase 'strumpet Fortune' recalls lines 245–46.

530   **Follies**   a variant spelling for *felloes* or *fellies*, the exterior rims on wooden wheels. But Shakespeare probably also intends a reference to the 'follies' (infidelities and deceits) that 'strumpet Fortune' (line 528) bequeaths to those who trust in her. See the note to lines 238–39. Modern editors normally emend to *fellies* (a reading introduced in the Fourth Folio, 1685).

531   **Nave**   hub. In the theatre, of course, *Nave* would be indistinguishable from *knave*.

532   **Fiends**   The word could be construed (a) Fiends, (b) Fiends', or (c) Fiend's.

Stoops to his Base, and with a hideous Crash
Takes prisoner Pyrrhus' Ear: for lo his Sword,
Which was declining on the milky Head
Of reverent Priam, seem'd i'th' Air to
    stick,
So as a painted Tyrant Pyrrhus stood   515
And, like a Neutral to his Will and Matter,
Did nothing.
But as we often see, against some Storm,
A Silence in the Heavens, the Rack stand
    still,
The bold Winds speechless, and the Orb below   520
As hush as Death, anon the dreadful Thunder
Doth rend the Region: so after Pyrrhus'
    Pause
A roused Vengeance sets him new a-work,
And never did the Cyclops' Hammers fall
On Mars's Armour, forg'd for Proof eterne,   525
With less Remorse than Pyrrhus' bleeding
    Sword
Now falls on Priam.
Out, out, thou strumpet Fortune; all you
    Gods
In general Synod take away her Power;
Break all the Spokes and Follies from her
    Wheel   530
And bowl the round Nave down the Hill of
    Heaven
As low as to the Fiends.'
POLONIUS   This is too long.
HAMLET   It shall to the Barber's with your Beard.

535   **Jig**   a song and dance routine following the play proper.

535– **Tale of Bawdry** bawdy story.
36

537   **mobled**   mobbled, muffled (with face covered). Hamlet's reaction in the next line suggests that he regards the word as obscure and affected; that does not bother Polonius, whose taste is more to the 'Fine' (overwrought) than to the 'Handsome' (line 479). See the note to lines 476–77, 489.

541   **Bison Rheum**   either (a) tears of the size and quantity a wild ox (bison) would discharge, or (b) tears enough to be blinding (bisson) to the Queen's own eyes. Both senses may be applicable to the Player's hyperbolic image. Here the Folio prints *bisson*, and most of today's editions adopt that spelling. Compare line 599.
     Clout   cloth. *Clout* could also refer to the centre of a target used in archery, a reminder that Hecuba's pate is vulnerable to the same kind of clout (blow) that fell on her husband's 'milky Head'.

542   **Diadem**   either a small crown or an ornamental headband.

543   **o'er-teemed**   exhausted from childbearing (52 children).

545   **Who this had seen**   whoever had seen this (rephrasing line 537).

546   **'Gainst . . . pronounc'd**   would have uttered treasonous pronouncements against the sway of Fortune.

552   **milch**   milky. The poet's point is that even the stars of Heaven would have been moved to compassion if they had seen Priam's widow in her lamentations. See the note to line 513.

553   **Passion**   compassion. In accordance with Epicurean philosophy, the Olympian Gods are here depicted as remote and uninvolved in human affairs.

554   **where**   both (a) whether, and (b) where.

557   **will you**   if you will, please.

558   **bestow'd**   lodged and cared for.

559   **used**   treated. Compare lines 565, 567.

560   **abstract**   both (a) brief, and (b) artful (extracting and preserving the essence of 'the Time').

– Prethee say on, he's for a Jig, or a Tale of   535
Bawdry, or he sleeps; say on, come to Hecuba.

PLAYER   'But who, ah Woe, had seen the mobled
Queen – '

HAMLET   'The mobled Queen'.

POLONIUS   That's good.

PLAYER   'Run barefoot up and down, threat'ning
    the Flames   540
   With Bison Rheum, a Clout upon that Head
   Where late the Diadem stood, and for a Robe
   About her lank and all o'er-teemed Loins
   A Blanket in the Alarm of Fear caught up;
   Who this had seen, with Tongue in Venom
       steep'd,   545
   'Gainst Fortune's State would Treason have
       pronounc'd.
   But if the Gods themselves did see her then,
   When she saw Pyrrhus make malicious Sport
   In mincing with his Sword her Husband's Limbs,
   The instant burst of Clamour that she made,   550
   Unless things Mortal move them not at all,
   Would have made milch the burning Eyes of
       Heaven
   And Passion in the Gods.'

POLONIUS   Look where he has not turn'd his Colour,
   and has Tears in's Eyes: prethee no more.   555

HAMLET   'Tis well, I'll have thee speak out the
   rest of this soon. – Good my Lord, will you
   see the Players well bestow'd. Do you hear,
   let them be well used, for they are the
   abstract and brief Chronicles of the Time;   560
   after your Death you were better have a bad
   Epitaph then their Ill Report while you live.

POLONIUS   My Lord, I will use them according to
   their Desert.

565 **God's Bodkin** God's little body; an oath alluding to the Crucifixion, and thus one that is appropriate to a speech in which Hamlet reminds Polonius that 'all have sinned and come short of the glory of God' (Romans 3:23) and 'scape' condemnation only through the 'Whipping' (Matthew 26:27) and sacrifice of Christ in their stead. Compare III.i.73.

566 **after his Desert** in accordance with what he deserves.
scape escape.

567 **Whipping** The punishment Hamlet chooses is apt; players who travelled and performed without a licence (usually secured through the patronage of a Lord) were subject to flogging, the penalty the law provided for those convicted of being vagabonds.

568– **the less . . . Bounty** Hamlet's phrasing echoes that of the
69 Apostle Paul in such passages as Romans 5:20 ('where sin abounded, grace did much more abound') and Ephesians 2:8 ('by grace are ye saved through faith; and that not of yourselves; it is the gift of God'). Both passages were central to the Lutheran theology promulgated at Wittenberg in 1517. Lines 565–69 recall I.v.156–7 and II.ii.53.

571 **hear a Play** In Shakespeare's time, discriminating audiences spoke of 'hearing' (attending to the 'Matter') rather than 'seeing' (being amused by the spectacle of) a play. See III.ii.1–52, where Hamlet reiterates this distinction between the 'Judicious' and those he dismisses as 'barren Spectators'. See III.ii. line 31.

575 **I** both 'Ay' and 'I' (as in lines 580, 586, and in II.i.52).

576 **hate** The Folio prints *ha't* (a contraction of *have it*), and that is Hamlet's meaning. But here, as in IV.vii.153 and V.ii.355, the Quarto spelling (and presumably the actor's pronunciation) keep the audience aware of the passion that drives the action forward. Hamlet will 'hate tomorrow night' as well as 'have it' then.

581 **look you** see that you.

586 **God buy** goodbye.

588 **monstrous** a violation of Nature's norms. Things that were monstrous were frequently regarded as portents, omens of disaster (from Latin *monere*, to warn).

589 **a Dream of Passion** an imagined set of emotions. *Dream* recalls I.ii.21, II.ii.10, 268–69.

HAMLET   God's Bodkin, Man, much better: use   565
every Man after his Desert, and who shall scape
Whipping? Use them after your own Honour and
Dignity: the less they deserve, the more Merit
is in your Bounty. Take them in.
POLONIUS   – Come, Sirs.   *Exit Polonius.*   570
HAMLET   – Follow him, Friends: we'll hear a Play
to morrow.   *[Exeunt all but one Player.]*
– Dost thou hear me, old Friend: can you play
the Murther of Gonzago?
PLAYER   I, my Lord.   575
HAMLET   We'll hate to morrow night; you could for
need study a Speech of some dozen Lines, or
sixteen Lines, which I would set down and
insert in't, could you not?
PLAYER   I, my Lord.   580
HAMLET   Very well, follow that Lord, and look you
mock him not.   *[Exit First Player.]*
– My good Friends, I'll leave you till Night,
You are welcome to Elsonoure.
ROSENCRAUS   Good my Lord.   585
HAMLET   I so, God buy to you.
                    Exeunt [Rosencraus and Guildenstern].
                    – Now I am alone.
O what a Rogue and Peasant Slave am I.
Is it not monstrous that this Player here,
But in a Fixion, in a Dream of Passion,

590   **Conceit**   here, a concept generated and elaborated by imagination.

591   **all the Visage wand**   his face paled to a completely wan (bloodless) complexion. Hamlet is probably combining *waned* and *wanned* here. *Working* recalls lines 141–44.

592   **Distraction . . . Aspect**   a distraught (semi-mad) condition manifested in his expression. Compare I.v.96.

593–   **his . . . Conceit**   all his bodily functions finding external
94   appearances in keeping with his ruling idea. *Conceit* (conception) echoes lines 189–91, 590; see the note to line 213.

595   **Hecuba**   Priam's wife and Troy's Queen.

598   **the Cue**   the prompting reason.

600   **cleave the general Ear**   split the ears of the general populace. Hamlet's imagery mirrors the picture of Pyrrhus in lines 504–27; *general* recalls line 529, and line 600 as a whole anticipates III.ii.9–15.

601   **appale the Free**   make pale (appal) the innocent (those free of guilt), by telling them the tale Hamlet has heard from the Ghost. *Free* echoes line 292 and recalls I.iii.91–93.

602   **Confound**   bewilder.

604   **muddy mettl'd**   equipped with a dull spirit, no better than a metal rendered inferior by its admixture of baser matter. See the note to I.i.91.
       peak   mope, look peaked.

605   **unpregnant of**   not filled to the bursting point with. Compare lines 216–20.

610   **Plucks . . . Beard**   See lines 454–55.

613   **'Swounds**   a contraction of 'God's wounds', an oath referring to the Crucifixion. Compare lines 393, 565.

617   **Offal**   entrails. The word literally means 'off-fall', waste.

618   **kindless**   abominable (see the note to III.ii.41), monstrous (see line 588).

Could force his Soul so to his own Conceit   590
That from her working all the Visage wand,
Tears in his Eyes, Distraction in his Aspect,
A broken Voice, an' his whole Function suiting
With Forms to his Conceit; and all for nothing,
For Hecuba.   595
What's Hecuba to him, or he to her,
That he should weep for her? What would he do
Had he the Motive and the Cue for Passion
That I have? He would drown the Stage with
     Tears
And cleave the general Ear with horrid Speech,   600
Make mad the Guilty and appale the Free,
Confound the Ignorant, and amaze indeed
The very Faculties of Eyes and Ears; yet I,
A dull and muddy mettl'd Rascal, peak
Like John-a-Dreams, unpregnant of my Cause,   605
And can say nothing; no, not for a King,
Upon whose Property and most dear Life
A damn'd Defeat was made. Am I a Coward?
Who calls me Villain, breaks my Pate a cross,
Plucks off my Beard, and blows it in my Face,   610
Tweaks me by the Nose, gives me the Lie i'th'
     Throat
As deep as to the Lungs? Who does me this?
Hah, 'Swounds, I should take it: for it cannot be
But I am Pigeon-liver'd and lack Gall
To make Oppression bitter, or ere this   615
I should 'a fatted all the region Kites
With this Slave's Offal. Bloody, bawdy Villain,
Remorseless, treacherous, lecherous, kindless Villain.
Oh Vengeance!
Why what an Ass am I? This is most brave,   620

621 **a Deer murthered** If this reading from the Second Quarto is correct (the Folio reads 'the Deere murthered'), it probably combines two senses: (a) a murdered deer (the hart, a stag, was sometimes treated as a symbol of royalty, as Hamlet does in III.ii.297), and (b) a dear one murdered. Modern editions normally follow the First and Third Quartos here and print 'a dear father murdered'. Neither of these texts has the authority of the Second Quarto and the First Folio. In line 623, the word *heart* is spelled *hart* in the Quarto. Other words reinforcing *deer* in this soliloquy include 'Rascal' (line 604) and 'dear' (line 607, where the Folio's *deere* is a reminder of the interchangeability of these homonyms); one early meaning of *rascal* is 'a young, lean, or inferior deer'. See the note to I.v.131.

625 **Stallion** a male drab (prostitute). Most modern editions adopt the Folio's *Scullion* (a kitchen servant).

626 **About** either (a) turn around, or (b) get on with it.
Braves bold, boastful displays of valour and defiance (compare line 620). This reading derives from the initial state of the Second Quarto; the revised Quarto reads *braines* (the word to be found in most of today's editions), and the First Folio reads *Brain*.

628 **Cunning** art, skill. See line 473.

629 **presently** immediately.

630 **Malefactions** evil-doings. *Tongue* (line 631) recalls I.ii.243–44, I.iii.59–60, 68–69.

635 **tent** probe.
blench flinch, wince (III.ii.267).

637 **Deale** Devil (compare *Eale* in I.iv.35). The powers Hamlet attributes to the Devil in lines 636–41 were widely assumed to be true. See the notes to I.i.25, 45, I.iv.42, I.v.3, 135, 156, and compare I.iii.125–30.

640 **such Spirits** the souls of persons weakened by melancholy.

641 **Abuses** both (a) deceives, and (b) misuses.

642 **relative** relating to verification. *Grounds* recalls I.v.150, where Hamlet says 'we'll shift our ground'.

That I, the Son of a Deer murthered,
Prompted to my Revenge by Heaven and Hell,
Must like a Whore unpack my Hart with Words
And fall a-Cursing like a very Drab;
A Stallion, fie upon't, foh.   625
About, my Braves. Hum, I have heard
That Guilty Creatures sitting at a Play
Have by the very Cunning of the Scene
Been strook so to the Soul that presently
They have proclaim'd their Malefactions: 630
For Murther, though it have no Tongue, will
   speak
With most miraculous Organ. I'll have these
   Players
Play something like the Murther of my Father
Before mine Uncle; I'll observe his Looks,
I'll tent him to the Quick; if 'a do blench,   635
I know my Course. The Spirit that I have seen
May be a Deale, and the Deale hath Power
T' assume a pleasing Shape, yea, and perhaps
Out of my Weakness, and my Melancholy,
As he is very potent with such Spirits,   640
Abuses me to damn me. I'll have Grounds
More relative than this: the Play's the thing
Wherein I'll catch the Conscience of the King.

                                                    Exit.

III.i   *This scene takes place in Elsinore Castle.*

1   **Conference**   conversation. Here the Folio prints *circumstance*. *Drift* recalls II.i.10, 37.

2   **puts on this Confusion**   adopts such a confused, disruptive mode of behaviour. The King's verb, 'puts on', implies a suspicion that Hamlet is only feigning. Compare I.v.163 and see the notes to I.iii.83, 111, II.i.19, II.ii.397–403, 486–97.

4   **dangerous**   Claudius implies that Hamlet's 'Lunacy' is a threat to the Prince himself (since a melancholic's despair could lead to suicide and thus damnation); but of course the King is primarily concerned about his own security. Compare *Julius Caesar*, I.ii.188–208.

5   **Distracted**   mentally and emotionally disturbed; distraught. We would probably use a word like 'neurosis' to describe what the Elizabethans called 'distraction'. Compare II.ii.592.

7   **forward to be sounded**   willing to have us test him with 'soundings'. The metaphor refers both to (a) verbal sounding (such as that in II.ii.230–341) and (b) nautical sounding, the lowering of lines to plumb for the depth of a body of water.

8   **crafty Madness**   Guildenstern too assumes that Hamlet's 'Madness' is a cunning defensive technique rather than genuine insanity. *Crafty* recalls II.ii.295–98.

9–10   **When ... State**   Guildenstern's remarks provide a reminder that Hamlet has already extracted 'a kind of Confession' from the King's spies (II.ii.295–98), and that the Prince is now plotting the indirect means by which he hopes to unmask 'Guilty Creatures sitting at a Play' (II.ii.627).

11–12   **forcing / Of his Disposition**   What Guildenstern probably means is that, though Hamlet was formally courteous, he also allowed his friends to see that it required some effort on his part to be so. *Disposition* recalls I.ii.168, I.iv.50–55, I.v.159–70, and II.ii.315–24.

12   **Niggard of Question**   not disposed to ask questions or initiate conversations.

13   **of our Demaunds**   in response to our inquiries.

14   **assay him to any Pastime**   attempt to interest him in any pastime. *Assay* recalls II.ii.71.

16   **o'er-raught**   overtook.

ACT III

Scene 1

Enter King, Queen, Polonius, Ophelia, Rosencraus,
Guildenstern, Lords.

KING   An' can you by no Drift of Conference
    Get from him why he puts on this Confusion,
    Grating so harshly all his Days of Quiet
    With turbulent and dangerous Lunacy?
ROSENCRAUS   He dooes confess he feels himself
    Distracted,   5
    But from what Cause 'a will by no means speak.
GUILDENSTERN   Nor do we find him forward to be
    sounded,
    But with a crafty Madness keeps aloof
    When we would bring him on to some Confession
    Of his true State.
QUEEN   Did he receive you well?   10
ROSENCRAUS   Most like a Gentleman.
GUILDENSTERN   But with much forcing
    Of his Disposition.
ROSENCRAUS   Niggard of Question,
    But of our Demaunds most free in his
    Reply.
QUEEN   Did you assay him to any Pastime?
ROSENCRAUS   Madam, it so fell out that certain
    Players   15
    We o'er-raught on the way; of these we told him,
    And there did seem in him a kind of Joy
    To hear of it. They are here about the Court,

22   **the Matter** the material to be performed. Compare I.v.101–3, II.i.70, II.ii.95, 199–201, 469–79, 515–17.

24   **Edge** spur, incitement. This word echoes I.iii.77 and anticipates III.ii.272–74. Claudius' advice in lines 24–25 recalls II.i.67–69 and II.ii.10–18.

26   **two** This is the reading of the Second Quarto; many editors follow the Folio and print *too*. If the Quarto reading is correct, it would appear that the King refers to himself and Polonius, the two who will remain once Ophelia has been 'loosed' to Hamlet. It is also possible, however, that the King simply overlooks Ophelia when calculating the number who really matter from his point of view. After all, in the eyes of the King, Polonius, and Laertes, Ophelia is only a lowly maiden.

28   **as 'twere** as if it were.
    Accident accident. Here the Quarto spelling suggests a derivation from Latin *cedere* (to yield) rather than from *cadere* (to fall). If so, the literal meaning of Polonius' phrase is 'by submitting to circumstance'. Compare III.ii.223, IV.vii.67, 118, V.ii.394.

29   **Affront** meet, encounter.

30   **bestow** stow, hide away. Compare line 41 and II.ii.557–58.

31   **frankly** freely and directly. *Encounter* (which recalls II.ii.167–69) is a word that sometimes carries copulative implications. Compare *Romeo and Juliet*, II.v.29.

36   **happy** fortunate. Compare I.i.129, II.ii.216–20, 238–39, 412.

37   **Wildness** ungovernable behaviour. This word recalls I.v.130, II.i.18, 22.

38   **Wonted** accustomed, normal.

40   **gracious so please you** in a gracious (pious) manner, if you please. Most editors assume that Polonius addresses this phrase and 'We will bestow ourselves' to the King. But nowhere else in Shakespeare is 'Gracious' used alone as a title.

41   **this Book** probably either a devotional manual or a Bible, in view of what Polonius says in lines 42–46 and what Hamlet says in lines 86–87.

42   **Exercise** activity (here referring to a religious meditation).
    colour account for, appear to conform to. Compare I.ii.68, II.ii.295–98, 554–55.

And, as I think, they have already order
This Night to play before him.

POLONIUS   'Tis most true: 20
 And he beseech'd me to entreat your Majesties
 To hear and see the Matter.

KING   With all my Heart,
 And it doth much content me to hear him so
  inclin'd.
 Good Gentlemen, give him a further Edge,
 And drive his Purpose into these Delights.   25

ROSENCRAUS We shall, my Lord.
       Exeunt Rosencraus and Guildenstern.

KING   Sweet Gertrard, leave us two,
 For we have closely sent for Hamlet hether,
 That he, as 'twere by Accedent, may here
 Affront Ophelia; her Father and my self,
 We'll so bestow our selves that, seeing unseen, 30
 We may of their Encounter frankly judge,
 And gather by him, as he is behav'd,
 If't be th' Affliction of his Love or no
 That thus he suffers for.

QUEEN   I shall obey you.
 – And for your part, Ophelia, I do wish   35
 That your good Beauties be the happy Cause
 Of Hamlet's Wildness: so shall I hope your
  Virtues
 Will bring him to his Wonted Way again,
 To both your Honours.

OPHELIA   Madam, I wish it may.

POLONIUS Ophelia, walk you here, gracious so
  please you: 40
 We will bestow our selves. Read on this Book,
 That Show of such an Exercise may colour

43 **Lowliness** pious humility. Modern editions normally adopt the
Folio's *loneliness* here. But what Ophelia is being asked to
'Show' (display) is 'Devotion's Visage' (line 44), the humility
characteristic of 'pious Action' (line 45).
too blame too much to blame, too blameworthy.

44 **prov'd** demonstrated by experience.

48 **plast'ring Art** cosmetics, the 'Art' whose purpose is to disguise
base 'Matter' (II.ii.95).

49 **to** either (a) in the eye of, or (b) compared to.

50 **painted Word** words that cover over ugly thoughts and deeds.

52 **withdraw my Lord** Polonius' phrasing in the Second Quarto
suggests that he and Claudius are standing far enough apart
that they retire to separate hiding places. The Folio reads 'let's
withdraw my Lord', and that would appear to indicate a
staging in which the two eavesdroppers retreat to the same
location.

54 **suffer** endure pain or injury patiently, without resistance.

57 **by opposing** It is not clear whether Hamlet is here referring to
direct self-slaughter or to a Quixotic attack against
overwhelming odds that will result in certain death. In either
event, the outcome will be a release from his 'Sea of
Troubles'.

57–58 **to . . . more** either (a) to 'die' figuratively no more, or (b) to die
in order to sleep no more. The Folio places a comma after die,
and modern editions usually follow suit. Neither of the
authoritative early texts places a comma in the same phrase in
line 61.

59 **Hart-ache** Here the Quarto's *hart* can mean either (a) hart (see
the notes to I.v.131, II.ii.621), or (b) heart (the Folio spelling).

60 **a Consummation** both (a) a conclusion, and (b) a consuming
(annihilation).

61 **Devoutly . . . sleep** The Quarto has no internal punctuation in
this line; the Folio places a full stop after *wish'd*.

62 **Rub** resistance, impediment. The term derives from the game
of bowls, and it refers to anything that throws a bowl off
course. See the second note to II.i.62. *Dream* echoes
II.ii.266–84, 589.

Your Lowliness. We are oft too blame in this,
'Tis too much prov'd, that with Devotion's
  Visage
And pious Action we do sugar o'er   45
The Devil himself.
KING   — O 'tis too true,
How smart a Lash that Speech doth give my
  Conscience.
The Harlot's Cheek beautied with plast'ring
  Art
Is not more ugly to the thing that helps it
Than is my Deed to my most painted Word: 50
O heavy Burthen.

                    Enter Hamlet.

POLONIUS   I hear him coming, withdraw, my Lord.
                    Exeunt [Claudius and Polonius].
HAMLET   To be or not to be, that is the Question;
Whether 'tis Nobler in the Mind to suffer
The Slings and Arrows of outrageous Fortune,   55
Or to take Arms against a Sea of Troubles,
And by opposing end them; to die to sleep
No more, and by a Sleep to say we end
The Hart-ache, and the thousand Natural Shocks
That Flesh is heir to; 'tis a Consummation   60
Devoutly to be wish'd to die to sleep,
To sleep, perchance to dream; ay there's the
  Rub,
For in that Sleep of Death what Dreams may
  come

64   **shuffled . . . Coil** sloughed off this skin (as does a snake when moulting). *Coil* suggests not only (a) the body, but (b) all the toils and turmoils of human life, and (c) a rope or chain coiled around a struggling prisoner. Compare the imagery in II.ii.312–14.

65   **Respect** consideration; matter to take into account.

66   **That . . . Life** (a) that makes suffering so long-lived, and (b) that makes a long life so dreadful.

68   **Contumely** scorn, insulting haughtiness.

70   **Spurns** kicks.

72   **Quietus** settlement of an account (with a play on *quietude*). Hamlet's words can apply either to suicide or to regicide (killing the King). He hesitates because he realizes that either action could result in his damnation. See the second note to I.ii.132.

73   **a bare Bodkin** a simple, unsheathed dagger. Compare II.ii.565. **Fardels** burdens, bundles. See line 64. *Weary* echoes I.ii.133–34.

76   **Borne** bourn; boundary, borders. The spelling in the early texts plays on *bear* (line 73), which itself plays on *bare* in the same line, and on the sense of *borne* that relates to birth. Compare *King Lear*, IV.vi.57, where Edgar uses this word to reinforce his suggestion that his father has just experienced spiritual regeneration.

77   **Traviler** both (a) traveller, and (b) travailer, weary labourer. Compare II.ii.353.

80   **Conscience** both (a) consciousness, and (b) the moral sense.

81   **Native Hew of Resolution** Hamlet puns on *hew* (a swinging stroke with an axe or blade to chop down or slaughter) and *hue* (colour, complexion, vigour), to describe both the natural expression and the in-born disposition (sanguine, blood-red) of courage and resolve.

82   **sickled . . . Thought** Here the Second Quarto's *sickled* combines two basic meanings: (a) sickened, and (b) cut down with a sickle (a curved blade). These cohere with two meanings for *Cast* to yield a complex of related implications: (a) replaced with a pale, sickly cast (complexion), and (b) cut down and left to languish under the cast-off stalks of what has now become a faded overlay of 'Thought'. The Folio's *sicklied* yields only the first set of meanings.

When we have shuffled off this Mortal Coil
Must give us Pause. There's the Respect   65
That makes Calamity of so long Life:
For who would bear the Whips and Scorns of
   Time,
Th' Oppressor's Wrong, the Proud Man's
   Contumely,
The Pangs of despis'd Love, the Law's Delay,
The Insolence of Office, and the Spurns   70
That patient Merit of th' Unworthy takes,
When he himself might his Quietus make
With a bare Bodkin? Who would Fardels bear,
To grunt and sweat under a weary Life,
But that the Dread of something after Death,   75
The undiscover'd Country from whose Borne
No Traviler returns, puzzles the Will,
And makes us rather bear those Ills we have,
Then fly to others that we know not of.
Thus Conscience dooes make Cowards of us all,   80
And thus the Native Hew of Resolution
Is sickled o'er with the Pale Cast of Thought,
And Enterprises of great Pitch and Moment

84 **Regard** consideration; compare *Respect* in line 65.
   their Currents turn awry divert their flow into a channel that
   leads away from 'Action' (the fulfilment of 'Will', line 77) into
   puzzled paralysis. After contemplating his dilemma from the
   perspective of either a Pyrrhus or an 'antique Roman'
   (V.ii.353), Hamlet has allowed Christian 'Regard' to stay his
   hand. Having done so, he now upbraids himself for
   cowardice.

85 **loose** both (a) release, dispense with, and (b) lose. Compare
   I.iii.31, 76 and II.ii.167.

85–86 **Soft . . . Orizons** This line is here punctuated as in the Quarto.
   The Folio places a question-mark after *Ophelia*. The usual
   interpretation of this moment is that Hamlet begins speaking
   to Ophelia only when he addresses her as 'Nymph'; but in the
   Foreword to this volume Derek Jacobi argues that the Prince's
   entire speech (lines 53–87) may be addressed to her.
   Orizons orisons, prayers; probably pronounced 'o-rý-zons'
   here; compare II.ii.489.

98 **Unkind** This is the play's first suggestion that Hamlet has been
   unkind to Ophelia; it probably signals to Hamlet that Ophelia
   is playing a scripted role and is thus not to be trusted.
   Meanwhile it is conceivable that Hamlet is to be represented
   as having heard what an unguarded Polonius says in
   II.ii.220–21. *Unkind* recalls II.ii.618.

112 **the Time gives it Proof** In lines 104–5 and 108–11 Hamlet has
   implied that Ophelia's 'Honesty' (chastity) is failing to shield
   her 'Beauty' from the kind of 'Discourse' that can corrupt a
   maiden. What he probably means is that Ophelia's 'Honesty'
   in another sense (her truthfulness) has been compromised.
   From the comments he made to Polonius in II.ii., it seems
   likely that Hamlet had already concluded that Ophelia's
   'Fishmonger' father is inserting himself into his daughter's
   affairs. When he says 'the Time gives it Proof', then, Hamlet
   probably means that Ophelia's devious behaviour now
   confirms those earlier suspicions. Ophelia's 'Honesty' has
   been transformed into a kind of 'Bawd' who 'looses' her
   Beauty to Hamlet in a way that serves not love but the will of
   her conniving father and his crafty King. What was once a
   'Paradox' (a statement to be treated sceptically) is now proven
   true.

With this Regard their Currents turn awry,
And loose the name of Action. Soft you now,   85
The fair Ophelia, Nymph, in thy Orizons
Be all my Sins rememb'red.

OPHELIA   Good my Lord,
How dooes your Honour for this many a Day?

HAMLET I humbly thank you well.

OPHELIA My Lord, I have Remembrances of yours   90
That I have longed long to redeliver;
I pray you now receive them.

HAMLET No, not I, I never gave you ought.

OPHELIA My honour'd Lord, you know right well you
      did,
And with them Words of so sweet Breath compos'd   95
As made these things more rich; their Perfume
      lost,
Take these again, for to the Noble Mind
Rich Gifts wax poor when Givers prove Unkind;
There my Lord.

HAMLET Ha, ha, are you Honest.   100

OPHELIA My Lord.

HAMLET Are you Fair?

OPHELIA What means your Lordship?

HAMLET That if you be Honest and Fair, your Honesty
should admit no Discourse to your Beauty.   105

OPHELIA Could Beauty, my Lord, have better
Commerce than with Honesty?

HAMLET Ay truly, for the Power of Beauty will
sooner transform Honesty from what it is to a
Bawd than the Force of Honesty can translate   110
Beauty into his Likeness; this was sometime a
Paradox, but now the Time gives it Proof. I
did love you once.

OPHELIA Indeed my Lord, you made me believe so.

115–   **Virtue . . . it**   we cannot graft virtue onto our original stock so
17   thoroughly as to remove all traces of the original plant.
        Hamlet echoes the same doctrines as in II.ii.565–69. The
        Second Quarto reading, *euocatat* (evocutate), is not
        impossible to defend; it could be a coinage deriving from
        evoke or evocate, 'to call up', and it could refer to an
        exorcism, a spiritual uprooting of 'our old Stock', rather than
        to the less radical remedy of inserting a new bud or 'eye' into
        a trunk (the original meaning of *inoculate*) that otherwise
        retains its original nature.

119   **Nunn'ry**   convent. *Nunnery* could also mean brothel, and that
        ambiguity colours even the lines in which Hamlet appears to
        be advising Ophelia to seclude herself from the 'Resort' of
        men (II.ii.148).

120–   **indifferent Honest**   as virtuous as (no different from) the next
21   person. *Indifferent* recalls II.ii.236.

124   **beck**   call, command.

133   **play the Fool**   be the fool he is. This phrase could refer to the
        activities of a 'Fishmonger' (II.ii.178), either a bawd or a
        frequenter of brothels, and to the role of a witting or
        unwitting sexual tool. See *Antony and Cleopatra*, I.i.13,
        where Antony is described as a 'Strumpet's Fool'.

136–   **this Plague for thy Dowry**   this curse as your wedding
37   settlement. *Chast* (*chaste*) recalls I.iii.31.

138   **Calumny**   slander.

140   **Fool**   Here Hamlet means a man who has been fooled (deceived
        and turned into a laughing-stock) by an unfaithful wife.

141   **Monsters**   horned cuckolds (cheated husbands). See II.ii.588.

145   **Paintings**   use of cosmetics. Compare lines 48–50.

147   **gig and amble**   move or dance in a lewd or suggestive way.
        Most editions emend *gig* to *jig*, of which it was a variant
        form; but the Folio spelling, *gidge*, suggests a different
        pronunciation here. Compare III.ii.131.
        list   (a) incline yourself in a seductive manner to men you seek
        to attract, and (b) listen to their blandishments as they seek to
        give you what you list (desire). See the note to I.v.21. Most of
        today's editions adopt the Folio's *lisp* in this passage.

HAMLET   You should not have believ'd me, for Virtue   115
cannot so inoculate our old Stock but we shall
relish of it; I loved you not.

OPHELIA   I was the more deceived.

HAMLET   Get thee to a Nunn'ry, why would'st thou be
a Breeder of Sinners? I am my self indifferent   120
Honest, but yet I could accuse me of such
things that it were better my Mother had not
borne me: I am very Proud, Revengeful,
Ambitious, with more Offences at my beck than
I have Thoughts to put them in, Imagination to   125
give them Shape, or Time to act them in. What
should such Fellows as I do crawling between
Earth and Heaven? We are arrant Knaves all, believe
none of us. Go thy ways to a Nunn'ry. Where's
your Father?   130

OPHELIA   At home, my Lord.

HAMLET   Let the Doors be shut upon him, that he
may play the Fool no where but in's own House.
Farewell.

OPHELIA   – O help him, you sweet Heavens.   135

HAMLET   If thou doost marry, I'll give thee this
Plague for thy Dowry: be thou as Chast as Ice,
as Pure as Snow, thou shalt not escape Calumny.
Get thee to a Nunn'ry, farewell. Or if thou
wilt needs marry, marry a Fool, for Wise Men   140
know well enough what Monsters you make of
them: to a Nunn'ry go, and quickly too,
farewell.

OPHELIA   – Heavenly Powers restore him.

HAMLET   I have heard of your Paintings well enough;   145
God hath given you one Face and you make your
selfs another; you gig and amble, and you list;

148 **nickname God's Creatures**   probably both (a) give wanton names to your lovers and their bodily parts, and (b) misname (by transforming into scorned victims) the men you use, trick, and ridicule. Compare IV.vii.164–67.

148– **make your Wantonness Ignorance**   both (a) when you get
49 caught, pretend that you didn't know what you were doing (see *As You Like It*, IV.i.162–87), and (b) become so inured to wantonness and to ignoring your conscience that you grow ignorant of the fact that you are lascivious. See *Othello*, III.iii.392–95, *Troilus and Cressida*, II.iii.31–34, *Romeo and Juliet*, III.iii.132, and *Macbeth*, I.v.58–60, for references to the ignorance that results from wilful neglect.

149– **I'll no more on't**   I'll have no more of it. Hamlet cannot bear to
50 be reminded of or to re-enact what his father suffered.

151 **moe**   more. Lines 150–53 echo 1 Corinthians 7:7–9, where the Apostle Paul says 'to the unmarried and widows, It is good for them if they abide even as I do. But if they cannot abstain, let them marry: for it is better to marry than to burn.'

156 **Th' Expectation . . . State**   the heir apparent and favourite of the state. The Folio prints *expectancy*.

157 **Glass of Fashion**   mirror (exemplar) of dress and appearance.

159 **Deject**   both (a) cast down, and (b) rejected.

161 **what**   Most editors adopt *that* from the Folio.

162 **out of Time**   with no order or rhythm. The Folio prints *out of tune*, an idea conveyed by *Harsh*. Compare III.iv.137–38. *Sovereign Reason* recalls I.iv.72–73.

163 **blown Youth**   youth in full bloom.

164 **Blasted with Ecstasy**   blighted with madness; beside itself. *Blasted* echoes I.iv.40; *Ecstasy* recalls II.i.98 and anticipates III.iv.72.

167 **Form**   formal order, the self-control of deliberate discourse. *Affections* recalls II.ii.475–77. Compare Polonius' comments in II.ii.212–14.

169 **sits on brood**   sits brooding, like a mother bird incubating eggs until they are ready to hatch and yield a brood of offspring.

you nickname God's Creatures, and make your
Wantonness Ignorance; go to, I'll no more
on't, it hath made me mad. I say we will have   150
no moe Marriage; those that are married
already, all but one shall live, the rest
shall keep as they are. To a Nunn'ry go.   *Exit.*
OPHELIA O what a Noble Mind is here o'erthown!
The Courtier's, Soldier's, Scholar's Eye,
  Tongue, Sword,   155
Th' Expectation and Rose of the fair State,
The Glass of Fashion and the Mould of Form,
Th' Observ'd of all Observers, quite quite
  down,
And I of Ladies most Deject and Wretched,
That suck'd the Honey of his Music'd Vows;   160
Now see what Noble and most Sovereign Reason,
Like sweet Bells jangled out of Time, and Harsh,
That unmatch'd Form, and Stature of blown Youth
Blasted with Ecstasy; O woe is me,
T' have seen what I have seen, see what I see.   165

Enter King and Polonius.

KING Love, his Affections do not that way tend,
Nor what he spake, though it lack'd Form a
  little,
Was not like Madness; there's something in his
  Soul
O'er which his Melancholy sits on brood,

170 **doubt** fear. See II.ii.56, 118–21.

Disclose disclosure [of what the egg contains]. Brutus uses a similar image to justify his decision to intercept another source of Danger 'in the Shell' before it can hatch (*Julius Caesar*, II.i.32–34).

172– **I have . . . down** This announcement, in which the King
73 imparts information new to Polonius, would seem most compatible with a staging in which they have watched Hamlet and Ophelia from different hiding places. See the note to line 52. We should also observe that the King and Polonius engage in private conversation, ignoring the distraught Ophelia. See the note to line 26.

174 **neglected Tribute** overdue payment. Claudius refers to the Danegeld, a fee the English paid the Vikings in exchange for a degree of security from complete domination; see IV.iii.58–65. Here the 'Tribute' is probably 'neglected', in part, because the Danes have been remiss about enforcing it.

175 **Haply** both (a) perhaps, and (b) happily (it is to be hoped). Compare line 36.

176 **variable Objects** new sights (to distract his attention).

177 **something settled** unidentified but somewhat firmly fixed. *Matter* echoes line 22.

179 **From Fashion of himself** away from his normal behaviour. *Fashion* recalls line 157.

182 **How now** how are you? *Sprung* echoes *Springes* (I.iii.114).

186 **entreat** urge.

187 **show his Grief** reveal what troubles him. Compare I.ii.3, 82, 94, II.i.115.
round open, unrestrained.

189 **find him not** fail to discover what is really on his mind. *Conference* (dialogue) echoes line 1.

192 **unmatch'd** unengaged, neglected. In due course Claudius and his nephew will be match'd even more emphatically; compare III.iv.205–6. Most of today's editions opt for the Folio's *unwatch'd* in this line.

And I do doubt the Hatch and the Disclose   170
Will be some Danger; which for to prevent,
I have in quick Determination
Thus set it down: he shall with speed to
    England
For the Demaund of our neglected Tribute.
Haply the Seas, and Countries different,   175
With variable Objects, shall expel
This something settled Matter in his Heart,
Whereon his Brains still beating puts him thus
From Fashion of himself. What think you on't?
POLONIUS   It shall do well. But yet do I believe   180
The Origin and Commencement of his Grief
Sprung from neglected Love. — How now,
    Ophelia?
You need not tell us what Lord Hamlet said,
We heard it all. — My Lord, do as you please,
But if you hold it fit, after the Play,   185
Let his Queen-Mother all alone entreat him
To show his Grief; let her be round with him,
And I'll be plac'd (so please you) in the Ear
Of all their Conference. If she find him not,
To England send him: or confine him where   190
Your Wisdom best shall think.
KING   It shall be so:
Madness in Great Ones must not unmatch'd go.
                                        Exeunt.

III.ii This scene takes place in the Castle. As it opens, Hamlet is advising the Players on how to perform their parts.

2 **trippingly** skippingly, with lightness, ease, and rapidity. In this line *pronounc'd* derives from the Folio. The Quarto's *pronoun'd* is probably a misprint, though it would be in keeping with the egotism of Hamlet's advice in this speech to have him 'pronoun' to the Players about a craft they practise as seasoned professionals and he pronounces upon only as an amateur critic and adapter of other dramatists' works.

3 **mouth it** speak it with laboured, exaggerated delivery.

4 **as live** as lief; as soon, as willingly.

6 **use all gently** moderate your gestures, in the manner of a suave gentleman.

8 **acquire and beget** obtain (through training) and deliver (in performance).

9 **Temperance** restraint, self-control. Compare III.iv.137.

10 **robustious** blustering, excessively histrionic.

11 **Periwig-pated** wig-covered (and thus looking pretentious). **Totters** tatters, scraps.

12 **spleet** split. Compare II.ii.597–603, where Hamlet offers a justification for 'Horrid Speech'.

13 **Groundlings** members of the audience who paid only a penny to enter and who stood in the pit, the yard surrounding the stage.

13–14 **capable of** able to appreciate.

14 **inexplicable Dumb-shows** inscrutable pantomimes. Hamlet's point seems to be that what the dumb-shows signify is beyond the comprehension of the groundlings. *Noise* probably refers to loud declamation, shouting, and excessive sound effects. See the passage cited in the note to line 12.

16 **Termagant** like Herod, a ranting tyrant in medieval mystery plays; he was a Saracen deity, traditionally presented as a counterpart to Muhammad.

20 **Discretion** judgement. Compare II.i.113, II.ii.502.

22 **Observance** concern, point of caution.

Scene 2

Enter Hamlet, and three of the Players.

HAMLET   Speak the Speech, I pray you, as I
pronounc'd it to you, trippingly on the Tongue;
but if you mouth it as many of our Players do,
I had as live the Town Crier spoke my Lines.
Nor do not saw the Air too much with your   5
Hand thus, but use all gently, for in the very
Torrent, Tempest, and, as I may say, Whirlwind
of your Passion, you must acquire and beget a
Temperance that may give it Smoothness. O it
offends me to the Soul to hear a robustious   10
Periwig-pated Fellow tear a Passion to Totters,
to very Rags, to spleet the Ears of the
Groundlings, who for the most part are capable
of nothing but inexplicable Dumb-shows, and
Noise. I would have such a Fellow whipp'd for   15
o'er-doing Termagant: it out-Herods Herod, pray
you avoid it.
PLAYER   I warrant your Honour.
HAMLET   Be not too Tame neither, but let your own
Discretion be your Tutor; suit the Action to   20
the Word, the Word to the Action, with this
special Observance, that you o'er-step not the

23   **Modesty of Nature** norms and manners of ordinary human behaviour. See the notes to II.ii.297, 473.

24   **from** a departure from.
    End objective, rationale; what Aristotle referred to as a 'final cause'. *Purpose* recalls II.ii.295.

26   **as 'twere** so to speak.

28   **Age and Body of the Time** historical setting and physical realities of the period (as represented both in the play and in the audience). Compare II.ii.363–95, 557–62, III.i.155–64.

28–29 **his Form and Pressure** its defining shape and impression (as in a seal). *Form* echoes III.i.167, *Pressure* I.v.98–100.

29–30 **come tardy off** underdone (performed with hesitancy or inadequacy).

30   **Unskilful** the unknowing, undiscriminating 'General' (II.ii.469).

31   **the Judicious** those with sophisticated taste and judgement. See II.ii.466–79.

32   **Censure** judgement (either approving or disapproving). This word recalls I.iii.69, I.iv.34–35, and anticipates line 94.
    Allowance reckoning, consideration.

34–35 **and . . . prais'd** heard that others praised. Most modern editions adopt the Folio's *praise* in line 35.

39–40 **Nature's Journeymen** Nature's day-labourers (rather than Nature or God).

41   **abhominably** the normal Shakespearean spelling of *abominably*. The word was thought to derive from *ab homine* (Latin for 'away from humanity', un-human).

42   **indifferently** well enough, tolerably. See III.i.120–21.

46   **set down** scripted. This phrase anticipates line 48 and recalls I.iii.121–22, I.iv.64, I.v.106–8, 180, II.ii.80, 208–9, 473, 576–79, III.i.168–77.

48   **barrain** barren. The Second Quarto spelling suggests wordplay on *bare*, *rain*, and *brain*. See the second note to III.iii.22, and compare *The Merchant of Venice*, I.iii.135.

49   **necessary Question** crucial issue. Compare II.ii.380–82.

Modesty of Nature: for anything so o'er-doone
is from the Purpose of Playing, whose End,
both at the first and now, was and is, to hold   25
as 'twere the Mirror up to Nature, to shew
Virtue her Feature, Scorn her own Image, and
the very Age and Body of the Time his Form and
Pressure. Now this over-done, or come tardy
off, though it makes the Unskilful laugh,   30
cannot but make the Judicious grieve, the
Censure of which One must in your Allowance
o'er-weigh a whole Theatre of Others. O there
be Players that I have seen play, and heard
others prais'd, and that highly, not to speak   35
it profanely, that neither having th' Accent
of Christians, nor the Gait of Christian,
Pagan, nor Man, have so strutted and bellowed
that I have thought some of Nature's
Journeymen had made Men, and not made them well,   40
they imitated Humanity so abhominably.

PLAYER   I hope we have reform'd that indifferently
with us.

HAMLET   O reform it altogether. And let those
that play your Clowns speak no more than is   45
set down for them, for there be of them that
will themselves laugh, to set on some quantity
of barrain Spectators to laugh too, though
in the mean time some necessary Question of
the Play be then to be considered; that's   50

51 **pitiful Ambition** lamentable arrogance (here the overweening audacity of a mere player who believes himself superior both to the play and to the intentions, the 'purpose', of the playwright). *Ambition* recalls II.ii.264–79, III.i.120–26.

52 **uses it** does it. See II.ii.559.

55 **presently** immediately.

S.D. **Exeunt they two** This stage direction, from the Second Quarto, indicates the departure of Rosencraus and Guildenstern.

59 **howe** ho. Hamlet is bidding Horatio to come. In the early texts that appear to derive from Shakespeare's own manuscripts, the 'how' spelling for 'ho' or 'hoa' is quite common.

61 **just** probably both (a) honest, and (b) judicious (line 31).

62 **As ... withal** as I have ever encountered in my dealings with people. *Copt withal* means 'coped with', encountered.

63 **flatter** curry favour by telling pleasing lies.

65 **Revenue** wealth, income; here accented on the second syllable.

68–69 **crook ... Fawning** curtsy where profit may derive from obsequious bowing and scraping. Here *crook* means 'bend'; *pregnant Hinges* refers to 'ready knee-joints', eager to discharge their devotion to 'absurd Pomp', fools in positions of power. Compare I.ii.50–56, II.ii.26–32. *Thrift* (thriving, prosperity) echoes I.ii.179–80.

70 **dear** precious. See the note to II.ii.621.
    Mistress of her Choice in a position to decide for herself.

71 **And could ... Election** and could make a selection from the men she had to choose from. Hamlet has spoken about the factors that inhibit 'Election' in I.iv.11–37; compare I.iii.14–28, 103–5, 122–35, I.v.94–103, II.ii.266–68, III.i.53–85.

74 **Buffets** blows (as from a boxer). *Suff'ring* echoes III.i.53–57.

Villainous, and shews a most pitiful Ambition
in the Fool that uses it. Go make you ready.

Exeunt Players.

Enter Polonius, Guildenstern, and Rosencraus.

– How now, my Lord, will the King hear this
piece of Work?

POLONIUS   And the Queen too, and that presently.   55

HAMLET   Bid the Players make haste. – Will you two
help to hasten them?

ROSENCRAUS   Ay my Lord.   *Exeunt they two.*

HAMLET   – What howe, Horatio.

Enter Horatio.

HORATIO   Here, sweet Lord, at your Service.   60

HAMLET   Horatio, thou art e'en as just a Man
As ere my Conversation copt withal.

HORATIO   O my dear Lord.

HAMLET   Nay do not think I flatter,
For what Advauncement may I hope from thee
That no Revenue hast but thy good Spirits   65
To feed and clothe thee? Why should the Poor
   be flatter'd?
No, let the candied Tongue lick absurd Pomp,
And crook the pregnant Hinges of the Knee
Where Thrift may follow Fawning. Doost thou
   hear,
Since my dear Soul was Mistress of her Choice,   70
And could of Men distinguish her Election,
S' hath seal'd thee for her self; for thou
   hast been
As one in suff'ring all that suffers nothing,
A Man that Fortune's Buffets and Rewards
Hast ta'en with equal Thanks; and blest are
   those   75

76 **Blood** emotions, passions. See I.iii.6, II.i.34.
co-meddled mingled. In lines 70–81 Hamlet defines Horatio as a man of exemplary objectivity and self-control.

78 **Stop** fingering for a particular note on a recorder or other musical instrument. Compare lines 372–402. *Fortune's Finger* is probably to be thought of as lustful and whorish; see II.ii.238–46. *Sound* recalls III.i.7.

80 **I** both 'I' and 'ay'. Compare II.ii.575, III.ii.305, 324.

82 **to night** tonight. See I.v.140.

83 **Circumstance** pertinent details. This word recalls I.v.124.

86 **Comment** noting; consideration, observation.

87 **occulted** hidden, secret.

88 **unkennel** come out of hiding (like a rabbit or fox being driven out of its hole or lair in a hunt).

90 **foul** filthy, besmudged, wicked.

91 **Vulcan's Stithy** the forge of Vulcan, blacksmith of the Gods. Vulcan's 'Imaginations' were 'foul' too, because he suspected, correctly, that his wife Venus was turning him into one of society's 'Monsters' (III.i.141) by sleeping with Mars. Eventually Vulcan caught the two lovers in a snare, as Hamlet hopes to do with his own 'Mousetrap' (line 261) for Claudius (and perhaps the Queen). Because of his blackness, Vulcan was also associated with Hell.
heedful Note attentive scrutiny.

93 **after** afterwards.

94 **Censure of his Seeming** This phrase can mean something as neutral as 'assessment of his behaviour'; but in fact Hamlet appears to have made up his mind already that the King will only be 'Seeming' (feigning) if he appears unaffected by the play. The 'Purpose' of Hamlet's 'Playing' (line 24) will be to obtain grounds for 'Censure' (condemnation) of a murderer. He assumes that his stagecraft will disclose the King's statecraft. *Censure* echoes line 32.

95 **steal ought** steal anything; manage to get away with any guilty behaviour that a good detective should catch (line 96).

96 **detected** either (a) being detected, or (b) having been detected. The Folio prints *detecting*, and most of today's editions follow suit.

Whose Blood and Judgement are so well co-meddled,
That they are not a Pipe for Fortune's Finger
To sound what Stop she please. Give me that
    Man
That is not Passion's Slave, and I will wear him
In my Heart's Core, I, in my Heart of Heart   80
As I do thee. Something too much of this.
There is a Play to night before the King;
One Scene of it comes near the Circumstance
Which I have told thee of my Father's Death;
I prethee when thou seest that Act a-foot,   85
Even with the very Comment of thy Soul
Observe my Uncle; if his occulted Guilt
Do not it self unkennel in one Speech,
It is a damned Ghost that we have seen,
And my Imaginations are as foul   90
As Vulcan's Stithy. Give him heedful Note,
For I mine Eyes will rivet to his Face,
And after we will both our Judgements join
In Censure of his Seeming.
HORATIO   Well, my Lord,
  If a' steal ought the whilst this Play is
    playing   95
  And scape detected, I will pay the Theft.

Enter Trumpets and Kettle-drums, King, Queen,
Polonius, Ophelia, Rosencraus, Guildenstern, and other
Lords Attendant, with his Guard carrying Torches.
Danish March. Sound a Flourish.

97–98 **be idle**   resume my antic disposition.

100–1 **of the Chameleon's Dish**   fed like a chameleon (thought to be able to draw sustenance from the air). The reference to feeding recalls I.ii.143–45, 179–80, I.v.30–33, 54–56, II.ii.52, 84, 472–78, and anticipates, III.iii.8–10.

101 **Promise-cramm'd**   Hamlet implies that the promises he has received are so much thin air (heir). He is alluding to the King's assurance that Hamlet is the heir apparent to the throne (I.ii.109) – rather than the rightful King even now. See the notes to I.ii.109, II.ii.213, 276–78, 304–5.

102 **Capons**   castrated male chickens, which are fattened up before being slaughtered and served.

103–4 **I have . . . mine**   I refuse to acknowledge that any of these words have anything to do with me.

110–11 **I . . . me**   The same actor who first spoke these lines as Polonius had probably performed Julius Caesar a few months before *Hamlet* joined *Julius Caesar* in the Globe repertory. Meanwhile the same actor who played Brutus (Richard Burbage) would surely have been playing Hamlet. An Elizabethan audience would thus have enjoyed multiple ironies in an exchange that proves both retrospective and prophetic.

112 **Brute part**   both (a) a brutish, brutal act, and (b) the part of Brutus. Shakespeare probably intends an additional reference to the ancestral Brutus, who feigned an antic disposition (idiocy) of his own in order to outwit and in time defeat the tyrannical Tarquins and found the Roman Republic in 509 BC. Hamlet may also be alluding to *Brutus* as a name meaning dull and brutish. See the note to I.v.163.

116–17 **Mettle more attractive**   Hamlet compares Ophelia to a magnetic metal. Compare I.i.91. *Lap* (line 118) recalls II.ii.238–39.

122 **Country Matters**   Hamlet puns on the sound of the first syllable to imply that Ophelia thought him to be referring to 'Women's matters' (*Julius Caesar*, I.i.27), female genitalia.

HAMLET   They are coming to the Play. I must be
   idle.
Get you a place.

KING   How fares our Cousin Hamlet?

HAMLET   Excellent i' faith, of the Chameleon's   100
   Dish: I eat the Air, Promise-cramm'd. You
   cannot feed Capons so.

KING   I have nothing with this Aunswer, Hamlet,
   these Words are not mine.

HAMLET   No, nor mine now, my Lord. – You play'd   105
   once i'th' University, you say.

POLONIUS   That did I, my Lord, and was accounted
   a good Actor.

HAMLET   What did you enact?

POLONIUS   I did enact Julius Caesar, I was kill'd   110
   i'th' Capital: Brutus kill'd me.

HAMLET   It was a Brute part of him to kill so
   Capital a Calf there. – Be the Players ready?

ROSENCRAUS   Ay my Lord, they stay upon your
   Patience.

QUEEN   Come hether, my dear Hamlet, sit by me.   115

HAMLET   No, good Mother, here's Mettle more
   attractive.

POLONIUS   – O ho, do you mark that.

HAMLET   Lady, shall I lie in your Lap?

OPHELIA   No, my Lord.

HAMLET   I mean, my Head upon your Lap?   120

OPHELIA   Ay, my Lord.

HAMLET   Do you think I meant Country Matters?

123 **Nothing** another common name for what lies 'between Maids' Legs' (lines 124–25) based on the Elizabethan jest that a female either has 'no thing' or has one that resembles the figure for nothing (o). In line 129 Hamlet may be playing on *I* and *eye* as figures for the male and female genitalia; meanwhile *onely* (only) in line 131 may be punning on *one* (1) as another symbol for the male member in its 'keen' state (line 272).

131 **Jig-maker** either (a) a composer, or (b) a performer of jigs, the comic song-and-dance routines that followed a play. *Jig* recalls *gig* in III.i.147.

132 **merry** mischievously (here erotically) playful, carefree. Hamlet alludes to such biblical passages as Ecclesiastes 8:15 ('Then I commended mirth, because a man hath no better thing under the sun, than to eat, and to drink, and to be merry'), Isaiah 22:13 ('let us eat and drink: for to morrow we shall die'), and Luke 12:19 ('And I will say to my soul, Soul, thou hast much goods laid up for many years; take thine ease, eat, drink, and be merry').

134 **within's two Hours** within these [last] two hours.

136– **Nay . . . Sables** In that case, let's cast my black mourning
37 apparel to the Devil [traditionally depicted as wearing black], because I'll now outfit myself in luxurious sable furs [also dark, but not associated with mourning]. See II.ii.486.

141 **build Churches** have his name memorialized in the chapels he has endowed.

142 **not thinking on** not being thought about (remembered).
with the Hobby-horse along with the Hobby-horse character in the May Day celebrations that took place in the English countryside before the Puritans put a stop to them. The tradition called for a man to wear a hooped costume resembling a horse; he chased and cornered maidens, and his actions were designed to suggest the movements of a male in pursuit of copulative fulfilment.

143 **Epitaph** tombstone memorial. The words Hamlet goes on to quote are from a ballad mourning the demise of May Day festivities.

146– **makes Shew of Protestation** puts on a display of her devotion.
47

OPHELIA   I think Nothing, my Lord.

HAMLET   That's a fair Thought to lie between Maids'
Legs.   125

OPHELIA   What is, my Lord?

HAMLET   Nothing.

OPHELIA   You are merry, my Lord.

HAMLET   Who, I?

OPHELIA   Ay, my Lord.   130

HAMLET   O God, your onely Jig-maker, what should
a man do but be merry? For look you how
cheerfully my Mother looks, and my Father
died within's two Hours.

OPHELIA   Nay, 'tis twice two Months, my Lord.   135

HAMLET   So long? Nay then let the Dev'l wear Black,
for I'll have a Suit of Sables. O Heavens, die
two Months ago, and not forgotten yet; then
there's Hope a Great Man's Memory may out-live
his Life half a Year. But by'r Lady 'a must   140
build Churches then, or else shall 'a suffer
not thinking on, with the Hobby-horse, whose
Epitaph is 'For O, for O, the Hobby-horse
is forgot.'

The Trumpet sounds. Dumb-show follows.

Enter a King and Queen very lovingly, the Queen   145
embracing him and he her. She kneels and makes
Shew of Protestation unto him. He takes her up, and

154   **passionate Action**   uncontrolled lamentation. In this line *with* functions as if it were *and*.

155   **condole**   mourn, commiserate.

158   **harsh**   The Folio substitutes *loath and unwilling* for this word. *Harsh* recalls III.i.162, where it means 'discordant'.

160   **munching Mallico**   mouthing malice (referring to the exaggerated 'munching' gestures of the dumb-show actors as they mime speech and enact malice). *Mallico* probably derives from *malhecho* (Spanish for malefaction, evil deed). Modern editors normally substitute the Folio's *Miching* (usually interpreted to mean 'sneaking') for *munching*, the adjective to be found in the Second Quarto text of the play. Compare 'make Mouths at' (II.ii.390–91) and 'mouth it' (III.ii.3).

162   **Belike**   likely, probably.
  imports the Argument   implies the theme (story). See II.ii.380–82.

165   **keep**   The Folio reads *keep Counsel* (maintain a secret); that spells out Hamlet's implication.

167   **Show**   display. As Ophelia's reply (line 170) makes clear, Hamlet refers to a show of flesh, and probably to an overt display of erotic behaviour. *Show*, spelled *shew* in the Folio, may involve wordplay on *shoe*, another term for the female pudendum; see *The Two Gentlemen of Verona*, II.iii.19–20, where Launce says that 'this Shoe with the Hole in it is my Mother'.

170   **naught**   naughty.
  mark   pay attention to. Ophelia's point is that rather than listen to Hamlet's bawdy innuendo, she will focus on the play.

173   **stooping to your Clemency**   bowing to beg your mercy.

175   **the Posy of a Ring**   a motto (usually in verse) engraved inside a ring. *Posy* is an abbreviated form of *poesy*, 'poetry'. *Ring* was another word that frequently referred to a woman's maidenhead, and Hamlet plays on that sense of 'the Posy of a Ring' in line 177. See the note to line 123, and compare II.ii.458–60. For similar play on *Ring*, see *The Merchant of Venice*, V.i.193–208, 258–59, 306–7.

declines his Head upon her Neck; he lies him
down upon a Bank of Flowers; she, seeing him
asleep, leaves him; anon comes in an other Man,   150
takes off his Crown, kisses it, pours Poison
in the Sleeper's Ears, and leaves him. The
Queen returns, finds the King dead, and makes
passionate Action. The Pois'ner with some
three or four come in again, seem to condole   155
with her. The dead Body is carried away. The
Pois'ner woos the Queen with Gifts; she seems
harsh awhile, but in the end accepts love.

OPHELIA   What means this, my Lord?
HAMLET   Marry this munching Mallico, it means   160
  Mischief.
OPHELIA   Belike this Show imports the Argument
  of the Play.
HAMLET   We shall know by this Fellow.

Enter Prologue.

The Players cannot keep, they'll tell all.   165
OPHELIA   Will 'a tell us what this Show meant?
HAMLET   Ay, or any Show that you will show him;
  be not you asham'd to show, he'll not shame
  to tell you what it means.
OPHELIA   You are naught, you are naught, I'll mark   170
  the Play.
PROLOGUE   For us and for our Tragedy,
                  Here stooping to your Clemency,
                  We beg your Hearing patiently.
HAMLET   Is this a Prologue, or the Posy of a Ring?   175
OPHELIA   'Tis brief, my Lord.
HAMLET   As Woman's Love.

Enter [the Player] King and Queen.

178 **Phoebus' Cart**   the chariot of the Sun God.

179 **Neptune's salt Wash**   the ocean, of which Neptune was the god
in Roman mythology. Compare I.i.113–15.
Tellus' orbed Ground   the Earth, of which Tellus was the
Roman goddess. *Orbed* echoes II.ii.520–21.

180 **borrowed Sheen**   reflected brightness.

182 **Hymen**   the Greek God of Marriage.

183 **Bands**   both (a) wedding bands (rings), and (b) the bonds of
matrimony. See I.ii.24, and see the note to I.ii.9.

185 **doone**   done; here spelled to rhyme with *Moon*.

187 **your**   This pronoun derives from the Folio printing. The Second
Quarto's *our* is not out of the question, however; it could
refer to the 'former State' of a couple who were once closer
and healthier than they are now. Since a husband and his wife
are ideally to be 'one flesh' (see the note to IV.iii.52), the
'State' of either party to a union would be shared by the other
party to what both would regard as 'our' condition.

188 **distrust you**   fear for your health.

189 **Discomfort**   worry, trouble.

191 **hold Quantity**   weigh equally in the balance.

192 **Either . . . Extremity**   either holding no quantity (neither
weighing anything) or both holding maximum quantity
(weighing as much as possible). The Player Queen's image
depicts Fear and Love as two quantities being weighed on a
set of scales. Her point is that, whether light or heavy, they
are of equal weight. See the note to II.ii.243, and compare
Hamlet's remarks on the need to avoid 'Extremity' in lines
1–52. *Ought* (aught) echoes line 95.

193 **Proof**   experience (which has proven it).

194 **is ciz'd**   is in size. The Quarto spelling recalls II.ii.497; here it
may play on an aphetic (frontally abbreviated) form of either
incis'd (engraved, as in line 175) or *exercised*.

198 **operant**   vital, living.
leave   begin ceasing. This sense of *leave* plays on that in line
197.

200 **haply**   both (a) perhaps, and (b) happily. Compare III.i.175.

[PLAYER] KING   Full thirty times hath Phoebus' Cart
   gone round
Neptune's salt Wash, and Tellus' orbed Ground,
And thirty dozen Moons with borrowed Sheen   180
About the World have times twelve thirties been
Since Love our Hearts, and Hymen did our Hands
Unite co-mutual in most sacred Bands.
[PLAYER] QUEEN   So many Journeys may the Sun
   and Moon
Make us again count o'er ere Love be doone.   185
But Woe is me, you are so Sick of late,
So far from Cheer, and from your former State,
That I distrust you: yet though I distrust,
Discomfort you, my Lord, it nothing must.
For Women fear too much, even as they love,   190
And Women's Fear and Love hold Quantity,
Either None, in neither Ought, or in Extremity;
Now what my Love is Proof hath made you know,
And as my Love is ciz'd, my Fear is so;
Where Love is great, the littlest Doubts are Fear,   195
Where little Fear grows great, great Love
   grows there.
[PLAYER] KING   Faith I must leave thee, Love, and
   shortly too,
My operant Powers their Functions leave to do,
And thou shalt live in this fair World behind,
Honour'd, belov'd, and haply one as kind   200
For Husband shalt thou –
[PLAYER] QUEEN   O confound the rest,
Such Love must needs be Treason in my Breast;
In Second Husband let me be accurst,

204 **None ... first** either (a) let none wed a second husband but those who killed their first, or (b) no women wed second husbands but those who killed their first husbands.

205 **Wormwood** Hamlet refers to a herb whose extract was a bitter-tasting oil. The Nurse says that she applied it to her dug to wean the infant Juliet (*Romeo and Juliet*, I.iii.26, 30). Hamlet probably means either (a) 'that's so much wormwood' or (b) 'that's the bitter truth'.

206-7 **The Instances ... Thrift** the considerations that motivate second marriage are base calculations of profit. *Respects* recalls III.i.65–66; *Thrift* echoes lines 68–69.

211 **determine** resolve to bring to pass.

213 **Validity** strength, health, staying power.

215 **Mellow** ripe. What the Player King says in lines 212–15 is that Purpose holds firm for about as long as it takes a fruit to ripen and fall to the ground of its own accord. *Purpose* echoes lines 23–29.

218 **propose** propose to do, state as our purpose.

220– **The Violence ... destroy** Because of the violent passions
21 (irrational impulses) they entail, both Grief and Joy sow the seeds of destruction for any 'Enactures' (avowed purposes) they prompt in the very moment when such vows are sworn; because as soon as the passion that gave rise to the vow subsides, the vow subsides with it.

223 **on slender Accident** on the basis of insupportable chance circumstances. The Second Quarto spelling, reproduced here, can mean either (a) accident, circumstance, or (b) accedence (from *accede*, 'agree to' or 'enter upon'). See the note to III.i.28. The Quarto form *griefes* (grieves) could have been dictated by a desire for rhetorical balance with *Grief*; but the *selfes* form in III.i.147 suggests that *-fes* endings may have been an authorial predilection.

224 **aye** ever.

226 **prove** put to the test. *Question* echoes line 49.

229 **The Poor ... Enemies** The unworthy man, once he is up in fortune, discovers that his former enemies are now eager to be his friends.

None wed the second, but who kill'd the first.

HAMLET That's Wormwood. 205

[PLAYER] QUEEN The Instances that second Marriage
    move
  Are base Respects of Thrift, but none of Love;
  A second time I kill my Husband dead
  When second Husband kisses me in Bed.

[PLAYER] KING I do believe you think what now you
    speak, 210
  But what we do determine, oft we break:
  Purpose is but the Slave to Memory,
  Of violent Birth, but poor Validity,
  Which now the Fruit Unripe sticks on the
    Tree,
  But fall unshaken when they Mellow be. 215
  Most necessary 'tis that we forget
  To pay our selves what to our selves is Debt;
  What to our selves in Passion we propose,
  The Passion ending, doth the Purpose lose;
  The Violence of either, Grief or Joy, 220
  Their own Enactures with themselves destroy;
  Where Joy most revels, Grief doth most lament,
  Grief joys, Joy griefes, on slender Accedent;
  This World is not for aye, nor 'tis not strange
  That even our Loves should with our Fortunes
    change; 225
  For 'tis a Question left us yet to prove,
  Whether Love lead Fortune, or else Fortune Love.
  The Great Man down, you mark his Favourite
    flies,
  The Poor, advaunc'd, makes Friends of Enemies;

230 **hetherto** hitherto, up to now.
    doth Love on Fortune tend does Love prove to be subservient
      to Fortune.

231 **not needs** needs none.

232 **Want** need, poverty.
    try put to test, call upon for help.

233 **Directly . . . Enemy** immediately turns him into, or proves him
    to be, an enemy (by applying the 'season' of 'Want', need, to
    him and finding him wanting). *Seasons* recalls II.i.28.

234 **orderly** in an orderly fashion.

235 **Wills and Fates** desires (motives) and fortunes.

236 **Devises still** devices (plans) always.

237 **their Ends** what will happen to them under the pressure of time
    and changing circumstances.

240 **Nor** neither.

243 **Anchor's . . . Scope** let my freedom and comfort be limited to
    that of a religious hermit's (anchorite's) fare in his solitude.
    Cheer can mean (a) disposition, well-being, (b) countenance,
    and (c) entertainment (food and hospitality).

244 **Each Opposite** every obstacle or reversal.
    blanks turns white (by removing blood from the complexion).

250 **fain I would beguile** gladly would I divert and thereby cheat
    (by escaping it through sleep). Compare *A Midsummer
    Night's Dream* V.i.39–41, where Theseus calls for an
    'Abridgement' to 'beguile / The Lazy Time'. See the notes to
    II.ii.450 (on 'Abridgement') and I.iii.130 (on 'beguide').

256 **the Argument** a thematic summary of the action to be
    dramatized. See line 162.

257 **Offence** offending (seditious or blasphemous) material.

258 **in jest** in sport. Hamlet means 'it's only a play', not real life.

And hetherto doth Love on Fortune tend,   230
For who not needs shall never lack a Friend;
And who in Want a Hollow Friend doth try
Directly seasons him his Enemy.
But orderly to end where I begun,
Our Wills and Fates do so contrary run   235
That our Devises still are overthrown;
Our Thoughts are ours, their Ends none of our
    own.
So think thou wilt no second Husband wed,
But die thy Thoughts when thy first Lord is
    dead.
[PLAYER] QUEEN   Nor Earth to me give Food, nor
    Heaven Light,   240
Sport and Repose lock from me Day and Night,
To Desperation turn my Trust and Hope,
And Anchor's Cheer in Prison be my Scope;
Each Opposite that blanks the Face of Joy
Meet what I would have well, and it destroy;   245
Both here and hence pursue me lasting Strife,
If, once I be a Widow, ever I be a Wife.
HAMLET   If she should break it now.
[PLAYER] KING   'Tis deeply sworn, Sweet, leave me
    here a while,
My Spirits grow Dull, and fain I would beguile   250
The tedious Day with Sleep.
[PLAYER] QUEEN   Sleep rock thy Brain,   *Sleeps.*
And never come Mischance between us Twain.
                                                      Exit.
HAMLET   Madam, how like you this Play?
QUEEN   The Lady doth protest too much, me thinks.
HAMLET   O but she'll keep her Word.   255
KING   Have you heard the Argument? Is there no
    Offence in't?
HAMLET   No, no, they do but jest, poison in jest,
    no Offence i'th' World.

261 **Mary** an oath referring to the Virgin Mary. By Shakespeare's time it was usually spelled *marry* and meant 'indeed' or 'truly'.

Tropically figuratively. The word derives from the Greek word *trope* (literally, turn or twist), and it refers to any use of language that is other than strictly straightforward. *Tropically* is itself a trope (play or spin) on *trap*, here a device to 'catch the Conscience of the King' (II.ii.643).

264 **knavish** Hamlet probably means 'depicting knavery'. But *knavish* could also mean (a) crude, amateurish (because produced by a mere knave, a young page), and (b) villainous, wicked (the usual modern sense of the word). *Piece of Work* echoes II.ii.324, III.ii.54.

266 **Free Souls** souls free of guilt, with free consciences. *Free* recalls I.iii.93, II.ii.291–92, 601, and III.i.13.

266– **Let the galled Jade winch** let the chafed jade (a worn-out
67 horse) wince. Compare II.ii.626–43.

267 **Withers** the ridges between a horse's shoulder blades.
unwrong not pinched tight (wrung) and thus chafed, rubbed sore, because not 'wrong' (guilty).

270– **I could . . . dallying** Hamlet compares himself to the Chorus
71 who 'interprets' (provides running commentary) for a puppet show. Here *dallying* refers to both (a) playful dangling, and (b) erotic foreplay. Compare the innuendo in lines 165–77 and in III.i.103–53.

272 **keen** Ophelia probably means (a) sharp-witted, but in line 273 Hamlet takes her to mean (b) sexually aroused (compare the play on 'point' in I.v.126). *Edge* echoes I.iii.77, III.i.24; *Groaning* recalls II.ii.123.

275 **Still better and worse** yet wittier and naughtier.

276 **mistake** Hamlet means 'mis-take' (deceive, abuse), with a reference to the phrase 'for better, for worse' in the marriage ceremony.

277 **leave** cease, abandon (compare lines 197–98).

KING   What do you call the Play?   260
HAMLET   The Mousetrap. Mary how? Tropically. This
  Play is the Image of a Murther doone in Vienna;
  Gonzago is the Duke's name, his Wife Baptista;
  you shall see anon. 'Tis a knavish Piece of
  Work, but what of that? Your Majesty, and we   265
  that have Free Souls, it touches us not. Let
  the galled Jade winch, our Withers are unwrong.

Enter Lucianus.

This is one Lucianus, Nephew to the King.
OPHELIA   You are as good as a Chorus, my Lord.
HAMLET   I could interpret between you and your   270
  Love if I could see the Puppets dallying.
OPHELIA   You are keen, my Lord, you are keen.
HAMLET   It would cost you a Groaning to take off
  mine Edge.
OPHELIA   Still better and worse.   275
HAMLET   So you mistake your Husbands. – Begin,
  Murtherer, leave thy damnable Faces and begin;

278 **Raven** a black bird of evil omen, proverbially associated with retribution. Compare *Julius Caesar*, V.i.83, and *The Tempest*, I.ii.320–22.

279 **Revenge** by introducing the theme of revenge, Hamlet manages a neat variation on both Claudius' crime and the crime depicted in 'The Murther of Gonzago' (there too the villain is motivated by lust and ambition rather than by revenge). Meanwhile, by presenting the 'Nephew to the King' (line 268) as the murderer, Hamlet sends Claudius a signal that another king's nephew is brooding over another regicide.

281 **Considerate Season** the time well considered (chosen prudently). The Folio prints *Confederate* (cooperative). *Season* echoes line 233.
else no Creature seeing otherwise no one else around to see.

282 **rank** foul, evil. Compare I.ii.136, I.v.33–37, II.i.20.
of out of, from.

283 **Hecat's Ban** the curse (probably with a play on *bane*, poison) of the Goddess associated with magical arts. Puck invokes 'Triple Hecate' (Cynthia, Diana, and Persephone) in the Epilogue to *A Midsummer Night's Dream*. *Hecat* also figures prominently in *Macbeth*; see II.i.50–51, III.v.1–36.
blasted blighted, withered. See III.i.164.
invected both (a) cursed (from *invective*, denunciation), and (b) imported, introduced. The Folio prints *infected*.

S.D. **Powres** pours (with the same wordplay on 'powers' as in *Macbeth*, I.v.28, IV.i.18).

292 **False Fire** a shot with a blank [empty] shell. This line occurs only in the First Folio.

297– **Why . . . play** The *Deer* and *Hart* imagery recalls II.ii.620–25.
98 See the note to I.v.131.

299 **watch** both (a) stay awake, and (b) observe.

302 **turn Turk with me** betray me. The Muhammadan Turks were viewed as untrustworthy infidels.

304 **Fellowship . . . Players** part ownership in an acting troupe. Hamlet alludes to the plumes ('Feathers') and rosette-adorned shoes worn by the players. *Cry*, a hunting term, compares the 'Players' to a pack of clamorous hounds in hot pursuit of the 'strooken Deer' (line 297). Compare IV.ii.31–32, where Hamlet says, 'Hide, Fox, and all after.'

come, the croaking Raven doth bellow for
Revenge.

LUCIANUS Thoughts black, Hands apt, Drugs fit,
    and Time agreeing, 280
Considerate Season, else no Creature seeing.
– Thou Mixture rank, of Midnight Weeds
    collected,
With Hecat's Ban thrice blasted, thrice
    invected,
Thy natural Magic, and dire Property,
On wholesome Life usurps immediately. 285

                  Powres the Poison in his Ears.

HAMLET 'A poisons him i'th' Garden for his Estate;
his name's Gonzago; the Story is extant, and
written in very choice Italian; you shall see
anon how the Murtherer gets the Love of
Gonzago's Wife. 290

OPHELIA The King rises.

HAMLET What, frighted with False Fire.

QUEEN How fares my Lord?

POLONIUS Give o'er the Play.

KING Give me some Light, away. 295

POLONIUS Lights, Lights, Lights.

              Exeunt all but Hamlet and Horatio.

HAMLET Why let the strooken Deer go weep,
       The Hart ungalled play,
    For some must watch while some must sleep,
       Thus runs the World away. 300
Would not this, Sir, and a Forest of Feathers,
if the rest of my Fortunes turn Turk with me,
with provincial Roses on my raz'd Shoes, get
me a Fellowship in a Cry of Players?

HORATIO Half a Share.

HAMLET   A whole one, I. 305

306 **Damon** a poetic shepherd's name here chosen, perhaps, to recall an era before the fall of the 'Realm'. *Dear* plays on *deer*, lines 297–98.

307–8 **This . . . himself** This clause is usually interpreted to mean 'this kingdom was stripped away [literally dis-mantled, its mantle stolen] from Jove himself [Hamlet's father]'. Another possibility is that *of* means 'from' or 'by', in which case Hamlet is saying that 'Jove himself' (the present King) is the usurping dismantler. In either case, Hamlet now feels sure he has the 'Grounds / More relative' he was seeking. Compare the *mantle* imagery in *Julius Caesar*, III.ii.172, 197–98.

309 **Pajock** a pun on (a) peacock, and (b) patchock (base savage).

310 **rim'd** The word *Ass* would have provided the expected rhyme in line 309; Hamlet's substitution allows him to convey both that notion and the stronger one he imports with *Pajock*.

311 **I'll . . . Word** Hamlet believes that the King's reaction has confirmed the truth of the Ghost's testimony. Whether this 'trial' has also proved the Ghost to be the spirit of Hamlet's father, however, is another question. In I.iii.121–22 of *Macbeth* Banquo notes that 'oftentimes to win us to our Harm, / The Instruments of Darkness tell us Truths.' It is conceivable that an 'honest' (truth-telling) ghost may not be 'an Honest Ghost' (I.v.135), a benign spirit.

316 **Recorders** wind instruments with eight air holes. Evidently Hamlet addresses this request to one or more of the Players; whether they are on stage at this point, however, is not clear. See the Quarto stage directions following lines 296, 370.

318 **perdy** by God (from the French *pardieu*).

320 **voutsafe** vouchsafe, grant.

326 **distemper'd** disturbed with a passion (in this case 'Choler', anger) beyond tempering or controlling by reason. See the note to line 9.

331 **Purgation** cure (a treatment to remove disease by bleeding). See the note to II.ii.18. Hamlet implies that if he purged the King, he would make his condition worse, (a) by submerging him in even more choler (the King's own bile), or (b) by subjecting him to even more bile (the rage prompting Hamlet to thrust a sword into him, or (c) by plunging him to his death in a hangman's collar. Compare *Romeo and Juliet*, I.i.1–5.

> For thou dcost know, O Damon dear,
>   This Realm dismantled was
> Of Jove himself, and now raigns here
>   A very very Pajock.

HORATIO   You might have rim'd.   310

HAMLET   O good Horatio, I'll take the Ghost's Word
for a thousand Pound. Did'st perceive?

HORATIO   Very well, my Lord.

HAMLET   Upon the Talk of the Poisoning.

HORATIO   I did very well note him.   315

HAMLET   – Ah ha, come some Music, come the
Recorders:

> For if the King like not the Comedy,
> Why then belike he likes it not perdy.

– Come, some Music.

Enter Rosencraus and Guildenstern.

GUILDENSTERN   Good my Lord, voutsafe me a Word   320
with you.

HAMLET   Sir, a whole History.

GUILDENSTERN   The King, Sir.

HAMLET   I Sir, what of him?

GUILDENSTERN   Is in his Retirement mervilous   325
distemp'red.

HAMLET   With Drink, Sir?

GUILDENSTERN   No, my Lord, with Choler.

HAMLET   Your Wisdom should shew it self more
richer to signify this to the Doctor, for for me to   330
put him to his Purgation would perhaps plunge
him into more Choler.

333– **put . . . Frame** control what you are saying. Compare the
34   King's remarks in III.i.166–68.

334– **stare . . . Affair** do not act like a wide-eyed madman when I
35   come to you on the King's affairs. Modern editors normally
      adopt the Folio's *start*, but *stare* conveys the crazed look that
      Guildenstern seems to be associating with Hamlet's 'wild and
      whirling Words' (I.v.130). Compare *Julius Caesar*,
      III.i.98–99, IV.ii.321–22.

339   **welcome** well come. Hamlet extends the courtesy due an
      ambassador.

340   **Curtesy** courtesy. But here as elsewhere Shakespeare plays on
      cur (see *Breed* in line 341).

342   **wholesome Aunswer** proper (polite) and fitting response. In
      lines 347–48 Hamlet plays on another sense of *wholesome*
      (healthy, a word that means 'whole').

348   **diseas'd** both (a) unhealthy, and (b) ill at ease (dis-eased),
      disturbed.

353   **Admiration** astonishment.

354   **wonderful** to be wondered at, marvelled over.

356   **Impart** disclose. This word recalls I.iv.58. Meanwhile the
      imagery of line 355 echoes I.ii.147–49.

358   **Closet** private chamber.

359– **We . . . Mother** I would obey her even if she were my mother
60   ten times over. Alluding to the commandment that children
      are to 'honour' their mothers (Exodus 20:12), Hamlet implies
      that he will obey the Queen despite the fact that she is his
      mother, rather than because of it.

360   **Trade** commerce. This word, combined with Hamlet's use of
      the royal plural ('us'), implies that he regards his old
      schoolmates as nothing more than the King's mercenaries. He
      has used similar terminology in II.ii.178 and III.i.104–11.

362   **Pickers and Stealers** hands. Hamlet alludes to the Anglican
      Catechism, which exhorts against 'picking and stealing'.

364   **Distemper** disturbance. See line 326.

364– **You do surely . . . Friend** Rosencraus probably means that
66   Hamlet fails to avail himself of a source of comfort if he
      denies himself the chance to unburden himself to a friend. But
      his words could also be interpreted as a threat that Hamlet
      risks incarceration if he does not become more forthcoming.

GUILDENSTERN   Good my Lord, put your Discourse
into some Frame, and stare not so wildly from
my Affair.   335
HAMLET   I am tame, Sir, pronounce.
GUILDENSTERN   The Queen your Mother, in most
great Affliction of Spirit, hath sent me to you.
HAMLET   You are welcome.
GUILDENSTERN   Nay good my Lord, this Curtesy   340
is not of the right Breed; if it shall please you
to make me a wholesome Aunswer, I will do your
Mother's Commaundement; if not, your Pardon and
my Return shall be the end of my Business.
HAMLET   Sir, I cannot.   345
ROSENCRAUS   What, my Lord?
HAMLET   Make you a wholesome Answer; my Wit's
diseas'd; but Sir, such Answer as I can make,
you shall commaund, or rather, as you say, my
Mother. Therefore no more, but to the Matter: 350
my Mother, you say.
ROSENCRAUS   Then thus she says: your Behaviour
hath strook her into Amazement and Admiration.
HAMLET   O wonderful Son, that can so 'stonish a
Mother; but is there no Sequel at the Heels   355
of this Mother's Admiration? Impart.
ROSENCRAUS   She desires to speak with you in her
Closet ere you go to Bed.
HAMLET   We shall obey, were she ten times our
Mother. Have you any further Trade with us?   360
ROSENCRAUS   My Lord, you once did love me.
HAMLET   And do still, by these Pickers and Stealers.
ROSENCRAUS   Good my Lord, what is your Cause of
Distemper? You do surely bar the Door upon
your own Liberty if you deny your Griefs to   365
your Friend.

367   **Advancement** promotion to my rightful position. Compare
      II.ii.255–78.

371   **I** both 'I' and 'Ay'. Compare line 80.
      While the Grass grows The proverb concludes with the words
      'the Steed starves'. See lines 99–102.

372– **O the Recorders** Hamlet addresses this line to one of the
 73   Players. He has called for them in lines 316 and 319; either
      they have taken this long to respond, or they have held back
      while Hamlet conversed with Rosencraus and Guildenstern.

373– **To withdraw with you** to speak privately. As he speaks,
 74   Hamlet probably draws Guildenstern aside.

374– **to recover the Wind of me** to get to the windward side of me.
 75   Hamlet compares Guildenstern to a hunter stalking prey and
      using the wind to carry his scent to the animal, thereby
      frightening it to run in the direction of the snare awaiting a
      victim.

375   **Toil** snare, net. See the notes to lines 91, 304.

376– **if my Duty . . . unmannerly** if in my show of duty I appear to
 77   be too forward, it is only because my love is so great that it
      sometimes offends as a result of excessive zeal.

384   **Touch** technique, skill.

386   **Ventages** vents, stops. Compare lines 74–78, where Hamlet
      commends Horatio for his ability to avoid being Fortune's
      plaything.

391   **utterance of Harmony** harmonious sound. To *utter* is to speak
      out. *Skill* echoes lines 29–33.

395   **the Heart of my Mystery** my essence, the core of my being.
      Here as elsewhere the Quarto spelling is *hart*. See the note to
      line 297.
      sound both (a) make a full gamut of sounds, and (b) measure
      depth. See line 78. *Top* (line 396) recalls II.ii.471 and
      anticipates line 415.

397   **Compass** range. Compare II.i.9–12.

398   **Organ** instrument (the recorder). Lines 392–402 echo
      II.ii.626–32.

HAMLET   Sir, I lack Advauncement.

ROSENCRAUS   How can that be, when you have the
Voice of the King himself for your Succession
in Denmark?   370

Enter the Players with Recorders.

HAMLET   I Sir, but 'While the Grass grows . . .'
The Proverb is something musty. – O the
Recorders, let me see one. – To withdraw with
you, why do you go about to recover the Wind
of me, as if you would drive me into a Toil?   375

GUILDENSTERN   O my Lord, if my Duty be too bold,
my Love is too unmannerly.

HAMLET   I do not well understand that: will you
play upon this Pipe?

GUILDENSTERN   My Lord, I cannot.   380

HAMLET   I pray you.

GUILDENSTERN   Believe me, I cannot.

HAMLET   I do beseech you.

GUILDENSTERN   I know no Touch of it, my Lord.

HAMLET   It is as easy as Lying. Govern these   385
Ventages with your Fingers and Thumb;
give it Breath with your Mouth, and it will
discourse most eloquent Music; look you,
these are the Stops.

GUILDENSTERN   But these cannot I commaund to   390
any utterance of Harmony, I have not the Skill.

HAMLET   Why look you now, how unwoorthy a thing
you make of me: you would play upon me, you
would seem to know my Stops, you would pluck
out the Heart of my Mystery, you would sound   395
me from my Lowest Note to the Top of my
Compass; and there is much Music, excellent
Voice, in this little Organ, yet cannot you
make it speak. 'Sblood, do you think I am

401–2 **though . . . me** even though you don't pretend to have the
expertise to manipulate me as a trained musician bows or
plucks a stringed instrument (one with 'frets', or bars of wood
or wire, to guide the positioning of the fingers), and even if
you manage to avoid vexing me (another meaning of 'fret')
with your invasions of my privacy, you will still not be able to
have your way with me, not only because of your lack of skill,
but also because I will not let you 'play upon me' as if I were
'what Instrument you will'. Hamlet is probably punning on a
third, architectural sense of 'fret': make ridges and furrows in
my brow like the fretwork (carved or embossed patterns made
up of intersecting lines) in a ceiling. Compare line 415, where
the protagonist says, 'They fool me to the top of my Bent.'

405 **presently** right away. *Shape* (line 407) recalls I.ii.82, I.iv.42,
I.v.53, II.ii.638, III.i.123–26.

411 **It is back'd** it has a back.

414 **by and by** shortly.

415 **fool me** toy with me. See the notes to III.i.140, 148.
top of my Bent to the limit of my ability to bear it patiently.
Bent recalls II.ii.30. Like a fully taut crossbow, Hamlet is at
the 'Sticking Place'; he is ready to 'bend up / Each corporal
Agent to [the] terrible Feat' he feels compelled toward
(*Macbeth*, I.vii.60, 79–80). *Top* echoes line 396.

419 **Witching Time** midnight, when the forces of evil are most
potent. Hamlet is thinking of the witches' sabbath, when
witches were said to drink human blood.

420 **breaks out** pops open (like a festering boil) and releases.
Compare III.iv.141–46 and IV.iv.24–26 for similar disease
imagery. The Folio prints *breaths*, and most modern editions
print *breathes*.

422 **bitter Day** Hamlet may be referring to Judgement Day. It
seems more likely, however, that his immediate subject is
daylight, which is now bitter for him because of the situation
in which he finds himself.

423 **Soft** hush. Hamlet summons himself to attention.

easier to be play'd on than a Pipe? Call me   400
what Instrument you will, though you fret me not,
you cannot play upon me. God bless you, Sir.

Enter Polonius.

POLONIUS   My Lord, the Queen would speak with
you, and presently.   405
HAMLET   Do you see yonder Cloud that's almost in
shape of a Camel?
POLONIUS   By th' Mass and 'tis, like a Camel
indeed.
HAMLET   Me thinks it is like a Weasel.   410
POLONIUS   It is back'd like a Weasel.
HAMLET   Or like a Whale.
POLONIUS   Very like a Whale.
HAMLET   Then I will come to my Mother by and by.
They fool me to the top of my Bent. I will   415
come by and by.
POLONIUS   I will say so.   *Exit.*
HAMLET   'By and by' is easily said. – Leave me,
Friends.   [*Exeunt all but Hamlet.*]
– 'Tis now the very Witching Time of Night,
When Churchyards yawn, and Hell it self
breaks out   420
Contagion to this World: now could I drink hote
Blood
And do such Business as the bitter Day
Would quake to look on. Soft, now to my Mother.

424   **loose** both (a) release, surrender, and (b) lose. Compare
        III.i.85. *Hart* (*Heart* in the Folio) echoes line 395.
        thy Nature your share of human nature. Hamlet is exhorting
        himself not to be so caustic with his mother that he forgets
        that he is her son.

425   **Nero** Nero executed his mother Agrippina after she poisoned
        her husband, the Emperor Claudius.

426   **Cruel** stern (III.iv.126), rigorous.

428   **Hypocrites** liars, deceivers (to each other). Hamlet may be
        aware that in Greek the word for actor is *hypocrite*; if so,
        what he is saying is that his tongue and his soul should play
        different roles and try thereby to keep each other separate, the
        tongue being cruel, the soul kind. Compare *Julius Caesar*,
        II.i.160–81, 222–26.

429– **How . . . consent** however she may be rebuked ('shent', put to
30   shame) in my words, to give them the seals of my approval
        without allowing my soul to become a party to the deeds the
        harsh judgements would seem to call for.

III.iii This scene takes place in the King's chambers of the Castle.

1   **I like him not** I am not pleased with his behaviour.

2   **range** have free rein.

3   **Commission** official authorization of responsibilities.
        dispatch prepare in an expeditious fashion.

5   **The terms of our Estate** my position as King.

7   **his Brows** Shakespeare frequently treats threatening brows
        (here symbolic of a brooding mind) as symbols of imminent
        danger. Compare I.ii.4, II.i.85–87.
        provide make ready.

8   **holy and religious Fear** Guildenstern alludes to the
        commonplace that the monarch is God's deputy on Earth, and
        that the good of the commonwealth is dependent on his
        health and security. This doctrine derives ultimately from
        Romans 13:1–7.

– O Hart, loose not thy Nature, let not ever
The Soul of Nero enter this firm Bosom;   425
Let me be Cruel, not Unnatural.
I will speak Daggers to her, but use none;
My Tongue and Soul in this be Hypocrites,
How in my Words somever she be shent,
To give them Seals, never my Soul consent.   *Exit.*   430

Scene 3

Enter King, Rosencraus, and Guildenstern.

KING   I like him not, nor stands it safe with us
  To let his Madness range: therefore prepare
     you,
  I your Commission will forthwith dispatch,
  And he to England shall along with you.
  The terms of our Estate may not endure   5
  Hazard so near's as doth hourly grow
  Out of his Brows.
GUILDENSTERN   We will our selves provide:
  Most holy and religious Fear it is
  To keep those many many Bodies safe

10 **That . . . Majesty** Guildenstern's imagery is interesting. It hints
at a kind of cannibalism, and it suggests that the King's
subjects are a 'Convocation of politic Worms' (IV.iii.19). It
also suggests a perversion of the Communion service
instituted at the Last Supper. See Matthew 26:26, where we
read that 'Jesus took the bread, and when he had blessed, he
brake it, and gave it to the disciples, and said, Take, eat: this
is my body.' See the note to III.ii.102.

11 **peculiar** individual (physical and mortal).

13 **Noyance** annoyance, mortal danger.

14 **Weal** well-being (literally, wealth, as in *commonweal*).
Rosencraus alludes to the doctrine that the King's mystical
body and the Body Politic are 'one flesh', in a relationship that
resembles holy matrimony and mirrors the 'marriage' between
Christ and his Church; see Ephesians 5:21–33. Hamlet
alludes to the political theology of the King's two bodies –
physical ('single and peculiar', line 11) and spiritual (lines
14–15) – in II.ii.276–78 and in IV.ii.26–31.

15 **Cesse** cessation, cease.

16 **Gulf** whirlpool.

17 **massy** massive.

18 **Somnet** summit. Compare I.iv.68–73.

20 **mortis'd** notched. *Adjoin'd* echoes I.ii.9, 20.

21 **Annexment** appendage.

22 **Attends** accompanies.
boist'rous Rain tumultuous downpour. Most of today's
editions adopt the Folio's *Ruine*. But the Quarto's *raine* may
be intended as an allusion to the parable of the house built
upon sand (Matthew 7:24–27). A number of Rosencraus'
phrases echo that narrative. It is possible that the 1623 Folio
reading was influenced by the version of the parable in other
translations. For example, in the 1611 King James Bible's
rendering of Luke 6:49, we are told about 'a man that
without a foundation built / an house upon the earth; against
which the stream did beat vehemently, and immediately it fell;
and the ruin of that house was great'. *Rain* is a homonym of
reign and *rein*, of course, and in Claudius' regime both will
soon become increasingly 'boist'rous'. See the notes to
III.ii.48, 307–8, V.i.229, and compare lines 45–46.

That live and feed upon your Majesty.   10
ROSENCRAUS   The single and peculiar Life is bound
  With all the Strength and Armour of the Mind
  To keep it self from Noyance, but much more
  That Spirit upon whose Weal depends and rests
  The Lives of many. The Cesse of Majesty   15
  Dies not alone, but like a Gulf doth draw
  What's near it with it; or it is a massy Wheel
  Fix'd on the Somnet of the highest Mount,
  To whose huge Spokes ten thousand lesser
    things
  Are mortis'd and adjoin'd, which when it falls   20
  Each small Annexment, petty Consequence,
  Attends the boist'rous Rain. Never alone

23 **sigh** suffer pain. *Groan* echoes III.ii.273–74.

24 **Viage** voyage.

25 **Fetters** shackles, to impede the leg movements of a prisoner.
Fear source of danger. Compare I.i.116.

29 **the Process** the proceedings, what transpires.
I'll . . . home I guarantee she'll take him to task.

31 **then** than. But once again *then* provides a meaning that will
prove ironically apt. Compare I.ii.228.

33 **of Vantage** from a more objective point of view (an
advantageous perspective that is not 'partial', line 32).
Farre Fare. But the Quarto spelling emphasizes that the
original sense of this word was 'travel'. Polonius little suspects
that he will be the one who embarks on a journey before the
King goes to bed.

36 **rank** rotten, foul. See III.ii.282.

37 **primal eldest Curse** the curse associated with the original
murder, Cain's slaughter of Abel (Genesis 4).

39 **as sharp as Will** as powerful as all that the human will can
summon. *Sharp* echoes *keen* (III.ii.272), and *Will* calls
attention to the lust that prompted Claudius' crimes; see the
note to I.ii.60. Meanwhile *Inclination* provides yet another
clue that the King's 'Will' will be difficult to put down; see
Pericles, IV.iii.104–6, 153–56, where Boult talks about how
Marina's 'Beauty stirs up the lewdly inclin'd'.

41 **to . . . bound** both (a) committed to two equally demanding
tasks, and (b) bound (directed) to conflicting destinations.

42 **I stand in Pause** Claudius' condition recalls that of Pyrrhus in
II.ii.509–17. The 'Mousetrap' *has* caught 'the Conscience of
the King' (II.ii.643), and now the issue is in doubt: will he or
won't he repent?

43 **both neglect** fail to do either. Compare III.i.180–82.

46 **wash . . . Snow** Claudius' words recall several biblical
passages, among them Isaiah 1:18 ('Come now, and let us
reason together, saith the Lord: though your sins be as scarlet,
they shall be as white as snow') and Matthew 27:24 ('When
Pilate saw that he could prevail nothing, but that rather a
tumult was made, he took water, and washed his hands
before the multitude, saying, I am innocent of the blood of
this just person'). *Rain* echoes line 22.

Did the King sigh, but with a general Groan.

KING   Arm you, I pray you, to this speedy Viage,

For we will Fetters put about this Fear,   25

Which now goes too free-footed.

ROSENCRAUS   We will haste us.

Exeunt Gentlemen.

Enter Polonius.

POLONIUS   My Lord, he's going to his Mother's
    Closet.

Behind the Arras I'll convey my self

To hear the Process. I'll warrant she'll tax
    him home;

And as you said, and wisely was it said,   30

'Tis meet that some more Audience then a
    Mother,

Since Nature makes them partial, should
    o'erhear

The Speech of Vantage. Farre you well, my Liege;

I'll call upon you ere you go to Bed,

And tell you what I know.

KING   Thanks, dear my Lord.   35

Exit [Polonius].

 — O my Offence is rank, it smells to Heaven,

It hath the primal eldest Curse upon't,

A Brother's Murther. Pray can I not,

Though Inclination be as sharp as Will:

My stronger Guilt defeats my strong Intent,   40

And like a Man to double Business bound,

I stand in Pause where I shall first begin,

And both neglect. What if this cursed Hand

Were thicker than it self with Brother's Blood,

Is there not Rain enough in the sweet Heavens   45

To wash it white as Snow? Whereto serves Mercy

49–50 **To . . . down** Claudius echoes the Lord's Prayer: 'And forgive us our debts, as we forgive our debtors. And lead us not into temptation, but deliver us from evil' (Matthew 6:12–13).

52 **serve my Turn** be of help in my situation. Again Claudius' phrasing provides an ironic counterpoint to his insufficiently 'strong Intent' to turn himself over to Heaven. *Turn* was a term for an illicit sexual encounter, as illustrated in *Titus Andronicus*, II.i.95–97, and *Othello*, IV.i.256–58.

54 **Effects** gains, possessions. *Possess'd* echoes I.v.67.

56 **retain th' Offence** Unless he surrenders what his guilt has gained him, Claudius observes he must retain the guilt itself.

57 **Currents** courses (with wordplay on *currencies*).

58 **guilded Hand** both (a) gold-covered (because of the wealth and hypocrisy of the offender), and (b) gold-bearing (to bribe Justice). Here as in *Macbeth*, II.ii.53–54, *guilded* plays on *guilt*.

shove by Justice push Justice aside. This reading is from the Folio; the Second Quarto's 'showe by iustice', while by no means impossible, is difficult to relate to the other imagery in this speech. Claudius seems to be thinking about a board game, now known as shove-halfpenny, in which players competed by shoving, or shuffling, small coins towards their desired positions.

59–60 **the . . . Law** the ill-gotten gains themselves are used to bribe the Law to look the other way. Claudius' own situation is an illustration of this principle; the Queen he has won through his crime has brought him a throne and the support of a Council that has 'freely gone / With this Affair along' (I.ii.15–16).

61 **There is no Shuffling** there no sleight of hand is allowed.

61–62 **there . . . Nature** there (before God) the case (legal 'Action') is presented in its true character, with no trickery. Since Claudius' 'Action' depends upon 'lies' for its success in 'this World', his words do 'double Business' here.

64 **rests** remains (with wordplay on resting a case). Claudius will soon conclude that 'the Rest is Silence' (V.ii.370).

65 **can** can do.

But to confront the Visage of Offence?
And what's in Prayer but this two-fold Force,
To be forestalled ere we come to fall,
Or pardon being down? Then I'll look up.   50
My Fault is past, but oh what form of Prayer
Can serve my Turn? Forgive me my foul Murther:
That cannot be, since I am still possess'd
Of those Effects for which I did the Murther,
My Crown, mine own Ambition, and my Queen.   55
May one be pardon'd and retain th' Offence?
In the corrupted Currents of this World,
Offence's guilded Hand may shove by Justice,
And oft 'tis seen the Wicked Prize it self
Buys out the Law. But 'tis not so Above: 60
There is no Shuffling, there the Action lies
In his true Nature, and we our selves compell'd,
Even to the Teeth and Forehead of our Faults,
To give in Evidence. What then, what rests?
Try what Repentance can. What can it not?   65
Yet what can it when one cannot repent?
O wretched State, O Bosom black as Death,

68   **limed**   trapped, as in a sticky snare of birdlime. Hamlet has succeeded in his effort to 'catch the Conscience of the King' (II.ii.643). Will he now wish to see Claudius set 'free' (see line 26, and compare III.ii.266) by a repentance that removes him from office, results in his public confession and execution, and sends a redeemed sinner to Heaven? See *Macbeth*, I.iv.1–11.

69   **make Assay**   make an attempt. Compare II.i.59–63.

70   **Hart**   both (a) heart, and (b) hart (king). Compare III.ii.297, 395.

71   **borne**   both (a) born, and (b) carried. Compare I.iv.14, I.v.180, V.i.155.

73   **but**   Most of today's editions adopt the Folio's *pat*. Since the Quarto reading makes good sense, there is no compelling reason to change it.

75   **scann'd**   examined more carefully.

79   **Hire and Salary**   Here the Folio reading is much more plausible than the Second Quarto's *base and silly*; it provides a suitable contrast to *Revenge* (opposing a noun with a noun phrase), and it coheres with the financial metaphors that dominate Hamlet's remarks as well as those of his adversary.

81   **broad blown**   in full flower ('flush', filled, with vigour). Compare III.i.163.

82   **Audit**   reckoning, account (when he comes to the Last Judgement). Behind Hamlet's imagery Elizabethans would have heard echoes of the New Testament parables of stewardship, among them the Parable of the Unjust Steward (Luke 16:1–13), the Parable of the Talents (Matthew 25:14–30), and the Parable of the Steward and his Servants (Luke 12:42–48, cited in the note to *King Lear*, I.v.55), all of them pertinent not only to a man's personal life but to his discharge of the responsibility he has for those subject to his care and supervision. Meanwhile Claudius' situation recalls the Parable of the Lost Sheep (Matthew 18:11–14), and of the Good Shepherd who will 'leave the ninety and nine' sheep who are safely in the fold and seek the rescue of 'that which is gone astray'. As Claudius notes in lines 45–50, no matter how dismal a man's 'Audit', if he truly repents before he dies he may have his debts forgiven. See Luke 5:30–32, Acts 9:1–31, and Matthew 5:43–6:15.

O limed Soul, that, struggling to be free,
Art more ingag'd. – Help, Angels, make Assay.
– Bow, stubborn Knees. – And Hart with
   Strings of Steel,   70
Be soft as Sinews of the new borne Babe.
All may be well.

Enter Hamlet.

HAMLET   Now might I do it, but now 'a is a-praying;
And now I'll do't; and so 'a goes to Heaven,
And so am I reveng'd. That would be scann'd: 75
A Villain kills my Father, and for that
I his sole Son do this same Villain send
To Heaven.
Why, this is Hire and Salary, not Revenge.
'A took my Father grossly full of Bread,   80
With all his Crimes broad blown, as flush as May,
And how his Audit stands who knows save Heaven?

83 **But ... Thought** but given the perspective we have, based on what we know and can infer. Compare the phrasing in I.i.62–64.

85 **in the Purging of his Soul** while he is purifying his soul of its guilt. Hamlet is now referring to Claudius.

86 **fit ... Passage** in proper spiritual condition for his departure to the next world (by contrast with his victim, who was caught unawares, out of season, bearing his sins on his soul unconfessed and unabsolved). *Season'd* echoes III.ii.281, and *Passage* recalls II.ii.441. As we learn in lines 97–98, Claudius only appears to be in a state of grace.

88 **know ... Hent** wait till you can seize on a more horrible occasion. *Hent* combines a verb meaning 'seize' and a noun meaning 'time' or 'opportunity'.

89 **Rage** This noun could refer to any surrender to passion, including lust; here, however, it seems most likely to mean an angry frenzy. Lines 89–92 recall II.i.17–59.

90 **incestious** incestuous. Compare I.ii.157, I.v.41.

92 **Relish** trace. But in view of the other culinary metaphors in the speech ('full of Bread', 'season'd'), the word probably means 'taste' as well. Compare III.i.115–17. *Game* (line 91) recalls II.i.24, 56.

95 **stays** awaits me.

96 **Physic** medication. Hamlet probably refers to Claudius' 'Purging of his Soul' (line 85). Compare III.ii.325–32, and see the note to III.ii.331.

III.iv This scene takes place in the Queen's Closet (private chamber).

1 **strait** straight; immediately (as in II.ii.462).
lay home to him rebuke him as only a mother can do.

3 **your Grace** both (a) an honorific for the Queen, and (b) a reference to her gracious (loving) intercessions for her wayward son. In this scene, unlike the rest of the play, the Quarto speech headings identify Hamlet's mother as 'Gertrard' rather than as 'Queen'.

4 **Heat** Polonius alludes to the smouldering wrath of the King. See the note to III.ii.381. The fire-screen image implies that if Claudius' dependency on Gertrard didn't confine him, at least figuratively, to the hearth of domesticity, he would burst into a conflagration that would incinerate his nettlesome nephew in roaring flames.
silence me both (a) cease speaking, and (b) seclude myself silently. Polonius' phrasing will prove ironically apt.

But in our Circumstance and Course of Thought,
'Tis Heavy with him: and am I then reveng'd
To take him in the Purging of his Soul,   85
When he is fit and season'd for his Passage?
No.
– Up, Sword, and know thou a more horrid Hent:
When he is Drunk, Asleep, or in his Rage,
Or in th' incestious Pleasure of his Bed,   90
At Game a-swearing, or about some Act
That has no Relish of Salvation in't,
Then trip him, that his Heels may kick at
    Heaven,
And that his Soul may be as damn'd and black
As Hell, whereto it goes. – My Mother stays;   95
This Physic but prolongs thy sickly Days.   *Exit*.
KING   My Words fly up, my Thoughts remain below;
    Words without Thoughts never to Heaven go.   *Exit*.

Scene 4

Enter Gertrard and Polonius.

POLONIUS   'A will come strait; look you lay home
    to him,
    Tell him his Pranks have been too broad to bear
    with,
    And that your Grace hath screen'd and stood
    between
    Much Heat and him. I'll silence me even here,

5 **round** completely open. See III.i.187.
 wait you serve you, do as you bid me to do. Most editors
  adopt the Folio's *warrant you*. Compare III.iii.95.
 fear me not don't worry.

10 **Idle** both (a) wilfully irrelevant (evading the issue), and (b)
  irreverent, insolent. Hamlet's reply (line 11) mimics the
  Queen's words 'with a Difference' (IV.v.185) that shocks her
  with its disrespect. See the note to III.ii.359–60.

13 **forgot me** forgotten who I am (and your relationship to me).
 Rood Cross.

14 **your ... Wife** Hamlet's point is that the Queen is guilty of
  incest.

16 **I'll ... speak** I'll turn you over to those who can command
  better behaviour from you. *Set* recalls III.ii.44–48 and
  anticipates lines 18, 59, 207.

18 **Glass** mirror.

21 **how** The word means 'ho' the first two times it is used in this
  line. Compare IV.iii.15.
 a Rat Hamlet alludes not only to the loathsomeness and
  sneakiness of this creature, but also to its tendency to make
  sounds that eventually attract attention and thereby get it
  killed. Having laid a 'Mousetrap', the Prince is elated at the
  discovery that he has caught an even larger rodent than he'd
  expected.

22 **for a Duckat** probably either (a) I'll wager a ducat (a gold
  coin), or (b) for the price of a ducat. Hamlet's image echoes
  the monetary metaphors of the previous scene (see the notes
  to III.iii.57, 58, 61, 61–62, 79, 82); he believes he has caught
  Claudius 'At Game' (III.iii.91) and plunged him 'into more
  Choler' (III.iii.331–32), the raging fires of Hell.

Pray you be round.

GERTRARD   I'll wait you, fear me not.   5
Withdraw, I hear him coming.

Enter Hamlet.

HAMLET   Now Mother, what's the matter?
GERTRARD   Hamlet, thou hast thy Father much offended.
HAMLET   Mother, you have my Father much offended.
GERTRARD   Come, come, you answer with an Idle
     Tongue.   10
HAMLET   Go, go, you question with a Wicked Tongue.
GERTRARD   Why how now, Hamlet?
HAMLET   What's the matter now?
GERTRARD   Have you forgot me?
HAMLET   No, by the Rood, not so:
   You are the Queen, your Husband's Brother's
     Wife,
   And, would it were not so, you are my Mother.   15
GERTRARD   Nay, then I'll set those to you that can
     speak.
HAMLET   Come, come, and sit you down. You shall
     not boudge;
   You go not till I set you up a Glass
   Where you may see the Inmost Part of you.
GERTRARD   What wilt thou do, thou wilt not murther
     me,   20
   Help, how.
POLONIUS   What how, help.
HAMLET   How now, a Rat,
   Dead for a Duckat, dead.   *Kills Polonius.*
POLONIUS   O I am slain.
GERTRARD   O me, what hast thou done?
HAMLET   Nay I know not,
   Is it the King?
GERTRARD   O what a rash and bloody Deed is this.   25

30   **I . . . Better**   What Hamlet means is 'I mistook you for the King'. Compare III.ii.275–76.

31   **Thou . . . Danger**   you discover that to be too much of a busybody is somewhat dangerous.

32   **Leave**   give over, quit. Hamlet speaks to Gertrard.

34   **Penitrable Stuff**   both (a) material that is not too hard to be wrung or pierced, (b) matter capable of penitence. Compare *The Merchant of Venice*, III.iii.18, where Solanio calls the immovably vengeful Shylock an 'impenitrable Cur'.

35   **damned Custom**   damnable habit (the vicious practices it has become accustomed to).
       bras'd   both (a) plated it with brass, and (b) burnished and hardened it with intense heat (compare line 42). See I.i.68, 90–91.

36   **Proof . . . Sense**   completely shielded against normal human feelings and common sense. Hamlet fears that his mother's conscience may be so calloused by sin, so hardened against the 'compunctious Visitings of Nature' (see the note to I.v.86–87), that it can no longer be pierced by remorse. In the previous scene Claudius has experienced his last pangs of guilt. Having spurned the good 'Angels' who have made him aware of his peril and urged him to repent, he will henceforth be 'free' (III.iii.68, 69), of doubt as he yields himself to the plots prompted by 'hard Use' (*Macbeth*, III.iv.141).

39   **blurs**   obscures. *Noise* (line 38) recalls III.ii.9–15. *Modesty* echoes III.ii.23.

40   **Calls Virtue Hypocrite**   turns Virtue into a hypocrite (by pretending to be virtuous). See III.ii.428.

42   **Blister**   Hamlet refers to the blister branded on the foreheads of whores to subject them to public shame. *Rose* echoes III.i.156.

43   **Dicer's Oaths**   the promises of habitual gamblers, proverbially unreliable. Compare I.iii.125–30, II.i.20–35, 51–63.

44   **Contraction**   contract-making, the swearing of solemn oaths. *Contraction* recalls I.ii.3–4, I.iii.119–33, and *plucks* echoes II.ii.610, III.ii.392–99.

45–46 **sweet . . . Words**   turns the beauty and order of religious observances into a uncontrolled jumble of 'Words without Thoughts' (III.iii.98).

HAMLET   A bloody Deed, almost as bad, good Mother,
  As kill a King, and marry with his Brother.
GERTRARD   As kill a King.
HAMLET   Ay Lady, it was my Word.
      [*Hamlet opens the Arras and discovers Polonius.*]
  – Thou wretched, rash, intruding Fool, farewell,
  I took thee for thy Better, take thy Fortune: 30
  Thou find'st to be too Busy is some Danger.
  – Leave wringing of your Hands, peace, sit you
      down,
  And let me wring your Heart: for so I shall
  If it be made of Penitrable Stuff,
  If damned Custom have not bras'd it so   35
  That it be Proof and Bulwark against Sense.
GERTRARD   What have I done, that thou dar'st wag thy
      Tongue
  In Noise so rude against me?
HAMLET   Such an Act
  That blurs the Grace and Blush of Modesty,
  Calls Virtue Hypocrite, takes off the Rose   40
  From the fair Forehead of an innocent Love,
  And sets a Blister there, makes Marriage Vows
  As false as Dicer's Oaths; O such a Deed
  As from the Body of Contraction plucks
  The very Soul, and sweet Religion makes   45
  A Rhapsody of Words. Heaven's Face dooes glow

47 **this Solidity and compound Mass**   the heart described in lines 33–36.

48 **as . . . Doom**   in anticipation of Judgement Day. Compare the phrasing in II.ii.518.

50 **That roars . . . Index**   Here *Index* probably refers to a prefatory summary of the contents of a book. If this line belongs to Hamlet (the Folio assigns it to the Queen), it is probably meant to illustrate the 'Rhapsody of Words' he describes in line 46. His point would seem to be either (a) that Heaven's present 'Visage' is only an index (prologue or dumb-show) of the 'Doom' to follow, or (b) that a description of the Queen's 'Act' is like a thundering table of contents, foretelling the fearful judgement to be detailed in the volume itself.

52 **counterfeit Presentment**   artificial rendering. Hamlet is probably holding up two portraits side by side.

54 **Front**   forehead, 'Brow' (compare III.iii.5–7). *Hyperion* (the Sun God) echoes I.ii.140. *Jove* (Jupiter or Zeus) was the ruler of the Gods; *Mars* was the God of War.

56 **Station**   bearing, upright posture (literally, 'standing').

57 **a Heave**   an up-swelling of the earth to 'kiss' the alighting Mercury (messenger of the Gods). Most editors adopt the Folio's *Heaven-kissing Hill* in this line.

62 **mildew'd Ear**   blighted ('blasting') ear of grain. *Ear* recalls I.v.35–37; *Blasting* echoes III.ii.283.

65 **batten on this Moor**   gorge on this wasteland (with a pun on *Blackamoor*). Hamlet is usually assumed to be referring to wet marshland; but *moor* could also mean 'heath', a barren tract of land covered primarily by heather.

67 **Heyday**   prime vigour (literally, 'high day').

68 **waits upon**   both (a) awaits direction from, and (b) serves. Compare line 5.

70 **Sense**   In this passage the word means (a) the senses by which one perceives, (b) common sense, and (c) sensual appetite.

O'er this Solidity and compound Mass
With heated Visage, as against the Doom,
Is Thought-sick at the Act –
GERTRARD   Ay me, what Act?
HAMLET   That roars so loud, and thunders in the
     Index.   50
Look here upon this Picture, and on this,
The counterfeit Presentment of two Brothers.
See what a Grace was seated on this Brow,
Hyperion's Curls, the Front of Jove himself,
An Eye like Mars, to threaten and command,   55
A Station like the Herald Mercury,
New lighted on a Heave, a kissing Hill,
A Combination and a Form indeed
Where every God did seem to set his Seal
To give the World assurance of a Man;   60
This was your Husband. Look you now what
     follows:
Here is your Husband, like a mildew'd Ear,
Blasting his wholesome Brother. Have you Eyes?
Could you on this fair Mountain leave to feed,
And batten on this Moor; ha, have you Eyes?   65
You cannot call it Love, for at your Age
The Heyday in the Blood is Tame, it's Humble,
And waits upon the Judgement: and what Judgement
Would step from this to this? Sense sure you
     have,
Else could you not have Motion, but sure that
     Sense   70

71   **apoplex'd**   paralysed, rendered inoperable. Like epilepsy, apoplexy was associated in Shakespeare's time with the deafness that resulted from a wilful neglect of the voice of conscience, a refusal to heed the word of God; see the notes to I.ii.77, III.i.148–49, and compare *2 Henry IV*, I.ii.112–39, where the arrogant Falstaff defines 'this whoreson Apoplexy' as 'the Disease of Not Listening, the Malady of Not Marking'. One reason Hamlet 'roars so loud' (line 50) is that he thinks it possible that Gertrard no longer has 'ears to hear' (Matthew 11:15), eyes to see, or senses to feel what a spiritually healthy person would register.

72   **Ecstasy**   a seizure in which one is beside oneself or enslaved (thrall'd) to another. See III.i.164. *Choice* recalls III.ii.70–71.

74   **serve . . . Difference**   both (a) permit you to make proper distinctions between 'two Brothers' (line 52) of such contrasting natures, and (b) allow you to see how far you've fallen from 'Grace' (line 53) by the foul 'Choice' you've made.

75   **cozen'd**   deceived, cheated (with play on 'cousined'). **Hoodman Blind**   blindman's buff.

77   **sans**   without (from the French).

78–79 **Or . . . mope**   or even a sickly portion of one properly functioning sense would have prevented such a dulled state.

81   **mutine**   lead a mutiny (rebellion). **in a Matron's Bones**   in the body of a respectable married woman.

84   **compulsive Ardure**   irresistible ardour (desire). **gives the Charge**   (a) urges you forward (like a captain ordering his soldiers into battle), (b) provides your commission to you, and (c) loads and fires you (as if you were a pistol or cannon). Compare I.iii.33–44.

86   **Reason pardons Will**   Reason (supposedly predominant in frosty-haired elders) serves as the go-between for, rather than the defence against, lust-driven Will, and absolves it from its sins like a corrupt confessor dispensing indulgences. Most of today's editions adopt the Folio's *panders* here; but *pardons* conveys the idea that vice is not only aided and abetted by but given the approval of 'sweet Religion' (line 45). It would be in character for a man who has studied at Wittenberg to reflect a Luther-like bias against the abuses of the Renaissance papacy.

Is apoplex'd, for Madness would not err,
Nor Sense to Ecstasy was ne'er so thrall'd,
But it reserv'd some quantity of Choice
To serve in such a Difference. What Devil was't
That thus hath cozen'd you at Hoodman Blind?   75
Eyes without Feeling, Feeling without Sight,
Ears without Hands or Eyes, Smelling sans all,
Or but a sickly Part of one true Sense,
Could not so mope.
– O Shame, where is thy Blush? – Rebellious Hell,   80
If thou canst mutine in a Matron's Bones,
To flaming Youth let Virtue be as Wax
And melt in her own Fire; proclaim no Shame
When the compulsive Ardure gives the Charge,
Since Frost it self as actively doth burn,   85
And Reason pardons Will.
GERTRARD   O Hamlet, speak no more:
Thou turn'st my very Eyes into my Soul,

88 **grieved** both (a) grievous, and (b) lamentable. The Folio reads
grained. Compare III.ii.364–6.

89 **Tinct** stain, taint.

90 **inseemed** enseamed (the Folio spelling); seamy, greasy.
Compare I.v.40–56. The Quarto spelling recalls I.ii.70–86,
where Hamlet says, 'I know not Seems', and III.ii.94, where
he recruits Horatio to 'join' him 'In Censure of' Claudius'
'Seeming'. It also suggests 'in-semened' (reeking with sexual
discharge).

95 **Kyth** kith, kin (kind of man). The Folio prints *tithe*.

96 **precedent** both (a) previous, and (b) of a higher order of
precedence. Here pronounced 'pre-cée-dent'.
a Vice of Kings a vice-ridden parody of a true king (like the
buffoonish Vice character in late-medieval morality plays).

97 **A Cutpurse ... Rule** a pickpocket [who has stolen] both the
empire (Denmark and its tributaries) and its throne.

98 **Diadem** crown.

100 **Of Shreds and Patches** Hamlet is probably thinking once more
of the Vice figure and his clown-like particoloured costume.
His point is that by comparison with the paragon of divinity
he supplanted (the epitome of human perfection), Claudius is
a beggarly thief (unworthy of being even so lowly a figure as
the court jester) rather than a man of king-like stature.

102 **Heavenly Guards** angels. Compare I.iv.38.

106 **important** urgent (as in 'importunate'). *Tardy* (line 104) echoes
III.ii.29–33, and lines 104–6 recall III.ii.210–39.

108 **whet** sharpen, as one does with a 'blunted' (dull) knife.

109 **Amazement** a maze-like bewilderment. See III.ii.352–56. The
Ghost's concern for Gertrard recalls I.v.83–87.

111 **Conceit** imagination (or, more literally, imaginary
conceptions). Compare II.ii.189–91, 588–95.

And there I see such black and grieved Spots
As will leave there their Tinct.

HAMLET   Nay but to live
In the rank Sweat of an inseemed Bed   90
Stew'd in Corruption, honeying and making love
Over the nasty Sty.

GERTRARD   O speak to me no more,
These Words like Daggers enter in my Ears,
No more, sweet Hamlet.

HAMLET   A Murtherer and a Villain,
A Slave that is not twenti'th part the Kyth   95
Of your precedent Lord: a Vice of Kings,
A Cutpurse of the Empire and the Rule,
That from a Shelf the precious Diadem stole
And put it in his Pocket.

GERTRARD   No more.

Enter Ghost.

HAMLET   A King
Of Shreds and Patches.   100
– Save me, and hover o'er me with your Wings,
You Heavenly Guards. – What would your Gracious
    Figure?

GERTRARD   – Alas, he's mad.

HAMLET   Do you not come your tardy Son to chide,
That, laps'd in Time and Passion, lets go by   105
Th' important Acting of your dread Command?
O say.

GHOST   Do not forget: this Visitation
Is but to whet thy almost blunted Purpose.
But look, Amazement on thy Mother sits;
O step between her and her fighting Soul;   110
Conceit in weakest Bodies strongest works,
Speak to her, Hamlet.

114 **bend your Eye on Vacancy** focus your eye on nothingness.
Bend recalls III.ii.415.

115 **incorporal** 'bodiless' (line 135).

116 **your Spirits** The Queen refers to the fluids that were thought to
permeate the blood and animate the brain. Hamlet has used
comparable phrasing in II.ii.640, III.ii.65–66; compare
II.ii.250.

117 **in th' Alarm** when the alarum (call to arms for battle) is
sounded.

118 **like Life in Excrements** as if there were life in outgrowths of
the body such as hair and nails.

119 **an** on.

120 **Distemper** imbalanced disposition. The Queen assumes that
Hamlet is experiencing a fit of madness. See III.ii.326, 364,
and compare line 137.

121 **Patience** self-control, to temper (regulate) the heat of passion.

123 **His Form and Cause conjoin'd** considering the combined
power of his form and the cause that brings him here.
Conjoin'd echoes III.iii.20.

124 **capable** capable of response. In Luke 19:40 Jesus says, 'I tell
you that, if these should hold their peace, the stones would
immediately cry out.' Compare III.ii.13–14.

125 **Least** lest.

126 **My stern Effects** my fierce impulses.

127 **Will want true Colour** will lack the resolve that bloodthirsty
passion would give them. See III.i.41–43.
Tears perchance for Blood shedding tears, perhaps, instead of
displaying the blood (ruddy complexion and courageous
passion) required for vengeance. Compare III.ii.76, 421.

132 **Habit** habitual apparel. This noun recalls I.iii.70, I.iv.28–29.

135– **This . . . in** This conjuring up of imaginary bodies is something
36 madness is very skilful in prompting. *Ecstasy* echoes line 72.

137 **temperately** moderately, not agitated with excitement.
Compare III.ii.9. *Time* recalls III.i.162, III.ii.28.

HAMLET   – How is it with you, Lady?

GERTRARD   Alas, how is't with you?

That you do bend your Eye on Vacancy,

And with th' incorporal Air do hold Discourse;   115

Foorth at your Eyes your Spirits wildly peep,

And, as the sleeping Soldiers in th' Alarm,

Your bedded Hair, like Life in Excrements,

Start up and stand an end. O gentle Son,

Upon the Heat and Flame of thy Distemper   120

Sprinkle cool Patience. Whereon do you look?

HAMLET   On him, on him; look you how Pale he
  glares;

His Form and Cause conjoin'd, preaching to
  Stones,

Would make them capable. – Do not look upon me

Least with this piteous Action you convert   125

My stern Effects: then what I have to do

Will want true Colour, Tears perchance for
  Blood.

GERTRARD   To whom do you speak this?

HAMLET   Do you see nothing there?

GERTRARD   Nothing at all, yet all that is I see.

HAMLET   Nor did you nothing hear?

GERTRARD   No, nothing but our selves.   130

HAMLET   Why look you there, look how it steals away,

My Father in his Habit as he lived;

Look where he goes, even now out at the Portal.

                                        Exit Ghost.

GERTRARD   This is the very Coinage of your Brain:

This bodiless Creation Ecstasy   135

Is very cunning in.

HAMLET   Ecstasy?

My Pulse as yours doth temperately keep Time,

And makes as healthful Music. It is not Madness

That I have uttered: bring me to the Test,

140 **reword** recount. Hamlet's point is that, if tested, he would be able to describe what he has seen in a coherent fashion that would prove that it was not the 'Coinage' (hallucination) of a disturbed brain.

140– **which Madness / Would gambol from** which madness would
41 make impossible, gambolling (leaping) away from the topic in an incoherent manner. Compare V.i.199.

142 **Lay not . . . Soul** do not deceive your soul by soothing it with an ointment that merely masks its disease in a deceptively flattering way without treating it.

144 **skin and film** cover over with a thin film of skin.
Ulcerous cancerous. See the note to III.iii.420.

145 **mining** undermining.

148 **Compost** organic fertilizer.

149 **ranker** more prolific. Compare line 90 and III.iii.36.

150 **Fatness** bloatedness. Compare I.v.31–33. *Fatness* can also refer to sweat (line 90); see V.ii.300.
Pursy pursed up, flabby, diseased, flatulent, incontinent.

152 **curb** bow, curtsy.
leave permission.

153 **cleft** split. Compare II.ii.596–603.

155 **leave** depart, probably with wordplay on *live* (the word to be found in the Folio and in most modern editions). Compare III.ii.277.

157 **Assume** act as if you have, as one assumes (puts on) a garment. Compare I.ii.238, II.ii.636–38.

159 **Of Habits Devil** who acts like a devil in devouring our 'Sense' (awareness) of the bad things we do habitually.
Habits are garments; compare line 132. Hamlet wants his mother to cast off her bad habits and don new ones based on alert 'Remembrance' of the instruction he has given her. Compare I.v.109–11, IV.v.177.

162 **to night** tonight. Compare III.ii.82.

163 **Easiness** Compare I.v.30–33.

165 **Stamp of Nature** character Nature has engraved or coined (line 134) in us. Compare I.iv.30.

And I the Matter will reword, which Madness   140
Would gambol from. Mother, for love of Grace,
Lay not that flattering Unction to your Soul,
That not your Trespass but my Madness speaks:
It will but skin and film the Ulcerous Place
Whiles rank Corruption, mining all within,   145
Infects unseen. Confess your self to Heaven,
Repent what's past, avoid what is to come,
And do not spread the Compost on the Weeds
To make them ranker. Forgive me this my Virtue,
For in the Fatness of these Pursy Times   150
Virtue it self of Vice must pardon beg,
Yea curb and woo for leave to do him good.

GERTRARD   O Hamlet, thou hast cleft my Heart in
    twain.

HAMLET   O throw away the Worser Part of it,
And leave the Purer with the other half.   155
Good night, but go not to my Uncle's Bed.
Assume a Virtue if you have it not:
That monster Custom, who all Sense doth eat,
Of Habits Devil, is Angel yet in this,
That to the use of Actions fair and good   160
He likewise gives a Frock or Livery
That aptly is put on. Refrain to night,
And that shall lend a kind of Easiness
To the next Abstinence, the next more easy:
For Use almost can change the Stamp of Nature,   165

166   **[shame]** The Quarto text appears to be missing a word; *shame* is used elsewhere in similar contexts and is thus supplied here. Compare *1 Henry IV*, III.i.54–58. Many editions follow the 1611 Third Quarto and print *master*; others supply *curb*, *house*, or *lodge*.

169   **I'll . . . you** Compare *King Lear*, IV.vi.55–57.

172   **their Scourge and Minister** their [Heaven's] agent. *Scourge* was often used to refer to an agent of Heaven who was himself evil, and who was cast off to damnation after punishing other evildoers. But Hamlet appears to be using the term as a synonym for *Minister* (a worthy instrument of divine justice). Strictly speaking, the same person could not be both a scourge and a minister; but Hamlet does not tend to think in rigorous theological terms. In II.ii.622, for example, he says, 'Prompted to my Revenge by Heaven and Hell.' As it turns out, the consequences of his inadvertent slaying do 'punish' Hamlet as well as Polonius (line 171).

173   **answer well** Hamlet probably means 'give a good answer for'; but he could also mean 'answer [pay for] thoroughly'.

176   **behind** still to come. Line 175 reiterates what Hamlet has said in III.ii.426.

178–   **Not . . . Craft.** Hamlet tells his mother neither to submit to the
85   King's lust, nor to let him know that Hamlet is sane.

179   **blowt** bloated; 'broad blown' (III.iii.81).

181   **reechy** reeky, filthy.

183   **rovel** ravel, unwind. *Craft* recalls III.i.8.

185   **'Twere good** It is to be expected, given a wife's vow to love and obey her husband [especially when that pledge is compounded by a subject's duty to a monarch].

187   **Paddock** toad. See *Macbeth*, I.i.8. In this line *from* has the force of 'even from [so base a husband and king as]'.
    Gib tomcat.

188   **such . . . hide** matter of such great concern to a dear one.
    do so withhold such crucial information.

And either [shame] the Devil or throw him out
With wondrous Potency. Once more good night,
And when you are desirous to be blest,
I'll Blessing beg of you. For this same Lord
I do repent; but Heaven hath pleas'd it so   170
To punish me with this, and this with me,
That I must be their Scourge and Minister.
I will bestow him and will answer well
The Death I gave him. So again good night.
I must be cruel only to be kind: 175
This Bad begins, and Worse remains behind.
One Word more, good Lady.
GERTRARD   What shall I do?
HAMLET   Not this by no means that I bid you do:
Let the blowt King tempt you again to Bed,
Pinch wanton on your Cheek, call you his Mouse,   180
And let him for a pair of reechy Kisses,
Or paddling in your Neck with his damn'd
    Fingers,
Make you to rovel all this Matter out,
That I essentially am not in Madness
But Mad in Craft. 'Twere good you let him
    know,   185
For who that's but a Queen, fair, sober, wise,
Would from a Paddock, from a Bat, a Gib,
Such dear Concernings hide? Who would do so?

189–
93 **No . . . down** No, despite the claims of 'Sense' (desire) and 'Secrecy' (a wife's obligation to share her secrets with her husband, especially when he is the King), if you open the basket and let the birds (my secret) out, the conclusion of your story will be like that of the ape who fell off the roof and broke his neck by creeping into a basket in a foolish effort to imitate the birds that flew out of it.

195 **breath** give breath (words) to; breathe. Compare II.i.31, 43 and IV.vii.65.

198 **seal'd** written and certified with the King's official seal in wax.

199 **Adders fang'd** poisonous snakes with their fangs at the ready.

200 **Mandate** commission, the King's commands.
sweep my Way Hamlet implies that Rosencraus and Guildenstern will combine the functions of a 'Whiffler 'fore the King' to 'prepare his way' (*Henry V*, V.Chorus.12–13) and a Marshal to conduct him to his place.

201 **marshal** conduct. One of the duties of the Marshal at formal occasions was to see that participants were properly bestowed (seated). Compare II.ii.557–58.
to Knavery Hamlet probably means 'to some kind of knavish plot against me'. But he may also mean the knavish plot he will devise to counter them. See the note to III.ii.264. He assumes that Rosencraus and Guildenstern are themselves privy to the King's 'Mandate'. The play provides no indisputable evidence that they are.
Let it work let their plans go forward.

202 **Enginer** engineer (agent) of the plot.

203 **Hoist with his own Petar** blown up by his own explosive. A *Petar* or *petard* was a kind of bomb.
an't shall go hard and it will be difficult.

204 **delve** dig.
Mines tunnels (used to undermine fortifications, among other things by the planting of bombs). Compare line 145.

206 **in one Line** straight on, in head-to-head confrontation.

209 **good night indeed** Hamlet means that he is now ready to say goodnight in earnest.

No, in despight of Sense and Secrecy,
Unpeg the Basket on the House's Top,   190
Let the Birds fly, and, like the famous Ape,
To try Conclusions, in the Basket creep
And break your own Neck down.

GERTRARD   Be thou assur'd,
If Words be made of Breath, and Breath of Life,
I have no Life to breath what thou hast said   195
To me.

HAMLET   I must to England, you know that.

GERTRARD   Alack, I had forgot. 'Tis so concluded on.

HAMLET   There's Letters seal'd, and my two
    Schoolfellows,
Whom I will trust as I will Adders fang'd,
They bear the Mandate, they must sweep my Way   200
And marshal me to Knavery: let it work,
For 'tis the Sport to have the Enginer
Hoist with his own Petar, an't shall go hard
But I will delve one Yard below their Mines,
And blow them at the Moon. O 'tis most sweet   205
When in one Line two Crafts directly meet.
This Man shall set me packing:
I'll lug the Guts into the neighbour Room.
Mother, good night indeed. This Counsellor

210 **Still** Hamlet alludes to the idea that Counsellors were expected
to be solemn and attentive. The Quarto spelling, *Counsayler*,
may entail another allusion to Polonius' role as 'Fishmonger'
(II.ii.178). Compare *Measure for Measure*, I.ii.110, where
Pompey the Clown tells Mistress Overdone, a bawd, to have
no fear about the future of her brothel since 'Good
Counsellors lack no Clients'. There 'Coun-sellers' are those
who arrange for the sale of *cunnus* (see the note to I.ii.60).
Secret confidential (able to keep secrets).
Grave sober, wise. One of Hamlet's implications is that the
only place where Polonius could be truly grave is in the grave.

212 **to . . . you** Hamlet puns on a rhetorical formula, comparable
to 'in few' (I.iii.125), 'Brief let me be' (I.v.58), 'in brief'
(II.ii.68), 'I will be brief' (II.ii.92), and 'to end where I begun'
(III.ii.234). *Draw* recalls II.i.87, and *End* echoes III.ii.23–29.

S.D. **Exit . . . Polonius.** The words 'tugging in Polonius' appear only
in the Folio text. It is not clear whether the Second Quarto's
Exit applies to Hamlet only or to Hamlet and Gertrard. In the
Quarto, like the other early texts of Shakespeare, *Exit* is
frequently used to refer to the departure of more than one
character (see IV.i.37, where the Folio prints '*Exit Gent.*').

Is now most Still, most Secret, and most Grave,   210
Who was in Life a most foolish prating Knave.
– Come Sir, to draw toward an End with you.
– Good night, Mother.

Exit Hamlet tugging in Polonius.
[*Exit Gertrard.*]

IV.i   This scene takes place immediately after the just-concluded
        Closet Scene. The Quarto stage directions and dialogue
        suggest that Gertrard has gone to tell the King what has just
        happened in her chamber, and may now be escorting Claudius
        and his two confidants back into her closet. See line 9, where
        she probably points to 'the Arras', and line 28, where
        Claudius (thinking about what he has said in lines 12–13)
        says 'come away' and probably escorts the Queen to a less
        threatening locale. The Folio text implies a different staging of
        the scene. It follows '*Exit Hamlet tugging in Polonius*' with
        '*Enter King*' and makes no mention of Rosencraus and
        Guildenstern. Having cut Hamlet's reference to them in
        III.iv.198–206, it also deletes IV.i.4. For another instance of
        alternate Quarto–Folio staging patterns, see the note to
        III.i.52.

1   **profound Heaves**   deep heaving motions. Compare III.iv.57.
        Matter recalls III.i.22, 177, III.ii.350, III.iv.7, 12, 140, 183,
        and anticipates IV.v.96, 102, 176, IV.vi.28, V.i.159, 302,
        307, V.ii.166, 224.

4   **Bestow . . . while**   Leave us in solitude. *Bestow* echoes
        III.iv.173.

5   **What . . . to night?**   Most of today's editions substitute an
        exclamation point for the question mark in the original
        printings. But Gertrard is probably still wondering what she
        has seen tonight. And her query gives her a moment to decide
        how to respond to her husband's insistence (line 2) that she
        'rovel all this Matter out' (III.iv.183).

7   **Mad**   The Queen's first words about the preceding interview
        indicate that she has indeed shifted her loyalty to Hamlet, at
        least to the extent of protecting him from the charge that
        what he did was intentional. She is now a willing party to his
        'Antic Disposition' (I.v.163), his use of a pretence of insanity
        to excuse actions that would otherwise be regarded as capital
        crimes.

8   **lawless Fit**   uncontrolled seizure, 'Ecstasy' (III.iv.72, 135).

ACT IV

Scene 1

Enter King and Queen, with Rosencraus and Guildenstern.

KING There's Matter in these Sighs, these profound
    Heaves,
  You must translate; 'tis fit we understand them.
  Where is your Son?
GERTRARD – Bestow this place on us a little while.
                [Exeunt all but the King and Queen.]
  – Ah mine own Lord, what have I seen to night?   5
KING What, Gertrard, how dooes Hamlet?
GERTRARD Mad as the Sea and Wind when both
    contend
  Which is the mightier, in his lawless Fit,
  Behind the Arras hearing some thing stir,
  Whips out his Rapier, cries 'A Rat, a Rat,'   10

11 **brainish Apprehension** misjudgement, based on a figment of his imagination. The Queen implies that Hamlet thought Polonius really was a rat.

16 **answer'd** both (a) explained, and (b) responded to. See III.iv.173.

17 **Providence** 'providing', management of the royal household. This word anticipates V.ii.231–32.

18 **short** on a short leash.
out of haunt sequestered from society. Compare II.ii.147–49.

20 **fit** suitable, appropriate. This word echoes line 8.

22 **divulging** being disclosed. Hamlet has used a similar disease image in III.iv.144–46.

23 **Pith** vital core.

25 **Ore** either (a) a piece of pure metal (usually referring to gold), or (b) a vein of a particular metal in a mine. This word plays on *O'er* (at the beginning of the line), and it recalls I.i.91.

26 **Mineral** either (a) a piece of unrefined extract from a mine (ore in the more usual modern sense), or (b) a mine itself. Compare III.iv.145, 202–5.

27 **pure** both (a) unmixed with baser metals (in this case any touches of sanity), and (b) pure in heart, innocent.
'a weeps for what is done. Again, the Queen appears to be attempting to 'screen' Hamlet (III.iv.3). Nothing in the previous scene suggests that Hamlet 'weeps' over his deed, regret it though he may.

29 **The Sun . . . touch** as soon as morning comes. Claudius' imagery echoes III.iv.51–65.

32 **countenance and excuse** tolerate and explain satisfactorily. *Countenance* recalls I.ii.228, I.iii.112.

33 **go . . . Aid** go assemble some others to help you.

35 **dregg'd** dragged, drawn apart (line 24), as if he were no more than a bagful of dregs (compare the phrasing in III.iv.208).

36 **speak fair** speak gently (not reprovingly or threateningly). *Fair* recalls I.i.43, I.ii.62, 121, II.ii.60, 401, 436, III.i.102–5, 156, III.ii.124, 199, III.iv.41, 64, 160, 186, and anticipates IV.v.89, V.i.252, 255, V.ii.32, 34.

And in this brainish Apprehension kills
The unseen good Old Man.

KING   O heavy Deed!
It had been so with us had we been there:
His Liberty is full of Threats to all,
To you your self, to us, to every one.   15
Alas, how shall this bloody Deed be answer'd?
It will be laid to us, whose Providence
Should have kept short, restrain'd, and out of
    haunt
This mad Young Man; but so much was our Love
We would not understand what was most fit,   20
But like the Owner of a foul Disease,
To keep it from divulging, let it feed
Even on the Pith of Life. Where is he gone?

GERTRARD   To draw apart the Body he hath kill'd,
O'er whom his very Madness, like some Ore   25
Among a Mineral of Metals Base,
Shows it self pure; 'a weeps for what is done.

KING   O Gertrard, come away,
The Sun no sooner shall the Mountains touch
But we will ship him hence, and this vile Deed   30
We must with all our Majesty and Skill

Enter Rosencraus and Guildenstern.

Both countenaunce and excuse. – Ho Guildenstern,
Friends both, go join you with some further Aid:
Hamlet in madness hath Polonius slain,
And from his Mother's Closet hath he dregg'd him.   35
Go seek him out, speak fair, and bring the Body
Into the Chapel; I pray you haste in this.

                              Exeunt Gentlemen.
– Come Gertrard, we'll call up our wisest
    Friends,

39   **mean** intend. Compare IV.iii.29.

41   **Whose Whisper** rumours of which ('what's untimely doone').
      Modern editors tend to assume that a phrase is missing from
      the preceding line. Perhaps, but it seems equally likely that
      Shakespeare deliberately inserted a short (metrically
      'untimely') line at this point to signal a brief pause after
      'doone' for dramatic emphasis. The word *doone* provides a
      near rhyme for *do* in line 39 (a word it balances rhetorically).
      o'er the World's Diameter Claudius depicts the world as flat,
      and he means 'from one extreme to the other'.

42   **Blank** target; literally, a white spot in the target one aims at
      when firing at blank (level) range, as opposed to the arched
      trajectory required for shooting at longer ranges.

44   **Woundless Air** unwoundable air. Claudius hopes that the
      'Whisper' (the news of Polonius' death) will find a target other
      than the King. Compare I.i.140–41.

45   **My . . . Dismay** Claudius' words recall III.i.161–64,
      III.iv.136–37; they also remind us that the fearful Claudius is
      still experiencing 'sickly Days' (III.i.96). Compare *Macbeth*,
      III.i.102–6.

IV.ii This scene shifts to another part of the Castle, probably one near
       the 'neighbour Room' (III.iv.208) adjacent to the Queen's
       Closet.

1   **stow'd** bestowed (see III.iv.173, IV.i.4), stored away.

6   **Compound it** mix (or mixed) it. Modern editions normally
       follow the Folio here and print *Compounded*. But since
       Hamlet hasn't buried the corpse, it is quite possible that he
       answers Rosencraus' question with a command for
       Rosencraus to take care of the burial. Hamlet remains 'antic'
       in his behaviour, and we should not expect any of his replies
       to adhere to conventional logic. An alternative possibility here
       is that *Compound* means 'compounded'. The metre is
       awkward in the Second Quarto version, and it may be that
       the Folio's *Compounded* was an editorial emendation to
       repair it. If a syllable was inadvertently omitted from the First
       Quarto version of the line, however, it may have been a *the*
       before *Dust* rather than an *-ed* after *Compound*.

6–7   **Dust whereto 'tis Kin** Hamlet alludes to Genesis 3:19, 'dust
       thou art, and unto dust shalt thou return'. *Dust* echoes
       I.ii.70–7, I.iv.17, II.ii.329–30. *Kin* recalls '*Kyth*', III.iv.95.

And let them know both what we mean to do
And what's untimely doone,   40
Whose Whisper o'er the World's Diameter,
As level as the Cannon to his Blank
Transports his poison'd Shot, may miss our Name
And hit the Woundless Air. O come away,
My Soul is full of Discord and Dismay.   *Exeunt.*   45

Scene 2

Enter Hamlet.

HAMLET   Safely stow'd.
GENTLEMEN *within*   Hamlet, Lord Hamlet.
HAMLET   But soft, what Noise? Who calls on Hamlet?

Enter Rosencraus and Guildenstern.

O here they come.
ROSENCRAUS   What have you doone, my Lord,
   with the dead Body?   5
HAMLET   Compound it with Dust whereto 'tis
   Kin.
ROSENCRAUS   Tell us where 'tis, that we may take
   it thence
And bear it to the Chapel.
HAMLET   Do not believe it.
ROSENCRAUS   Believe what?

10 **keep your Counsel** act in accordance with your counsel (advice or judgement), with wordplay on the more usual sense 'keep your secrets'. Compare III.ii.165, and see the note to III.iv.210.

11 **demaunded of a Spunge** ordered around by a sponge.

12 **Replication** reply. But Hamlet is probably playing on other senses of *replication*, among them (a) fold or bend (to squeeze), and (b) echo or reverberate (as in a musical tone repeated an octave higher or lower). Murellus uses the word to mean 'echo' in I.i.52 of *Julius Caesar*.

15 **I** both 'I' [do], and 'Ay'. Compare III.ii.371.

16 **Countenaunce** both (a) favour, face, and (b) indulgence (as in IV.i.32).

17–18 **in the end** in the final reckoning (with play on a sense that relates *end* to 'posterior' and 'in the end' to defecation). Compare III.iv.212. *End* recalls I.v.18, II.i.91–92, II.ii.300, 345–46, III.i.56–60, III.ii.23–26, 234–37, 344, III.iv.119, 212, and anticipates IV.iii.23–24, IV.v.60, 187–88, IV.vii.154, V.ii.10–11. Hamlet is saying that Rosencraus' 'Return shall be the end of [his] Business' (III.ii.344).

20 **glean'd** picked up, as with leftovers from a harvested field. The King has used this verb in II.ii.16.

24 **sleeps** is to no avail (because it doesn't awaken the hearing). See the notes to I.ii.77, III.i.148–49, III.iv.36, 71, 86. *Knavish* recalls III.ii.264, III.iv.201.

28–29 **The Body . . . Body** Hamlet alludes to the doctrine of 'the King's two bodies', the idea that a monarch has both a normal, mortal body and a mystical, spiritual body as the epitome of his realm. See the notes to II.ii.276–78, III.iii.10, 14. As usual, Hamlet's meanings are equivocal and multiple. One implication is that the body of Claudius is now attached to the Kingship, but that the true King (either the elder Hamlet or the younger Hamlet) is not identical with the Body (Claudius) who is now pretending to be King. In that sense, this 'King' is 'a thing of nothing' (lines 30, 32), a Body that is not the thing it is taken to be. The obscene innuendo in 'nothing' (see the note to III.ii.123) anticipates Hamlet's calling Claudius 'Mother' in IV.iii.49.

31–32 **Hide . . . after** a hunting call appropriate for the 'Fox' (Claudius) whom Hamlet is warning to hide. See the note to III.ii.304.

HAMLET   That I can keep your Counsel and not mine   10
own; besides, to be demaunded of a Spunge, what
Replication should be made by the Son of a
King.

ROSENCRAUS   Take you me for a Spunge, my Lord?

HAMLET   I Sir, that soaks up the King's   15
Countenaunce, his Rewards, his Authorities. But
such Officers do the King best Service in the
end: he keeps them like an Apple in the Corner
of his Jaw, first mouth'd to be last swallow'd.
When he needs what you have glean'd, it is but   20
squeezing you, and, Spunge, you shall be dry
again.

ROSENCRAUS   I understand you not, my Lord.

HAMLET   I am glad of it: a Knavish Speech sleeps
in a Foolish Ear.   25

ROSENCRAUS   My Lord, you must tell us where the
Body is, and go with us to the King.

HAMLET   The Body is with the King, but the King
is not with the Body. The King is a thing –

GUILDENSTERN   A Thing, my Lord?   30

HAMLET   Of nothing: bring me to him. Hide, Fox,
and all after.   *Exeunt.*

IV.iii This scene takes place immediately after IV.ii in another room of the Castle. The 'two or three' with whom Claudius enters are probably the 'wisest Friends' he has referred to in IV.i.38.

3 put . . . him prosecute him to the full extent of the law. *Body* (line 2) echoes IV.ii.26–29; *goes loose* recalls IV.i.17–19.

4 distracted not rational, easily diverted from an objective appraisal. But Claudius may be concerned about the masses becoming 'distracted' in a more severe sense (frenzied) once they hear about and become agitated over the death of Polonius. See III.i.5.

5 like form their preferences. Compare III.iii.1.

6 th' Offender's Scourge the punishment given the criminal. *Scourge* echoes III.iv.170–72.
   wayed both (a) registered, given its way (put on course), and (b) weighed, taken into consideration. Compare I.iii.17, 29, 48.

7 To bear all smooth and even (a) to carry everything smoothly over an even way (road or terrain), and (b) to keep things peaceful and calm. Compare III.ii.1–9, 19–33.

9 Deliberate Pause the result of a dispassionate weighing of all the alternatives. The King is saying that a reaction that must be 'sudden' must seem to be 'deliberate' (unhurried, reflective). In fact the King's plans for Hamlet have been devised with some deliberation: Claudius told Polonius of his scheme to send Hamlet to England immediately after the two of them eavesdropped on the conversation between Hamlet and Ophelia (III.i.168–74). Claudius is trying to avoid any 'Censure of his Seeming' (III.ii.94) by those who think he has failed to 'use all gently', with a 'Temperance' that may give his actions 'Smoothness' (III.ii.6, 9). *Pause* recalls II.ii.509–27, 587–625, III.i.80–85, III.ii.210–37.
   desperate grown at the critical stage (where the patient is desperate, at the point where life is in the balance). Compare the imagery in IV.i.16–23.

10 By desperate Appliance by the application of desperate measures (measures equal to the severity of the crisis).

Scene 3

Enter King, and two or three.

KING   I have sent to seek him, and to find the
   Body.
   How dangerous is it that this Man goes loose,
   Yet must not we put the strong Law on him:
   He's lov'd of the distracted Multitude,
   Who like not in their Judgement but their Eyes,   5
   And where 'tis so, th' Offender's Scourge is
      wayed,
   But never the Offence. To bear all smooth and
      even,
   This sudden sending him away must seem
   Deliberate Pause; diseases desperate grown
   By desperate Appliance are reliev'd   10
   Or not at all.

       Enter Rosencraus and all the Rest.

              – How now, what hath befall'n?
ROSENCRAUS   Where the dead Body is bestow'd, my
   Lord,
   We cannot get from him.
KING   But where is he?

14   **Without**   just outside the chamber. Compare *Macbeth*,
      III.i.44–45.
      guarded   under guard.
      to know your Pleasure   to learn what you have decided to do
      with him.

15   **How**   ho. Compare III.iv.21. The stage direction following this
      line derives from the Second Quarto. The Folio reads '*Enter
      Hamlet and Guildensterne.*'

19   **Convocation**   solemn assembly.
      politic Worms   worms who are occupied with affairs of state.
      See the note to III.iii.10.

20   **Your . . . Diet**   Hamlet plays on two senses of *Diet*: (a) food,
      and (b) a council or convocation. He alludes in particular to
      the Diet of Worms (a famous council in the German city of
      Worms); here the Holy Roman Emperor presided over an
      assembly at which Martin Luther was condemned for heresy
      in 1521. Hamlet adopts the colloquial *your* throughout this
      dialogue; it is a familiar, informal way of saying 'the', and
      here it reinforces the satirical reductiveness of everything
      Hamlet utters about matters that are normally treated with
      formal reverence and stately reserve.

21   **fat**   feed to make fat. See the note to III.iii.10. *Fat* recalls I.v.31,
      II.ii.614–17.

23   **Variable Service**   different dishes or servings. *End* (line 24)
      echoes III.iv.212; Hamlet hints at his desire to 'draw toward
      an End' with the 'Fat King', a capon who is now plump
      enough to be harvested and served (see III.ii.99–102).

31   **go a Progress**   Hamlet alludes to the pompous ceremonies
      whereby royal personages were welcomed when they went on
      progresses, official state journeys; he suggests that a king's
      final progress may be somewhat less dignified than the ones he
      grew accustomed to in life. *Beggar* echoes II.ii.276–78, 288.

35   **other place**   Hell.

36   **nose**   smell. *Lobby* (line 37) recalls II.ii.165–66.

41   **tender**   treat with careful regard. Compare I.iii.99–110.
      as   both (a) at the same time as, and (b) just as much as.

ROSENCRAUS   Without, my Lord, guarded to know
    your Pleasure.
KING   Bring him before us.
ROSENCRAUS   – How, bring in the Lord.   15

            They enter.

KING   Now, Hamlet, where's Polonius?
HAMLET   At Supper.
KING   At Supper, where?
HAMLET   Not where he eats, but where 'a is eaten;
    a certain Convocation of politic Worms are e'en
    at him. Your Worm is your onely Emperor for Diet.   20
    We fat all Creatures else to fat us, and we fat
    our selves for Maggots. Your Fat King and your
    Lean Beggar is but Variable Service, two Dishes
    but to one Table, that's the End.
KING   Alas, alas.   25
HAMLET   A Man may fish with the Worm that hath eat
    of a King, and eat of the Fish that hath fed of that
    Worm.
KING   King. What doost thou mean by this?
HAMLET   Nothing but to shew you how a King may   30
    go a Progress through the Guts of a Beggar.
KING   Where is Polonius?
HAMLET   In Heaven, send thether to see; if your
    Messenger find him not there, seek him i'th'
    other place your self; but if indeed you find   35
    him not within this Month, you shall nose him
    as you go up the Stairs into the Lobby.
KING   – Go seek him there.
HAMLET   'A will stay till you come.
                        [*Exeunt Attendants.*]
KING   Hamlet, this Deed, for thine especial
    Safety,   40
    Which we do tender, as we dearly grieve

43 **With fiery Quickness** This phrase, which may or may not be authorial, occurs only in the Folio printing of the play.

44 **Bark** boat. Lines 44–45 echo I.iii.1–4, 55–57, 83.
at help in a favourable disposition.

45 **Th' Associates tend** those who will go with you are at your service. *Bent* recalls III.iv.114.

48 **Cherub** presiding angel.

48–49 **but . . . England** This sentence may be addressed to 'Th' Associates', as is almost certainly true of line 53.

52 **Man and Wife is one Flesh** Hamlet alludes to the marriage ceremony and to such biblical passages as Genesis 2:24 and Matthew 19:5–6. Here the reference is a reminder that the 'one Flesh' created by this incestuous marriage is a grotesque parody of 'holy matrimony'. See the note to III.iii.14.
so my Mother therefore it follows that you are my mother. Hamlet implies that it is as appropriate to call Claudius his mother as it is to call him his father or his King. Here and in line 49 *Mother* becomes charged with innuendo that anticipates an Oedipal expletive that entered mainstream culture in the 1960s. Compare II.ii.403–4.

54 **at foot** at his heels (keeping a close eye on him).
tempt incite, spur. Compare I.iv.68.

55 **to night** tonight. But Claudius' phrasing can also carry more sinister implications. Compare I.iv.7, III.iv.162, IV.i.5, and see *Macbeth*, I.v.33, 60–63, II.iii.59.

58 **at ought** at any value. Compare III.ii.95, 192.

60 **Cicatrice** scar. Claudius implies that Danish forces have recently disciplined 'England' (here referring primarily to the English King). See the note to III.i.174.

61 **free Awe** uncoerced reverence, fear, and obedience. *Free* recalls III.ii.266, III.iii.68.

62 **coldly set** aloofly disregard. Claudius' phrasing recalls I.ii.180 and III.iv.16, 18, 59, 207.

63 **Our Sovereign Process** the command ('Mandate', III.iv.200) that I, as the King of England's sovereign, am dispatching. *Process* echoes I.v.35–37, III.iii.28–29.
which imports at full spells out with complete clarity. *Imports* recalls I.ii.23–24, III.ii.162–63, III.iv.106.

64 **congruing to that Effect** in accordance with that objective.

For that which thou hast done, must send thee
  hence
With fiery Quickness. Therefore prepare thy self;
The Bark is ready, and the Wind at help;
Th' Associates tend, and every thing is bent   45
For England.
HAMLET   For England.
KING   Ay Hamlet.
HAMLET   Good.
KING   So is it if thou knew'st our Purposes.
HAMLET   I see a Cherub that sees them; but come,
  for England. Farewell, dear Mother.
KING   Thy loving Father, Hamlet.   50
HAMLET   My Mother: Father and Mother is Man and
  Wife, Man and Wife is one Flesh, so my Mother.
  – Come, for England.   *Exit.*
KING   – Follow him at foot, tempt him with Speed
  aboard,
  Delay it not: I'll have him hence to night.   55
  Away, for every thing is seal'd and done
  That else leans on th' Affair; pray you make
    haste.   *[Exeunt all but the King.]*
  – And England, if my Love thou hold'st at ought,
  As my great Power thereof may give thee Sense,
  Since yet thy Cicatrice looks raw and red   60
  After the Danish Sword, and thy free Awe
  Pays Homage to us, thou may'st not coldly set
  Our Sovereign Process, which imports at full
  By Letters congruing to that Effect

66   **the Hectic**   a severe, unbroken fever.

68   **How ere my Haps**   however my fortunes have been (a) before,
      or (b) ever in the past.
      will nere begin   *Nere* echoes *ere*, and here it means 'ne'er' (with
      a suggestion that Claudius hopes the day when he will be
      secure in his joys is now quite 'near'). Most editions adopt the
      Folio reading, *were ne're begun*, which conforms to
      Shakespeare's frequent practice of concluding a scene-ending
      soliloquy with a rhymed couplet (compare I.iii, I.v, II.i, II.ii,
      III.ii, and III.iii).

IV.iv This scene takes place on the way to the harbour, just prior to
      the departure for England. The Folio includes only the first
      eight lines.

2   **Licence**   authorization.

3   **Craves ... March**   requests an official Danish escort for the
      conduct of a march across Danish territory for which
      permission has already been requested and granted
      (II.ii.60–82). *Conveyance* recalls I.iii.1–4.

4   **the Rendezvous**   Fortinbrasse may mean (a) where we will meet
      him, but he probably means (b) where to meet us after you
      have delivered your message to him.

5   **would ... us**   either (a) would like to speak directly to me, or
      (b) has any business to conduct with us. *Ought* (aught) echoes
      IV.iii.58.

6   **in his Eye**   to his face, in his presence. Fortinbrasse's phrasing
      hints at effrontery. See IV.vii.44–45, where a jaunty Hamlet
      uses similar language, and compare II.ii.454–55, 610.

8   **Powers**   military forces.

9   **purpos'd**   directed, intended. Compare III.ii.19–29.

12   **Main**   primary territory.

14   **Addition**   exaggeration.

16   **Profit**   value, advantage.

17   **farm**   either (a) lease, rent, or (b) cultivate (farm in the usual
      modern sense). *Duckets* (ducats) recalls II.ii.392.

The present Death of Hamlet. Do it, England,   65
For like the Hectic in my Blood he rages,
And thou must cure me; till I know 'tis done,
How ere my Haps, my Joys will nere begin.   *Exit.*

Scene 4

Enter Fortinbrasse with his Army over the Stage.

FORTINBRASSE   Go, Captain, from me greet the
   Danish King,
Tell him that by his Licence Fortinbrasse
Craves the Conveyance of a promis'd March
Over his Kingdom; you know the Rendezvous,
If that his Majesty would ought with us,   5
We shall express our Duty in his Eye,
And let him know so.
               I will do't, my Lord.
FORTINBRASSE   Go softly on.   *Exit.*

Enter Hamlet, Rosencraus, &c.

HAMLET   Good Sir, whose Powers are these?
CAPTAIN   They are of Norway, Sir.
HAMLET   How purpos'd, Sir, I pray you?
CAPTAIN   Against some part of Poland.
HAMLET   Who commaunds them, Sir?   10
CAPTAIN   The Nephew to old Norway: Fortinbrasse.
HAMLET   Goes it against the Main of Poland, Sir,
Or for some Frontier?
CAPTAIN   Truly to speak, and with no Addition,
We go to gain a little Patch of Ground   15
That hath in it no Profit but the Name.
To pay five Duckets, five, I would not farm it;

19   **ranker Rate**   higher return. *Ranker* echoes III.iv.148–49.
      in Fee   outright.

21   **garrison'd**   fortified with armed soldiers.

23   **Will not debate**   will not be sufficient to contest.

24   **Impostume**   abscess, festering sore. Hamlet uses yet another
      image from the vocabulary of disease. See IV.iii.9–11, 65–67.

25   **inward breaks**   erupts within the body. Compare Hamlet's
      similar reference to an 'Ulcerous Place' in III.iv.144–46.

27   **God buy you**   God be with you.

28   **before**   ahead of me.

29   **How . . . me**   How everything that happens and everyone I
      encounter both (a) spies upon and (b) bears witness against
      me. Hamlet is employing a metaphor from legal terminology.

31   **Market**   profitable use. Lines 30–32 echo II.ii.315–32.

33   **large Discourse**   ample powers of reasoning. Compare
      I.ii.150–51.

34   **Looking before and after**   with an eye to both the past and the
      future. The ambiguous syntax permits this phrase to modify
      both *he* (God) and *Discourse*. See the note to I.ii.222.

36   **fust**   grow musty.

37   **Bestial Oblivion**   beastlike forgetfulness. Compare
      III.ii.131–44, 210–39.
      craven Scruple   slavish, cowardly doubt. See III.i.80–85.

38   **Of . . . Event**   of dwelling excessively on the outcome.

39   **quarter'd**   both (a) broken into fourths (as with the shield on a
      coat of arms), (b) cornered like a prey, and (c) dismembered,
      as with a convict who has been hanged, drawn, and
      quartered.

41   **to do**   yet to be accomplished.

42   **Sith**   since (as in II.ii.6, 12).

43   **gross**   both (a) obvious, and (b) dirty, foul.

44   **Mass and Charge**   massive numbers and expenditure.

47   **Makes . . . Event**   defies the unknown risks he undertakes.
      Compare II.ii.389–93.

Nor will it yield to Norway or the Pole
A ranker Rate, should it be sold in Fee.
HAMLET   Why then the Polack never will defend it.   20
CAPTAIN   Yes, it is already garrison'd.
HAMLET   Two thousand Souls, and twenty thousand
    Duckets
    Will not debate the Question of this Straw:
    This is th' Impostume of much Wealth and Peace,
    That inward breaks, and shows no Cause without   25
    Why the Man dies. I humbly thank you, Sir.
CAPTAIN   God buy you, Sir.   *[Exit.]*
ROSENCRAUS   Will't please you go, my Lord?
HAMLET   I'll be with you straight, go a little
    before.
    – How all Occasions do inform against me,
    And spur my dull Revenge. What is a Man   30
    If his chief Good and Market of his Time
    Be but to Sleep and Feed? A Beast, no more.
    Sure he that made us with such large Discourse,
    Looking before and after, gave us not
    That Capability and God-like Reason   35
    To fust in us unus'd. Now whether it be
    Bestial Oblivion, or some craven Scruple
    Of thinking too precisely on th' Event,
    A Thought which, quarter'd, hath but one part
        Wisdom,
    And ever three parts Coward, I do not know   40
    Why yet I live to say this thing's to do
    Sith I have Cause, and Will, and Strength, and
        Means
    To do't. Examples gross as Earth exhort me:
    Witness this Army of such Mass and Charge,
    Led by a delicate and tender Prince,   45
    Whose Spirit, with divine Ambition puff'd,
    Makes Mouths at the invisible Event,
    Exposing what is Mortal, and Unsure,

51   **great Argument** a significant cause or reason for the combat. *Argument* echoes III.ii.162, 256.

53   **at the Stake** both (a) staked, as in a wager, and (b) tied to the stake, like a bear attacked by baying dogs in a baiting arena.
    stand stand still; pause, delay. Compare IV.iii.9. Hamlet is 'looking before and after' (line 34), patiently 'at the Stake', when everything he sees conspires to 'exhort' him to 'stir' and 'be Bloody' (lines 43, 53, 63).

55   **Blood** passion. A number of Hamlet's phrases suggest analogies with manly 'Excitements' of a different kind. See III.ii.76, and compare the genital senses *Argument* carries in *Romeo and Juliet*, II.iii.95–108, and *Troilus and Cressida*, IV.v.26–29.

58   **a Fantasy . . . Fame** an illusory 'Argument' and a trifling cause prompted by a desire for 'Fame'. Fortinbrasse is here presented as the kind of soldier the melancholy Jaques describes as 'Seeking the Bubble Reputation / Even in the Cannon's Mouth' (*As You Like It*, II.vii.152–53).

60   **Cause** case (*causa* in Latin); another legal metaphor. *Try* recalls III.iv.138–41.

61   **Continent** container. Hamlet's point in lines 59–62 is that the plot of ground being fought over is too small to hold the massive numbers who will 'debate' it.

IV.v   This scene returns us to the Castle, where the Queen has just received word that Ophelia wishes to talk with her.

1   **Importunate** impatiently demanding; an echo of I.iii.32, IV.iii.63–64.

2   **Distract** deranged. See II.ii.592, III.i.5, IV.iii.4.
    Mood agitated emotional and mental state. Normally this word refers to a fit of passion, usually anger.

6   **Spurns enviously** kicks maliciously.
    Straws trifling things. This word, picking up on Hamlet's two uses of it in the previous scene (IV.iv.23, 52), hints at a relationship between Hamlet's situation and that of Ophelia.
    in Doubt (a) in her state of doubt (suspicion, fear, uncertainty), (b) that have doubtful meaning at best.

8   **unshaped use of it** incoherent way of speaking. This phrase recalls I.ii.82, I.iv.39–43, I.v.53, II.ii.636–38, III.i.123–26, III.ii.406–7, and anticipates IV.vii.88–89, V.ii.10–11.

To all that Fortune, Death, and Danger dare,
Even for an Eggshell. Rightly to be Great   50
Is not to stir without great Argument,
But greatly to find Quarrel in a Straw
When Honour's at the Stake: how stand I then
That have a Father kill'd, a Mother stain'd,
Excitements of my Reason and my Blood,   55
And let all sleep, while to my Shame I see
The imminent Death of twenty thousand Men
That for a Fantasy and Trick of Fame
Go to their Graves like Beds, fight for a Plot
Whereon the Numbers cannot try the Cause,   60
Which is not Tomb enough and Continent
To hide the Slain? O from this Time forth
My Thoughts be Bloody, or be nothing worth.   *Exit.*

Scene 5

Enter Horatio, Gertrard, and a Gentleman.

QUEEN   I will not speak with her.
GENTLEMAN   She is Importunate,
  Indeed Distract; her Mood will needs be pitied.
QUEEN   What would she have?
GENTLEMAN   She speaks much of her Father, says she
    hears
  There's Tricks i'th' World, and hems, and beats
    her Heart,   5
  Spurns enviously at Straws, speaks things in
    Doubt
  That carry but half Sense. Her Speech is nothing,
  Yet the unshaped use of it doth move

9 **to Collection** to attempt to put the fragments together into something that makes sense.

yawn gape, listen in open-mouthed concentration. Most editors follow the Folio and print *aim*, conjecture. Compare III.ii.419–21.

10 **botch the Words ... Thoughts** patch the words together in a way that conforms to their own notions of what she is trying to say. *Fit* recalls IV.i.8, 20.

11 **yield them** yield up words (produce words to accompany them). In this line *Which* refers to *Words* (line 10).

13 **sure** secure, certain.
unhappily unaptly, incoherently. See II.ii.216–20, 412.

14 **strew** spread. This verb, which echoes *straw*, will recur in V.i.259.

15 **ill breeding Minds** minds inclined to thoughts that might endanger the security of the throne. Horatio is advising the Queen to allow Ophelia to be admitted. Compare II.ii.185–86, III.ii.340–41.

18 **Toy** trifle. See I.iii.6.
Amiss misfortune.

19 **artless Jealousy** uncontrollable anxiety.

20 **spills** both (a) undoes, destroys, and (b) pours out, reveals. The quotation marks enclosing lines 16–20 derive from the Second Quarto. They are apparently meant to indicate that the Queen is reciting a verse she has memorized. The actor playing the Queen was probably meant to speak with more formality than usual when delivering these lines.

S.D. **Enter Ophelia distracted** The word *distracted* derives from the First Folio stage direction; here it means 'beside herself', 'deranged'. The First Quarto, which undoubtedly preserves some authentic staging detail despite its generally unreliable rendering of the text of the play, indicates that Ophelia enters 'playing on a Lute', singing, and with her 'hair down' (a conventional sign of madness). The songs she sings in this scene are probably snatches from ballads that would have been familiar to the original audience.

22 **How now** both (a) how are you, and (b) what may I do for you.

The Hearers to Collection: they yawn at it,
And botch the Words up fit to their own
   Thoughts,   10
Which, as her Winks, and Nods, and Gestures yield
   them,
Indeed would make one think there might be
   Thought,
Though nothing sure, yet much unhappily.
HORATIO   'Twere good she were spoken with, for she
   may strew
Dangerous Conjectures in ill breeding Minds.   15
Let her come in.

Enter Ophelia distracted.

QUEEN   'To my Sick Soul, as Sin's true Nature is,
   Each Toy seems Prologue to some great Amiss;
   So full of artless Jealousy is Guilt,
   It spills it self in fearing to be spilt.'   20
OPHELIA   Where is the beauteous Majesty of Denmark?
QUEEN   How now, Ophelia?
OPHELIA *sings*

   ' "How should I your True-love know
     From another one?"

25   **Cockle Hat**   a hat with a cockle shell on it. Such hats were worn by pilgrims who had visited the shrine of Saint James of Compostela in Spain. *Cockle* and *Staff* are both words that hint at the dead lover's physical endowments; see the notes to lines 42, 64.

26   **Shoone**   an archaic (poetic) plural for *shoes*.

27   **imports**   signifies. See IV.iii.63–65.

32   **Stone**   gravestone. The placement of the marker at the feet, rather than the head, of the deceased anticipates other irregularities to be dwelled on later in the ballad, and then later in the play. *Stone* can also mean 'testicle'; see *Romeo and Juliet*, I.iii.53, and *The Merchant of Venice*, II.viii.23–24. In this song the word is a reminder that Ophelia laments both the death of her father and the loss of her 'True-love' (Hamlet).

36   **Shrowd**   shroud; burial cloth. The Quarto spelling suggests a relationship with *shrewd*, 'cursed' or 'sharp'; compare I.iv.1, where the word usually rendered *shrowdly* in modern editions is spelled *shroudly*.

38   **Larded**   bestrewn, covered over.

39–40 **Which ... Showers**   Ophelia's song implies that the 'True-love' who has died has not been properly mourned. Spoken in the Queen's presence, these words are a reminder of the insufficiency of her devotion to the elder Hamlet. But they have a more direct bearing on another recent burial whose circumstances are hinted at in lines 87–88.

42   **good-dild**   a garbled version of 'God yield' (bless).

42–43 **They say ... Daughter**   Ophelia is probably quoting some version of a folk-tale in which a baker's daughter, having been stingy when asked for bread by a beggar who was actually Christ in disguise (see Matthew 25:31–46), was transformed into an owl. Bakers' daughters appear to have been held in low esteem generally, and in many ballads and tales they are depicted as lascivious.

46   **Conceit upon her Father**   The King means that Ophelia's words reflect her grief for her father.

50   **betime**   early.

"By his Cockle Hat and Staff,   25
  And his Sandal Shoone." '
QUEEN   Alas, sweet Lady, what imports this Song?
OPHELIA   Say you? Nay pray you mark:

' "He is dead and gone, Lady,
  He is dead and gone;   30
  At his Head a Grass-green Turf,
  At his Heels a Stone." '

O ho.
QUEEN   Nay but Ophelia.
OPHELIA   Pray you mark: 35
  'White his Shrowd as the Mountain Snow.'

Enter King.

QUEEN   Alas, look here, my Lord.
OPHELIA   'Larded all with sweet Flowers,
  Which, beweept to the Ground, did not go
    With True-love Showers.'   40
KING   How do you, pretty Lady?
OPHELIA   Well, good-dild you. They say the Owl was
a Baker's Daughter; Lord, we know what we are,
but know not what we may be. God be at your
Table.   45
KING   Conceit upon her Father.
OPHELIA   Pray let's have no Words of this, but when
they ask you what it means, say you this.

'To morrow is Saint Valentine's Day,
  All in the Morning betime,   50
And I a Maid at your Window
  To be your Valentine.

    Then up he rose,
    And donn'd his Clothes,

55   **dupp'd** opened. Compare lines 53–58 with *King Lear*,
      I.v.54–55.

61   **Gis** an abbreviation of 'Jesus'.
      Saint Charity holy love (from Latin *caritas*).

64   **Cock** both (a) a corruption of God, and (b) a reference to the
      male member. See line 25.
      too blame too much to blame.

65   **tumbled me** took my maidenhead.

69   **And** if.

73   **lay . . . Ground** place him without proper ceremony in the
      earth, rather than accord him the dignity of a stone vault.

76   **God night** like *good night*, an abbreviation of 'God give you
      good night'.

79–80 **O this . . . behold** The King's momentary lapse into prose is an
      indication of his own disturbed condition; he has temporarily
      lost his secure command of the discourse habitual to him. In
      the speech that follows, moreover, there are several lines
      (among them 86–87) that contain enough metrical
      irregularities to make them seem like eruptions of prose
      beneath an otherwise smooth overlay of verse. Compare
      II.i.48–51.

82   **single Spies** as individual scouts to gather intelligence for the
      army preparing an attack. See IV.iv.29–30.

84   **Author** originator; instigator, responsible party.

85   **muddied** stirred up, agitated.

And dupp'd the Chamber Door;   55
   Let in the Maid
   That out a Maid
Never departed more.'

KING   Pretty Ophelia.

OPHELIA   Indeed without an Oath I'll make an end on't.   60

'By Gis and by Saint Charity,
   Alack and fie for Shame,
Young Men will do't if they come to't,
   By Cock they are too blame.'

Quoth she, "Before you tumbled me,   65
   You promis'd me to wed." '

He answers:
' "So would I 'a done, by yonder Sun,
   And thou hadst not come to my Bed." '

KING   How long hath she been thus?   70

OPHELIA   I hope all will be well; we must be
patient, but I cannot choose but weep to think
they would lay him i'th' cold Ground. My
Brother shall know of it, and so I thank you
for your good Counsel. – Come, my Coach.   75
– God night, Ladies, God night. Sweet Ladies,
God night, God night.   *Exit.*

KING   Follow her close, give her good Watch, I pray
   you.   *[Exit Horatio.]*
O this is the Poison of deep Grief; it springs
all from her Father's Death, and now behold,   80
O Gertrard, Gertrard,
When Sorrows come, they come not single Spies
But in Battalions. First her Father slain;
Next your Son gone, and he most violent Author
Of his own just Remove; the People muddied,   85
Thick, and unwholesome in their Thoughts, and
   Whispers

87   **greenly**   foolishly (like a naive child).

88   **In hugger mugger**   with haste, secrecy, and little if any
         ceremony.

90   **Pictures**   only images of human beings. *Fair* (line 89) recalls
         IV.i.36.

93   **keeps himself in Clouds**   hides himself away in a suspicious
         obscurity. Claudius' imagery recalls I.ii.66–73. *Containing*
         (line 91) echoes IV.iv.61.

94   **wants . . . Ear**   is not lacking for gossips and malcontents to
         incite him to rebellion. *Buzzers* is an echoic word to imitate
         the sound of those who whisper; it also suggests buzzing
         insects (pests) and buzzards as they infect Laertes' ear. See the
         notes to II.ii.415, 421. Line 94 recalls such previous passages
         as I.v.35–37 and IV.ii.24–25. *Feeds* echoes IV.iii.16–31.

95   **pestilent**   both (a) contagious, and (b) pest-borne.

96–98 **Wherein . . . Ear**   with which [Polonius' death] those who have
         no real 'Matter' (substantive basis) for their discontent, and
         need to find a justification for it, will not hesitate to blame
         'our Person' (Claudius) in one ear after another. *Matter* recalls
         IV.i.1; *beggar'd* (impoverished) echoes IV.iii.22–24, 31.

99   **a Murd'ring-piece**   a type of cannon that discharged a
         scattering of shots and could thus hit many men with one
         firing.

100   **superfluous Death**   enough blows to kill me many times over.
         The literal meaning of *superfluous* is 'overflowing', and that
         sense will prove applicable not only to Claudius but to 'poor
         Ophelia' (line 88).

101   **Swissers**   Swiss guards, mercenaries from Switzerland.

103   **over-peering of his List**   looking over its boundary (overflowing
         its shore). Compare line 100. *List* echoes I.i.93, I.iii.30, I.v.21,
         168, III.i.147.

104   **Flats**   flat land, beaches.
         impitious   both (a) pitiless, and (b) impetuous. Compare II.i.78,
         90, III.iv.125.

105   **in a riotous Head**   at the head of an uncontrollable force.

106   **O'erbears**   overwhelms. Compare lines 100, 103.

107   **as**   as if.

For good Polonius' Death; and we have done
  but greenly
In hugger mugger to inter him; poor Ophelia
Devided from her self, and her fair Judgement,
Without the which we are Pictures, or mere Beasts;   90
Last, and as much containing as all these,
Her Brother is in secret come from Fraunce,
Feeds on this Wonder, keeps himself in Clouds,
And wants not Buzzers to infect his Ear
With pestilent Speeches of his Father's Death,   95
Wherein Necessity, of Matter beggar'd,
Will nothing stick our Person to arraign
In Ear and Ear. O my dear Gertrard, this,
Like to a Murd'ring-piece, in many places
Gives me superfluous Death.   *A Noise within.* 100

Enter a Messenger.

KING Attend, where is my Swissers, let them guard
  the Door.
  – What is the matter?
MESSENGER   Save your self, my Lord.
  The Ocean over-peering of his List
  Eats not the Flats with more impitious Haste
  Than young Laertes in a riotous Head   105
  O'erbears your Officers. The Rabble call him
    Lord,
  And as the World were now but to begin,

244

108   **Antiquity forgot**   all age and tradition forgotten or disregarded. See I.v.90–103.

109   **The Ratifiers . . . Word**   the basis and support for every pledge and compact in civilized society.

113   **cheerfully**   excitedly (like baying dogs 'crying' after their prey).

114   **Counter**   To run counter was to pursue the scent in the wrong direction, to pursue nothing. See the notes to I.ii.60, III.ii.123, and compare III.iv.52, IV.i.32.

117   **give me leave**   permit me [to speak with the King alone]. Compare I.ii.49–61.

121–   **brands . . . Mother**   places the brand of a whore even here
23   [probably accompanied by a gesture to the centre of Laertes' forehead] between the chaste, unblemished brows of my virtuous mother. Hamlet has used a similar image in III.iv.42. *Chast* (*chaste*) echoes III.i.137.

124   **looks so Giant-like**   manifests itself in such an audacious fashion. The King alludes to the rebellion of the ancient Giants of the Earth, who piled Mount Pelion atop Mount Ossa in an attempt to storm Heaven and overthrow the Olympian Gods. Shakespeare would have known the story from Ovid's *Metamorphoses* (Book I) and *Fasti* (Book V). See the notes to V.i.266, 295.

125   **fear our Person**   be afraid for me or for the 'Person' (body) of Majesty itself. See the note to IV.ii.28–29.

126–   **There's . . . Will**   A king, being God's deputy on Earth, is so
28   thoroughly surrounded with divine power that Treason can do no more than lift its head without having its will suppressed. In view of what 'Treason' has done to Claudius' predecessor, the King's words are undercut by an irony that is lost on Laertes but not on the audience.

127   **but . . . would**   merely (a) show the top of its head and utter a chick-like peep through the eggshell (compare III.i.168–74) from which it seeks to hatch, and (b) peer through a crack in the 'hedge' it would like to penetrate. *Peep* echoes III.iv.113–16.

129   **incens'd**   inflamed with choler. Compare V.ii.61, 316, and see the note to III.ii.331.

Antiquity forgot, Custom not known,
The Ratifiers and Props of every Word,
They cry 'Choose we, Laertes shall be King,   110
Caps, Hands, and Tongues applaud it to the
    Clouds,
Laertes shall be King, Laertes King.'

                    A Noise within.

QUEEN   How cheerfully on the False Trail they cry.
  – O this is Counter, you false Danish Dogs.

       Enter Laertes with Others.

KING   The Doors are broke.
LAERTES   Where is this King?   115
  – Sirs, stand you all without.
ALL   No, let's come in.
LAERTES   I pray you give me leave.
ALL   We will, we will.
LAERTES   I thank you, keep the Door. – O thou
  vile King,
  Give me my Father.
QUEEN   Calmly, good Laertes.
LAERTES   That Drop of Blood that's calm proclaims
    me Bastard,   120
  Cries Cuckold to my Father, brands the Harlot
  Even here between the chast unsmirched Brow
  Of my true Mother.
KING   What is the Cause, Laertes,
  That thy Rebellion looks so Giant-like?
  – Let him go, Gertrard, do not fear our Person: 125
  There's such Divinity doth hedge a King
  That Treason can but peep to what it would,
  Acts little of his Will. – Tell me, Laertes,
  Why thou art thus incens'd. – Let him go,
    Gertrard.
  – Speak, Man.

132   **juggled with**   subjected to tricks and sleight of hand, abused (II.ii.641).

133   **To Hell, Allegiance**   What Laertes says here and in the following lines is that he is prepared to forswear his Christian faith, and particularly the injunction that subjects leave vengeance to God and obey their rulers (see Romans 12, 13), and risk damnation in order to avenge his father's death.

135   **To this Point I stand**   to this pledge I commit myself, and I will not be moved. *Stand* echoes IV.iv.53; *Point* recalls I.v.126; and both words emphasize the virile assertiveness of Laertes' refusal to be treated as a weaker vessel. Compare the erotic analogies in IV.iv.36–63 and in lines 126–28, 131 (where Claudius depicts Kingship as invulnerable to assault by aggressive 'Will'), and in line 134 (where 'Pit' suggests both Hell and the 'Sulphurous' female 'Pit' of *King Lear*, IV.vi.126).

136   **That . . . Negligence**   that I will henceforth refuse to concern myself with either Heaven or Hell, 'Let come what comes' (line 137).

137   **onely**   only. But here, as in III.ii.131, the spelling in the early texts reinforces the kind of phallic one-liness that figures in similar contexts elsewhere; compare *Julius Caesar*, I.ii.153–54, and *Macbeth*, I.vii.72–74.

138   **throughly**   thoroughly.

140   **husband**   manage; conserve and employ. *Will* (line 139, echoing lines 126–28) recalls such previous passages as I.ii.60, I.v.43–45, II.i.98–102, III.i.75–79, III.iii.39, III.iv.80–86, IV.iv.36–43. Compare Sonnets 135, 136, and see *Julius Caesar*, II.ii.71.

144   **Soopstake**   swoopstake, a variant of *sweepstake*, a word that describes a winner's scooping up all the stakes (money wagered) in a betting game. Laertes is ready to sweep not only what he is entitled to but everything else as well. Compare IV.iv.43–53. *Draw* echoes IV.i.24.

145   **Looser**   both (a) loser, and (b) releaser (the one who gives away the stakes). Compare III.ii.424.

LAERTES   Where is my Father?
KING   Dead.   130
QUEEN   But not by him.
KING   Let him demaund his Fill.
LAERTES   How came he Dead? I'll not be juggled with.
  To Hell, Allegiance; Vows, to the blackest Devil;
  Conscience and Grace, to the profoundest Pit.
  I dare Damnation. To this Point I stand,   135
  That both the Worlds I give to Negligence,
  Let come what comes, onely I'll be reveng'd
  Most throughly for my Father.
KING   Who shall stay you?
LAERTES   My Will, not all the World's:
  And for my Means, I'll husband them so well,   140
  They shall go far with little.
KING   Good Laertes,
  If you desire to know the Certainty
  Of your dear Father, is't writ in your Revenge
  That, Soopstake, you will draw both Friend and
      Foe,
  Winner and Looser?
LAERTES   None but his Enemies.   145
KING   Will you know them then?
LAERTES   To his good Friends thus wide I'll ope my
      Arms,

148 **Life-rend'ring Pelican** Laertes alludes to the bestiary fable
about the mother Pelican who, in order to preserve her
starving offspring, feeds them the blood of her own breast. An
emblem of self-sacrifice, the Pelican was a popular medieval
symbol for a Christ-like ruler's devotion to the well-being of
his commonwealth.

149 **Repast** feed. Shakespeare's wording in this passage reminds us
that the Pelican's sacrifice is an emblem of the Pastor
(shepherd) who opened his arms wide on the Cross and laid
down 'his life for his friends' (John 15:13).

152 **sensibly** feelingly (with all my senses). *Grief*, which can here
mean 'grievance', recalls III.ii.223, 364–66.

153 **level** even, clear. The King may be thinking of himself as a
target (with his pure heart as the 'blank' or centre) at which
Laertes' 'Judgement' may 'level' (take aim). His implication is
that because he is innocent, he can withstand the most
penetrating scrutiny. Compare lines 98–100, and see
IV.i.38–44.
'pear appear. This word plays on *peer* and echoes lines 103,
127.

157 **Sense and Virtue** sensation and operative power.

158– **paid ... Beam** Laertes promises to pile enough 'Weight' of
59 revenge on 'our Scale' (his family's) to tip the balance beam in
his favour. It will not be enough to get 'even'; Laertes insists
on more than compensatory damages. The phrase *turn the
Beam* can also mean 'divert the beam of the most searing
eyesight'.

163– **Nature ... loves** Nature (and human nature in particular) is
65 shown to be most 'fine' (pure, refined) when it manifests itself
through Love; and where it is present in its noblest form (as in
Ophelia's love for her father), it sends some precious part or
sign ('Instance') of itself (in this case, Ophelia's 'Wits' or
sanity) to the object of its devotion (the 'Poor Man's Life').

170 **persuade Revenge** urge me by arguments to commit revenge.

And like the kind Life-rend'ring Pelican,
Repast them with my Blood.
KING   Why now you speak
  Like a good Child, and a true Gentleman.   150
  That I am Guiltless of your Father's Death,
  And am most sensibly in Grief for it,
  It shall as level to your Judgement 'pear
  As Day dooes to your Eye.
A Noise within: Let her come in.

Enter Ophelia.

LAERTES   How now? What Noise is that?   155
  – O Heat, dry up my Brains; Tears seven times
    salt
  Burn out the Sense and Virtue of mine Eye.
  – By Heaven, thy Madness shall be paid with
    Weight
  Till our Scale turn the Beam. O Rose of May,
  Dear Maid, kind Sister, sweet Ophelia.   160
  – O Heavens, is't possible a Young Maid's Wits
  Should be as mortal as a Poor Man's Life?
  Nature is fine in Love, and where 'tis fine
  It sends some precious Instance of it self
  After the thing it loves.   165
OPHELIA   'They bore him Bare-fac'd on the Bier,   *Song.*
  Hey non nonny nonny, hey nonny:
    And in his Grave rain'd many a Tear.'
  Fare you well, my Dove.
LAERTES   Hadst thou thy Wits, and didst persuade
    Revenge,   170
  It could not move thus.

172 **A-down** Like the nonsense words in line 167, this refrain would normally function simply as melodic filler; in this context, however, it reminds us that, like Ophelia's father, Ophelia's wits are now 'quite quite down' (III.i.158). She is 'of Ladies most Deject and Wretched', and her own 'Noble and most Sovereign Reason, / Like sweet Bells jangl'd out of Time, and Harsh', is 'Blasted with Ecstasy' (III.i.159–64).

173 **Wheel** refrain (but with an echo of the Wheel of Fortune, also 'down').

175 **Steward** household manager, 'husband' (line 140). This word recalls the parables on stewardship cited in the note to III.iii.82.

177 **Remembrance** mindfulness; fidelity to one's obligations; commitment to those to whom one is indebted. Compare I.ii.1–7, 143, I.iii.84–85, I.v.90, 94–96, 110, II.ii.26, 468, 474, III.i.90, III.ii.210–47, V.ii.2, 3, 107. *Rosemary* is also associated with 'Grace and Remembrance' in *The Winter's Tale*, IV.iv.74–77.

182 **Fennel** a herb associated with (a) flattery, and (b) weddings. **Columbines** flowers associated with (a) ingratitude, and (b) infidelity.

180 **Document** Laertes probably has in mind a written record, comparable to the 'Tables' with which Hamlet resolves to 'remember' the Ghost's commands; see I.v.94–110. Ophelia's madness will 'persuade Revenge' (line 170) for Laertes in a way that parallels the Ghost's charge to Hamlet. The literal meaning of *document* is 'lesson' (from Latin *docere*, to teach).

183 **Rue** a herb associated with sorrow and repentance.

184 **Herb of Grace** another name for Rue. The Gardener uses this same phrase in III.iv.104 of *Richard II*.

185 **with a Difference** Ophelia's words derive from heraldry; a difference (such as the Daisy she now presents along with the Rue) was a variation in a coat of arms to allow individual members of a family to be distinguished by their heraldic insignia.

188 **made . . . End** died well (in a state of grace). Compare I.v.73–79, III.iii.73–96. *End* recalls IV.iii.24.

OPHELIA   You must sing 'A-down a-down,' and you
call him 'A-down-a'. O how the Wheel becomes
it; it is the false Steward that stole his Maister's
Daughter.   175
LAERTES   This Nothing's more than Matter.
OPHELIA   There's Rosemary, that's for Remembrance;
pray you, Love, remember; and there is Pansies,
that's for Thoughts.
LAERTES   A Document in Madness, Thoughts and   180
Remembrance fitted.
OPHELIA   There's Fennel for you, and Columbines;
there's Rue for you, and here's some for me.
We may call it Herb of Grace a' Sundays; you
may wear your Rue with a Difference. There's a   185
Daisy; I would give you some Violets, but they
wither'd all when my Father died; they say 'a
made a good End.

189 **bonny sweet Robin** The song Ophelia quotes here is likely to
have been a bawdy one (similar to the Valentine song she sang
in IV.v.49–69), with Robin referring to both a lover and a
male organ. But, as Laertes points out in the next speech,
Ophelia's pitiful innocence in madness can turn 'Hell it self' to
'Favour and to Prettiness'. Because there is not any 'Method'
in Ophelia's 'Madness' (II.ii.212–13), what would otherwise
sound like 'documents' of wantonness come across instead as
indications of unfulfilled hopes for 'Joy' (erotic fulfilment, line
189).

192 **come again** both (a) return, and (b) ejaculate any more. See the
note to line 140.

198 **Flaxen** white.
Pole poll (head), with play on the kind of 'pole' that 'Robin'
signifies.

200 **Mone** moan, here spelled in a way that provides an eye-rhyme
with *gone*.

201 **'a** have.

202 **buy** be with.

204 **commune with** share in; accented on the first syllable. *Grief*
(both sorrow and grievance) recalls I.ii.3, 82, 94, II.i.115,
III.i.180–82, 186–87, III.ii.220–23, 364–66, IV.v.79, 151–54,
and anticipates V.i.267–68.

208 **collateral Hand** indirect involvement (that is, through an agent
or associate).

209 **us touch'd** me touched (implicated) with guilt [of the crimes
you wish to avenge]. *Touch'd* recalls I.i.21, I.iii.89, I.v.134,
II.i.12, III.ii.265–66, 384, IV.i.29–32.

211 **in Satisfaction** to satisfy your honour and its demand that you
have justice.

214 **due Content** proper rest (as a result of its achieving
satisfaction).

215 **Obscure Funeral** secret burial service. The word *obscure*
literally means 'covered over'; what Laertes is implying is that
the manner of his father's hasty disposal was shady. See lines
87–88.

     'For bonny sweet Robin is all my Joy.'

LAERTES   Thoughts and Afflictions, Passion, Hell
   it self,   190
   She turns to Favour and to Prettiness.

OPHELIA   'And will 'a not come again,   *Song.*
               And will 'a not come again;
               No, no, he is dead,
               Go to thy Death-bed,   195
               He never will come again.

               His Beard was as white as Snow,
               All Flaxen was his Pole;
               He is gone, he is gone,
               And we cast away Mone.   200
               God 'a mercy on his Soul,'
   And of all Christians' Souls, God buy you.   *Exit.*

LAERTES   – Do you see this, O God?

KING   Laertes, I must commune with your Grief,
   Or you deny me Right. Go but apart,   205
   Make choice of whom your wisest Friends you
     will,
   And they shall hear and judge 'twixt you and
     me;
   If by direct or by collateral Hand
   They find us touch'd, we will our Kingdom give,
   Our Crown, our Life, and all that we call Ours   210
   To you in Satisfaction; but if not,
   Be you content to lend your Patience to us,
   And we shall jointly labour with your Soul
   To give it due Content.

LAERTES   Let this be so.
   His Means of Death, his Obscure Funeral,   215

216   **Hatchment**   a memorial tablet above the tomb, bearing the
          deceased's coat of arms. Compare line 185, and see the note
          to line 127, where Claudius refers to another kind of
          'Hatchment'.

217   **Right**   rite, ritual.
          Ostentation   public ceremony.

218   **Cry . . . Earth**   Claudius alludes to Genesis 4:10, where the
          Lord tells the author of the 'primal eldest Curse' (III.iii.37)
          that 'the voice of thy brother's blood crieth unto me from the
          ground'. He also echoes Luke 19:37–40, where the Pharisees
          tell Jesus to rebuke his disciples for referring to him as King;
          Jesus replies that 'if these should hold their peace, the stones
          would immediately cry out'. Line 218 recalls I.ii.125–28.

219   **That**   so that.

220   **the great Axe**   the axe of the executioner. Claudius assumes
          that the order he has sent to England will shortly provide for
          the fulfilment of this pledge; he expects to hear soon that
          Hamlet has been beheaded.

IV.vi   This scene is probably to be thought of as occurring somewhere
          in the Castle.

1   **What**   what kind of messengers.

10   **Embassador**   The 'ambassador' the Sailor refers to is Hamlet.

12   **let**   caused, made.

14   **Means**   way of transporting my letters.

16   **were two Days old at Sea**   had been at sea for two days.

17   **Appointment**   appearance and equipment.

18–19 **put on a compelled Valour**   fought bravely out of necessity.

19   **boorded**   boarded.

No Trophy Sword, nor Hatchment o'er his Bones,
No Noble Right, nor Formal Ostentation,
Cry to be heard, as 'twere from Heaven to Earth,
That I must call't in Question.

KING   So you shall,
And where th' Offence is, let the great Axe fall.   220
I pray you go with me.   *Exeunt.*

Scene 6

Enter Horatio and Others.

HORATIO   What are they that would speak with me?
GENTLEMAN   Sea-faring Men, Sir: they say they have
Letters for you.
HORATIO   Let them come in.
I do not know from what part of the World   5
I should be greeted, if not from Lord Hamlet.

Enter Sailors.

SAILOR   God bless you, Sir.
HORATIO   Let him bless thee too.
SAILOR   'A shall, Sir, and't please him. There's a
Letter for you, Sir: it came from th' Embassador   10
that was bound for England, if your name be
Horatio, as I am let to know it is.
HORATIO [*reads*]   'Horatio, when thou shalt have
over-look'd this, give these Fellows some Means
to the King: they have Letters for him. Ere we   15
were two Days old at Sea, a Pirate of very
warlike Appointment gave us Chase; finding our
selves too slow of sail, we put on a compelled
Valour, and in the Grapple I boorded them, on the

22   **Thieves of Mercy**   thieves who are gracious to their victims.

22–23 **but they knew what they did**   but they did it in the knowledge
         that it would be to their advantage to do so.

23   **Turn**   favour. The Folio prints 'good turne'. See III.iii.51–52.

25–26 **as thou wouldst fly Death**   as you would use if you were fleeing
         death.

27   **make thee Dumb**   stun you to speechlessness.

27–28 **too light . . . the Matter**   Hamlet compares his words to bullets
         that are too tiny for the bore (width) of the gun from which
         they are to be shot. Here *the Matter* refers to the subject that
         occasions the words. Compare I.i.65–73, I.ii.131–32,
         I.iii.34–35, I.iv.6 (stage direction), III.iv.83–86, 201–6,
         IV.i.41–44, IV.iii.40–43, IV.v.153–54.

33   **give you way**   guide you (to someone who will bear your letters
         to the King).

IV.vii This scene takes us to another room in the Castle, where the
         King is concluding a meeting with Laertes.

1   **my Acquittance seal**   give its seal to (formal recognition of) my
         innocence (acquittal). Here *Conscience* means both (a) mind,
         consciousness, and (b) conscience (the moral sense that
         requires a son to 'remember' his father by seeing that his
         slayer receives a just recompense for his crime). Compare
         II.ii.643, III.i.47, 80, IV.v.134, V.ii.58, 67–68, 309. *Seal*
         recalls I.ii.132, III.iv.59, and anticipates V.ii.50. Compare
         I.i.81, I.ii.60, III.ii.72, 430, III.iv.198, IV.iii.56, V.ii.47.

3   **Sith**   since.

6   **proceeded**   This reading derives from the First Folio; the Second
         Quarto prints *proceed*.
       Feats   deeds, particularly evil ones.

7   **Capital**   punishable by death (literally decapitation, cutting off
         the *capus*, head, of the offender).

9   **mainly**   both (a) powerfully, and (b) especially.

10   **unsinowed**   unsinewed, lacking in strength. Compare I.v.93.

instant they got clear of our Ship, so I alone   20
became their Prisoner. They have dealt with me
like Thieves of Mercy, but they knew what they
did: I am to do a Turn for them. Let the King
have the Letters I have sent, and repair thou
to me with as much speed as thou wouldest fly   25
Death; I have Words to speak in thine Ear will
make thee Dumb, yet are they much too light
for the Bore of the Matter. These good Fellows
will bring thee where I am. Rosencraus and
Guildenstern hold their Course for England;   30
of them I have much to tell thee. Farewell.

   So that thou knowest thine Hamlet.'
HORATIO Come, I will give you way for these your
  Letters,
And do't the speedier that you may direct me
To him from whom you brought them. *Exeunt.* 35

Scene 7

Enter King and Laertes.

KING Now must your Conscience my Acquittance seal,
 And you must put me in your Heart for Friend,
 Sith you have heard, and with a knowing Ear,
 That he which hath your Noble Father slain
 Pursued my Life.
LAERTES   It well appears: but tell me   5
 Why you proceeded not against these Feats
 So Criminal and so Capital in nature,
 As by your Safety, Greatness, Wisdom, all things else
 You mainly were stirr'd up.
KING   O for two special Reasons,
 Which may to you, perhaps, seem much
  unsinowed,   10

11 **th'are** they are.

14 **conjunctive to** joined to. This is one of many images of jointure
    in the play. Claudius is saying that he is as totally devoted to
    his wife as she is to her son. The King's phrasing is yet
    another reminder that his illegitimate union with Gertrard
    constitutes his principal claim to legitimacy as Denmark's
    monarch. See the notes to I.ii.9, 20, III.iii.20, III.iv.123.

15 **as the Star . . . Sphere** Claudius alludes to the Ptolemaic
    conception of the Universe, whereby each of the heavenly
    bodies revolved around the Earth fixed in a crystalline sphere.
    Compare I.iv.31, II.ii.146.

17 **Count** both (a) recounting (telling of what happened), and (b)
    accounting (trial and execution of the murderer). See IV.v.114
    for references to other words related to *Count*.

18 **General Gender** common people. Here *Gender* means 'kind'.

20 **the Spring . . . Stone** These are springs and wells in England
    that coat objects in carbonate of lime and thereby petrify
    them; one such location is Matlock Bath in Derbyshire.

21 **Gives** Claudius means 'gyves', shackles (see II.i.76), here used
    as symbols of Hamlet's criminality. But the Second Quarto
    spelling reminds us that it is because of Hamlet's gifts (one
    meaning of *gives*) that his fetters are converted to 'Graces'
    (endearing qualities).
    Graces virtues, signs of favour.

22 **Too slightly timber'd** made with too light a shaft.
    loud strong and noisy. The loud wind is an apt metaphor for
    the currents of popular feeling as Claudius depicts them.

23 **reverted** blown back.

24 **But . . . them** but not hit the targets I'd aimed for.

26 **into Desp'rate Terms** into a desperate (hopeless) condition.

27 **if Praises may go back again** Laertes' phrase can be interpreted
    in two ways: (a) if praises may return to an earlier condition
    (what Ophelia was before she went mad), and (b) if I may be
    forgiven for seeming to praise myself in praising one so near
    to me. Both ideas echo the King's image of the reverted
    arrows (lines 21–23). Hamlet will employ a similar metaphor
    in V.ii.252–56.

And yet to me th'are strong. The Queen his
   Mother
Lives almost by his Looks; and for my self,
My Virtue or my Plague, be it either which,
She's so conjunctive to my Life and Soul
That as the Star moves not but in his Sphere,   15
I could not but by her. The other Motive,
Why to a Public Count I might not go,
Is the great Love the General Gender bear him,
Who, dipping all his Faults in their Affection,
Work, like the Spring that turneth Wood to
   Stone,   20
Convert his Gives to Graces, so that my Arrows,
Too slightly timber'd for so loud a Wind,
Would have reverted to my Bow again,
But not where I have aim'd them.
LAERTES And so have I a Noble Father lost,   25
  A Sister driven into Desp'rate Terms,
  Whose Worth, if Praises may go back again,

28 **Stood ... Age** could stand on the top of the highest mountain for all the ages and challenge all comers. Compare III.iv.51–65, IV.v.133–38, V.i.262–67, 286–96.

31 **Flat and Dull** undistinguished (like the unreflecting 'foil', the dun-coloured backdrop that sets off a shiny jewel) and leaden. Compare II.ii.604, where Hamlet calls himself 'A dull and muddy-mettl'd Rascal', and V.ii.267–69, where the Prince says, 'I'll be your Foil, Laertes'. *Flat* can also mean 'unelevated' and 'stale'; see I.ii.133, IV.v.104, V.i.264–67. For other instances of *Dull* see I.iii.64, 77, I.v.30–33, IV.iv.29–30, V.i.59–60.

33 **Pastime** a matter of idle interest. *Beard* recalls II.ii.454–55, 608–18.
You ... more The King expects an ambassador to come soon with word of Hamlet's execution in England. Ironically, a messenger enters almost as he speaks, but with news of a very different nature. See the note to IV.v.220.

44 **Naked** unattended, alone. But in fact there is a 'naked' (unceremonious, unadorned) quality to Hamlet's whole letter. 'High and Mighty' sounds jauntily familiar, if not downright contemptuous, and it implies that the King is to be regarded as an overweening usurper rather than revered as a monarch deserving of his exalted position. In this edition the letter is rendered as it appears in the Second Quarto. The less 'naked' version in the Folio (adopted by most modern editions) adds the phrase *and more strange* before *Return*. It also affixes the name *Hamlet* to the end of the message. Lines 44–45 echo IV.iv.1–7. *Set* recalls IV.iii.62 and anticipates line 128.

46 **thereunto** for it. Because of the ambiguity of Hamlet's syntax, 'first asking you Pardon' can relate to either (a) Hamlet's recounting (telling) of his story, or (b) his 'Return'. See the note to I.ii.222.

49 **Abuse** deception, trick, lie. Compare II.ii.636–41.

50 **Character** handwriting. See I.iii.58–59.

52 **devise me** explain it to me.

Stood Challenger on Mount of all the Age
For her Perfections; but my Revenge will come.
KING   Break not your Sleeps for that; you must
   not think   30
That we are made of Stuff so Flat and Dull
That we can let our Beard be shook with Danger,
And think it Pastime; you shortly shall hear
   more;
I loved your Father, and we love our self,
And that I hope will teach you to imagine –   35

Enter a Messenger with Letters.

– How now? What News?
MESSENGER   Letters, my Lord, from Hamlet.
These to your Majesty, this to the Queen.
KING   From Hamlet, who brought them?
MESSENGER   Sailors, my Lord, they say; I saw them
   not.
They were given me by Claudio: he receiv'd them   40
Of him that brought them.
KING   – Laertes, you shall hear them.
– Leave us.   *Exit Messenger.*
   [*Reads*] 'High and Mighty, you shall know I
   am set Naked on your Kingdom. To morrow shall
   I beg leave to see your Kingly Eyes, when I   45
   shall, first asking you Pardon, thereunto
   recount the Occasion of my sudden Return.'
What should this mean: are all the rest come back,
Or is it some Abuse, and no such thing?
LAERTES   Know you the Hand?
KING   'Tis Hamlet's Character. Naked,   50
And in a Postscript here he says alone.
Can you devise me?
LAERTES   I am lost in it, my Lord, but let him come:
It warms the very Sickness in my Heart
That I shall live and tell him to his Teeth   55

56 **didst** Modern editions normally adopt the Folio's *diest* here. The implications are much the same: in charging and challenging Hamlet, Laertes would in effect be telling him that he must die at the hands of an avenger. It may be that as he speaks this line Laertes thrusts his sword in a manner that mimics what Hamlet did to his father.

58 **I** both 'I' [will], and 'Ay'. Compare IV.ii.15.

59 **to a Peace** to be reconciled with my enemy.

61 **checking at his Voyage** reproving, rejecting the idea of his voyage, like a hawk that checks at (attacks) any prey it sees. See the note to II.ii.461.

62–63 **I will . . . Devise** I will manipulate him into undertaking an exploit, the idea for which has just matured in my thinking (though the seeds for it were present before this moment). *Devise*, 'devising' or 'device', echoes line 52 and anticipates line 68.

65 **breath** breathe, give breath (rhyming with *Death*). Compare III.iv.195.

66 **uncharge the Practice** exonerate the activity. Here *uncharge* means the opposite of *charge* (accuse). See the note to III.iv.84, and compare IV.iv.44. *Practice* can refer to the execution of any kind of plan; but here it carries the connotation of a trick or stratagem.

67 **Accident** accident, here 'that which accedes (yields) to circumstance'. Compare III.i.28, III.ii.223, IV.vii.118, V.ii.394.

68 **The rather** and all the more so.

69 **Organ** agent, instrument. Compare III.ii.398, and see the notes to IV.v.135, 137, 140.

70 **Travail** travel. The Elizabethan spelling reminds us that travel in the Renaissance involved considerable effort. Compare II.ii.353, III.i.76–77.

72 **Parts** abilities, accomplishments.

75 **unworthiest Siege** least importance. Here *Siege* is used in the earlier sense of 'seat' (throne) or 'rank'. *Regard* (opinion) recalls II.ii.79, III.i.84.

'Thus didst thou.'

KING   If it be so, Laertes,
As how should it be so, how otherwise,
Will you be rul'd by me?

LAERTES   I my Lord,
So you will not o'errule me to a Peace.

KING   To thine own Peace; if he be now returned   60
As checking at his Voyage, and that he means
No more to undertake it, I will work him
To an Exploit, now ripe in my Devise,
Under the which he shall not choose but fall;
And for his Death no Wind of Blame shall
          breath,   65
But even his Mother shall uncharge the Practice
And call it Accedent.

LAERTES   My Lord, I will be rul'd,
The rather if you could devise it so
That I might be the Organ.

KING   It falls right,
You have been talk'd of since your Travail much,   70
And that in Hamlet's Hearing, for a Quality
Wherein they say you shine; your Sum of Parts
Did not together pluck such Envy from him
As did that One, and that in my Regard
Of the unworthiest Siege.

LAERTES   What Part is that, my Lord?   75

76 **Ribaud** both (a) ribald (ribaldry, a toy or trifle, not excluding a bawdy 'Light and Careless' Livery', line 78, echoing III.iv.157–64), and (b) riband (ribbon, decorative flourish). Compare I.iii.5–10, 99–110, II.ii.238–40, III.i.90–99. Most editions follow the 1611 Third Quarto and emend the Quarto's *ribaud* to *riband*; see the note to I.ii.83.

79 **Sables** dark fur coats. Compare III.ii.136–37. Lines 76–79 echo II.i.107–13.
   Weeds apparel. This word recalls I.ii.132–37.

80 **Importing . . . Graveness** signifying maturity and dignity. Compare IV.v.27. *Graveness* recalls IV.v.29–32, 215–19.
   since ago.

83 **can well** are highly skilled. Here *can* combines knowledge and capability.

86–87 **Incorps'd . . . With** combined into a single composite body. *Incorps'd* provides another reminder of Polonius' corpse.

87 **topp'd** excelled. Compare III.ii.415.

88 **in Forgery . . . Tricks** in an attempt to forge an adequate description with all the flourishes that rhetoric supplies. *Forgery* recalls II.i.19–20.

90 **Lamord** This name may be intended to suggest both *le mords* (Old French for a horse's bit by which a rider controls his mount) and *La Mort* (French for 'death'). Some editions follow the Folio and print *Lamound* (which would suggest *le monde* and describe an ideal man of the world).

91 **Brooch** ornament, here one to be worn in the hat of a courtier. Compare lines 76–80.

92 **He . . . of you** he confessed his inferiority to you.

93 **Masterly Report** testimony to your mastery.

94 **Art and Exercise in your Defence** technique and execution in the courtly arts of self-defence.

97 **Scrimures** scrimers, fencers (from *escrimeurs* in French).

98 **Motion, Guard, nor Eye** offensive manoeuvres, defensive skills, nor precision in thrusting.

100 **Envy** both (a) sense of rivalry, and (b) malice.

KING   A very Ribaud in the Cap of Youth,
    Yet needful too, for Youth no less becomes
    The Light and Careless Livery that it wears
    Than settled Age his Sables, and his Weeds
    Importing Health and Graveness. Two Months
        since   80
    Here was a Gentleman of Normandy.
    I have seen my self, and serv'd against, the
        French,
    And they can well on Horseback, but this
        Gallant
    Had Witchcraft in't: he grew unto his Seat,
    And to such Wondrous Doing brought his Horse   85
    As had he been Incorps'd and Demi-natur'd
    With the brave Beast. So far he topp'd, me
        thought,
    That I in Forgery of Shapes and Tricks
    Come short of what he did.
LAERTES   A Norman was't?
KING   A Norman.
LAERTES   Upon my Life, Lamord.
KING   The very same.   90
LAERTES   I know him well, he is the Brooch indeed
    And Gem of all the Nation.
KING   He made Confession of you,
    And gave you such a Masterly Report
    For Art and Exercise in your Defence,
    And for your Rapier most especial,   95
    That he cried out 'twould be a Sight indeed
    If one could match you; the Scrimures of their
        Nation
    He swore had neither Motion, Guard, nor Eye,
    If you oppos'd them. Sir, this Report of his
    Did Hamlet so envenom with his Envy   100
    That he could nothing do but wish and beg
    Your sudden coming o'er to play with you.

105   **the Painting of a Sorrow**   a mere imitation of true sorrow.
Compare IV.v.88–90, and see such previous passages as
I.ii.147–49, 198, I.v.95–103, II.ii.4–7, III.i.48–50, 145–49,
157–58, III.ii.14, III.iii.46–47, III.iv.17–19, 51–65.

109   **in Passages of Proof**   through proven experience (evidence that
has accumulated over the passage of time).

110   **qualifies**   moderates and thus lessens. This passage echoes a
theme of 'The Mousetrap', especially III.ii.210–39.

112   **Weeke**   wick.
Snuff   either (a) a device for snuffing out a flame, or (b) the
cutting off of the end of a wick.
abate   diminish or extinguish.

113   **at a like Goodness still**   at the same intensity forever.

114   **Plurisy**   surfeit, superfluity ('too much'). The King is thinking of
pleurisy (an inflammation of the pleura, the thin membrane
enveloping the lungs); its discharges were thought to result
from the excessive consumption of fluids. Compare
III.iv.150–52.

115   **too much**   excess, overgrowth. See the note to IV.v.100, and
compare IV.iv.24–26.

117   **Abatements**   legal impediments, quashing forbidden practices.
Delays   This word recalls 'the Law's Delay' (III.i.69); and
Claudius' speech as a whole echoes several of Hamlet's
soliloquies. Like his nephew, the King is aware that 'the
Native Hew of Resolution' (III.i.81) may itself be hewn down
by any of a variety of 'Accidents'.

118   **Accidents**   accidents. See line 67.

119–   **Spendthrift's Sigh . . . easing**   Every sigh was thought to cause
20   the loss of a drop of blood.

122   **indeed**   both (a) truly, and (b) in deed (by what you do).

124   **should Murther sanctuarize**   should provide (a) asylum for a
murderer (an ironic reminder of Hamlet's words in the Prayer
Scene, III.iii.73–96), and (b) security against a murder enacted
in retaliation.

125   **have no Bounds**   acknowledge no limits on its scope.

Now out of this —
LAERTES   What out of this, my Lord?
KING Laertes, was your Father dear to you?
  Or are you like the Painting of a Sorrow,   105
  A Face without a Heart?
LAERTES   Why ask you this?
KING Not that I think you did not love your Father,
  But that I know Love is begun by Time,
  And that I see in Passages of Proof
  Time qualifies the Spark and Fire of it.   110
  There lives within the very Flame of Love
  A kind of Weeke, or Snuff that will abate it,
  And nothing is at a like Goodness still,
  For Goodness, growing to a Plurisy,
  Dies in his own too much. That we would do   115
  We should do when we would: for this 'would'
    changes,
  And hath Abatements and Delays as many
  As there are Tongues, are Hands, are Accidents.
  And then this 'should' is like a Spendthrift's
    Sigh,
  That hurts by easing. But to the Quick of th'
    Ulcer,   120
  Hamlet comes back: what would you undertake
  To show your self indeed your Father's Son
  More than in Words?
LAERTES   To cut his Throat i'th' Church.
KING No place indeed should Murther sanctuarize,
  Revenge should have no Bounds. But good Laertes,   125

126 **Will you do this** if you will do this.

128 **put . . . praise** commission courtiers who will commend.

130 **in fine** in the end. Compare II.ii.69, 479, IV.v.163–65.

131 **Remiss** neglectful, lacking in prudence.

133 **Foils** fencing swords.

135 **unbated** its end not blunted with a button to cover the tip.
     a pace of Practice a rapid thrust in a practice match for sport.
     Pace may be a Shakespearean spelling for *pass* (the fencing
     term that appears in the Folio, echoing *Passages*, line 109),
     but it seems equally likely to be a pun to convey the kind of
     fast-paced 'Shuffling' required to accomplish the shift
     Claudius is plotting. *Shuffling* recalls III.iii.60–64.

138 **an Unction . . . Mountebank** an ointment from an itinerant
     drug salesman. *Unction* echoes III.iv.142.

139 **Mortal** deadly.

140 **Cataplasm** poultice; a soft, moist plaster applied to a wound or
     sore.

141 **Simples** herbal extracts (from single plants rather than
     combinations thereof) for use as drugs.
     Virtue power (to cure).

143 **withal** therewith. *Touch* recalls IV.v.209.

144 **Contagion** poison. Compare I.iii.41–42, III.ii.420–21.
     gall chafe, scratch. See I.iii.39, III.ii.267, 298, V.i.148.

146 **Convenience** expedient; literally, a coming together of 'Time
     and Means'.

147 **fit us to our Shape** suit us to our roles (as avengers). *Fit* recalls
     IV.v.10; *Shape* echoes line 88 and III.ii.407.

148– **And . . . assay'd** and should our intention be disclosed as a
49   result of our inept performance [of this 'play' we are scheming
     to produce], it would be better for us if we hadn't attempted it
     in the first place. Here *And that* means 'If'. *Drift* recalls
     II.i.10, 37, III.i.1; *assay'd* echoes II.i.62, II.ii.71, III.i.14,
     III.iii.69.

150 **Back or Second** backup plan.

Will you do this, keep close within your Chamber;
Hamlet return'd shall know you are come home;
We'll put on those shall praise your Excellence,
And set a double Varnish on the Fame
The Frenchman gave you, bring you in fine
    together,   130
And wager o'er your Heads; he being Remiss,
Most Generous, and free from all Contriving,
Will not peruse the Foils, so that with ease,
Or with a little Shuffling, you may choose
A Sword unbated, and in a pace of Practice   135
Requite him for your Father.
LAERTES   I will do't,
And for that Purpose I'll anoint my Sword.
I bought an Unction of a Mountebank
So Mortal that, but dip a Knife in it,
Where it draws Blood, no Cataplasm so rare,   140
Collected from all Simples that have Virtue
Under the Moon, can save the thing from Death
That is but scratch'd withal. I'll touch my
    Point
With this Contagion, that if I gall him slightly,
It may be Death.
KING   Let's further think on this.   145
Weigh what Convenience both of Time and Means
May fit us to our Shape if this should fail;
And that our Drift look through our bad
    Performance,
'Twere better not assay'd; therefore this
    Project
Should have a Back or Second, that might hold   150

151 **blast in Proof**   fail (literally, blight) in execution, like a cannon that explodes while it is being test-fired. *Blast* recalls III.iv.62–63. *Proof* echoes line 109.

152 **Cunnings**   abilities, skills. Compare II.ii.473, 628, III.iv.136, V.ii.395.

153 **hate**   ha't (have it). Compare II.ii.576, V.ii.355.
hote   hot. See II.ii.137, III.ii.421.

154 **As make**   as you should contrive to make.
Bouts   individual rounds of fencing.

155 **prefarr'd**   preferred, offered.

156 **A Chalice for the nonce**   a goblet for the occasion (literally, 'the once'). *Chalice* often carries religious connotations.

157 **Stuck**   sword thrust. Compare *stucatho* (stoccato) in *Romeo and Juliet*, III.i.77. *Purpose* (line 158) echoes III.ii.23–29; it thereby reminds us that the 'Playing' Claudius and Laertes are plotting will hold up a 'Mirror' of the 'Nature' of their 'bad Performance' (line 148).

162 **ascaunt**   aslant (askance) over. The Folio prints *aslant*.

163 **his hoary**   its whitish.

164 **fantastic**   intricately wrought, the product of fantasy.

165 **Long Purples**   probably a kind of wild orchid with an extended phallus-like purple spike, (hence the 'grosser Name' provided by 'liberal' (free-speaking) peasants.

167 **cull-cold**   chaste (cold to 'culling', embracing).

168 **pendant**   hanging.
Cronet Weeds   weeds formed into crowns (with a play on *weeds*, 'apparel', echoing line 79). The Quarto spelling, a contraction of *coronet* (the spelling in the Folio), echoes *Crowflowers* (line 165) and suggests that these 'Weeds' have become a 'crow-net' to snare the hapless Ophelia. Compare I.iii.114, III.ii.373–75, and see the note to III.ii.91.

169 **envious**   malicious. Compare lines 99–102.

170 **Trophies**   the precious garlands she had woven from flowers. This word echoes IV.v.216.

171 **weeping Brook**   The Queen poetically absolves the water from blame. Compare IV.i.27.

If this did blast in Proof. Soft, let me see,
We'll make a solemn Wager on your Cunnings;
I hate, when in your Motion you are hote and dry,
As make your Bouts more violent to that end,
And that he calls for drink, I'll have prefarr'd
   him   155
A Chalice for the nonce, whereon but Sipping
If he by chance escape your venom'd Stuck,
Our Purpose may hold there. But stay, what
   Noise?

Enter Queen.

QUEEN   One Woe doth tread upon another's Heel,
   So fast they follow; your Sister's drown'd,
   Laertes.   160
LAERTES   Drown'd, O where?
QUEEN   There is a Willow grows ascaunt the Brook
   That shows his hoary Leaves in th' glassy Stream;
   Therewith fantastic Garlands did she make
   Of Crowflowers, Nettles, Daisies, and Long
     Purples,   165
   That liberal Shepherds give a grosser Name,
   But our cull-cold Maids do Deadmen's Fingers
     call them.
   There on the pendant Boughs, her Cronet Weeds
   Clamb'ring to hang, an envious Sliver broke,
   When down her weedy Trophies and her self   170
   Fell in the weeping Brook; her Clothes spread
     wide,
   And Marmaid-like awhile they bore her up,

173 **Lauds** hymns of praise.

174 **incapable . . . Distress** unable to recognize her own danger.

175– **native . . . Element** born in and accustomed to that
76 environment. Compare I.ii.47, I.iv.13–14.

175 **indewed** both (a) in-dewed (submerged in 'dew'), and (b)
endued (clothed, endowed, harmonized). See the notes to
I.v.90, 109; Ophelia has now been 'loosed' to return to her
'Element' (see II.ii.167), resolved 'into a Dew' (I.ii.130).

178 **melodious Lay** Here the liquids ('l'-sounds) in the Queen's
description evoke the element in which Ophelia sang her last
'Lay' (song).

183 **our Trick** an involuntary manifestation of weakness in keeping
with the 'Custom' of human nature: to cry despite the 'Shame'
a man feels when acting 'The Woman' (line 185). See the
notes to I.ii.101, 146, II.ii.587–625, IV.v.135.

185 **will be out** will come out.
Adiew adieu. See the note to line 175.

186 **fain** gladly, fervently.
blaze both (a) burn fiercely, and (b) proclaim itself. Compare
I.iii.116, I.v.20, and see the note to IV.v.216.

187 **Folly** Laertes refers to his 'foolish' lack of manly self-control.
He exits because he can no longer suppress his tears. Hamlet
appears to use *Foolery* with the same implications (womanish)
in V.ii.226. Compare *The Merchant of Venice*, II.iii.13–14,
Macbeth, IV.ii.27–29, *King Lear*, I.iv.315–18, IV.vii.43–46,
57–58.

Which time she chaunted Snatches of old Lauds,
As one incapable of her own Distress,
Or like a Creature native and indewed   175
Unto that Element; but long it could not be
Till that her Garments, heavy with their Drink,
Pull'd the poor Wretch from her melodious Lay
To muddy Death.
LAERTES   Alas, then she is drown'd.
QUEEN   Drown'd, drown'd.   180
LAERTES   – Too much of Water hast thou, poor
    Ophelia,
And therefore I forbid my Tears; but yet
It is our Trick, Nature her Custom holds,
Let Shame say what it will; when these are gone,
The Woman will be out. – Adiew, my Lord,   185
I have a Speech a' Fire that fain would blaze,
But that this Folly drowns it.   *Exit.*
KING   – Let's follow, Gertrard.
How much I had to do to calm his Rage;
Now fear I this will give it start again,
Therefore let's follow.   *Exeunt.*   190

V.i This scene takes place in a graveyard. The two 'Clowns' referred
to in the opening stage direction are a pair of rustics – one the
parish sexton and chief gravedigger, the other apparently his
assistant. They enter carrying spades and mattocks, and it
soon becomes evident that they are here to prepare for the
burial of Ophelia.

2 **Salvation** release. If the Clown is a genuine bumpkin, he
probably means to say 'damnation'. But if Ophelia 'made a
good End' (IV.v.188), she has achieved the only 'Salvation'
available to someone in her circumstances. See the note to
I.iii.103–4. At issue is whether Ophelia committed suicide; if
it had been determined that she did, she would be regarded as
one who was guilty of mortal sin (as Hamlet notes in
I.ii.131–32 and III.i.53–86) and would thus not be entitled to
Christian burial rites.

4 **Crowner** Coroner, the official who ruled on the cause of death
for anyone whose demise was not clearly by normal means.
This word echoes IV.vii.168.
sate on her sat on her (conducted a formal inquest into her
death).

7 **in her own Defence** while attempting to save her life.

8 **found so** so determined by the Coroner's inquest.

9 **so offended** The Clown probably means 'so defended' (thus
accounted for). Most editions follow the Folio, which prints
Se offendendo, another malapropism (for *se defendendo*, in
self-defence). In either case, the Clown may mean precisely
what he says: that Ophelia 'offended' against both herself and
the divine prohibition against self-slaughter.

11 **wittingly** knowingly. An 'Act' requires the conscious will of its
agent. See the note to I.v.43.

13 **or all** or all three at once. Most of today's editions follow the
Folio and print *argal*; see line 20.

14 **Goodman Delver** a title more or less equivalent to 'Neighbour
Digger'. *Delver* echoes III.iv.204, and it reminds us that
Hamlet is a 'Delver' too.

17–18 **will he nill he** will he or will he not.

18 **he goes** it is he that goes (he who is accountable for his act).
What the Clown fails to note is that *nill he* would not apply
to an act for which the victim was responsible.

ACT V

Scene 1

Enter two Clowns.

CLOWN   Is she to be buried in Christian Burial,
when she wilfully seeks her own Salvation?
OTHER   I tell thee she is, therefore make her
Grave straight; the Crowner hath sate on her,
and finds it Christian Burial.   5
CLOWN   How can that be, unless she drown'd her
self in her own Defence?
OTHER   Why 'tis found so.
CLOWN   It must be so offended, it cannot be else,
for here lies the Point. If I drown my self   10
wittingly, it argues an Act, and an Act hath
three Branches; it is to act, to do, to perform,
or all; she drown'd her self wittingly.
OTHER   Nay, but hear you, Goodman Delver.
CLOWN   Give me leave. Here lies the Water, good.   15
Here stands the Man, good. If the Man go to
this Water and drown himself, it is, will he
nill he, he goes; mark you that. But if the
Water come to him, and drown him, he drowns

20   **argall**   a rustic pronunciation of *ergo*, Latin for 'therefore'.
        Shakespeare is probably having an extra measure of fun with
        a pun on the name of an Elizabethan scholar, John Argall,
        who wrote learned treatises on logic.

23   **Quest**   inquest. The Clown's contraction keeps us mindful that
        a 'Quest' (search) for 'Law' is highly problematical in this
        case.

24   **Will . . . an't**   If you will have the truth of it. Compare
        IV.vii.126.

28   **have Count'naunce**   be indulged (have their deeds
        countenanced or overlooked). Compare IV.i.30–32.

30   **even Christen**   ordinary fellow Christians.

35   **bore Arms**   was entitled to bear a coat of arms as a gentleman
        (a distinction still conferred by the College of Arms in
        London, as in Shakespeare's England).

41   **to the Purpose**   with an answer that directly and truthfully
        addresses the question. Hamlet has used this expression
        earlier in his first conversation with Rosencraus and
        Guildenstern (II.ii.295).
        confess thy self   The Clown alludes to a proverb, 'Confess thy
        self and be hanged.' See *Othello*, IV.i.38–40.

42   **Go to**   come now, get out of here. *Go to* is usually an
        expression of disapprobation or protest, often used mockingly
        to express disbelief in or to dismiss what another speaker has
        just said.

45   **Frame**   structure. Compare I.ii.19–20, II.ii.317–24,
        III.ii.333–35.

46   **Tenants**   occupants (hanged criminals). *Tenant* literally means
        'holder', and it can also refer to that which 'hangs from'
        something.

48   **dooes well**   answers the question well. But in the next sentence
        the Clown gives a different twist to the expression, with *it*
        now referring not to the assistant's answer but to the Gallows
        made by the Gallows-maker.

49   **It dooes well**   it does its job well. Behind the dialogue on *well* is
        the sense of the word that means 'in Heaven'; see the note to
        II.ii.441.

not himself; argall, he that is not guilty of   20
his own Death shortens not his own Life.

OTHER   But is this Law?

CLOWN   Ay marry is't, Crowner's Quest Law.

OTHER   Will you ha' the Truth an't, if this had
not been a Gentlewoman, she should have been   25
buried out a' Christian Burial.

CLOWN   Why there thou say'st, and the more Pity
that Great Folk should have Count'naunce in
this World to drown or hang themselves, more
then their even Christen. Come, my Spade,   30
there is no auncient Gentlemen but Gard'ners,
Ditchers, and Grave-makers: they hold up
Adam's Profession.

OTHER   Was he a Gentleman?

CLOWN   'A was the first that ever bore Arms.   35

OTHER   Why he had none.

CLOWN   What, art a Heathen? How dost thou
understand the Scripture? The Scripture says
Adam digg'd; could he dig without Arms? I'll
put another Question to thee; if thou answerest   40
me not to the Purpose, confess thy self.

OTHER   Go to.

CLOWN   What is he that builds stronger than either
the Mason, the Shipwright, or the Carpenter?

OTHER   The Gallows-maker, for that Frame outlives a   45
thousand Tenants.

CLOWN   I like thy Wit well, in good faith, the
Gallows dooes well; but how dooes it well?
It dooes well to those that do ill. Now thou

50   **doost ill** doest evil. The Clown's jest is based on the notion
      that if his companion confesses his 'ill' before he is hanged,
      the Gallows will do 'well' for him by sending his redeemed
      soul to Paradise. This theology is also implicit in such
      passages as I.v.73–79, III.iii.73–96, IV.v.188, and V.ii.26–47.

55   **unyoke** be freed from further labour (like an ox), and (b) be
      cut down from the gallows.

56   **Marry** truly. This expression probably originated as an oath
      referring to the Virgin Mary. Like *Mass*, referring to the
      Eucharist (line 58, echoing II.i.50, III.ii.408), it was a very
      mild oath by Shakespeare's time.

60   **your dull Ass** a stupid ass. The Clown uses the familiar article.
      mend improve. *Pace* echoes IV.vii.135.

63   **soope** soup, brew (perhaps a mixed one, such as the 'pottle of
      Sack' with 'Eggs' that Falstaff rejects in III.v.30–34 of *The
      Merry Wives of Windsor*). This word echoes *Soopstake*,
      IV.v.144. Most of today's editions adopt the Folio's *stoupe*.

65–68 **In Youth . . . meet** The song that the Clown begins here and
      continues later is a garbled version of 'The Aged Lover
      Renounceth Love', a poem by Thomas Lord Vaux that had
      been printed in a popular anthology, *Tottel's Miscellany*, in
      1557. Many of the *O* and *a* words appear to be the Clown's
      grunts as he digs.

67   **To . . . Behove** to shorten the time for my benefit.

69   **no Feeling of his Business** no sensitivity to the kind of work he
      does. Compare IV.v.151–52.

71–72 **Custom . . . Easiness** Long habit has made it something he does
      with complete ease (without thinking deeply about it). See the
      Ghost's words about 'Ease' in I.v.30–33; and compare
      III.iv.32–36, 63–85, 153–67.

73–74 **the Hand . . . Sense** the hand that has been little employed is
      more sensitive (dainty), because it is not yet calloused.

74   **Dintier** both (a) daintier, and (b) dentier (with a greater
      disposition to put dents in the skulls it tosses and cudgels (line
      80). See *Antony and Cleopatra*, II.vi.39, where Pompey refers
      to 'Targes undinted'.

76   **claw'd** gripped.

doost ill to say the Gallows is built stronger   50
than the Church: argall, the Gallows may do well
to thee. To't again, come.

OTHER Who builds stronger than a Mason, a
Shipwright, or a Carpenter?

CLOWN Ay, tell me that and unyoke.   55

OTHER Marry now I can tell.

CLOWN To't.

OTHER Mass, I cannot tell.

CLOWN Cudgel thy Brains no more about it, for
your dull Ass will not mend his Pace with Beating.   60
And when you are ask'd this Question next, say
'A Gravemaker: the Houses he makes lasts till
Doomsday.' Go get thee in, and fetch me a soope
of Liquor.   [*Exit Other Clown.*]
　　　'In Youth when I did love, did love,   *Song.*   65
　　　　　Me thought it was very sweet
　　　To contract, O, the Time for a my
　　　　　Behove,
　　　　　O me thought there a was nothing a
　　　　　　meet.'

　　　　　　Enter Hamlet and Horatio.

HAMLET Has this Fellow no Feeling of his Business?
'A sings in Grave-making.   70

HORATIO Custom hath made it in him a Property of
Easiness.

HAMLET 'Tis e'en so: the Hand of little Employment
hath the Dintier Sense.

CLOWN 'But Age with his stealing Steps   *Song.*   75
　　　　　Hath claw'd me in his Clutch,

77 **intill the Land** into the land. The Clown's phrase suggests 'into the grave'; it also plays on *till*, cultivate.

80 **jowls it to the Ground** dashes its jowls to the ground. The Clown is digging up old bones to make room for the fresh corpse.

81 **Cain's Jawbone** This reference to the first murder (Genesis 4) reminds us of a more recent fratricide and of the murderer's own awareness of 'the primal eldest Curse' (III.iii.37). See IV.v.218.

82 **the Pate of a Politician** the head of a crafty intriguer (not limited to one involved in politics in the modern sense).

83 **o'er-reaches** Hamlet enjoys the irony that one who sought to undo others with his plots is now being bumped by a bumpkin.

83–84 **one that would circumvent God** one so overweening in his arrogance that he sought to get around (outwit) God himself. Compare *Macbeth*, II.iii.9–12, where the Porter derides the 'Equivocator' who 'committed Treason enough for God's sake, yet could not equivocate to Heaven'.

93 **Chop-less** without 'chops' (jaws).
Massene probably a variant of *mazzard*, head, and *mazer*, bowl or cup. The Folio prints *mazard*.

94–95 **and we . . . see't** if we had the skill to perceive it.

96 **Loggets** a game in which pieces of wood were tossed at a stake.

99 **Shrowding Sheet** burial shroud. See the notes to I.iv.1, IV.v.36.

103 **Quiddities** subtle arguments, fine legal distinctions.

104–5 **his Quillites . . . Tricks** Hamlet notes that none of the Lawyer's tricks will be of any use to him in the court of last resort presided over by the Gravedigger. Like quiddities, 'Quillites' are quibbles over minutiae. 'Tenures' are titles to real estate. Compare lines 45–46.

106 **Sconce** head, but with a pun on a type of fine.

107–8 **his Action of Battery** the Clown's liability for a suit (action) for his action of battery (battering the Lawyer's skull). Compare *Measure for Measure*, II.i.188–92.

> And hath shipp'd me intill the Land
> As if I had never been such.'

HAMLET   That Skull had a Tongue in it, and could
sing once; how the Knave jowls it to the Ground,   80
as if 'twere Cain's Jawbone, that did the first
Murder. This might be the Pate of a Politician,
which this Ass now o'er-reaches; one that would
circumvent God, might it not?

HORATIO   It might, my Lord.   85

HAMLET   Or of a Courtier, which could say 'Good
Morrow, sweet Lord; how doost thou, sweet Lord?'
This might be My Lord Such-a-One, that prais'd
My Lord Such-a-One's Horse when 'a went to beg
it, might it not?   90

HORATIO   Ay my Lord.

HAMLET   Why e'en so, and now My Lady Worm's
Chop-less, and knock'd about the Massene with a
Sexton's Spade; here's fine Revolution, and we
had the Trick to see't. Did these Bones cost   95
no more the Breeding but to play at Loggets
with 'em? Mine ache to think on't.

CLOWN   'A Pickaxe and a Spade, a Spade,   *Song*.
          For and a Shrowding Sheet.
          O a Pit of Clay for to be made   100
          For such a Guest is meet.'

HAMLET   There's another; why may not that be the
Skull of a Lawyer? Where be his Quiddities now,
his Quillites, his Cases, his Tenures, and his
Tricks? Why dooes he suffer this mad Knave now   105
to knock him about the Sconce with a dirty
Shovel, and will not tell him of his Action of
Battery? Hum, this Fellow might be in's Time

109– **Buyer of Land . . . Recoveries** Lawyers were notorious for
11 using their expertise to amass great holdings. 'Statutes' and
'Recognizances' were bonds in which debts had been secured
with land and property. 'Fines' and 'Recoveries' were
procedures for transferring land and property. 'Vouchers'
were devices to guarantee (vouch for) an owner's title.

111– **Is this . . . Dirt?** Is this the end of his fines, and the final return
13 from his recoveries, to have his fine head full of fine-grained
dirt? *Dirt* anticipates V.ii.87–89. *Fine* echoes IV.vii.130.

113– **Will . . . ha?** 'Indentures' were duplicate copies of a deed,
18 inscribed on a single sheet of parchment which was then cut
in an indented (toothlike) line so that the buyer's and seller's
halves could later be matched, if necessary, to prove their
authenticity. The Lawyer's final estate (the 'Box' he is buried
in) is too small to hold even the pieces of parchment (the
'Conveyances') that record the 'Dirt' he went to so much
effort to acquire. So much for the 'Assurance' (security) to be
found in 'Sheep-skins'. *Dirt* carries the same implications as
Dust in I.ii.68–73. Compare Hamlet's remarks in lines
213–29 and in II.ii.315–30, IV.ii.6, IV.iii.16–35.

114 **Doubles** 'double Vouchers' (line 110). Most of today's editions
adopt the Folio reading for this passage: 'Purchases, and
double ones too'.

124 **Sirrah** a mode of address for a social inferior. Hamlet also uses
thee, *thou*, and *thine* forms with familiar condescension; the
Clown, on the other hand, employs respectful *you*, *your*, and
yours forms.

128 **on't** of it. Here *lie* means 'stand' or 'reside'.

132 **the Quick** the living (with wordplay on quick-witted, cheeky).

134 **Quick Lie** The Clown probably means a lie that spurts back
and forth with the rapidity of quicksilver (mercury). In lines
126–33 he and Hamlet have used *lie* to mean (a) tell a lie, (b)
stand, and (c) lie down, thereby demonstrating that *lie* is not a
word to lie still. Since *Quick Lie* was a term for the kind of
woman with whom one could have an easy sexual encounter
(whence the name Mistress Quickly, a pun on 'Quick-lie', in *1*
and *2 Henry IV*), the Clown is also implying that the word
Lie is itself a wanton.

143 **Absolute** uncompromising in his insistence on absolute
precision. Lines 136–42 echo II.ii.330–32.

a great Buyer of Land, with his Statutes, his
Recognizances, his Fines, his double Vouchers,   110
his Recoveries. Is this the Fine of his Fines,
and the Recovery of his Recoveries, to have his
fine Pate full of fine Dirt? Will his Vouchers
vouch him no more of his Purchases and Doubles
than the Length and Breadth of a Pair of   115
Indentures? The very Conveyances of his Lands
will scarcely lie in this Box, and must th'
Inheritor himself have no more, ha?

HORATIO   Not a iot more, my Lord.

HAMLET   Is not a Parchment made of Sheep-skins?   120

HORATIO   Ay my Lord, and of Calve-skins too.

HAMLET   They are Sheep and Calves which seek out
Assurance in that. I will speak to this Fellow.
– Whose Grave's this, Sirrah?

CLOWN   Mine, Sir, or a Pit of Clay for to be made.   125

HAMLET   I think it be thine indeed, for thou liest
in't.

CLOWN   You lie out on't, Sir, and therefore 'tis
not yours. For my part, I do not lie in't, yet
it is mine.   130

HAMLET   Thou doost lie in't, to be in't and say it
is thine. 'Tis for the Dead, not for the Quick:
therefore thou liest.

CLOWN   'Tis a Quick Lie, Sir: 'twill away again
from me to you.   135

HAMLET   What Man doost thou dig it for?

CLOWN   For no Man, Sir.

HAMLET   What Woman then?

CLOWN   For none neither.

HAMLET   Who is to be buried in't?   140

CLOWN   One that was a Woman, Sir; but rest her
Soul, she's dead.

HAMLET   – How Absolute the Knave is, we must speak

144 **by the Card** perhaps an allusion to the 'Shipman's Card'
(*Macbeth*, I.iii.16), a chart used by sailors to navigate the seas.
Equivocation ambiguity; literally, speaking one word with two
or more equally possible meanings. Hamlet is a master of
equivocation himself, and in the world of this play
equivocation is a way of life and death. See the note to lines
83–84.

145– **this three . . . it** during the last three years I have noticed. *Age*
46 (era) recalls II.ii.557–62, III.ii.23–29; it also echoes
II.i.110–13, IV.vii.25–29, 76–80.

146 **Picked** picky, finicky in its use of language.

149 **galls his Kibe** chafes his chilblain (inflamed sore on the heel).
Compare IV.vii.144.

155 **borne** born.

161 **seen** noticed. *Matter* (line 159) echoes IV.vi.27–28 and
anticipates lines 302, 307.

165 **How strangely?** Strangely in what way or sense?

166 **loosing** The Clown means (a) 'losing', but (b) 'loosing'
(liberating, freeing from normal restraints) is closer to the
truth.

167 **Upon what Ground?** For what reason or cause?

173 **pocky Corses** pock-marked corpses. The Clown is probably
referring to victims of the pox (syphilis).

175 **A Tanner** a craftsman who tans hide to make leather. The
Clown goes on to point out that by his use of tannin (a
substance from the barks of oak trees) to tan the hides of
animals, a tanner tans (and thereby waterproofs) his own skin
as well.

by the Card, or Equivocation will undo us. By
the Lord, Horatio, this three Years I have took   145
note of it, the Age is grown so Picked that the
Toe of the Peasant comes so near the Heel of
the Courtier he galls his Kibe. – How long hast
thou been Grave-maker?

CLOWN   Of the Days i'th' Year I came to't that Day   150
that our last King Hamlet overcame Fortinbrasse.

HAMLET   How long is that since?

CLOWN   Cannot you tell that? Every Fool can tell
that, it was that very Day that young Hamlet
was borne: he that is mad and sent into England.   155

HAMLET   Ay marry, why was he sent into England?

CLOWN   Why because 'a was mad. 'A shall recover
his Wits there; or if 'a do not, 'tis no great
matter there.

HAMLET   Why?   160

CLOWN   'Twill not be seen in him there, there the
men are as mad as he.

HAMLET   How came he mad?

CLOWN   Very strangely, they say.

HAMLET   How strangely?   165

CLOWN   Faith, e'en with loosing his Wits.

HAMLET   Upon what Ground?

CLOWN   Why here in Denmark: I have been Sexton
here, Man and Boy, thirty Years.

HAMLET   How long will a man lie i'th' Earth ere   170
he rot?

CLOWN   Faith, if 'a be not Rotten before 'a die,
as we have many pocky Corses nowadays that will
scarce hold the laying in, 'a will last you some eight
Year, or nine Year. A Tanner will last you nine   175
Year.

HAMLET   Why he more than another?

CLOWN   Why Sir, his Hide is so tann'd with his
Trade that 'a will keep out Water a great while;

180 **sore**   severe.

181 **whoreson**   bastard, a mild expletive that was often used with jocular familiarity.

182 **lyen**   lain.

188 **a flagon of Renish**   a pitcher of Rhine wine.

191 **This?**   As Hamlet speaks this line, he probably takes the skull from the Gravedigger's hand. In the next line the Clown shifts from *This* (line 189) to *that* in reference to Yorick's head. The Folio adds the clause 'Let me see,' at the beginning of line 193.

195 **Fancy**   invention (imagination, wit).

196 **abhorred**   abhorrent (literally, to be shuddered away from).

197 **my Gorge rises**   my gullet threatens to regurgitate.

199 **Gibes**   sarcastic jests.
    Gambols   skipping movements. Compare III.iv.140–41.

201 **wont**   accustomed.

202 **Grinning**   Hamlet refers to the exposed teeth of the skull.
    Chop-fall'n   fallen down in the jaws; literally, down in the mouth. Compare line 93.

204 **paint**   apply cosmetics. See the note to IV.vii.105.
    Favour   Hamlet is probably combining such senses as (a) facial appearance, (b) beauty, (c) love-token, and (d) social standing.

208 **Alexander**   Alexander the Great (356–323 BC), King of Macedonia, who amassed more territory than anyone prior to him; he sat down and wept when he realized that there were no more lands for him to conquer. *Fashion* satirizes the emphasis on success and appearance that leads to such manifestations of human vanity as cosmetics, courtliness, and conquest. It recalls I.iii.5–6, 109–11, II.ii.366, III.i.157, 179.

211 **pah**   an expression of disgust.

216 **Bunghole**   the spout hole in a cask for beer or wine. The word could also refer to the anus, and that may be a secondary implication.

and your Water is a sore Decayer of your   180
whoreson dead Body. Here's a Skull now hath
lyen you i'th' Earth three and twenty Years.

HAMLET   Whose was it?

CLOWN   A whoreson Mad Fellow's it was; whose do
you think it was?   185

HAMLET   Nay I know not.

CLOWN   A Pestilence on him for a Mad Rogue, 'a
pour'd a flagon of Renish on my Head once;
this same Skull, Sir, was Sir Yorick's Skull,
the King's Jester.   190

HAMLET   This?

CLOWN   E'en that.

HAMLET   Alas, poor Yorick, I knew him, Horatio,
a Fellow of infinite Jest, of most excellent
Fancy. He hath bore me on his Back a thousand   195
times, and now how abhorred in my Imagination
it is: my Gorge rises at it. Here hung those
Lips that I have kiss'd I know not how oft.
– Where be your Gibes now? Your Gambols, your
Songs, your flashes of Merriment, that were   200
wont to set the Table on a Roar? Not one now
to mock your own Grinning, quite Chop-fall'n.
Now get you to my Lady's Table, and tell her,
let her paint an Inch thick, to this Favour she
must come; make her laugh at that. – Prethee,   205
Horatio, tell me one thing.

HORATIO   What's that, my Lord?

HAMLET   Doost thou think Alexander look'd a' this
Fashion i'th' Earth?

HORATIO   E'en so.   210

HAMLET   And smelt so, pah.

HORATIO   E'en so, my Lord.

HAMLET   To what base Uses we may return,
Horatio? Why may not Imagination trace the
Noble Dust of Alexander till 'a find it stopping a   215
Bunghole?

217   **curiously**   ingeniously, precisely.

219   **iot**   jot; from the Greek word *iota*, the name of the letter corresponding to our *i*.

220   **Modesty**   rational and measured deliberation. Compare III.ii.23, III.iv.39.

223   **Loam**   a mortar or plaster 'Clay' (line 226) comprised of earth, sand, and straw. Shakespeare alludes to conversions similar to those in lines 219–29 in *Antony and Cleopatra*, I.i.35–37.

226   **Imperious Caesar**   Here *Imperious* means both (a) imperial (possessing the power and attributes of an emperor), and (b) haughty. Hamlet is probably referring to Julius Caesar (100–44 BC), but he may also be thinking of Octavius Caesar (63 BC–AD14), who assumed the title Caesar Augustus after he became Emperor in 27 BC. After Augustus every Roman emperor was known as Caesar, and the name became synonymous with *monarch*. Hamlet may well be meditating on that as he plots to undo an 'Imperious Caesar' who keeps 'the World in Awe' in his own time. *Awe* echoes IV.iii.58–65.

229   **t'expel the Water's Flaw**   to keep out the rain. Here *Flaw* is probably either a variant of *flow* (so spelled to rhyme with *Awe*) or a word referring to a shaft of ice. Most editors adopt the Folio's *Winter's flaw*, referring either to a shaft of ice or to a squall of gusty wind.

232   **maimed Rites**   curtailed ceremony.

234   **Foredo it**   destroy its.
      of some Estate   of high station.

235   **Couch we**   let us conceal ourselves (in a crouching position).

239   **DOCTOR**   Doctor of Divinity. Priest.
      Obsequies   funeral ceremonies. See I.ii.92.

241   **great . . . Order**   an order from the King supersedes the proper 'Order' (liturgical practice) of the Church.

243   **For**   instead of.

244   **Shards**   bits of shattered pottery.
      Peebles   pebbles.

245   **Virgin Crants**   garlands strewn on an unblemished maiden.

HORATIO 'Twere to consider too curiously to
consider so.
HAMLET No faith, not a iot, but to follow him
thether with Modesty enough, and Likelihood to   220
lead it, as thus: Alexander died, Alexander was
buried, Alexander returneth to Dust, the Dust
is Earth, of Earth we make Loam; and why of
that Loam whereto he was converted might they
not stop a Beer-barrel?   225
Imperious Caesar, dead and turn'd to Clay,
Might stop a Hole, to keep the Wind away.
O that that Earth which kept the World in Awe
Should patch a Wall t'expel the Water's Flaw.

Enter King, Queen, Laertes, and the Corse.

But soft, but soft a while, here comes the King,   230
The Queen, the Courtiers. Who is this they
  follow?
And with such maimed Rites? This doth betoken
The Corse they follow did with desp'rate Hand
Foredo it own Life; 'twas of some Estate.
Couch we a while and mark.   235
LAERTES What Ceremony else?
HAMLET That is Laertes, a very Noble Youth, mark.
LAERTES What Ceremony else?
DOCTOR Her Obsequies have been as far enlarg'd
As we have Warranty; her Death was doubtful,   240
And but that great Commaund o'er-sways the
  Order,
She should in Ground Unsanctified been lodg'd
Till the Last Trumpet. For charitable Prayers,
Shards, Flints, and Peebles should be thrown on her:
Yet here she is allow'd her Virgin Crants,   245

246 **Her . . . Burial** the strewing of flowers symbolic of maidenhood, and the bell-ringing and earthen burial that befit a person who has died in a state of grace and is returning to her earthly 'home' to await 'the Last Trumpet' (line 243) that summons her to her new home in Heaven. See the note to line 50.

250 **a Requiem** a solemn Mass for the peaceful repose of the deceased. *Rest* anticipates V.ii.370.

251 **Peace-parted Souls** souls that departed at peace with God. Suicides were regarded as souls who died in despair, with no trust in God's grace. See lines 232–34.

255 **howling** a state proverbially associated with the damned.
the fair Ophelia This is Hamlet's first realization that Ophelia is dead. His words echo III.i.86.

256 **Sweets to the Sweet** sweet flowers to the sweet soul. In Shakespeare *sweet* frequently means 'blessed with grace'.

258 **thought** expected. The Queen's sentiments in lines 257–59 not only endear her to the audience; they also remind us that Ophelia was the victim of tragically misguided interference by both her brother and her father.

259 **treble** triple.

261 **most ingenious Sense** sanity. Laertes uses *ingenious* in the Latin sense referring to intellectual vitality.

264 **Quick** living. Compare lines 132–35.

266 **Pelion** the mountain the primordial Giants piled on Mount Ossa in their challenge to the Olympian Gods. Claudius has associated an earlier outburst from Laertes with 'Giant-like' rebellion in IV.v.124.

267 **blew** blue. But the spelling in the Quarto and Folio texts may entail a pun on the past tense of *blow*, a word that can mean (a) in full bloom (as in III.i.163 and III.iii.81), (b) blown up or blasted open (as in III.iv.205), or (c) blown by wind (as in V.ii.203–4). *Grief* (both sorrow and grievance) recalls IV.v.204 and anticipates V.ii.79.

269 **Conjures** casts under its spell.

Her Maiden Strewments, and the bringing home
Of Bell and Burial.

LAERTES   Must there no more be doone?

DOCTOR   No more be doone.
We should profane the Service of the Dead
To sing a Requiem and such Rest to her   250
As to Peace-parted Souls.

LAERTES   Lay her i'th' Earth,
And from her fair and unpolluted Flesh
May Violets spring. I tell thee, churlish
    Priest,
A minist'ring Angel shall my Sister be
When thou liest howling.

HAMLET   What, the fair Ophelia.   255

QUEEN   Sweets to the Sweet, farewell,
I hop'd thou should'st have been my Hamlet's
    Wife;
I thought thy Bride-bed to have deck'd, sweet
    Maid,
And not t' have strew'd thy Grave.

LAERTES   O treble Woe
Fall ten times double on that cursed Head   260
Whose wicked Deed thy most ingenious Sense
Depriv'd thee of. – Hold off the Earth a while,
Till I have caught her once more in mine Arms.
                                    Leaps in the Grave.
Now pile your Dust upon the Quick and Dead,
Till of this Flat a Mountain you have made   265
T' o'ertop old Pelion, or the skyish Head
Of blew Olympus.

HAMLET   What is he whose Grief
Bears such an Emphasis, whose Phrase of Sorrow
Conjures the wand'ring Stars, and makes them
    stand

270 **Wonder-wounded** struck with amazement, from 'wand'ring' (orbiting) to arrested 'Wonder' at such a display of *hubris* (overweening pride). *Hearers* recalls such previous passages as I.ii.77, 148–9, 170, II.i.173, II.ii.571, III.i.147, III.iv.37–94, 153–67, IV.v.215–19, and IV.vi.26–28, and anticipates V.ii.220–37.

271 **Hamlet the Dane** Hamlet's phrasing echoes earlier uses of 'the Dane' by Claudius, and implies that Hamlet is not only asserting his superiority to Laertes but staking his claim to the Crown itself.

274 **spleenative Rash** Hamlet uses the adjective *spleenative* (splenitive) to refer to the kind of passion that was thought to derive from the spleen, the seat of the impulsive emotions. The Folio adds an *and* before *Rash* to yield a metrically regular line, and modern editors normally follow suit. It may be, however, that Shakespeare deliberately inserted a truncated line here in keeping with the short-tempered rashness Hamlet describes.

277 **a sunder** asunder, apart. The Quarto spelling imitates the action the King's words demand.

280 **wag** move up and down (traditionally regarded as the last sign of life).

285 **forbear** restrain (literally, bear away). By this point, both young men are probably being held to keep them from attacking each other physically.

286 **S'wounds** God's wounds, an oath referring to the Crucifixion.

287 **Woo't** wilt thou.

288 **Esill** vinegar. Hamlet may be alluding to the bitter gall given to Jesus on the Cross (Matthew 27:34).

291 **quick** alive.

292 **prate** speak idly and boastfully. Compare III.iv.210–11.

294 **Singeing . . . Zone** pushing its head so high that it will be singed by the heat of the Sun. *Pate* echoes line 82.

295 **Ossa** another reference to the Giants' rebellion (see the note to line 266).
mouth both (a) prate, rant, and (b) make mouths (insulting grimaces). Compare II.ii.389–95, III.ii.3–4, IV.iv.47. In this line *and* means 'if'.

Like Wonder-wounded Hearers? This is I, 270
Hamlet the Dane.
LAERTES　The Devil take thy Soul.
HAMLET　　　　　　　　　Thou pray'st not well.
I prethee take thy Fingers from my Throat,
For, though I am not spleenative Rash,
Yet have I in me something Dangerous, 275
Which let thy Wisdom fear. Hold off thy Hand.
KING　Pluck them a sunder.
QUEEN　　　　　　　　Hamlet, Hamlet.
ALL　　　　　　　　　　　　Gentlemen.
HORATIO　Good my Lord, be quiet.
HAMLET　Why, I will fight with him upon this Theme
Until my Eyelids will no longer wag. 280
QUEEN　O my Son, what Theme?
HAMLET　I loved Ophelia. Forty thousand Brothers
Could not with all their Quantity of Love
Make up my Sum. – What wilt thou do for her?
KING　O he is mad, Laertes.
QUEEN　　　　　　　For love of God, forbear him. 285
HAMLET　S'wounds, shew me what thou't do:
Woo't weep? Woo't fight? Woot't fast? Woo't tear
　thy self?
Woo't drink up Esill, eat a Crocodile?
I'll do't. Doost come here to whine?
To out-face me with leaping in her Grave? 290
Be buried quick with her, and so will I.
And if thou prate of Mountains, let them throw
Millions of Acres on us, till our Ground,
Singeing his Pate against the Burning Zone,
Make Ossa like a Wart. Nay and thou'lt mouth, 295
I'll rant as well as thou.

296   **mere**   pure, absolute.

298   **Anon**   in a short while. *Fit* (seizure) recalls IV.i.8–10. Compare
       IV.vii.147.
       Patient   passive, contented.

299   **golden Cuplets**   the golden-downed couplets (offspring) of the
       Dove, a traditional symbol of peace, love, deliverance, and
       divine grace (see Genesis 8:8–12 and Matthew 3:16).
       disclosed   hatched. Doves normally lay two eggs at a time.

300   **drooping**   with eyelids lowered, spent. The Queen's words
       imply that Hamlet will also feel remorse for his outburst.

304   **The Cat will mew**   the cat is bound to meow (despite the efforts
       of even the most powerful man on earth).
       and Dog will have his Day   and the dog, too, will act in
       accordance with his nature. What Hamlet means by this
       parting line is unclear. He may be saying that he and Laertes
       have just gone at each other like a dog and a cat; he may be
       trying to excuse his own passion; or he may be warning
       Laertes that 'his Day' (Hamlet's) will come (to finish what he
       was prevented from doing on this occasion). *Hercules* recalls
       I.ii.152–53, II.ii.387–88, and it suggests that 'Hamlet the
       Dane' (line 271) is now beginning to assert the prerogatives he
       believes himself to have inherited from his father.

305   **wait upon him**   tend to him.

307   **We'll . . . Push**   The King is speaking privately to Laertes, and
       he is telling him 'we'll strike while the iron is hot'. *Matter*
       echoes lines 159, 302.

310   **thereby**   as a result. The King implies to the Queen that he will
       place a memorial over Ophelia's grave to ensure a period of
       harmony ('An Hour of Quiet'); meanwhile he is probably
       implying to Laertes that true 'Quiet' will result from a more
       fitting 'Monument' to Ophelia, namely the death of Hamlet.

V.ii   This scene returns us to the Castle, where Hamlet is telling
       Horatio what happened aboard the ship to England.

1   **now shall you see the other**   now shall I tell you about the other
       matter (the 'Words' Hamlet promised Horatio in the letter
       delivered in IV.vi).

QUEEN   This is mere Madness,
  And thus a while the Fit will work on him;
  Anon as Patient as the female Dove
  When that her golden Cuplets are disclosed,
  His Silence will sit drooping.
HAMLET   — Hear you, Sir,   300
  What is the reason that you use me thus?
  I lov'd you ever, but it is no matter:
  Let Hercules himself do what he may,
  The Cat will mew, and Dog will have his Day.
KING   — I pray thee, good Horatio, wait upon him.   305
                   Exit Hamlet, and Horatio.
  — Strengthen your Patience in our last night's
    Speech,
  We'll put the Matter to the present Push.
  — Good Gertrard, set some Watch over your Son;
  This Grave shall have a living Monument,
  An Hour of Quiet thereby shall we see;   310
  Till then in Patience our Proceeding be.   *Exeunt.*

Scene 2

Enter Hamlet and Horatio.

HAMLET   So much for this, Sir, now shall you see the
  other;
  You do remember all the Circumstance.
HORATIO   Remember it, my Lord.
HAMLET   Sir, in my Heart there was a kind of
  Fighting
  That would not let me sleep; me thought I lay   5

6 **Mutines in the Bilbo** mutineers shackled to the bilbo, the long
iron bar with which Renaissance ships were equipped to
discourage insurrections. The Folio prints *bilboes.*
rashly irrationally, instinctively, intuitively.

8 **Indiscretion** impulsive behaviour; 'rashness'. Compare
III.ii.19–20, where Hamlet tells the Players 'let your own
Discretion be your Tutor'; see also I.ii.5–7, II.i.112–13,
II.ii.501–2.

9 **deep Plots** deeply meditated, deliberate plans. As Hamlet
speaks, the audience is aware that Claudius and Laertes have
laid 'deep Plots' against him; see IV.vii.53–158.
fall either (a) fall short of their targets (compare IV.vii.21–24)
or (b) fall to the ground (like trees that have been hewn down,
lines 10–11). The Folio reads *paule* (pall) here, and most of
today's editions follow suit; *pall* would echo II.ii.601.
learn teach.

10–11 **There's . . . will** Hamlet's metaphor suggests a number of
related ways in which Providence 'shapes our Ends': (a) it
gives our lives a well-carved shape, despite our own tendency
to 'hew' (chop) them in a rough, shapeless manner; (b) it
takes our 'Ends' (intentions) and gives them a shape we can
only approach in a rough-hewn fashion; and (c) it takes the
'Ends' of our lives (both literally, and in the sense pertaining
to God's purpose for them) and gives them a shape (fits them
into a design) that we can at best approximate with our
rough-hewn plans and actions. *Rough-hew* echoes Hamlet's
earlier reference to 'the Native Hew of Resolution' (III.i.81).
Ends echoes III.ii.237, where the Player King says, 'Our
Thoughts are ours, our Ends none of their own.' Compare
IV.v.188, IV.vii.154.

13 **scarf'd** wrapped.

15 **in fine** in the end, eventually. Compare V.i.108–13.

17 **unfold** open up. Most editors adopt the Folio's *unseal* here.
Manners alludes to the etiquette that normally prohibits
invasions of another person's privacy. Compare *King Lear*,
IV.vi.256–58.

19 **A** Most editions construe this word to mean 'Ah'; compare
V.i.67–68. The Folio prints *Oh. Knavery* echoes IV.ii.24–25.

20 **Larded** garnished (as in IV.v.38).

Worse than the Mutines in the Bilbo, rashly,
And prais'd be Rashness for it; let us know,
Our Indiscretion sometime serves us well
When our deep Plots do fall, and that should
   learn us
There's a Divinity that shapes our Ends   10
Rough-hew them how we will.
HORATIO   That is most certain.
HAMLET   Up from my Cabin,
   My Sea-gown scarf'd about me in the Dark,
   Grop'd I to find out them, had my Desire,
   Finger'd their Packet, and in fine withdrew   15
   To mine own Room again, making so bold,
   My Fears forgetting Manners, to unfold
   Their graund Commission; where I found, Horatio,
   A Royal Knavery, an exact Command,
   Larded with many several sorts of Reasons,   20

21   **Importing** pertaining to. Hamlet plays on the literal sense,
      'porting (carrying) in', to pun on *Larded*, which can also
      mean 'loaded', 'stuffed', or 'fattened' (as in IV.iii.16–31).
      Importing recalls IV.vii.80.

22   **With . . . Life** with more bugbears than I've ever heard in all
      my life. *Goblins* echoes I.iv.39.

23   **Supervise** overlooking, perusal [of the document].
      no Leisure bated with no time deducted (abated) for leisure.
      Compare IV.vii.111–18.

24   **stay** wait for.

29   **benetted round** caught in a net. See the note to IV.vii.168.
      Villains Most editions emend to *villainies*. But Hamlet seems to
      be thinking primarily of the enemies arrayed against him at
      this moment, the two agents he assumes to be privy to the
      King's intentions: Rosencraus and Guildenstern.

30   **Or** before; an alternative spelling of *ere*.

32   **fair** in a neat hand, similar to the calligraphy of a professional
      scribe. See the note to IV.i.36.

33   **Statists** 'statesmen', men in high office. *Devis'd* recalls
      IV.vii.52, 63, 68.

34   **A Baseness** a demeaning skill. In V.i.213–14 Hamlet has noted
      the 'base Uses' to which 'we may return'.

36   **Yeman's Service** the benefit accruing to a reliable craftsman
      (yeoman).

37   **I** both 'I' [will] and 'Ay'. Compare IV.vii.58.

39   **Tributary** dependent. See the note to III.i.174.

40   **As** so that. In line 39 *As* means 'whereas'. *Palm* recalls
      I.i.108–12.

42   **a Comma . . . Amities** a link to tie them together in friendship.

43   **As, Sir, of great Charge** As clauses, Sir, of great weight and
      importance. The Folio prints *Assis*, which suggests a pun on
      'Ases' and 'Asses'. *Charge* echoes IV.vii.66.

Importing Denmark's Health and England's too,
With ho such Bugs and Goblins in my Life,
That on the Supervise, no Leisure bated,
No, not to stay the Grinding of the Axe,
My Head should be strook off.

HORATIO   Is't possible?   25

HAMLET   Here's the Commission, read it at more
    Leisure;
But wilt thou hear now how I did proceed?

HORATIO   I beseech you.

HAMLET   Being thus benetted round with Villains,
Or I could make a Prologue to my Brains,   30
They had begun the Play; I sat me down,
Devis'd a new Commission, wrote it fair.
I once did hold it as our Statists do,
A Baseness to write fair, and labour'd much
How to forget that Learning; but Sir now   35
It did me Yeman's Service. Wilt thou know
Th' Effect of what I wrote?

HORATIO   I, good my Lord.

HAMLET   An earnest Conjuration from the King,
As England was his faithful Tributary,
As Love between them like the Palm might
    flourish,   40
As Peace should still her wheaten Garland wear
And stand a Comma 'tween their Amities,
And many such like As, Sir, of great Charge,
That on the View and Knowing of these Contents,
Without Debatement further more or less,   45
He should those Bearers put to sudden Death,

47   **Not Shriving-time allow'd**   without allowing enough time for
them to confess their sins and prepare their souls for death.
The haste Hamlet calls for parallels that of the commission
calling for his own execution (line 24). We must remember
that at the time Hamlet wrote his death order he was
assuming that he would arrive in England with his former
schoolmates; he would thus have wanted them silenced before
they could say anything that would jeopardize his own life.
Even so, however, the harshness of Hamlet's sentence (going
beyond that of even so evil a character as Claudius in its
explicit call for what the Prince assumes will be the
damnation of his victims) is surely designed by the playwright
to give the audience pause. See the note to V.i.50.

48   **ordinant**   ordering matters.

52   **Subscrib'd it**   signed it (literally, 'wrote under' it). *Seal* (line 50)
recalls IV.vii.1.

53   **Changeling**   Hamlet compares the exchanged document to a
mischievous imp substituted by fairies for a stolen child. See
the note to I.i.158.

57   **make love to**   woo, aggressively solicit.

59   **Insinuation**   winding into affairs of state; obsequious flattery.
Employment (line 57) echoes V.i.73–74.

61   **Pass . . . Points**   thrust of the fierce, enraged, sword-tips. *Pass*
echoes IV.vii.135, *fell* II.ii.508, *incensed* IV.v.129. *Points*
recalls IV.v.135 and IV.vii.143–45; compare I.ii.199,
I.v.126–27, V.i.10.

65   **Popp'd . . . Hopes**   inserted himself between the throne and my
expectations. The copulative imagery of lines 64–65 charges
Election with an echo of *erection*. See the notes to
IV.ii.28–29, 52, IV.iv.53, IV.v.114, 135, 139. *Election* recalls
III.ii.69–78 and anticipates line 367.

66   **Thrown . . . Life**   cast out his hook for my own ('proper') life.

67   **Cus'nage**   a pun on (a) cozenage (trickery), and (b) cousin-like
behaviour. Any relative, including an uncle or a nephew,
could be called a cousin.

68   **quit him**   both (a) requite (repay) him, and (b) kill him.
Compare IV.vii.1.

69   **Canker**   here either (a) a cancer or (b) a cankerworm.

Not Shriving-time allow'd.
HORATIO How was this seal'd?
HAMLET Why even in that was Heaven ordinant;
 I had my Father's Signet in my Purse,
 Which was the Model of that Danish Seal;   50
 Folded the Writ up in the Form of th' other,
 Subscrib'd it, gave't the Impression, plac'd
  it safely,
 The Changeling never known. Now the next Day
 Was our Sea-fight, and what to this was sequent
 Thou knowest already.   55
HORATIO So Guildenstern and Rosencraus go to't.
HAMLET Why Man, they did make love to this
  Employment:
 They are not near my Conscience. Their
  Defeat
 Dooes by their own Insinuation grow:
 'Tis Dangerous when the Baser Nature comes   60
 Between the Pass and fell incensed Points
 Of Mighty Opposites.
HORATIO Why what a King is this!
HAMLET Dooes it not, think thee, stand me now upon?
 He that hath kill'd my King, and whor'd my
  Mother,
 Popp'd in between th' Election and my Hopes,   65
 Thrown out his Angle for my proper Life,
 And with such Cus'nage, is't not perfect
  Conscience
 To quit him with this Arm? And is't not to be
  damn'd
 To let this Canker of our Nature come
 In further Evil?   70
HORATIO It must be shortly known to him from
  England
 What is the Issue of the Business there.

73   **the Interim's mine** I'll succeed within the brief interval I have
to work with. Fittingly, this line is one metrical foot 'short'
see the notes to II.ii.90–91, 516–17.

74   **no more than to say one** lasts no longer than it takes a person
either to say the word *one* or to count to one.

76   **I forgot my self** I lost control of my true nature.

77–78 **by the Image . . . his** for if I look at my own situation, I now
recognize that the one he faces is identical with it. Like the
Latin word *causa*, *cause* can mean both 'cause' and 'case'.

78   **I'll count his Favours** I'll weigh (take into full account, as in
line 74) his virtues and the kindnesses he has done me.
Modern editions normally emend *count* to *court*. Compare
III.ii.184–85, IV.vii.16–18.

79   **the Bravery of his Grief** the bravado with which Laertes
proclaimed his 'Grief' (grievances) against 'the cursed Head'
(V.i.260) responsible for his griefs (sorrows). *Bravery* recalls
II.ii.626, where Hamlet forswears his own 'Braves' and begins
devising a mousetrap. *Grief* echoes V.i.267.

80   **a Tow'ring Passion** Hamlet uses *Tow'ring* with nice precision
here. To avoid having Laertes 'out-face' him (V.i.290), he
engaged his opponent in a match to see whose grief and rage
could be more 'Giant-like'.

84   **gracious** blessed with divine favour. Compare I.i.159, I.ii.56,
II.ii.45, III.i.40, III.iv.102.

86–87 **his Crib . . . Mess** his trough will have a place in the King's
dining hall. Hamlet's point is that obsequious flatterers,
however base, are more than welcome in a degenerate court
that depends on such abominable creatures for its survival.

87   **Chough** either a crow or a jackdaw (a smaller bird that could
be taught to speak).

89   **Dirt** See the note to V.i.113–18.

91   **impart** disclose. Compare I.i.164, I.ii.112, 206, I.iv.58–59,
III.ii.356.

HAMLET   It will be short; the Interim's mine,
And a man's Life's no more than to say one.
But I am very sorry, good Horatio,   75
That to Laertes I forgot my self:
For by the Image of my Cause, I see
The Portraiture of his. I'll count his Favours;
But sure the Bravery of his Grief did put me
Into a Tow'ring Passion.
HORATIO   Peace, who comes here?   80

Enter a Courtier.

COURTIER   Your Lordship is right welcome back to
Denmark.
HAMLET   I humbly thank you, Sir.
– Doost know this Water-fly?
HORATIO   No, my good Lord.
HAMLET   Thy State is the more gracious, for 'tis a
Vice to know him. He hath much Land and fertile: 85
let a Beast be Lord of Beasts, and his Crib
shall stand at the King's Mess. 'Tis a Chough,
but, as I say, spacious in the Possession of
Dirt.
COURTIER   Sweet Lord, if your Lordship were at   90
Leisure, I should impart a thing to you from
his Majesty.
HAMLET   I will receive it, Sir, with all Diligence

94 **Bonnet** hat. The Courtier has removed his bonnet out of
    deference, and Hamlet is telling him to put it back on. In line
    206 we learn that the Courtier's name is Ostricke (probably a
    play on Ostrich), and it seems likely that his headdress in the
    original staging was designed to make him resemble a bird
    stupid enough to believe itself invisible if its head were buried.

99 **indifferent** somewhat. Compare III.ii.42.

100 **Sully** Possibly either a misreading for or a variant of *sultry* (the
    Folio reads *soultry*, which Ostricke appears to understand,
    line 102). But Hamlet may be coining an adjective that
    combines *sultry* (humid) and *sullied* (soiled, dirty).

104 **bad** bade.

107 **remember** be reminded. Prompted, perhaps, by 'great Wager
    on your Head', Hamlet tells Ostricke once more to cover his
    head. *Matter* recalls IV.vi.27–28, V.i.159, 302, 307, and
    anticipates lines 166, 224.

111 **Differences** distinctions. But Laertes is also full of 'Differences'
    in another sense: quarrels (see *King Lear*, I.iv.97). Compare
    III.iv.74, IV.v.184–85.
    soft Society refined, delicate manners.

112 **Showing** appearance.
    sellingly as if to market him. Compare II.i.58. This reading
    derives from the first imprint of the Second Quarto; the
    revised Q2 text reads *fellingly*, and most of today's editions
    emend to *feelingly*, the reading in the 1611 Third Quarto.

113 **Card or Calendar of Gentry** chart or inventory of gentlemanly
    attributes. *Card* echoes V.i.143–44.

114 **Continent** container. See IV.iv.61.

116– **Sir . . . more** Hamlet parodies Ostricke's ridiculously
25 pretentious vocabulary. Here *Definement* means 'definition',
    Perdition means 'loss', *dazzy* means 'dizzy', *Raw* means
    'unripe', *verity of Extolment* means 'truth of praise', *Article*
    means 'substance', *Infusion* means 'quality', and *Dearth*
    means 'preciousness'. *Arithmatic*, the usual Shakespearean
    form of *arithmetic*, was probably accented on the penultimate
    syllable. *Devide* (line 117) echoes I.i.71.

of Spirit; your Bonnet to his right Use, 'tis
for the Head.   95
COURTIER   I thank your Lordship, it is very Hot.
HAMLET   No, believe me, 'tis very Cold, the Wind
   is Northerly.
COURTIER   It is indifferent Cold, my Lord, indeed.
HAMLET   But yet me thinks it is very Sully and Hot,   100
   or my Complexion –
COURTIER   Exceedingly, my Lord, it is very Soultery,
   as 'twere, I cannot tell how: My Lord his
   Majesty bad me signify to you that 'a has laid
   a great Wager on your Head: Sir, this is the   105
   Matter.
HAMLET   I beseech you remember.
COURTIER   Nay good my Lord, for my Ease, in good
   faith. Sir, here is newly come to Court Laertes,
   believe me an absolute Gentleman, full of most   110
   excellent Differences, of very soft Society,
   and great Showing; indeed, to speak sellingly
   of him, he is the Card or Calendar of Gentry:
   for you shall find in him the Continent of what
   Part a Gentleman would see.   115
HAMLET   Sir, his Definement suffers no Perdition
   in you, though I know to devide him
   inventorially would dazzy th' Arithmatic of

119 **Raw** unripe, immature ('of unimproved Mettle', I.i.91), not fully developed. The first imprint of Q2 reads *yaw*, a nautical term for a veering off course. Here *neither* means 'nevertheless' or 'notwithstanding'.

120 **Saile** both (a) sale (see line 112), and (b) sail (sailing ability), a sense that can be related to either *raw* or *yaw*.

123 **make true Diction** speak truly.
Semblable mirror image.

124 **who else would trace him** and anyone else who would attempt to follow in his footsteps.

125 **Umbrage** shadow. Hamlet anticipates the later sense of 'taking umbrage' (being offended). He and Laertes have been rivals, suspicious and envious of one another, from the inception of the action, and the Prince's remarks remind us that he has been 'envenomed' both by the praise Laertes has received for his courtly skills (IV.vii.70–102) and by Laertes' behaviour at Ophelia's funeral (V.i.259–311).

128 **The Concernancy** what is this all about?

129 **our more rawer Breath** our crude, inadequate words. See lines 119–20.

133– **What . . . Gentleman?** What is the significance of your naming
34 of this gentleman? Why are we talking about him now?

141 **much approve me** prove much about me (go far toward proving it true that I am 'not ignorant'). *Approve* recalls I.i.24–25.

144 **least** lest. Hamlet continues to present himself as the 'least I' in this conversation about noble 'Excellence'.

145 **compare** appear to have the audacity to compare myself.

147– **in the Imputation laid on him** in the reputation he bears.
48

148 **them in his Meed** those of comparable merit.

149 **unfellowed** unequalled.

152 **well** let that pass without dispute.

Memory, and yet but Raw neither, in respect of
his quick Saile, but in the verity of Extolment   120
I take him to be a Soul of great Article, and
his Infusion of such Dearth and Rareness as, to
make true Diction of him, his Semblable is his
Mirror, and who else would trace him, his
Umbrage, nothing more.   125

COURTIER   Your Lordship speaks most infallibly of
him.

HAMLET   The Concernancy, Sir, why do we wrap the
Gentleman in our more rawer Breath?

COURTIER   Sir.   130

HORATIO   Is't not possible to understand in another
Tongue? You will do't, Sir, really.

HAMLET   What imports the Nomination of this
Gentleman?

COURTIER   Of Laertes.   135

HORATIO   His Purse is empty already, all's Golden
Words are spent.

HAMLET   Of him, Sir.

COURTIER   I know you are not Ignorant.

HAMLET   I would you did, Sir; yet in faith if you   140
did, it would not much approve me; well, Sir.

COURTIER   You are not Ignorant of what Excellence
Laertes is.

HAMLET   I dare not confess that, least I should
compare with him in Excellence: but to know a   145
Man well were to know himself.

COURTIER   I mean, Sir, for this Weapon; but in the
Imputation laid on him, by them in his Meed,
he's unfellowed.

HAMLET   What's his Weapon?   150

COURTIER   Rapier and Dagger.

HAMLET   That's two of his Weapons, but well.

COURTIER   The King, Sir, hath wager'd with him six
Barbary Horses, against the which he has

155 **inpawn'd** pledged, staked in equal wager.

156 **Poynards** poniards (daggers). The spelling in the Second
Quarto text may reflect Shakespeare's preferred
pronunciation.
Assigns appurtenances.
Girdle belt.
Hanger the apparatus (usually one or two straps) attached to a
courtier's girdle to hold his rapier and poniard.

157 **Carriages** normally meaning gun-carriages, for cannon, here
used as an affected term for sword hangers.

158 **dear to Fancy** pleasing to the eye.

158– **responsive to the Hilts** matching the sword hilts in design.
59 Compare the imagery in I.ii.82.

160 **liberal Conceit** elaborate design. *Liberal* echoes IV.vii.166;
Conceit recalls III.iv.111, IV.v.46.

162 **edified by the Margent** informed by the explanatory notes in
the margin (Horatio alludes to the glosses in weighty tomes
such as the Bibles of Shakespeare's day).

164 **Carriage** carriages.

165 **German** germane, relevant; probably with an allusion to
German cannon. In the opening scene Marcellus has referred
to the 'daily cost of Brazen Cannon / And foreign Mart for
Implements of War' (I.i.68–69). The Second Quarto spelling,
Ierman, may indicate a pronunciation that echoes *Yeman*, line
36.

168 **Barbary Horses** a breed known for its swiftness and quality.

171 **impon'd** both (a) imposed, wagered, and (b) impawn'd.
Hamlet appears to be mocking the Courtier's accent. The
phrase *impon'd, as* appears only in the Folio, which also has
impon'd in line 155.

178 **vouchsafe the Answer** grant a response to the invitation
(challenge).

183– **the Breathing . . . me** the time of day when I ordinarily
84 exercise. *Breathing* echoes I.iii.129–30 and IV.vii.65.

186 **and** if. *Purpose* echoes IV.vii.153–58.

187 **odd Hits** the hits by which his total exceeds mine, given the
odds upon which the King has wagered; compare lines
273–75.

impawn'd, as I take it, six French Rapiers and   155
Poynards, with their Assigns, as Girdle, Hanger,
and so. Three of the Carriages in faith are
very dear to Fancy, very responsive to the
Hilts, most delicate Carriages, and of very
liberal Conceit.   160

HAMLET   What call you the Carriages?

HORATIO   I knew you must be edified by the Margent
ere you had done.

COURTIER   The Carriage, Sir, are the Hangers.

HAMLET   The Phrase would be more German to the   165
Matter if we could carry a Cannon by our sides;
I would it might be Hangers till then. But on,
six Barbary Horses against six French Swords,
their Assigns, and three liberal conceited
Carriages: that's the French Bet against the   170
Danish. Why is this all impon'd, as you call
it?

COURTIER   The King, Sir, hath laid, Sir, that in
a dozen Passes between your self and him, he
shall not exceed you three Hits; he hath laid   175
on Twelve for Nine, and it would come to
immediate Trial, if your Lordship would
vouchsafe the Answer.

HAMLET   How if I answer no?

COURTIER   I mean, my Lord, the Opposition of   180
your Person in Trial.

HAMLET   Sir, I will walk here in the Hall; if it
please his Majesty, it is the Breathing Time of
Day with me. Let the Foils be brought, the
Gentleman willing, and the King hold his Purpose.   185
I will win for him and I can; if not, I will
gain nothing but my Shame, and the odd Hits.

188   **deliver you so**   deliver this message from you.

194   **for's Turn**   who will speak for him, commending (praising) his
      duty. Compare III.iii.51–52, IV.vi.23.

195– **This Lapwing ... Head**   Horatio compares Ostricke to a bird
96   that was proverbially ludicrous and was said to run around
      with its eggshell on its head almost as soon as it was hatched.
      See the notes to III.i.169, V.ii.94, 119.

197   **comply with his Dug**   compliment (bow politely to) his
      mother's nipple. Compare II.ii.399–403.

198   **Breed**   The Folio reads *Bevy*, a flock of birds. Compare
      III.ii.340–41.

199   **drossy**   worthless.

199– **only got the Tune of the Time**   [have] only mastered the tune
200   (without the words, the substance) of the time's fashions.
      Compare III.iv.137–38.

200–1 **and ... Encounter**   and based on a superficial manner of social
      interaction with no understanding of what society's customs
      really signify. Here *Habit* probably refers to a fashionable
      mode of dress that serves as a kind of uniform for members of
      the group. Compare III.iv.132, 159.

201   **a ... Collection**   a combination of foppish gestures that makes
      them resemble the yeasty froth on a mug of beer or ale. Here
      histy, which may be a variant spelling for *yeasty*, also suggests
      hesty, a word that can mean 'commanding' (as in *behest*) or
      'promising with vows'. Most editions adopt the Folio reading
      in lines 200–1 and print *an outward habit* and *a yeasty
      collection*.

202–3 **profane ... Opinions**   heretical and newly fabricated opinions.
      Here *profane* probably means 'irreverent' or (perhaps
      unintentionally) 'unsound'. *Trennowed* may be either a
      variant or a misreading of *treenailed* (fastened together with
      treenails, cylindrical wooden pegs for use with the timbers
      required in shipbuilding) or a coinage to combine that word
      with *trendled* (trinnelled), a word meaning 'rolled' or
      'revolved'. Most editions follow the Folio and print *fond and
      winnow'd Opinions*.

203–4 **and do ... out**   so that if you try (test) them by blowing on
      them, all you get are empty bubbles.

COURTIER   Shall I deliver you so?
HAMLET   To this Effect, Sir, after what Flourish
  your Nature will.   190
COURTIER   I commend my Duty to your Lordship.
HAMLET   Yours, yours.   *Exit Courtier.*
  – He dooes well to commend it himself:
  there are no Tongues else for's Turn.
HORATIO   This Lapwing runs away with the Shell on   195
  his Head.
HAMLET   'A did comply with his Dug before 'a suck'd
  it: thus has he, and many more of the same Breed
  that I know the drossy Age dotes on, only got
  the Tune of the Time, and out of an Habit of   200
  Encounter, a kind of histy Collection, which
  carries them through and through the most profane
  and trennowed Opinions; and do but blow them to
  their Trial, the Bubbles are out.

Enter a Lord.

LORD   My Lord, his Majesty commended him to you   205
  by young Ostricke, who brings back to him that
  you attend him in the Hall; he sends to know if
  your pleasure hold to play with Laertes, or that
  you will take longer Time?
HAMLET   I am constant to my Purposes, they follow   210
  the King's Pleasure; if his Fitness speaks,
  mine is ready; now or whensoever, provided I be
  so able as now.
LORD   The King and Queen and all are coming down.
HAMLET   In happy Time.   215

216–   **The Queen . . . Laertes**   the Queen requests that you exchange
17   some courteous words with Laertes to welcome him back into
       your good favour.

220   **You . . . Lord**   What Horatio means, in the words of the Folio
       text, is 'You will lose this Wager, my Lord.' But in the Second
       Quarto version of the line, which has no internal punctuation,
       Horatio's words can also mean 'You will release (or unleash)
       my Lord.' See IV.v.145, and compare the imagery of
       IV.vii.21–24 and V.ii.9.

221–   **since . . . Practice**   Whether Hamlet has been practising for the
22   reasons the King suggested in his conversation with Laertes
       (IV.vii.92–102) is impossible to determine. Hamlet has had
       better reasons to sharpen his skills with the rapier. But the
       Prince's words suggest that envy of Laertes' reputation may
       have been at least one motivating factor.

226   **Foolery**   something foolish, not to be taken seriously. See the
       note to IV.vii.187. What Hamlet describes here is very similar
       to the 'Fighting / That would not let [him] sleep' (V.ii.4–5)
       aboard the ship for England. That may have been a rash
       'Indiscretion', another kind of 'Foolery', but his decision to
       act on it would probably have saved the Prince's life when he
       arrived in England.

227   **Gamgiving**   misgiving. The Folio prints *gaingiving*, of which the
       Second Quarto spelling is likely to be a dialectal variant. The
       Gam in *Gamgiving* probably derives from *game*, and
       specifically from those games that involve the wagers and
       misgivings associated with gambling; compare II.i.24–26, 56,
       and III.iii.88–95.
       trouble a Woman   Elizabethans who had seen *Julius Caesar*
       would probably have recalled how the title character
       disregards Calphurnia's fears, a series of omens, his
       well-wishers' warnings, and his own misgivings when he
       resolves to play the role of 'mighty Caesar' and proceed to the
       Capitol. See the notes to *Julius Caesar*, I.ii.195, 208–9,
       II.ii.49, 105, II.iii.9, III.i.68.

228   **If your Mind . . . obey it**   Horatio's words recall Hamlet's
       observations about 'God-like Reason' in IV.iv.33–36.

LORD   The Queen desires you to use some gentle
   Entertainment to Laertes before you fall to
   play.
HAMLET   She well instructs me.   *[Exit Lord.]*
HORATIO   You will loose my Lord.   220
HAMLET   I do not think so; since he went into France
   I have been in continual Practice; I shall win
   at the Odds. Thou would'st not think how ill
   all's here about my Heart, but it is no matter.
HORATIO   Nay good my Lord.   225
HAMLET   It is but Foolery, but it is such a kind of
   Gamgiving as would perhaps trouble a Woman.
HORATIO   If your Mind dislike any thing, obey it.
   I will forestall their Repair hether, and say
   you are not fit.   230

231 **we defy Augury** I refuse to be guided by omens. Hamlet
presents himself as one who is not influenced by pagan
superstitions. But what he dismisses as 'Augury' can be
construed as the prudence prompted by a rational assessment
of circumstantial evidence; if so, Hamlet shows himself to be
too 'apoplexed' by his own vanity (see IV.iv.43–63) to permit
his 'ears to hear' (Matthew 11:15) a providential warning (see
IV.iv.33–36). See the note to V.i.270.

231– **There . . . Sparrow** Hamlet alludes to Matthew 10:29–31. But
32   his words also recall *Julius Caesar*, II.ii.26–27, where Caesar
says 'What can be avoided / Whose End is purpos'd by the
mighty Gods?'

238 **this Hand** Most interpreters infer that the King is speaking of
Laertes' hand, and that he then places it in Hamlet's hand.
That is the most plausible reading of this line. Another
possibility is that the King offers his own hand to Hamlet. If
so, whatever Hamlet does, he says nothing to Claudius in
response.

242 **a sore Distraction** a painful tendency to fall into fits of
madness. *Sore* echoes V.i.180–81.

244 **Exception** objection, difference (see the note to line 111).
Hamlet refers to an injury so severe that a man of honour
would feel that he had no choice but to requite it.

250 **Faction** party.

252 **in this Audience** in the presence of all these noble witnesses.

254 **that** as if. *Purpos'd* (line 253) echoes line 185.

254– **I . . . Brother** The analogy Hamlet cites is one that would
56   excuse what he did as a terrible accident: something for which
he was the cause but not the willing agent, and something for
which he is as sorry as he would be if he had shot his own
brother. Compare IV.i.38–44. Here *generous* means both (a)
magnanimous, forgiving, and (b) noble (as in I.iii.74).
Compare IV.vii.131–36, where Claudius predicts that those
qualities in Hamlet will make him so trusting that he will be
'Remiss' in prudence, another virtue.

HAMLET   Not a whit, we defy Augury. There is special
  Providence in the Fall of a Sparrow. If it be
  now, 'tis not to come; if it be not to come, it
  will be now; if it be not now, yet it will come;
  the Readiness is all. Since no Man of ought he   235
  leaves knows, what is't to leave betimes? Let
  be.

A Table prepar'd, and Flagons of Wine on it; Trumpets,
Drums, and Officers with Cushions; King, Queen, and all
the State; Foils, Daggers, and Laertes.

KING   Come, Hamlet, come and take this Hand from
  me.
HAMLET   – Give me your Pardon, Sir, I have done you
  Wrong,
  But pardon't as you are a Gentleman;   240
  This Presence knows, and you must needs have
  heard,
  How I am punish'd with a sore Distraction.
  What I have done that might your Nature, Honour,
  And Exception roughly awake, I here
  Proclaim was Madness. Was't Hamlet wrong'd
  Laertes?   245
  Never Hamlet. If Hamlet from himself
  Be ta'en away, and when he's not himself
  Dooes wrong Laertes, then Hamlet dooes it not,
  Hamlet denies it. Who dooes it then? His
  Madness.
  If't be so, Hamlet is of the Faction   250
  That is wrong'd, his Madness is poor Hamlet's
  Enemy. Sir, in this Audience, let my
  Disclaiming from a purpos'd Evil free me
  So far in your most generous Thoughts that I
  Have shot my Arrow o'er the House and hurt   255
  My Brother.
LAERTES   I am satisfied in Nature,

256– **I am . . . Revenge** you have satisfied the part of me that would
58   most vigorously spur me to revenge: my human feelings. *Stir*
      echoes I.i.7, 156, I.v.30–33, IV.i.7–12, and IV.iv.50–53.

258– **but . . . ungor'd** but I am not prepared to say that the demands
62   of my honour are satisfied until I have had an opportunity to
      submit the case to some venerable higher authorities in these
      matters and obtain their assurance that I can accept your
      apology without permanent injury to my good name. *Voice*
      recalls I.i.123–24, I.ii.44–45, I.iii.19–24, 68, II.ii.458–59,
      592–95, III.ii.367–70, 397–99, and anticipates lines 368,
      403–4. Here as elsewhere *President* means 'precedent',
      authoritative warrant.

262   **But all that Time** but in the meantime.

263   **receive . . . like Love** accept your offer of reconciliation in the
      spirit in which it is tendered.

265   **And . . . play** Hamlet says that he will now treat Laertes as he
      would a brother; *frankly* means 'freely', generously trusting,
      taking Laertes' word that he'll not 'wrong' Hamlet. *Freely*
      echoes line 253 and recalls IV.iii.61, IV.vii.132.

266   **Foils** fencing swords.

267   **your Foil** Hamlet plays on another sense of *Foil*, a dull
      background to set off the bright lustre of a precious gem. See
      the note to IV.vii.31.
      Ignorance lack of skill and knowledge in the art of the rapier.
      But *Ignorance* can also refer to culpable negligence. See the
      note to III.i.148–49, and compare V.ii.139–41.

269   **Stick** stand out. Hamlet puns on the kind of 'sticking'
      (piercing) a sword does. The wit of his jest derives from the
      fact that a sporting foil (with its point blunted or dulled) will
      not stick. What Hamlet is saying, in other words, is that he
      will be the kind of foil that permits Laertes' foil to be the
      opposite of a normal fencing foil: a foil that sticks. As it
      happens, Hamlet's wit unwittingly points back to the Prince
      himself as target. The 'Foil' that Laertes uses *will* 'Stick fiery
      off indeed', and Hamlet will fall victim to it because 'He,
      being Remiss, / Most Generous, and free from all Contriving,
      / Will not peruse the Foils' (IV.vii.131–33). *Fiery* echoes
      II.i.33, IV.iii.40–43.

273   **laid the Odds** staked the higher wager (the Barbary Horses).

Whose Motive in this Case should stir me most
To my Revenge, but in my Terms of Honour
I stand aloof, and will no Reconcilement
Till by some elder Maisters of known Honour   260
I have a Voice and President of Peace
To keep my Name ungor'd. But all that Time
I do receive your offer'd Love like Love,
And will not wrong it.

HAMLET   I embrace it freely,
And will this Brother's Wager frankly play.   265
– Give us the Foils, come on.

LAERTES   Come, one for me.

HAMLET   I'll be your Foil, Laertes: in mine
    Ignorance
Your Skill shall like a Star i'th' darkest
    Night
Stick fiery off indeed.

LAERTES   You mock me, Sir.

HAMLET   No, by this Hand.   270

KING   Give them the Foils, young Ostricke. – Cousin
    Hamlet,
You know the Wager.

HAMLET   Very well, my Lord.
Your Grace has laid the Odds a'th' Weaker Side.

KING   I do not fear it, I have seen you both:
But since he is better, we have therefore
    Odds.   275

LAERTES   – This is too heavy: let me see another.

277   **likes** pleases.

      have all a Length are all the same length. Most of today's editions substitute a question mark for the full stop that ends this sentence in the Second Quarto and First Folio texts. It is by no means clear that the incautious Hamlet is asking a question, notwithstanding Laertes' reply in line 278.

281   **quit . . . Exchange** requite (return a hit) in the third bout (having lost the first two). *Quit* echoes line 68.

284   **Union** a large pearl of the most exquisite quality.

287   **Kettle** kettledrum. Lines 286–89 echo I.ii.125–28.

291   **wary** This word recalls I.ii.133–34.

293   **Judgement** Hamlet is appealing to the judges (umpires, line 291), for a ruling.

S.D.   **a Piece goes off** a cannon fires.

300   **Fat** The Queen probably means 'sweating'. But she may also be saying that Hamlet is overweight and therefore not a match for Laertes' stamina. See the note to IV.iii.21.

HAMLET — This likes me well, these Foils have
   all a Length.

LAERTES   Ay my good Lord.   *Prepare to play.*

KING   Set me the stoups of Wine upon that Table.
   If Hamlet give the first or second Hit,   280
   Or quit in Answer of the third Exchange,
   Let all the Battlements their Ordnance fire.
   The King shall drink to Hamlet's better Breath,
   And in the Cup an Union shall he throw,
   Richer than that which four successive Kings   285
   In Denmark's Crown have worn: give me the Cups,
   And let the Kettle to the Trumpet speak,
   The Trumpet to the Cannoneer without,
   The Cannons to the Heavens, the Heaven to Earth,
   Now the King drinks to Hamlet. Come begin.   290
                                    Trumpets the while.
   — And you the Judges bear a wary Eye.

HAMLET   Come on, Sir.

LAERTES   Come, my Lord.   *They play.*

HAMLET   One.

LAERTES   No.

HAMLET   — Judgement.

OSTRICKE   A Hit, a very palpable Hit.
                     Drum, Trumpets, and Shot.
                     Flourish: a Piece goes off.

LAERTES   Well, again.

KING   Stay, give me Drink. — Hamlet, this Pearl is
   thine: 295
   Here's to thy Health. — Give him the Cup.

HAMLET   I'll play this Bout first, set it by a while.
                               [They play again.]
   — Come, another Hit. What say you?

LAERTES   A Touch,
   A Touch, I do confess't.

KING   — Our Son shall win.

QUEEN   He's Fat and scant of Breath.   300

301 **Napkin** handkerchief.

302 **carouses** offers a toast and then drinks a full cup without
pausing for breath. Compare I.ii.125–28, I.iv.7–11, II.i.56.

308 **I do not think't.** This line would appear to be a reply to what
Laertes has just said to the King. But another, equally likely
possibility is that the playwright wrote these words to be
spoken as an indication that the King is still reacting to what
the Queen has done a moment earlier: 'I can't bring myself to
believe what has just happened: I've lost my beloved Queen.'
It is conceivable that Claudius' words do 'double Business'
here (III.iii.41).

311 **pass** thrust. See the note to IV.vii.135. What will appear to be
a 'pass' delivered in 'practice' (sport or 'play', line 297) will in
fact be a 'Practice' in the more sinister sense: a cunning
deception. See *King Lear*, V.iii.151–54, where Goneril calls
Edmund a victim of his adversary's 'Practice' and says, 'Thou
art not vanquish'd, / But cozen'd and beguil'd.'

312 **make a Wanton of me** indulge me by toying with me.

316 **incens'd** enflamed with rage. See line 61.

317 **how** ho. So also in line 324.

319 **Springe** snare. Earlier in the play, Laertes' father has employed
the same proverb when warning Ophelia to avoid Hamlet
(I.iii.114).

321 **sounds** both (a) sounds (moans), and (b) s'ounds (swoons).

322 **O my dear Hamlet** The Queen realizes what has happened to
her, who was responsible for it, and who the intended victim
was to be; then, significantly, she turns away from her
husband to address herself to her son. Contrary to Claudius'
expectation, the Prince's mother does not 'uncharge the
Practice' (IV.vii.66). Instead she implicitly charges the
usurping King with treachery and attempted murder.

– Here Hamlet, take my Napkin, rub thy Brows;
The Queen carouses to thy Fortune, Hamlet.
HAMLET   Good Madam.
KING   Gertrard, do not drink.
QUEEN   I will, my Lord, I pray you pardon me.
KING   – It is the poison'd Cup, it is too late.   305
HAMLET   I dare not drink yet, Madam; by and by.
QUEEN   Come, let me wipe thy Face.
LAERTES   My Lord, I'll hit him now.
KING   I do not think't.
LAERTES   And yet it is almost 'gainst my Conscience.
HAMLET   Come for the third, Laertes, you do but
   dally.   310
   I pray you pass with your best Violence:
   I am sure you make a Wanton of me.
LAERTES   Say you so? Come on.   *Play.*
OSTRICKE   Nothing neither way.
LAERTES   Have at you now.   *[Laertes thrusts Hamlet.]*   315
                     In scuffling, they change Rapiers.
KING   Part them, they are incens'd.
HAMLET   Nay come again.
                  [They fight again. The Queen collapses.]
OSTRICKE   Look to the Queen there, how.
HORATIO   They bleed on both sides.
   – How is it, my Lord?
OSTRICKE   – How is't, Laertes?
LAERTES   Why as a Woodcock to mine own Springe,
   Ostricke:
   I am justly kill'd with mine own Treachery.   320
HAMLET   – How dooes the Queen?
KING   She sounds to see them bleed.
QUEEN   No, no, the Drink, the Drink, O my dear
   Hamlet,
   The Drink, the Drink: I am poisoned.
HAMLET   O Villainy; how, let the Door be lock'd,
   Treachery, seek it out.   325

330   **Unbated and envenom'd**   unprotected and poisoned. See IV.vii.99–102, 131–36.

333   **can**   am able to say.
       too blame   too blameworthy.

335   **Treason**   What the onlookers appear to mean is that Hamlet is committing treason in attacking the King. Only Hamlet and Horatio know how Claudius obtained his throne and maintained his hold on it. And, apart from Horatio, there is no one else in the Castle with any reason to feel loyal to Hamlet rather than to the man they regard as their duly anointed sovereign.

338   **Is . . . here?**   Hamlet refers not only to the pearl the King has placed in the poisoned chalice, but also to the 'Union' (marriage) that has poisoned all of Denmark. See the notes to I.ii.9, I.iv.89, I.v.35–37, IV.iii.52. Here *of* may mean *off*, the word to be found in the Folio and in most modern editions (compare II.ii.310, V.ii.269, where the Folio's *off* is adopted in this edition in preference to the Quarto's *of*); but since Horatio says, 'Here's yet some Liquor left' (line 354) a few moments hence, it may be that Hamlet dispatches Claudius without compelling him to 'Drink off' (swallow all) 'this Potion.'

340   **temper'd**   mixed, prepared.

341   **Exchange Forgiveness**   This exchange concludes the cycle initiated by Hamlet at the beginning of the scene when he requested pardon of Laertes. It seals the bond between two would-be brothers, and it completes the transfer of Laertes' loyalty from Claudius to Hamlet. See lines 252–65.

345   **Wretched Queen adiew**   The early texts do not specify when the Queen dies. It may be that she expires only now, as Hamlet bids farewell. *Adiew* (adieu) echoes I.ii.130, I.v.90, 110, IV.vii.175.

346   **Chance**   mischance, catastrophe.

347   **Mutes**   unspeaking actors. Within the play-world, Hamlet is speaking metaphorically; but in the theatre imitating that play-world, the actor playing Hamlet is speaking literally to his mute fellow actors who are pretending to be 'Audience to this Act'.

348   **as**   since, now that.

LAERTES It is here, Hamlet; thou art slain,
  No Med'cine in the World can do thee good;
  In thee there is not half an hour's Life.
  The treacherous Instrument is in thy Hand,
  Unbated and envenom'd: the foul Practice   330
  Hath turn'd it self on me. Lo here I lie,
  Never to rise again; thy Mother's poison'd;
  I can no more. The King, the King's too blame.
HAMLET The Point envenom'd too.
  – Then Venom to thy work.   *Hurts the King.*
ALL   Treason, Treason.   335
KING O yet defend me, Friends, I am but hurt.
HAMLET Here, thou incestious, murd'rous, damned
    Dane:
  Drink of this Potion. Is thy Union here?
  Follow my Mother.   *King dies.*
LAERTES   He is justly serv'd,
  It is a Poison temper'd by himself.   340
  Exchange Forgiveness with me, Noble Hamlet:
  Mine and my Father's Death come not upon thee,
  Nor thine on me.   *Dies.*
HAMLET Heaven make thee free of it, I follow thee.
  – I am dead, Horatio. – Wretched Queen, adiew.   345
  – You that look pale, and tremble at this Chance,
  That are but Mutes, or Audience to this Act,
  Had I but Time, as this fell Sergeant Death
  Is strict in his Arrest, O I could tell you –
  But let it be. – Horatio, I am dead,   350

351 **Cause** both case and cause (Hamlet's justification for 'this Act'). See the note to lines 77–78.

352 **the Unsatisfied** those who will believe that Hamlet committed treason unless they hear his 'Cause aright'.

353 **antique Roman** Horatio wishes to depart in what a later Shakespearean character calls 'the high Roman Fashion' (*Antony and Cleopatra*, IV.xv.86). Horatio bears the name of an ancient Roman, so there is a special appropriateness to his words. Here as in I.v.163 the Second Quarto spelling is *anticke*.

355 **hate** ha't (have it). Compare IV.vii.153.

359 **Felicity** escape from 'this harsh World' (line 360).

S.D. **Osrick** Here, for the first time in the Second Quarto, this courtier bears the name he is given consistently in the First Folio. It is conceivable that at this point Shakespeare simply decided to change the character's name to something more noble (Osric is a name with dignified Anglo-Saxon roots). But it is also possible that the name change is meant to signal a stage metamorphosis in which a character who exits as a foppish youth (probably at line 325) re-enters as a stately messenger to announce the arrival of another young man who appears to have matured into a more august role. Since the name is never spoken in its new form, the change would be registered solely in manner and bearing.

365 **o'er-crows** crows over (like a triumphant cock). See the note to IV.vii.168.

367 **Election** selection as Denmark's next King. Hamlet's 'dying Voice' (recommendation) will probably ensure that the Crown 'lights' (alights) on Fortinbrasse. See line 65.

369– **th' Occurrants . . . solicited** the occurrences, great and small,
70 that have urged us to this pass. *Rest* means both (a) remainder, and (b) repose (death).

371 **Good night** This farewell recalls the play's earlier 'good nights' (among them Hamlet's in III.iv and Ophelia's IV.v), and it also echoes 'To die to sleep, / To sleep, perchance to dream' (III.i.61–62).

372 **And . . . Rest** Horatio's benediction is in a very different mode from the 'Roman' sentiments he uttered a moment earlier. See the note to lines 369–70. *Angels* recalls V.i.249–51.

Thou livest; report me and my Cause aright
To the Unsatisfied.
HORATIO   Never believe it:
  I am more an antique Roman then a Dane;
  Here's yet some Liquor left.
HAMLET   As th'art a Man,
  Give me the Cup; let go, by Heaven I'll hate.   355
  O God, Horatio, what a wounded Name,
  Things standing thus unknown, shall I leave
      behind me?
  If thou did'st ever hold me in thy Heart,
  Absent thee from Felicity a while
  And in this harsh World draw thy Breath in Pain   360
  To tell my Story.   *A March afar off, and shout within.*
              What warlike Noise is this?

              Enter Osrick.

OSRICK   Young Fortinbrasse, with Conquest come
      from Poland,
  To th' Embassadors of England gives
  This warlike Volley.
HAMLET   O I die, Horatio,
  The potent Poison quite o'er-crows my Spirit;   365
  I cannot live to hear the News from England,
  But I do prophesy th' Election lights
  On Fortinbrasse, he has my dying Voice;
  So tell him, with th' Occurrants more and less
  Which have solicited; the rest is Silence.   370
                                        Dies.
HORATIO   Now cracks a Noble Hart. – Good night,
      sweet Prince,
  And flights of Angels sing thee to thy Rest.

S.D.   **the Embassadors** the ambassadors from England. It is only by coincidence that they arrive at the same time as Fortinbrasse returns from his expedition to Poland.

375   **ought** anything.
    Woe or Wonder events evoking pity or amazement.

376   **This Quarry . . . Havoc** Fortinbrasse combines a hunting metaphor (*Quarry* usually refers to a heap of deer or other game killed in a hunt) with a military one (*Havoc* is a war-cry signalling slaughter without mercy), and what he means is 'this pile of corpses proclaims that someone cried havoc'.

377   **toward** in the offing.

378   **Princes** persons of princely rank. *Shot* (single blow) echoes lines 252–56.

381   **senseless** without sense, unable to function. *Ears* recalls such previous passages as III.iv.49–86.

382   **his Commandement** The ambassadors assume, of course, that 'his' refers to Claudius. Horatio doesn't specify who 'gave Commandement for their Death' (line 386).

387   **jump** simultaneously.
    this bloody Question the carnage that has resulted from the 'Question' (issue) debated here. Horatio's phrasing recalls Hamlet's earlier references to 'some necessary Question' (III.ii.49) and 'the Question of this Straw' (IV.iv.23).

390   **Stage** Within the play-world, Horatio means 'platform'. But within the Elizabethan theatre, the character playing Horatio refers literally to a part of the Globe stage.

394   **accidental Judgements** judgements guided by miscalculations or chance.
    casual Slaughters deaths resulting from chance or from misreadings of the circumstances (as illustrated by lines 379–86).

395   **put on by Cunning** incited by deviousness.
    for no Cause without justification. The Folio prints *forc'd Cause*, and most of today's editions do likewise.

Why dooes the Drum come hether?

*Enter Fortinbrasse, with the Embassadors with Drum, Colours,
and Attendants.*

FORTINBRASSE   Where is this Sight?
HORATIO   What is it you would see:
   If ought of Woe or Wonder, cease your Search.   375
FORTINBRASSE   This Quarry cries on Havoc.
      – O proud Death,
   What Feast is toward in thine eternal Cell,
   That thou so many Princes at a Shot
   So bloodily hast strook?
EMBASSADORS   The Sight is dismal,
   And our Affairs from England come too late;   380
   The Ears are senseless that should give us
      Hearing
   To tell him his Commandement is fulfill'd,
   That Rosencraus and Guildenstern are dead.
   Where should we have our Thanks?
HORATIO   Not from his Mouth,
   Had it th' Ability of Life to thank you: 385
   He never gave Commandement for their Death.
   But since so jump upon this bloody Question
   You from the Polack Wars, and you from England,
   Are here arriv'd, give order that these Bodies
   High on a Stage be placed to the View,   390
   And let me speak to th' yet unknowing World
   How these things came about. So shall you hear
   Of carnal, bloody, and unnatural Acts,
   Of accedental Judgements, casual Slaughters,
   Of Deaths put on by Cunning and for no Cause,   395

396 **this Upshot**   the outcome you see here.

396– **Purposes mistook ... Heads**   Horatio probably means plans
97   mis-taken (not only mistakenly conceived, but conceived out
of evil intent) that have boomeranged on the perpetrators,
Claudius and Laertes in particular. But to a lesser degree,
Horatio's words can be applied to Hamlet's 'rough-hewn'
purposes too; see the notes to lines 220–31.

401 **some Rights of Memory**   Fortinbrasse's words remind us that
the wheel has now come full circle: like Hamlet, and like
Laertes, Fortinbrasse has had a father's honour to reinstate,
and he now claims not only the Norwegian territory the elder
Fortinbrasse had lost to the elder Hamlet, but the elder
Hamlet's kingdom in its entirety.

406 **wild**   dangerously ungoverned, unruly. Compare III.i.37. Here,
as in line 144, *least* means 'lest'.

409 **put on**   placed on the throne. This phrase echoes line 395;
compare I.iii.94, I.v.163, II.i.19–20, 29, III.iv.161–62,
IV.iii.3, IV.vi.18–19, IV.vii.128.

410 **for his Passage**   to honour his passing (death). See the note to
II.ii.441.

411 **Right**   both (a) deserved custom, and (b) rite, ritual. Line 412 is
probably to be followed by a pause for 'the Soldier's Music'.

414 **Becomes the Field**   would be appropriate for the battlefield.

And in this Upshot, Purposes mistook
Fall'n on th' Inventors' Heads. All this can I
Truly deliver.

FORTINBRASSE   Let us haste to hear it,
And call the Noblest to the Audience.
For me, with Sorrow I embrace my Fortune: 400
I have some Rights of Memory in this Kingdom,
Which now to claim my Vantage doth invite me.

HORATIO   Of that I shall have also cause to speak,
And from his Mouth whose Voice will draw no
    more;
But let this same be presently perform'd   405
Even while men's Minds are wild, least more
    Mischance
On Plots and Errors happen.

FORTINBRASSE   Let four Captains
Bear Hamlet like a Soldier to the Stage,
For he was likely, had he been put on,
To have proved most Royal; and for his Passage,   410
The Soldier's Music and the Right of War
Speak loudly for him.
Take up the Bodies: such a Sight as this
Becomes the Field, but here shows much amiss.
Go bid the Soldiers shoot.   415

> *Exeunt marching: after the which a Peal of*
> *Ordenance are shot off.*

FINIS

PERSPECTIVES ON
Hamlet

For eighteenth-century commentators, Shakespeare's tragedies posed difficulties because, as John Dennis put it in an essay published in London in 1712, they were thought to be 'wanting in the exact distribution of poetical justice'. All too often, Dennis said,

> the guilty and the innocent perish promiscuously, as Duncan and Banquo in *Macbeth*, as likewise Lady Macduff and her children, Desdemona in *Othello*, Cordelia, Kent, and King Lear in the tragedy that bears his name, Brutus and Portia in *Julius Caesar*, and young Hamlet in the *Tragedy of Hamlet*. For though it may be said in defence of the last, that Hamlet had a design to kill his uncle who then reigned, yet this is justified by no less than a call from heaven, and raising up one from the dead to urge him to it.

The net effect, according to Dennis, was to 'call the government of providence into question' and to encourage 'sceptics and libertines' in their heresy that the universe is ruled solely by 'chance'.

In the notes accompanying his edition of *The Plays of William Shakespeare* (London, 1765), Samuel Johnson endorsed Dennis' criticism of *Hamlet*, and carried it one step further.

> The poet is accused of having shown little regard to poetical justice, and may be charged with equal neglect of poetical probability. The apparition left the regions of the dead to little purpose; the revenge which he demands is not obtained but by the death of him that was required to take it; and the gratification which would arise from the destruction of an usurper and a murderer, is abated by the untimely death of Ophelia, the young, the beautiful, the harmless, and the pious.

But Johnson's opinions about the Danish play were not all negative.

If the dramas of Shakespeare were to be characterized, each by the particular excellence which distinguishes it from the rest, we must allow to the tragedy of *Hamlet* the praise of variety. The incidents are so numerous, that the argument of the play would make a long tale. The scenes are interchangeably diversified with merriment and solemnity; with merriment that includes judicious and instructive observations, and solemnity, not strained by poetical violence above the natural sentiments of man. New characters appear from time to time in continual succession, exhibiting various forms of life and particular modes of conversation. The pretended madness of Hamlet causes much mirth, the mournful distraction of Ophelia fills the heart with tenderness, and every personage produces the effect intended, from the apparition that in the first act chills the blood with horror, to the fop in the last, that exposes affectation to just contempt.

The conduct is perhaps not wholly secure against objections. The action is indeed for the most part in continual progression, but there are some scenes which neither forward nor retard it. Of the feigned madness of Hamlet there appears no adequate cause, for he does nothing which he might not have done with the reputation of sanity. He plays the madman most, when he treats Ophelia with so much rudeness, which seems to be useless and wanton cruelty.

Hamlet is, through the whole play, rather an instrument than an agent. After he has, by the stratagem of the play, convicted the King, he makes no attempt to punish him, and his death is at last effected by an incident which Hamlet has no part in producing.

The catastrophe is not very happily produced; the exchange of weapons is rather an expedient of necessity, than a stroke of art. A scheme might easily have been formed, to kill Hamlet with the dagger, and Laertes with the bowl.

Within a decade of Johnson's edition, essays such as William Richardson's *A Philosophical Analysis and Illustration of some of Shakespeare's Remarkable Characters* (London, 1774) were beginning to signal a more sympathetic view of both *Hamlet* and its title character. 'The death of his father', Richardson said, is 'a natural evil' that the Prince is able to endure. 'That he is excluded from succeeding immediately to the royalty that belongs to him', moreover, 'seems to affect him slightly; for to vehement and vain ambition he appears superior.' No, insisted Richardson, Hamlet

> is moved by finer principles, by an exquisite sense of virtue, of moral beauty and turpitude. The impropriety of Gertrude's behaviour, her ingratitude to the memory of her former husband, and the depravity she discovers in the choice of a successor, afflict his soul, and cast him into utter agony. Here then is the principle and spring of all his actions. . . . Surprise, on a discovery so painful and unexpected, adds bitterness to his sorrow; and led by the same moral principle to admire and glory in the high desert of his father, even this admiration contributes to his uneasiness. Aversion to his uncle, arising from the same origin, has a similar tendency, and augments his anguish. All these feelings and emotions, uniting together, are rendered still more violent, exasperated by his recent interview with the Queen, struggling for utterance, but restrained. Agitated and overwhelmed with afflicting images, no soothing, no exhilarating affection can have admission into his heart. His imagination is visited by no vision of happiness; and he wishes for deliverance from his afflictions, by being delivered from a painful existence.

Before Richardson wrote, a similar note was being sounded by one of his contemporaries, Henry Mackenzie, who published an important article in *The Mirror* (London, 1770). According to Mackenzie:

> Of all the characters of Shakespeare, that of Hamlet has been generally thought the most difficult to be reduced to any fixed or settled principle. With the strongest purposes of revenge, he is irresolute and inactive; amidst the gloom of the deepest melancholy, he is gay and jocular; and while he is described as a passionate lover, he seems indifferent about the object of his affections. . . .
>
> The basis of Hamlet's character seems to be an extreme sensibility of mind, apt to be strongly impressed by its situation, and overpowered by the feelings which that situation excites. Naturally of the most virtuous and most amiable disposition, the circumstances in which he was placed unhinged those principles of action, which, in another situation, would have delighted mankind, and made himself happy. . . . His misfortunes were not the misfortunes of accident, which, though they may overwhelm at first, the mind will soon call up

reflections to alleviate, and hopes to cheer: they were such as reflection only serves to irritate, such as rankle in the soul's tenderest part, her sense of virtue, and feelings of natural affection; they arose from an uncle's villainy, a mother's guilt, a father's murder! – Yet amidst the gloom of melancholy, and the agitation of passion, in which his calamities involve him, there are occasional breakings-out of a mind richly endowed by nature, and cultivated by education. We perceive gentleness in his demeanour, wit in his conversation, taste in his amusements, and wisdom in his reflections.

That Hamlet's character, thus formed by nature, and thus modelled by situation, is often variable and uncertain, I am not disposed to deny. I will content myself with the supposition that this is the very character which Shakespeare meant to allot him. Finding such a character in real life, of a person endowed with feelings so delicate as to border on weakness, with sensibility too exquisite to allow of determined action, he has placed it where it could be best exhibited, in scenes of wonder, of terror, and of indignation, where its varying emotions might be most strongly marked amidst the workings of imagination, and the war of the passions.

. . . Had Shakespeare made Hamlet pursue his vengeance with a steady determined purpose, had he led him through difficulties arising from accidental causes, and not from the doubts and hesitation of his own mind, the anxiety of the spectator might have been highly raised; but it would have been anxiety for the event, not for the person. As it is, we feel not only the virtues, but the weaknesses of Hamlet, as our own. . . .

. . . The incident of the Ghost, which is entirely the poet's own, and not to be found in the Danish legend, not only produces the happiest stage effect, but is also of the greatest advantage in unfolding that character which is stamped on the young prince at the opening of the play. In the communications of such a visionary being, there is an uncertain kind of belief, and a dark unlimited horror, which are aptly suited to display the wavering purpose and varied emotions of a mind endowed with a delicacy of feeling that often shakes its fortitude, with sensibility that overpowers its strength.

By the end of the century Mackenzie's portrayal of the title character as a 'delicate and tender Prince' (*Hamlet*, IV.iv.45) was dominant not only in Britain but in Germany. In *Wilhelm Meister's Apprenticeship* (1795), translated by Thomas Carlyle

(London, 1824), Johann Wolfgang von Goethe included a description of Hamlet as a young man 'not reflective or sorrowful by nature' but made so by what has 'become for him a heavy obligation'.

> . . . To me it is clear that Shakespeare meant, in the present case, to represent the effects of a great action laid upon a soul unfit for the performance of it. In this view the whole piece seems to me to be composed. There is an oak-tree planted in a costly jar, which should have borne only pleasant flowers in its bosom; the roots expand, the jar is shivered.
>
> A lovely, pure, noble and most moral nature, without the strength of nerve which forms a hero, sinks beneath a burden which it cannot bear and must not cast away. All duties are holy for him; the present is too hard. Impossibilities have been required of him; not in themselves impossibilities, but such for him. He winds, and turns, and torments himself; he advances and recoils; is ever put in mind, ever puts himself in mind; at last does all but lose his purpose from his thoughts; yet still without recovering his peace of mind.

Soon another German Romantic, August Wilhelm von Schlegel, was speaking in similar terms. In his 1808 *Lectures on Dramatic Art and Literature*, translated by John Black (London, 1846), Schlegel defined *Hamlet* as

> a tragedy of thought inspired by continual and never-satisfied meditation on human destiny and the dark perplexity of the events of this world, and calculated to call forth the very same meditation in the minds of the spectators. This enigmatical work resembles those irrational equations in which a fraction of unknown magnitude always remains, that will in no way admit of solution. . . . The whole is intended to show that a calculating consideration, which exhausts all the relations and possible consequences of a deed, must cripple the power of acting. . . .

But Schlegel went on to say that he could not 'pronounce altogether so favourable a sentence' on Hamlet's character 'as Goethe does'. In Schlegel's view, Hamlet's 'weakness' was

> too apparent: he does himself only justice when he implies that there is no greater dissimilarity than between himself and Hercules. He is not

solely impelled by necessity to artifice and dissimulation, he has a natural inclination for crooked ways; he is a hypocrite towards himself; his far-fetched scruples are often mere pretexts to cover his want of determination. . . . He has been chiefly condemned both for his harshness in repulsing the love of Ophelia, which he himself had cherished, and for his insensibility at her death. But he is too much overwhelmed with his own sorrow to have any compassion to spare for others. . . . [W]e evidently perceive in him a malicious joy, when he has succeeded in getting rid of his enemies. . . . Hamlet has no firm belief either in himself or in anything else: from expressions of religious confidence he passes over to sceptical doubts; he believes in the Ghost of his father as long as he sees it, but as soon as it has disappeared, it appears to him almost in the light of a deception. He has even gone so far as to say, 'there is nothing either good or bad, but thinking makes it so;' with him the poet loses himself here in labyrinths of thought, in which neither end nor beginning is discoverable. The stars themselves, from the course of events, afford no answer to the question so urgently proposed to them. A voice from another world, commissioned, it would appear, by heaven, demands vengeance for a monstrous enormity, and the demand remains without effect; the criminals are at last punished, but, as it were, by an accidental blow, and not in the solemn way requisite to convey to the world a warning example of justice; irresolute foresight, cunning treachery, and impetuous rage, hurry on to a common destruction; the less guilty and innocent are equally involved in the general ruin. The destiny of humanity is there exhibited as a gigantic Sphinx, which threatens to precipitate into the abyss of scepticism all who are unable to solve her dreadful enigmas.

A few years after Schlegel delivered his observations about the Prince of Denmark, Samuel Taylor Coleridge offered a series of lectures on Shakespeare and Milton. John Payne Collier took notes, and four and a half decades later (London, 1856) he published an edited collection of the comments Coleridge had made in 1811–12. Coleridge, a sometimes frustrated poet and critic who confessed to having more than a little of the melancholy Dane in himself, hypothesized that Shakespeare's purpose in creating so engaging a protagonist as Hamlet was to portray a person, in whose view the external world, and all its incidents and objects, were comparatively dim, and of no interest in themselves, and which began to interest only when they were reflected in the mirror of his mind. Hamlet beheld external things in the same way that a man of vivid imagination, who shuts his eyes, sees what has previously made an impression on his organs. . . .

The poet places him in the most stimulating circumstances that a human being can be placed in. He is the heir apparent of a throne; his father dies suspiciously; his mother excludes her son from the throne by marrying his uncle. This is not enough; but the ghost of the murdered father is introduced, to assure the son that he was put to death by his own brother. What is the effect upon the son? – instant action and pursuit of revenge? No: endless reasoning and hesitating – constant urging and solicitation of the mind to act, and so constant an escape from action; ceaseless reproaches of himself for sloth and negligence, while the whole energy of his resolution evaporates in these reproaches. This, too, not from cowardice, for he is drawn as one of the bravest of his time – not from want of forethought or slowness of apprehension, for he sees through the very souls of all who surround him, but merely from that aversion to action, which prevails among such as have a world in themselves. . . .

There is no indecision about Hamlet, as far as his own sense of duty is concerned; he knows well what he ought to do, and over and over again he makes up his mind to do it. . . . Yet with all this strong conviction of duty, and with all the resolution arising out of strong conviction, nothing is done. This admirable and consistent character, deeply acquainted with his own feelings, painting them with such wonderful power and accuracy, and firmly persuaded that a moment ought not to be lost in executing the solemn charge committed to him, still yields to the same retiring from reality. . . .

Coleridge defended his vacillating Prince from the charge Samuel Johnson had levelled in his comments about 'the scene where Hamlet enters and finds his uncle praying, and refuses to take his life, excepting when he is in the height of his iniquity'.

This conduct, and this sentiment, Dr. Johnson has pronounced to be so atrocious and horrible as to be unfit to be put into the mouth of a human being. The fact, however, is that Dr. Johnson did not understand the character of Hamlet, and censured accordingly: the determination to allow the guilty King to escape at such a moment is only part of the indecision and irresoluteness of the hero. Hamlet seizes hold of a pretext for not acting, when he might have acted so instantly and effectually: therefore, he again defers the revenge he was bound to seek, and declares his determination to accomplish it at some time

> When he is drunk, asleep, or in his rage,
> Or in th' incestuous pleasures of his bed.

This, allow me to impress upon you most emphatically, was merely the excuse Hamlet made to himself for not taking advantage of this particular and favourable moment for doing justice upon his guilty uncle, at the urgent instance of the spirit of his father. . . .*

Even after the scene with Osrick, we see Hamlet still indulging in reflection, and hardly thinking of the task he has just undertaken: he is all dispatch and resolution, as far as words and present intentions are concerned, but all hesitation and irresolution, when called upon to carry his words and intentions into effect; so that, resolving to do everything, he does nothing. He is full of purpose, but void of that quality of mind which accomplishes purpose.

Anything finer than this conception, and working out of a great character, is merely impossible. Shakespeare wished to impress upon us the truth that action is the chief end of existence – that no faculties of intellect, however brilliant, can be considered valuable, or indeed otherwise than as misfortunes, if they withdraw us from or render us repugnant to action, and lead us to think and think of doing, until the time has elapsed when we can do anything effectually. In enforcing this moral truth, Shakespeare has shown the fullness and force of his powers: all that is amiable and excellent in nature is combined in Hamlet, with the exception of one quality. He is a man living in meditation, called upon to act by every motive human and divine, but

---

* The general thrust of Coleridge's reply to Johnson's remarks on the Prayer Scene had been anticipated by William Richardson, who in his *Essays on Shakespeare's Dramatic Characters* (London, 1784) had said: 'You ask me, why he did not kill the Usurper? And I answer, because he was at that instant irresolute. This irresolution arose from the inherent principles of his constitution, and is to be accounted natural: it arose from virtuous, or at least from amiable sensibility, and therefore cannot be blamed. His sense of justice, or his feelings of tenderness, in a moment when his violent emotions were not excited, overcame his resentment. But you will urge the inconsistency of this account, with the inhuman sentiments he expresses. . . . In reply to this difficulty, and it is not inconsiderable, I will venture to affirm, that these are not his real sentiments. There is nothing in the whole character of Hamlet that justifies such savage enormity.'

the great object of his life is defeated by continually resolving to do, yet doing nothing but resolve.

A member of Coleridge's circle made explicit a sense of identification with Hamlet that had remained largely implicit in his friend's lecture about Shakespeare's most philosophical hero. In *Characters of Shakespear's Plays* (London, 1817), William Hazlitt said that Hamlet's 'speeches and sayings' are more than 'the idle coinage of the poet's brain' because

> They are as real as our own thoughts. Their reality is in the reader's mind. It is *we* who are Hamlet. This play has a prophetic truth, which is above that of history. Whoever has become thoughtful and melancholy through his own mishaps or those of others; whoever has borne about with him the clouded brow of reflection, and thought himself 'too much i'th' sun'; whoever has seen his golden lamp of day dimmed by envious mists rising in his own breast, and could find in the world before him only a dull blank with nothing left remarkable in it; whoever has known the 'pangs of despised love, the insolence of office, or the spurns which patient merit of the unworthy takes'; he who has felt his mind sink within him, and sadness cling to his heart like a malady, who has had his hopes blighted and his youth staggered by the apparitions of strange things; who cannot be well at ease while he sees evil hovering near him like a spectre; whose powers of action have been eaten up by thought, he to whom the universe seems infinite, and himself nothing; whose bitterness of soul makes him careless of consequences, and who goes to a play as his best resource to shove off, to a second remove, the evils of life by a mock representation of them – this is the true Hamlet.

We have been so used to this tragedy that we hardly know how to criticise it any more than we should know how to describe our own faces. But we must make such observations as we can. It is the one of Shakespear's plays that we think of the oftenest, because it abounds most in striking reflections on human life, and because the distresses of Hamlet are transferred, by the turn of his mind, to the general account of humanity. Whatever happens to him we apply to ourselves, because he applies it to himself as a means of general reasoning. He is a great moraliser; and what makes him worth attending to is, that he moralises on his own feelings and experience. If *Lear* is distinguished by the greatest depth of passion, *Hamlet* is the most remarkable for the ingenuity, originality, and unstudied development of character. Shakespear had more magnanimity than any other poet, and he has shewn more of it in this play than in any other. . . .

The character of Hamlet stands quite by itself. It is not a character marked by strength of will or even of passion, but by refinement of thought and sentiment. Hamlet is as little of the hero as a man can well be: but he is a young and princely novice, full of high enthusiasm and quick sensibility – the sport of circumstances, questioning with fortune and refining on his own feelings, and forced from the natural bias of his disposition by the strangeness of his situation. He seems incapable of deliberate action, and is only hurried into extremities on the spur of the occasion, when he has no time to reflect, as in the scene where he kills Polonius, and again, where he alters the letters which Rosencraus and Guildenstern are taking with them to England, purporting his death. At other times, when he is most bound to act, he remains puzzled, undecided, and sceptical, dallies with his purpose, till the occasion is lost, and finds out some pretence to relapse into indolence and thoughtfulness again. For this reason he refuses to kill the King when he is at his prayers, and by a refinement in malice, which is in truth only an excuse for his own want of resolution, defers his revenge to a more fatal opportunity, when he shall be engaged in some act 'that has no relish of salvation in it.'

The first great critic of the twentieth century, A. C. Bradley, built on the insights of his eminent eighteenth- and nineteenth-century predecessors. In *Shakespearean Tragedy* (London, 1904), Bradley stressed Hamlet's melancholy, which he traced to 'the moral shock of the sudden ghastly disclosure of his mother's true nature, falling on him when his heart was aching with love, and his body doubtless was weakened by sorrow'. Having seen his mother marry 'a man utterly contemptible and loathsome in his eyes', and marry him 'not for any reason of state, nor even out of old family affection, but in such a way that her son was forced to see in her action not only an astounding shallowness of feeling but an eruption of coarse sensuality', Hamlet discovers that

His whole mind is poisoned. He can never see Ophelia in the same light again: she is a woman, and his mother is a woman: if she mentions the word 'brief' to him, the answer drops from his lips like venom, 'as woman's love.'. . .

If we still wonder, and ask why the effect of this shock should be so tremendous, let us observe that *now* the conditions have arisen under which Hamlet's highest endowments, his moral sensibility and his genius, become his enemies. A nature morally blunter would have felt even so dreadful a revelation less keenly.... But Hamlet has the imagination which, for evil as well as good, feels and sees all things in one. Thought is the element of his life, and his thought is infected. He cannot prevent himself from probing and lacerating the wound in his soul....

'Melancholy,' I said, not dejection, nor yet insanity. That Hamlet was not far from insanity is very probable. His adoption of the pretence of madness may well have been due in part to fear of the reality; to an instinct of self-preservation, a fore-feeling that the pretence would enable him to give some utterance to the load that pressed on his heart and brain, and a fear that he would be unable altogether to repress such utterance.... If we like to use the word 'disease' loosely, Hamlet's condition may truly be called disease. No exertion of will could have dispelled it. Even if he had been at once to do the bidding of the Ghost he would doubtless have still remained for some time under the cloud....

... But Hamlet's melancholy ... is a totally different thing from the madness which he feigns; and he never, when alone or in company with Horatio alone, exhibits the signs of that madness.

[Hamlet's melancholy accounts for his] inaction. For the *immediate* cause of that is simply that his habitual feeling is one of disgust at life and everything in it, himself included, – a disgust which varies in intensity, rising at times into a longing for death, sinking often into weary apathy, but is never dispelled for more than brief intervals. Such a state of feeling is inevitably adverse to *any* kind of decided action; the body is inert, the mind indifferent or worse....

[But if the protagonist's melancholy explains his 'lethargy', it also accounts for] his own inability to understand why he delays. This emerges in a marked degree when an occasion like the player's emotion or the sight of Fortinbras's army stings Hamlet into shame at his inaction. '*Why*,' he asks himself in genuine bewilderment, 'do I linger? Can the cause be cowardice? Can it be sloth? Can it be thinking too precisely on the event? And does *that* again mean cowardice? What is it that makes me sit idle when I feel it is shameful to do so, and when I have *cause, and will, and strength, and means,* to act?' A man irresolute merely because he was considering a proposed action too minutely would not feel this bewilderment. A man might feel it whose conscience secretly condemned the act which his explicit consciousness approved; but we have seen that there is no sufficient evidence to justify us in conceiving Hamlet thus. These are the questions of a man stimulated for the moment to shake off the weight of his melancholy, and, because for the moment he is free from it, unable to understand the paralysing pressure which it exerts at other times.

I have dwelt thus at length on Hamlet's melancholy because, from the psychological point of view, it is the centre of the tragedy, and to omit it from consideration or to underrate its intensity is to make Shakespeare's story unintelligible. But the psychological point of view is not equivalent to the tragic; and having once given its due weight to the fact of Hamlet's melancholy, we may freely admit, or rather may be anxious to insist, that this pathological condition would excite but little, if any, tragic interest if it were not the condition of a nature distinguished by that speculative genius on which the Schlegel–Coleridge type of theory lays stress. Such theories misinterpret the connection between that genius and Hamlet's failure, but still it is this connection which gives to his story its peculiar fascination and makes it appear (if the phrase may be allowed) as the symbol of a tragic mystery inherent in human nature. Wherever this mystery touches us, wherever we are forced to feel the wonder and awe of man's godlike 'apprehension' and his 'thoughts that wander through eternity,' and at the same time are forced to see him powerless in his petty sphere of action, and powerless (it would appear) from the very divinity of his thought, we remember Hamlet. And this is the reason why, in the great ideal movement which began towards the close of the eighteenth century, this tragedy acquired a position unique among Shakespeare's drama, and shared only by Goethe's *Faust*. It was not that *Hamlet* is Shakespeare's greatest tragedy or most perfect work of art; it was that *Hamlet* most brings home to us at once the sense of the soul's infinity, and the sense of the doom which not only circumscribes that infinity but appears to be its offspring.

Less than two decades after Bradley's bold suggestion that *Hamlet* was not 'Shakespeare's greatest tragedy or most perfect work of art', T. S. Eliot weighed in with an even more shocking assertion: that 'So far from being Shakespeare's masterpiece, the play is almost certainly an artistic failure. In several ways', Eliot asserted, *Hamlet* 'is puzzling, and disquieting. . . . Of all the plays it is the longest and is possibly the one on which Shakespeare spent most pains; and yet he has left in it superfluous and inconsistent scenes which even hasty revision should have noticed.'

Writing in an article entitled 'Hamlet and his Problems' (1919), later reprinted in his *Selected Essays, 1917–1932* (London, 1932), Eliot went on to coin and illustrate a term that has achieved a lasting place in the lexicon of literary and dramatic criticism.

The only way of expressing emotion in the form of art is by finding an 'objective correlative'; in other words, a set of objects, a situation, a chain of events which shall be the formula of that *particular* emotion; such that when the external facts, which must terminate in sensory experience, are given, the emotion is immediateiy evoked. If you examine any of Shakespeare's more successful tragedies, you will find this exact equivalence; you will find that the state of mind of Lady Macbeth walking in her sleep has been communicated to you by a skilful accumulation of imagined sensory impressions; the words of Macbeth on hearing of his wife's death strike us as if, given the sequence of events, these words were automatically released by the last event in the series. The artistic 'inevitability' lies in this complete adequacy of the external to the emotion; and this is precisely what is deficient in *Hamlet*. Hamlet (the man) is dominated by an emotion which is inexpressible, because it is in *excess* of the facts as they appear. And the supposed identity of Hamlet with his author is genuine to this point: that Hamlet's bafflement at the absence of objective equivalent to his feelings is a prolongation of the bafflement of his creator in the face of his artistic problem. Hamlet is up against the difficulty that his disgust is occasioned by his mother, but that his mother is not an adequate equivalent for it; his disgust envelops and exceeds her. It is thus a feeling which he cannot understand; he cannot objectify it, and it therefore remains to poison life and obstruct action. None of the possible actions can satisfy it; and nothing that Shakespeare can do with the plot can express Hamlet. And it must be noticed that the very nature of the *données* of the problem precludes objective equivalence. To have heightened the criminality of Gertrude would have been to provide the formula for a totally different emotion in Hamlet; it is just *because* her character is so negative and insignificant that she arouses in Hamlet the feeling which she is incapable of representing.

What Eliot defined as an artistic problem was eventually redefined as a psychological dilemma, and one that could be stated in such a way as not only to exonerate but even to commend the dramatic form Shakespeare devised to depict it. In a Freudian analysis, *Hamlet and Oedipus* (New York, 1949), Ernest Jones argued that Hamlet was afflicted by an Oedipal complex, a long-forgotten but none the less debilitating youthful fantasy about murdering his father and marrying his mother.

That Hamlet is suffering from an internal conflict the essential nature of which is inaccessible to his introspection is evidenced by the following considerations. Throughout the play we have the clearest picture of a man who sees his duty plain before him, but who shirks it at every opportunity and suffers in consequence the most intense remorse. To paraphase Sir James Paget's well-known description of hysterical paralysis: Hamlet's advocates say he cannot do his duty, his detractors say he will not, whereas the truth is that he cannot will. Further than this, the deficient will-power is localized to the one question of killing his uncle; it is what may be termed a *specific abulia*. Now instances of such specific abulias in real life invariably prove, when analyzed, to be due to an unconscious repulsion against the act that cannot be performed (or else against something closely associated with the act, so that the idea of the act becomes also involved in the repulsion). In other words, whenever a person cannot bring himself to do something that every conscious consideration tells him he should do – and which he may have the strongest conscious desire to do – it is always because there is some hidden reason why a part of him doesn't want to do it; this reason he will not own to himself, and is only dimly if at all aware of. That is exactly the case with Hamlet. . . .

In Jones' interpretation of the action, everything is fine with Hamlet until his father's death and his mother's hasty second marriage. From this point on, however,

The association of the idea of sexuality with his mother, buried since infancy, can no longer be concealed from his consciousness. . . . Feelings which once, in the infancy of long ago, were pleasurable desires can now, because of his repressions, only fill him with repulsion. The long 'repressed' desire to take his father's place in his mother's affection is stimulated to unconscious activity by the sight of someone usurping this place exactly as he himself had once longed to do. More, this someone was a member of the same family, so that the actual usurpation further resembled the imaginary one in being incestuous. Without his being in the least aware of it these ancient desires are ringing in his mind, are once more struggling to find conscious expression, and need such an expenditure of energy again to 'repress' them that he is reduced to the deplorable mental state he himself so vividly depicts. . . .

The intensity of Hamlet's repulsion against women in general, and Ophelia in particular, is a measure of the powerful 'repression' to which his sexual feelings are being subjected. The outlet for those feelings in the direction of his mother has always been firmly dammed, and now that the narrow channel in Ophelia's direction has also been closed the increase in the original direction consequent on the awakening of early memories tasks all his energy to maintain the 'repression'. His pent-up feelings find a partial vent in other directions. The petulant irascibility and explosive outbursts called forth by his vexation at the hands of Guildenstern and Rosencrantz, and especially of Polonius, are evidently to be interpreted in this way, as also is in part the burning nature of his reproaches to his mother. Indeed, towards the end of his interview with his mother the thought of her misconduct expresses itself in that almost physical disgust which is so characteristic a manifestation of intensely 'repressed' sexual feeling. . . .

It will be seen from the foregoing that Hamlet's attitude towards his uncle-father is far more complex than is generally supposed. He of course detests him, but it is the jealous detestation of one evil-doer towards his successful fellow. Much as he hates him, he can never denounce him with the ardent indignation that boils straight from his blood when he reproaches his mother, for the more vigorously he denounces his uncle the more powerfully does he stimulate to activity his own unconscious and 'repressed' complexes. . . . His own 'evil' prevents him from completely denouncing his uncle's, and in continuing to 'repress' the former he must strive to ignore, to condone, and if possible even to forget the latter; *his moral fate is bound up with his uncle's for good or ill.* . . .

The explanation, therefore, of the delay and self-frustration exhibited in the endeavour to fulfil his father's demand for vengeance is that to Hamlet the thought of incest and parricide combined is too intolerable to be borne. One part of him tries to carry out the task, the other flinches inexorably from the thought of it. How fain would he blot it out in that 'bestial oblivion' which unfortunately for him his conscience contemns. He is torn and tortured in an insoluble inner conflict.

Nearly two decades prior to Jones' psychoanalytic study of *Hamlet*, G. Wilson Knight had indicted the Prince even more emphatically as an 'evil-doer'. In *The Wheel of Fire* (London, 1930), Knight asserted that

Except for the original murder of Hamlet's father, the *Hamlet* universe is one of healthy and robust life, good-nature, humour, romantic strength, and welfare: against this background is the figure of Hamlet pale with the consciousness of death. He is the ambassador of death walking amid life. The effect is at first primarily one of separation. But it is to be noted that the consciousness of death, and consequent bitterness, cruelty, and inaction, in Hamlet not only grows in his own mind distintegrating it as we watch, but also spreads its effects outward among the other persons like a blighting disease, and, as the play progresses, by its very passivity and negation of purpose, insidiously undermines the heart of the state, and adds victim to victim until at the end the stage is filled with corpses. . . .

If we are to attain a true interpretation of Shakespeare we must work from a centre of consciousness near that of the creative instinct of the poet. We must think less in terms of causality and more in terms of imaginative impact. Now Claudius is not drawn as totally evil – far from it. We see the government of Denmark working smoothly. Claudius shows every sign of being an excellent diplomatist and king. He is troubled by young Fortinbras, and dispatches ambassadors to the sick King of Norway demanding that he suppress the raids of his nephew. . . .

Throughout the first half of the play Claudius is the typical kindly uncle, besides being a good king. His advice to Hamlet about his exaggerated mourning for his father's death is admirable common sense . . . [as] opposed to the extreme misery of a sensitive nature paralysed by the facts of death and unfaithfulness. This contrast points the relative significance of the King and his court to Hamlet.

They are of the world – with their crimes, their follies, their shallownesses, their pomp and glitter; they are of humanity, with all its failings, it is true, but yet of humanity. They assert the importance of human life, they believe it, in themselves. Whereas Hamlet is inhuman, since he has seen through the tinsel of life and love, he believes in nothing, not even himself, except the memory of a ghost, and his black-robed presence is a reminder to everyone of the fact of death. There is no question but that Hamlet is right. The King's smiles hide murder, his mother's love for her new consort is unfaithfulness to Hamlet's father, Ophelia has deserted Hamlet at the hour of his need. Hamlet's philosophy may be inevitable, blameless, and irrefutable. But it is the negation of life. It is death. . . .

. . . Claudius, as he appears in the play, is not a criminal. He is – strange as it may seem – a good and gentle king, enmeshed by the chain of causality linking him with his crime. And this chain he might, perhaps, have broken except for Hamlet, and all would have been well.

In the Prayer Scene, III.iii, Shakespeare shows Claudius as a man stricken by remorse, and in Knight's view his words are 'the fine flower of a human soul in anguish'. Then, said Knight, the dramatist lets us see

the entrance of Hamlet, the late joy of torturing the King's conscience still written on his face, his eye a-glitter with the intoxication of conquest, vengeance on his mind; his purpose altered only by the devilish hope of finding a more damning moment in which to slaughter the King. . . . Which then, at this moment in the play, is nearer the Kingdom of Heaven? Whose words would be more acceptable of Jesus' God? Which is the embodiment of spiritual good, which of evil? The question of the relative morality of Hamlet and Claudius reflects the ultimate problem of this play.

For Knight the 'sweet Prince' who had been the darling of the Romantic poets and critics was more properly to be viewed as a cold, hard man who 'is not of flesh and blood':

he is a spirit of penetrating intellect and cynicism and misery, without faith in himself or anyone else, murdering his love of Ophelia, on the brink of insanity, taking delight in cruelty, torturing Claudius, wringing his mother's heart, a poison in the midst of the healthy bustle of the court. He is a superman among men. And he is a superman because he has walked and held converse with death. . . . He has seen the truth, not alone of Denmark, but of humanity, of the universe: and the truth is evil. . . .

. . . Thus Hamlet spends a great part of his time watching, analysing, and probing others. He unhesitatingly lances each in turn in his weakest spot. He is usually quite merciless. But all he actually accomplishes is to torment them all, terrorize them. . . . He exposes faults everywhere. But he is not tragic in the usual Shakespearean sense; there is no surge and swell of passion pressing onward through the play to leave us, as in *King Lear,* with the mighty crash and backwash of a tragic peace. . . .

. . .The Ghost may or may not have been a 'goblin damned'; it certainly was no 'spirit of health' (I.iv.40). The play ends with a dead march. The action grows out of eternity, closes in it. The ominous discharge of ordnance thus reverberates three times: once, before Hamlet sees the Ghost, and twice in Act V. The eternity of death falls as an abyss at either end, and Hamlet crosses the stage of life aureoled in his ghostly luminence.

While commentators such as T. S. Eliot, Ernest Jones, and G. Wilson Knight sought to look into the soul of the title character for the heart of *Hamlet*'s mystery, Theodore Spencer directed attention instead to the non-theatrical realm the play's creator shared with his audience. In 'Hamlet and the Nature of Reality' (*Journal of English Literary History*, Vol. 5, 1938), Spencer observed that

The average Elizabethan lived in a world very different from ours; a world in which the fundamental assumption was that of hierarchical order. There was a cosmological hierarchy, a political and social hierarchy, and a psychological hierarchy, and each was a reflection of the others. The governing of the state could be seen as an image of the order of the stars, and the order of the stars was reflected in the order of the faculties of man. The Ptolemaic heavens revolved around the earth; and as the sun was the largest and most resplendent of the planets, so the king was the center of the state. Similarly, as the earth was the center of the universe, so justice was the immovable center of political virtue. The cosmological and political orders were reflected in the order of nature. . . . The scale rose from inanimate matter, through the vegetative soul of plants, the sensible soul of animals, the rational soul operating through the body of man, the pure intelligence of angels, up to the pure actuality of God. Man was an essential link in the chain – the necessary mixture of body and soul to complete the order. . . . And man was more than this: he was the end for which the rest of the universe had been created. . . .

So described, the system appears, as indeed it was, not only orderly but optimistic. Yet underneath this tripartite order, of which man was the center, there were, in the sixteenth century, certain disturbing conceptions which painted the scene in different colors. In the first place, the earth could be seen, according to the Ptolemaic system, not only as the center and most important part of the universe, but as exactly the opposite. It could be regarded, to use Professor Lovejoy's words, as 'the place farthest removed from the Empyrean, the bottom of the creation, to which its dregs and baser elements sank.' . . . In the second place, man, the chief inhabitant of this tiny and remote globe, could be regarded as equally unworthy and corrupt, for since the fall of Adam he had only a faint glimmering of its original gift of natural reason, and hence, through his own fault, he was the only creature who had disrupted the system. . . .

Thus, in the inherited, . . . Christian view of man and his universe there was an implicit conflict between man's dignity and [his] wretchedness. . . . But there was another conflict, more particular to the sixteenth century, and since it was new, perhaps more emotionally and intellectually disturbing. It consisted in this: that in the sixteenth century each one of the interrelated orders – cosmological, political, and natural – which were the frame, the basic pattern, of all Elizabethan thinking, was being punctured by a doubt. Copernicus had questioned the cosmological order, Machiavelli had questioned the political order, Montaigne had questioned the natural order. The consequences were enormous.

In order to understand what the theory of Copernicus implied, it is necessary to have as vivid a picture as possible of the difference between his system and the Aristotelian or Ptolemaic. Upon the structure of the Ptolemaic system with the earth in the center, everything had been built; the order of creation, astrology, the theory of the macrocosm and the microcosm, the parallels between the universe and the state. But when the sun was put at the center, and the earth set between Mars and Venus as a mobile and subsidiary planet, the whole elaborate structure, with all its interdependencies, so easy to visualize, so convenient for metaphor and allusion, lost its meaning. . . .

The reasons for Machiavelli's reputation can perhaps best be realized by comparing *The Prince* with the *De Officiis* of Cicero. . . . For the *De Officiis*, as much as the *Politics* of Aristotle, from which it was partly derived, represents the official sixteenth century doctrine. Prudence, justice, liberality, greatness of soul, these and other virtues characterized the public man; the life of reason, in public as in private, implied the pursuit of virtue. But Machiavelli . . . was fundamentally practical. He regarded human history divorced from revelation, and human nature divorced from grace; he looked at man, as Bacon said, not as he should be, but as he is, and he found that man was naturally evil and that the best way to govern him for his own good was by fear and by force. . . .

Montaigne's position is less easy to summarize. But the implication of his ideas, at least those in the *Apology for Raymond Sebonde*, could be just as devastating to the inherited view of man's place in the natural sphere as the ideas of Copernicus and Machiavelli might be to man's place in the spheres of cosmology and politics. . . . Man can know nothing by himself, says Montaigne; he cannot know God, he cannot know his own soul, he cannot know nature. His senses are hopelessly unreliable, there are no satisfactory standards of beauty or of anything else, everything is in a flux, and the only way man can rise from his ignorant and ignominious position is by divine assistance. His purpose in writing the essay, says Montaigne, is to make people 'sensible of the inanity, the vanity, and insignificance of man; to wrest out of their fists the miserable weapon of their reason; to make them bow the head and bite the dust under the authority and reverence of the divine majesty.'

Spencer notes that, according to Ophelia, the Hamlet she'd known earlier was a youth who exemplified 'the courtier's, soldier's, scholar's, eye, tongue, sword'.

. . . In other words, he was an ideal Renaissance nobleman, himself an idealist, with – to use Bradley's somewhat romantic expression – 'an unbounded delight and faith in everything good and beautiful.' But the discovery of his mother's lust and the fact that the kingdom is in the hands of an unworthy man . . . these facts shatter his picture of the world, the state, and the individual. His sense of the evil in all three spheres is as closely interwoven in his first soliloquy as all three spheres were interwoven in sixteenth century thought. It is character-istic of Shakespeare's conception of Hamlet's universalizing mind that he should make Hamlet think, first, of the general rottenness: to him all the uses of the world are weary, stale, flat, and unprofitable, and things rank and gross in nature possess it entirely. . . . In other words, in first presenting Hamlet to his audience, Shakespeare uses an interwoven series of references to the world, the state, and the individual, and one reason this first soliloquy is so broken, its rhythms so panting, is that it reflects Hamlet's disillusionment about all three spheres at once. So closely were they related in contemporary thought that to smash one was to smash the others as well. . . .

But the occasion on which Hamlet speaks at greatest length of the heavens is, of course, when he describes his state of mind to Rosencrantz and Guildenstern in the second act. . . . To understand the force of his remarks we should have clearly in our minds the thousand and one sixteenth century repetitions of the old teaching, with which every member of Shakespeare's audience must have been familiar, that the surest way to understand man's place in the world and to realize the magnificence of God's creation, was to contemplate the glory of the superior heavens which surrounded the earth. But what Hamlet says is exactly the opposite.

During the last half-century those who have written about *Hamlet* have generally conceded that the Prince of the first four acts of the play is a man who says and does things that are difficult to square with Goethe's sentimental image of him as a youth of 'lovely, pure, noble, and most moral nature'. But the majority of recent interpreters have nevertheless found ways to salvage the hero's traditional stature by the way they've construed the drama's concluding scenes. In what has proven to be one of the most influential readings of the tragedy, for example ('The World of *Hamlet*', *Yale Review*, Vol. 41, 1952), Maynard Mack says that

In the last act of the play (or so it seems to me, for I know there can be differences on this point), Hamlet accepts his world and we discover a different man. Shakespeare does not outline for us the process of acceptance any more than he has done with Romeo or was to do with Othello. But he leads us strongly to expect an altered Hamlet, and then, in my opinion, provides him. We must recall that at this point Hamlet has been absent from the stage during several scenes, and that such absences in Shakespearean tragedy usually warn us to be on the watch for a new phase in the development of the character.... Furthermore, and this is an important matter in the theatre – especially in a play in which the symbolism of clothing has figured largely – Hamlet now looks different. He is wearing a different dress – probably, as Granville-Barker thinks, his 'seagown scarf'd' about him, but in any case no longer the disordered costume of his antic disposition. The effect is not entirely dissimilar to that in *Lear*, when the old king wakes out of his madness to find fresh garments on him.

Still more important, Hamlet displays a considerable change of mood. This is not a matter of the way we take the passage about defying augury, as Mr. Tillyard among others seems to think. It is a matter of Hamlet's whole deportment, in which I feel we may legitimately see the deportment of a man who has been 'illuminated' in the tragic sense. Bradley's term for it is fatalism, but if this is what we wish to call it, we must at least acknowledge that it is fatalism of a very distinctive kind – a kind that Shakespeare has been willing to touch with the associations of the saying in St. Matthew about the fall of a sparrow.... The point is not that Hamlet has suddenly become religious; he has been religious all through the play. The point is that he has now learned, and accepted, the boundaries in which human action, human judgment, are enclosed.

Till his return from the voyage he had been trying to act beyond these, had been encroaching on the role of providence, if I may exaggerate to make a vital point. He had been too quick to take the burden of the whole world and its condition upon his limited and finite self. Faced with a task of sufficient difficulty in its own right, he had dilated it into a cosmic problem – as indeed every task is, but if we think about this too precisely we cannot act at all. The whole time is out of joint, he feels, and in his young man's egocentricity, he will set it right. Hence he misjudges Ophelia, seeing in her only a breeder of sinners. Hence he misjudges himself, seeing himself a vermin crawling between earth and heaven. Hence he takes it upon himself to be his mother's conscience, though the ghost has warned that this is no fit task for him, and returns to repeat the warning: 'Leave her to heaven, And to those thorns that in her bosom lodge.' Even with the king, Hamlet has sought to play at God. *He* it must be who decides the issue of Claudius's salvation, saving him for a more damnable occasion. Now, he has learned that there are limits to the before and after that human reason can comprehend. Rashness, even, is sometimes good. Through rashness he has saved his life from the commission for his death, 'and prais'd be rashness for it.' This happy circumstance and the unexpected arrival of the pirate ship make it plain that the roles of life are not entirely self-assigned. 'There is a divinity that shapes our ends, Roughhew them how we will.' Hamlet is ready now for what may happen, seeking neither to foreknow it nor avoid it. 'If it be now, 'tis not to come; if it be not to come, it will be now; if it be not now, yet it will come: the readiness is all.'

The crucial evidence of Hamlet's new frame of mind, as I understand it, is the graveyard scene. Here, in its ultimate symbol, he confronts, recognizes, and accepts the condition of being man. It is not simply that he now accepts death, though Shakespeare shows him accepting it in ever more poignant forms: first, in the imagined persons of the politician, the courtier, and the lawyer, who laid their little schemes 'to circumvent God,' as Hamlet puts it, but now lie here; then in Yorick, whom he knew and played with as a child; and then in Ophelia. This last death tears from him a final cry of passion, but the striking contrast between his behavior and Laertes's reveals how deeply he has changed. . . .

After the graveyard and what it indicates has come to pass in him, we know that Hamlet is ready for the final contest of mighty opposites. He accepts the world as it is, the world as a duel, in which, whether we know it or not, evil holds the poisoned rapier and the poisoned chalice waits; and in which, if we win at all, it costs not less than everything. I think we understand by the close of Shakespeare's *Hamlet* why it is that unlike the other tragic heroes he is given a soldier's rites upon the stage. For as William Butler Yeats once said, 'Why should we honor those who die on the field of battle? A man may show as reckless a courage in entering into the abyss of himself.'

In an article that parallels Maynard Mack's in its ultimate assessment of the protagonist, Fredson Bowers depicts 'Hamlet as Minister and Scourge' (*Publications of the Modern Language Association*, Vol. 70, 1955). Bowers draws his title from a statement the Prince makes shortly after he stabs Polonius in the Closet Scene. As he ponders the implications of a deed that has resulted from mistaken identity, Hamlet says (III.iv.170–72) that

> Heaven hath pleas'd it so
> To punish me with this, and this with me,
> That I must be their Scourge and Minister.

Bowers maintains that much of what transpires from this moment forward in *Hamlet* depends upon the difference Renaissance Christians would have perceived between a 'Scourge' and a 'Minister'.

> . . . The standard religious concept of the time was that God intervened in human affairs in two ways, internally and externally. Internally, God could punish sin by arousing the conscience of an individual to a sense of grief and remorse, which might in extraordinary cases grow so acute as to lead to madness. Externally, God worked through inanimate, or at least subhuman objects, through the forces of Nature, and through the agency of human beings. . . . When a human agent was selected to be the instrument of God's vengeance, and the act of vengeance on the guilty necessitated the performance by the agent of a crime, like murder, only a man already damned for his sins was selected, and he was called a scourge. . . .
>
> Although some writers . . . used scourge and minister interchangeably, there was a general tendency to distinguish them. The references in the concordance show, for our purposes, that Shakespeare always means minister in a good sense unless he specifies that the minister is of hell. A minister of God, in contrast to a scourge, is an agent who directly performs some good. In this sense, heavenly spirits are ministers of grace, as Hamlet calls them. . . . The distinction between minister and scourge, thus, lies in two respects. First, a retributive minister may visit God's wrath on sin but only as the necessary final act to the overthrow of evil, whereas a scourge visits wrath alone, the delayed good to rest in another's hands. To take a rough and ready example, Richard III was thought of as a scourge for England, the final agent of God's vengeance for the deposition and murder of the anointed Richard II; but the good wishes of the ghosts make young Henry Richmond, in Raleigh's description, 'the immediate instrument of God's justice,' that is, a minister who will bring to a close God's

wrath by exacting public justice in battle on the tyrant Richard, this triumph to be followed by a reign of peace and glory under the Tudor dynasty. . . .

We are now in a position to examine Hamlet's 'scourge and minister.' We must recognize that the Ghost's command, though not explicit, was at first interpreted by Hamlet as a call to an act of private blood-revenge. . . . If Hamlet hopes to right the wrong done him and his father, and to ascend the throne of Denmark with honor, he must contrive a public vengeance which will demonstrate him to be a minister of Heaven's justice. . . . Since divine permission alone could free the Ghost to revisit the earth, the Ghost's demand for the external punishment of Claudius, and its prophecy of the internal punishment of Gertrude, is not alone a personal call but in effect the transmission of a divine command, appointing Hamlet as God's agent to punish the specific criminal, Claudius.

. . . Hamlet at the start finds himself in this peculiarly depressing position. He has been set aside from other human beings as an agent of God to set right the disjointed times, and he may reasonably assume from the circumstances of the ghostly visitation that he is a minister. Every private emotion urges him to a personal revenge of blood as the only means of solving his problem, and this revenge seems enforced by the secrecy of the original crime. But if he acts thus, he will be anticipating God's will, which in its good time will provide the just opportunity. If he anticipates and revenges, he risks damnation. . . .

With these considerations in mind, the two months' delay between the Ghost's visitation and the next appearance of Hamlet in Act II may seem to have more validity than certain rather bloodthirsty critics will allow. I suggest that this delay, which Shakespeare never explicitly motivates, was caused not alone by rising doubts of the Ghost, or by the physical difficulties of getting at Claudius, or by the repugnance of a sensitive young man to commit an act of murder, or by his examining the circumstances so over-scrupulously as to become lost in the mazes of thought, motive, and doubt; but instead as much as anything by Hamlet as minister waiting on the expected opportunity which should be provided him, and not finding it. . . . To satisfy at least one question, he contrives the mousetrap and secures his answer, in the process revealing himself. And immediately an opportunity is given him for private revenge in the prayer scene, but one so far different from divinely appointed public vengeance that Heaven would never have provided it for its minister, a sign that the time is not yet. He passes on, racking himself with bloodthirsty promises, and – no longer trusting to Heaven's delays – impulsively takes the next action upon himself. He kills Polonius, thinking him the King. He repents, but does not expect his repentance to alter the scales of justice. Heaven, it is clear, has punished him for anticipating by his own deed the opportunity that was designed for the future. . . . He has irretrievably stained his hands with innocent blood by his usurping action, and foreseeing Heaven withheld his proper victim as its punishment.

. . . Hamlet's own words show his own recognition that he had in part made himself a scourge by the mistaken murder; and I suggest that it is his acceptance of this part of his total role that leads him to send Rosencrantz and Guildenstern so cheerfully, at least on the surface, to their doom. . . .

When next we see Hamlet, after the interlude of the graveyard scene, a manifest change has taken place. When he left for England, as shown by his 'How all occasions do inform against me' soliloquy, he was still torn by his earlier dilemma of somehow reconciling the combat of his private emotions for revengeful action against the restraint of waiting on divine will. But it appears to him that very shortly Heaven reversed its course and actively demonstrated its guidance by preserving his life from the King's plot and returning him to Denmark, short-circuiting the delay of an English adventure. . . .

Immediately, Claudius' counterplot begins and the fencing match is arranged. Hamlet's assured feeling that he is only an instrument in the hands of God sustains him against the ominous portent of disaster that seizes on his heart. . . .

From the Elizabethan point of view, divine providence works out the catastrophe with justice. The plotters are hoist by their own villainous schemes; and then, triumphantly, the opportunity is given Hamlet to kill Claudius in circumstances which relieve him from immortal penalty for blood. By stage doctrine he must die for the slaying of Polonius, and, more doubtfully, for that of Rosencrantz and Guildenstern perhaps, the first in which he was inadvertently and the second consciously a scourge; and that penalty is being exacted. Since he cannot now ascend the throne over Claudius' body, all possible self-interest is removed. He has not plotted Claudius' death in cold blood, but seized an opportunity which under no circumstances he could have contrived by blood-revenge, to kill as a dying act of public justice a manifest and open murderer, exposed by the death of Gertrude, while himself suffering the pangs of death as his victim. The restitution of right lies only in him. Despite the terrible action of his forcing the poisoned cup between the King's teeth, Shakespeare takes great pains to remove the blood guilt from Hamlet by the expiation of his own death, and to indicate that the open killing was a ministerial act of public justice accomplished under the only possible circumstances. Hamlet's death is sufficient to expiate that of Polonius in the past and of Laertes in the present. With Christian charity Hamlet accepts Laertes' repentance and forgiveness accompanied by the prayer that 'Mine and my father's death come not upon thee' in the future life; and in turn he prays that Heaven will make Laertes free from the guilt of his own. Finally, Horatio's blessing, 'Flights of angels sing thee to thy rest,' are words of benediction for a minister of providence who died through anticipating heavenly justice but, like Samson, was never wholly cast off for his tragic fault and in the end was honored by fulfilling the divine plan in expiatory death. In more ways than one, but not necessarily more than he meant by his prophecy, Hamlet kept his promise for Polonius, 'I will answer well the death I gave him.'

In the years since Maynard Mack and Fredson Bowers published their essays a number of scholars have challenged the foundations upon which these and dozens of other critics have endeavoured to secure the Prince's standing as a hero who finally exhibits the way 'Rightly to be Great' (IV.iv.50). In *Hamlet and Revenge* (Stanford, 1967), for instance, Eleanor Prosser has offered evidence that many, if not most, Elizabethans would have been astonished by the now-traditional assumption that the Ghost's words to Hamlet are, to quote Bowers, 'in effect the transmission of a divine command'. Prosser cites a number of sixteenth- and seventeenth-century authorities who urged people to be sceptical about spectres claiming to be the ghosts of departed souls, and she notes that Barnardo, Horatio, and Marcellus are much more apprehensive than Hamlet is about a spirit who may be a demon with the power 'T' assume a pleasing Shape', deceive the unwary, and lead the Prince down the primrose path to damnation (see II.ii.636–43). Prosser also points out that while 'The Mousetrap', the play Hamlet stages before his uncle, does indeed 'catch the Conscience of the King' and thereby confirm the Ghost's testimony that Claudius is a fratricide and a regicide, it does not prove the Ghost 'honest' in any sense that would preclude its being a devil rather than the spirit of Hamlet's murdered father. Meanwhile Prosser argues that the kind of blood revenge the Ghost calls for, and the sinister subterranean voice with which it cries 'Swear' once Hamlet's companions rejoin him on the platform, would alone have made a Globe audience suspicious about such a visitor.

A number of recent commentators, among them several of those whose books and articles are listed under 'Further Reading' below, have questioned the confidence exemplified by Robert Ornstein's statement, in *The Moral Vision of Jacobean Tragedy* (Madison, Wisc., 1960), that the Prince of Denmark is 'the most noble, pure-minded, and blameless of Shakespeare's tragic protagonists' and that 'What is not near Hamlet's conscience is not near our own because he is our moral interpreter.' In the last few decades several critics have asked whether the Prince's demeanour in the graveyard and at the opening of the final scene of the play really does indicate the emergence of a mellower, wiser, and more stable Hamlet. Others have found reason to doubt that the trust Hamlet indicates in Providence is to be taken by the audience as an expression of genuine faith. And still others have wondered how much assurance a judicious playgoer in Shakespeare's theatre would have been expected to feel when Horatio invokes 'Flights of Angels' to 'sing' the title character's soul to its eternal 'Rest'.

All of which suggests that Shakespeare's most enigmatic tragedy will continue to elude our most earnest efforts to fix its 'shape'; at various times it may look like a 'Camel', or a 'Weasel', or a 'Whale', but if the first four centuries of its interpretive history are a reliable guide to the future, *Hamlet* will probably remain, for most of us, an ever-intriguing, ever-shifting 'Cloud' (III.ii.406–13).

SUGGESTIONS FOR FURTHER READING

Many of the works quoted in the preceding survey, or excerpts from those works, can be found in modern collections of criticism. Of particular interest or convenience are the following anthologies:

Bevington David (ed.), *Twentieth Century Interpretations of 'Hamlet'*, Englewood Cliffs, NJ: Prentice-Hall, 1968.

Bloom, Harold (ed.), *William Shakespeare's 'Hamlet': Modern Critical Interpretations*, New York: Chelsea House, 1990.

Hoy, Cyrus (ed.), *Hamlet*, (Norton Critical Edition), New York: Norton 1963.

Hubler, Edward (ed.), *Hamlet* (Signet Classic Edition), New York: New American Library, rev. 1987.

Jump, John (ed.), *Shakespeare, 'Hamlet': A Casebook*, London: Macmillan, 1968.

Muir, Kenneth, and Stanley Wells (eds), *Aspects of 'Hamlet'* (articles reprinted from *Shakespeare Survey*), Cambridge: Cambridge University Press, 1979 (includes Clifford Leech's 'Studies in *Hamlet*, 1901–1955').

Price, Joseph G. (ed.), *'Hamlet': Critical Essays*, New York: Garland, 1986.

Readers will also find a great deal of information about Shakespeare's most popular play in the annual *Hamlet Studies*, edited by R. W. Desai and published in New Delhi, India.

Other studies that include valuable discussions of *Hamlet*:

Alexander, Nigel, *Poison, Play, and Duel: A Study of 'Hamlet'*, Lincoln: University of Nebraska Press, 1971.

Alexander, Peter, *Hamlet, Father and Son*, Oxford: Clarendon Press, 1955.

Andrews, John F., ' "Dearly Bought Revenge": *Samson Agonistes*, *Hamlet*, and Elizabethan Revenge Tragedy', *Milton Studies*, 13 (1979), 81–107.

Bamber, Linda, *Comic Women, Tragic Men*, Stanford: Stanford University Press, 1982.

Barker, Francis, *The Tremulous Private Body: Essays on Subjection*, London: Methuen, 1984.

Battenhouse, Roy, *Shakespearean Tragedy: Its Art and Its Christian Premises*, Bloomington: Indiana University Press, 1969.

Berry, Ralph, 'Hamlet's Doubles', *Shakespeare Quarterly*, 37 (1986), 204–12.

Bertram, Paul, and Bernice W. Kliman (eds), *The Three-Text 'Hamlet': Parallel Texts of the First and Second Quartos and First Folio*, New York: AMS Press, 1991.

Booth, Stephen, 'On the Value of *Hamlet*', in *Reinterpretations of Elizabethan Drama*, ed. Norman Rabkin, New York: Columbia University Press, 1969.

Bulman, James C., *The Heroic Idiom of Shakespearean Tragedy*, Newark, Del.: University of Delaware Press, 1985.

Burckhardt, Sigurd, *Shakespearean Meanings*, Princeton: Princeton University Press, 1968.

Calderwood, James L., *To Be and Not to Be: Negation and Metadrama in 'Hamlet'*, New York: Columbia University Press, 1983.

Charlton, H. B., *Shakespearian Tragedy*, Cambridge: Cambridge University Press, 1948.

Charney, Maurice, *Hamlet's Fictions*, London: Routledge, 1988.

—— *Style in 'Hamlet'*, Princeton: Princeton University Press, 1969.

Conklin, Paul S., *A History of 'Hamlet' Criticism*, London: Routledge & Kegan Paul, 1947.

Danson, Lawrence, *Tragic Alphabet*, New Haven: Yale University Press, 1974.

De Madariaga, Salvador, *On 'Hamlet'*, London: Frank Cass & Co., 1964.

Dessen, Alan C., 'Hamlet's Poisoned Sword: A Study in Dramatic Imagery', *Shakespeare Studies*, 5 (1970), 53–69.

Dodsworth, Martin, *'Hamlet' Closely Observed*, London: Athlone Press, 1985.

Edwards, Philip, *'Hamlet'* (The New Cambridge Shakespeare), Cambridge: Cambridge University Press, 1985.

Frye, Roland Mushat, *The Renaissance Hamlet: Issues and Responses in 1600*, Princeton: Princeton University Press, 1984.

Gottshalk, Paul, *The Meanings of 'Hamlet'*, Albuquerque: University of New Mexico Press, 1972.

Granville-Barker, Harley, '*Hamlet*' in *Prefaces to Shakespeare*, Princeton: Princeton University Press, 1946–47.

Hallett, Charles A. and Elaine S., *The Revenger's Madness: A Study of Revenge Tragedy Motifs*, Lincoln: University of Nebraska Press, 1981.

Harrison, G. B., *Shakespeare's Tragedies*, New York: Oxford University Press, 1951.

Heilbrun, Carolyn G., *Hamlet's Mother and Other Women*, New York: Columbia University Press, 1990.

Hibbard, G. R. (ed.), *Hamlet* (The Oxford Shakespeare), Oxford: Clarendon Press, 1987.

Holland, Peter, '*Hamlet* and the Art of Acting', in *Drama and Symbolism*, ed. James Redmon, Cambridge: Cambridge University Press, 1982.

Honigmann, E. A. J., *Shakespeare: Seven Tragedies*, London: Macmillan, 1976.

Hunter, G. K., '*Hamlet* Criticism', *Critical Quarterly*, 1 (1959), 27–32.

Jardine, Lisa, ' "No offence i' th' world": *Hamlet* and Unlawful Marriage', in *Uses of History: Marxism, Postmodernism, and the Renaissance*, ed. Francis Barker et al., Manchester: Manchester University Press, 1991.

Jenkins, Harold (ed.), *Hamlet* (The Arden Edition), London: Methuen, 1982.

—— '*Hamlet* then till now', *Shakespeare Survey*, 18 (1965), 34–45.

Joseph, Bertram, *Conscience and the King*, London: Chatto & Windus, 1953.

Kastan, David, ' "His semblable is his mirror": *Hamlet* and the Imitation of Revenge', *Shakespeare Survey*, 19 (1987), 111–24.

King, Walter N., *Hamlet's Search for Meaning*, Athens, Ga: University of Georgia Press, 1982.

Kitto, H. D. F., *Form and Meaning in Drama*, London: Methuen, 1956.

Levin, Harry, *The Question of 'Hamlet'*, New York: Oxford University Press, 1959.

Levitsky, Ruth L., 'Rightly To Be Great', *Shakespeare Studies*, 1 (1965), 142–67.

Lewis, C. S., 'Hamlet – The Prince or the Poem?', *Proceedings of the British Academy*, 38, London: Oxford University Press, 1942.

McAlindon, T., 'Indecorum in *Hamlet*', *Shakespeare Studies*, 5 (1970), 70–96.

McGee, Arthur, *The Elizabethan Hamlet*, New Haven: Yale University Press, 1987.

Maher, Mary Z., *Modern Hamlets and Their Soliloquies*, Iowa City: University of Iowa Press, 1992.

Mander, Raymond, and Joe Mitchenson, *'Hamlet' Through the Ages: A Pictorial Record from 1709*, London: Rockliff, 1952.

Mercer, Peter, *'Hamlet' and the Acting of Revenge*, London: Macmillan, 1987.

Miller, Jonathan, *Subsequent Performances*, New York: Viking, 1986.

Mills, John A., *'Hamlet' on Stage: The Great Tradition*, Westport, Conn.: Greenwood Press, 1985.

Morris, Harry, *'Hamlet* as a *Memento Mori* Poem', *PMLA*, 85 (1970), 1035–40.

Proser, Matthew N., *The Heroic Image in Five Shakespearean Tragedies*, Princeton: Princeton University Press, 1965.

Rabkin, Norman, *Shakespeare and the Common Understanding*, New York: Free Press, 1967.

Ribner, Irving, *Patterns in Shakespearean Tragedy*, London: Methuen, 1960.

Righter, Anne, *Shakespeare and the Idea of the Play*, London: Chatto & Windus, 1962.

Rossiter, A. P., *Angel With Horns*, London: Longmans Green, 1961.

Sacks, Peter M., *The English Elegy: Studies in the Genre from Spenser to Yeats*, Baltimore: Johns Hopkins University Press, 1985.

Scofield, Martin, *The Ghosts of 'Hamlet': The Play and Modern Writers*, Cambridge: Cambridge University Press, 1980.

Sewall, Arthur, *Character and Society in Shakespeare*, Oxford: Clarendon Press, 1951.

Showalter, Elaine, 'Representing Ophelia: Women, Madness, and the Responsibilities of Feminist Criticism', in *Shakespeare and the Question of Theory*, ed. Patricia Parker and Geoffrey Hartman, London: Methuen, 1985.

Spencer, T. J. B., 'The decline of *Hamlet*', in *Hamlet* (Stratford-upon-Avon Studies), ed. John Russell Brown and Bernard Harris, London: Edward Arnold, 1963. (Also see Stanley Wells' 'A Reader's Guide to *Hamlet*' in the same volume.)

Stirling, Brents, *Unity in Shakespearean Tragedy*, New York: Columbia University Press, 1956.

Stoll, E. E., *Art and Artifice in Shakespeare*, Cambridge: Cambridge University Press, 1933.

Sypher, Wylie, *Four Stages of Renaissance Style*, Garden City, NY: Doubleday, 1955.

Trewin, J. C., *Five and Eighty Hamlets*, London: Hutchinson, 1987.

Van Doren, Mark, *Shakespeare*, New York: Henry Holt, 1939.

Walker, Roy, *The Time Is Out of Joint: A Study of 'Hamlet'*, London: A. Dakers, 1948.

Weitz, Morris, *'Hamlet' and the Philosophy of Literary Criticism*, Chicago: University of Chicago Press, 1964.

West, Rebecca, *The Court and the Castle*, New Haven: Yale University Press, 1958.

Whitaker, Virgil K., *The Mirror Up to Nature: The Technique of Shakespeare's Tragedies*, San Marino, Cal.: Huntington Library, 1965.

Wilshire, Bruce, *Role Playing and Identity: The Limits of Theatre as Metaphor*, Bloomington: Indiana University Press, 1982.

Wilson, J. Dover, *What Happens in 'Hamlet'*, Cambridge: Cambridge University Press, 1959.

Background studies and useful reference works:

Abbott, E. A., *A Shakespearian Grammar*, New York: Haskell House, 1972 (information on how Shakespeare's grammar differs from ours).

Allen, Michael J. B., and Kenneth Muir (eds), *Shakespeare's Plays in Quarto: A Facsimile Edition*, Berkeley: University of California Press, 1981.

Andrews, John F. (ed.), *William Shakespeare: His World, His Work, His Influence*, 3 vols, New York: Scribners, 1985 (articles on 60 topics).

Barroll, Leeds, *Politics, Plague, and Shakespeare's Theater*, Ithaca: Cornell University Press, 1992.

Bentley, G. E., *The Profession of Player in Shakespeare's Time, 1590–1642*, Princeton: Princeton University Press, 1984.

Blake, Norman, *Shakespeare's Language: An Introduction*, New York: St Martin's Press, 1983 (general introduction to all aspects of the playwright's language).

Bullough, Geoffrey (ed.), *Narrative and Dramatic Sources of Shakespeare*, 8 vols, New York: Columbia University Press, 1957–75 (printed sources, with helpful summaries and comments by the editor).

Campbell, O. J., and Edward G. Quinn (eds), *The Reader's Encyclopedia of Shakespeare*, New York: Crowell, 1966.

Cook, Ann Jennalie, *The Privileged Playgoers of Shakespeare's London*: Princeton: Princeton University Press, 1981 (argument that theatre audiences at the Globe and other public playhouses were relatively well-to-do).

De Grazia, Margreta, *Shakespeare Verbatim: The Reproduction of Authenticity and the Apparatus of 1790*, Oxford: Clarendon Press, 1991 (interesting material on eighteenth-century editorial practices).

Eastman, Arthur M., *A Short History of Shakespeare's Criticism*, New York: Random House, 1968.

Gurr, Andrew, *Playgoing in Shakespeare's London*, Cambridge: Cambridge University Press, 1987 (argument for changing tastes, and for a more diverse group of audiences than Cook suggests).

—— *The Shakespearean Stage, 1574–1642*, 2nd edn, Cambridge: Cambridge University Press, 1981 (theatres, companies, audiences, and repertories).

Hinman, Charlton (ed.), *The Norton Facsimile: The First Folio of Shakespeare's Plays*, New York: Norton, 1968.

Muir, Kenneth, *The Sources of Shakespeare's Plays*, New Haven: Yale University Press, 1978 (a concise account of how Shakespeare used his sources).

Onions, C. T., *A Shakespeare Glossary*, 2nd edn, London: Oxford University Press, 1953.

Partridge, Eric, *Shakespeare's Bawdy*, London: Routledge & Kegan Paul, 1955 (indispensable guide to Shakespeare's direct and indirect ways of referring to 'indecent' subjects).

Schoenbaum, S., *Shakespeare: The Globe and the World*, New York: Oxford University Press, 1979 (lively illustrated book on Shakespeare's world).

—— *Shakespeare's Lives*, 2nd edn, Oxford: Oxford University Press, 1992 (readable, informative survey of the many biographers of Shakespeare, including those believing that someone else wrote the works).

—— *William Shakespeare: A Compact Documentary Life*, New York: Oxford University Press, 1977 (presentation of all the biographical documents, with assessments of what they tell us about the playwright).

Spevack, Marvin, *The Harvard Concordance to Shakespeare*, Cambridge, Mass.: Harvard University Press, 1973.

Whitaker, Virgil K., *Shakespeare's Use of Learning*, San Marino, Cal.: Huntington Library, 1963.

Wright, George T., *Shakespeare's Metrical Art*, Berkeley: University of California Press, 1988.

PLOT SUMMARY

1.1 At midnight on the battlements of Elsinore Castle in Denmark, Barnardo relieves Francisco from guard duty. Marcellus enters with Horatio, a friend of Prince Hamlet.

The ghost that Barnardo and Marcellus have previously seen re-appears, looking like the recently deceased King of Denmark, Hamlet's father. Horatio tries unsuccessfully to speak with it before it leaves.

Horatio takes its appearance as a bad omen for Denmark. He explains how Fortinbrasse, the Prince of Norway, is making preparations to attack Denmark.

The ghost re-enters, still silent, and vanishes as dawn breaks. The men leave to tell Hamlet what has happened.

1.2 Claudius, King of Denmark, enters his court, in the company of his Queen, officials, courtiers, and Hamlet. Claudius explains that he has married, with the court's permission, Gertrude, who was King Hamlet's Queen, and so – as Old Hamlet was Claudius' brother – Claudius' sister-in-law. He sends courtiers to the King of Norway, to inform him that Fortinbrasse intends to make war on Denmark. Laertes, son of Polonius, the Lord Chamberlain, asks leave to return to France, and Claudius grants it.

The King and Queen then try to persuade Hamlet to stop mourning for his father, and manage to persuade him not to go to Wittenberg.

Everyone apart from Hamlet leaves. He laments the haste with which his mother has remarried. Barnardo, Marcellus and Horatio enter, and Horatio explains that they have seen King Hamlet's ghost. Hamlet decides he will watch with them during the coming night.

1.3 Near Polonius' chambers, Laertes, who is about to embark, warns his sister not to believe that Hamlet loves her. Polonius enters, and gives his son advice on how to conduct himself. Laertes leaves. Polonius, agreeing with Laertes' advice to Ophelia, insists that she never speak with Hamlet again.

1.4 Just before midnight on the battlements, the ghost appears. Hamlet asks it to speak, and it beckons him to follow, which he does, leaving the others.

1.5 The ghost claims to be Hamlet's father and to have been murdered by Claudius. It asks Hamlet to seek revenge on Claudius, which Hamlet promises to do, and as morning approaches the ghost leaves. Horatio and Marcellus arrive, and Hamlet makes them swear never to speak of what they have seen.

2.1 In his quarters, Polonius sends Reynaldo, his man, to find out how Laertes occupies his time in Paris. Ophelia enters frightened; Hamlet has been to her private chamber, looking and acting as if he were mad. Polonius, taking Ophelia with him, leaves to warn the King of Hamlet's overwrought condition.

2.2 At court, the King and Queen welcome Rosencraus and Guildenstern, and send them to find out what is troubling Hamlet. The courtiers who were sent to the King of Norway return with news that Norway has forbidden Fortinbrasse to attack Denmark.

Polonius explains to the King and Queen that he believes Hamlet's madness is due to Ophelia's rejection of his love. The Prince enters and Polonius, having asked the King and Queen to leave, speaks to him. Polonius leaves to arrange a meeting between Ophelia and Hamlet which he and the King will be able to overhear.

Rosencraus and Guildenstern enter, and are greeted by Hamlet as old friends. The Prince forces them to admit they were summoned. Rosencraus informs him that his favourite company of actors are on their way to the court.

Polonius comes to announce the arrival of the actors, who enter shortly after and are welcomed by Hamlet. One recites a favourite speech of Hamlet's at the Prince's request. Hamlet asks Polonius to find them lodgings, and all but one of the actors leave. Hamlet asks this man if the company can play 'The Murther of Gonzago' on the following night and whether they could add some lines of the Prince's own. The actor says they can and leaves.

Alone, Hamlet compares the actor's ability to be moved by a false passion with his own reaction to a true cause for passion. He explains that he is having the play acted so that he can judge Claudius' reaction to its plot, which is similar to the way in which his father was murdered.

3.1 Elsewhere in the castle, Rosencraus and Guildenstern discuss how Hamlet has acted towards them with the King and Queen. The King is happy to hear that a play will be performed that night. When the rest have left, the King and Polonius hide themselves within earshot of Ophelia.

Hamlet enters, debating the relative merits of life and death. Ophelia returns some of the tokens of love he gave her, which he refuses angrily, and then he leaves. The King enters, and, worried at what Hamlet might do, decides to send the Prince to England. Polonius suggests that Hamlet's mother first be given a chance to speak with the Prince alone.

3.2 Prior to the performance, Hamlet lectures three actors about techniques of acting. After they leave, Horatio enters, and Hamlet, having praised his friend, asks him to watch the King's reaction to the play.

The King and Queen, with various members of the court, take their places for the play. Hamlet sits by Ophelia, and the dumb show is played. Then the play begins, to be stopped when the King rises in anger at the sight of the player King being murdered. Everyone exits, leaving Hamlet to discuss the King's reaction with Horatio.

Rosencraus and Guildenstern return to tell Hamlet that his mother, the Queen, has sent for him. Shortly thereafter Polonius returns with the same message.

3.3 In his chambers, the King gives Rosencraus and Guildenstern orders for escorting Hamlet to England. Polonius brings news that Hamlet is going to see his mother. Polonius will hide in the Queen's room to hear what happens.

Alone, the King tries to pray for forgiveness for murdering his brother. Hamlet enters unseen, and holds back from killing the King while he is praying, in case his soul should go to heaven and not hell.

3.4 Polonius hides himself behind a tapestry in the Queen's private chamber. Hamlet enters and rebukes his mother for her conduct. She tries to leave, but he restrains her. She calls for help, a call Polonius takes up, at which noise Hamlet, thinking him the King, thrusts at him through the tapestry and kills him.

Hamlet then shames his mother by making her consider her conduct in marrying Claudius, her husband's brother. The ghost enters, unseen by the Queen, to urge Hamlet on to revenge. Hamlet leaves, dragging Polonius.

4.1 The Queen, in her chamber, tells the King of Polonius' murder. Claudius sends Rosencraus and Guildenstern to find the Prince and the body.

4.2 When they find Hamlet, he refuses to answer their questions and runs away.

4.3 Rosencraus brings Hamlet under guard to the King. Claudius finds out where Polonius' body is hidden and tells Hamlet that he is ordered to go to England.

4.4 While being escorted to the harbour, Hamlet sees the army of Fortinbrasse on its way to attack Poland. He wonders again at his own delay in taking revenge.

4.5 In the castle, Ophelia, who is now mad, visits the Queen. The King sends Horatio to look after her when she leaves. Laertes breaks in, at the head of a rebellious crowd, demanding to know what happened to his father. Claudius explains that he is guiltless of Polonius' death.

Ophelia re-enters, gives out flowers and herbs, and departs. Claudius leaves to explain to Laertes what happened to his father.

4.6 Sailors bring Horatio a letter from Hamlet, and take him back with them to the Prince.

4.7 Claudius explains to Laertes that he could not act against Hamlet because of the Queen's and the people's love for him. A messenger brings letters from Hamlet, announcing his return. The King plans with Laertes to kill Hamlet at a fencing match. The Queen enters with news that Ophelia has drowned.

5.1 Two gravediggers talk as they dig Ophelia's grave. Hamlet and Horatio come in, and the Prince speaks with the chief gravedigger. Ophelia's funeral procession enters, and the body is laid in the grave. Laertes jumps in after it, followed by Hamlet; they begin to fight and have to be separated.

5.2 In the castle, Hamlet tells Horatio how Rosencraus and Guildenstern carried orders from Claudius asking the English King to kill Hamlet, how he changed these orders to demand that Rosencraus and Guildenstern be killed, and how he managed to escape from the ship.

A courtier comes to invite Hamlet to a fencing match with Laertes, explaining that the King has bet on the Prince. Hamlet accepts.

Everyone arrives, and Hamlet apologizes for his behaviour to Laertes at Ophelia's grave. The two prepare to fence, Laertes taking an unblunted and poisoned rapier. They fence and Hamlet scores a hit. The King asks Hamlet to drink a cup of wine (which he has poisoned). Hamlet declines and he and Laertes fence, Hamlet again winning. The Queen drinks to his health with the poisoned wine. Hamlet and Laertes fence again, and then fall to scuffling, during which Laertes wounds Hamlet and then Hamlet, their rapiers having been exchanged, wounds Laertes. The Queen dies, poisoned. Laertes confesses that he has poisoned Hamlet, and that the King is responsible for what is happening. Hamlet stabs the king, and then forces him to drink the poisoned wine. Laertes dies. Osrick brings news that Fortinbrasse has arrived, and Hamlet, as he dies, recommends the throne be given to the Norwegian Prince.

Fortinbrasse enters, and Horatio promises to explain what has happened. Fortinbrasse orders the bodies be borne away.

ACKNOWLEDGEMENTS

The editor and publishers wish to thank the following for permission to use copyright material:

Mervyn Jones and W. W. Norton & Company, Inc for material from Ernest Jones, *Hamlet and Oedipus*, Gollancz. Copyright © 1949 by Ernest Jones;

The Johns Hopkins University Press for material from Theodore Spencer, 'Hamlet and the Nature of Reality', *English Literary History*, 5 (1938);

Maynard Mack for material from his article, 'The World of Hamlet', *The Yale Review*, 41 (1952);

Modern Language Association of America for material from Fredson Bowers, 'Hamlet as Minister and Scourge', *PMLA*, 70 (1955) pp.740-49;

Routledge for material from G. Wilson Knight, *The Wheel of Fire* (1930), Methuen & Co.;

Every effort has been made to trace all the copyright holders, but if any have been inadvertently overlooked the publishers will be pleased to make the necessary arrangement at the first opportunity.